BLACK FAMILIES

BLACK FAMILIES

Interdisciplinary Perspectives

Edited by
Harold E. Cheatham and James B. Stewart

Transaction Publishers
New Brunswick (U.S.A.) and London (U.K.)

Library of Congress Catalog Number: 89-35248
ISBN: 0-88738-812-4
Printed in the United States of America

Library of Congress Cataloging-in-Publication Data

  Black families : interdisciplinary perspectives / edited by Harold E.
    Cheatham and James B. Stewart.
        p.   cm.
    ISBN 0-88738-812-4
    1. Afro-Americans--Families. I. Cheatham, Harold E.
II. Stewart, James B. (James Benjamin), 1947–.
E185.86.B5255 1989
306.85′008996073—dc20   89-35248
                                                                    CIP

To our families of origin and our parents:
the late Elinor A. and Thomas G. Cheatham, Sr., and
Clora A. and the late Reuben M. Stewart,
who taught us how to love.
To our own families:
Arlene, Mark, and Brian Cheatham, and
Sharon, Kristin, Lorin, and Jaliya Stewart,
who convoke what we were taught.

CONTENTS

ACKNOWLEDGMENTS

Upon completion of this book we express our thanks first to our colleague Dr. Linda M. Burton, who together with the second author, James B. Stewart, conceived and organized the 1985 conference that was the genesis of the papers eventually collected for this volume. Dr. Burton also contributed very significantly to the early stages of the manuscript selection and development. Although Dr. Burton's own research and scholarly commitments led to her decision to withdraw from the project, we consider her contributions central to this final product.

Special thanks to Kay Burd, Administrative Aide, Black Studies Program, whose loyalty, diligence, and efficiency were invaluable in bringing the 1985 conference and this volume to fruition. Eileen Williams and Claire Markham, as well as support staff in the Individual and Family Studies Program, have provided us critical clerical assistance.

Gratitude is due to units of Pennsylvania State University that have provided financial and other support for the 1985 conference and an institutional climate of support that enabled this research and scholarship.

Our sincere thanks to our contributors who stayed the course, maintaining the commitment, diligence, resilience, and resourcefulness exemplary of black families.

FOREWORD

In 1960, black families lived in strictly segregated communities, un-protected by the extensive set of civil rights laws and Great Society programs that were established and implemented during the following decade. Yet, 75 percent of black children lived in families headed by married couples, often in households with additional adults — grandparents, aunts, uncles, etcetera. Black institutions such as the church were a major focus of community life, reinforcing family values and providing support when the family could not. Schools, hospitals, and other community institutions were segregated and had fewer resources than those in the white community, yet they provided employment for black professionals and other workers. Since most blacks were restricted in their choice of housing, workers throughout the income distribution lived and worked in close proximity, allowing children to observe a variety of lifestyles and occupational options.

The general expectation was that the political, economic, and social changes that would result from the legislative initiatives of the 1960s and 1970s would expand opportunities for blacks and increase the well-being of members of the black community, especially the children. However, the evidence shows quite clearly that the expected improvements have not taken place across the board. The majority of black children now live in single-parent families, usually with their mother. Two-thirds of them do not have other adults in the household, which decreases their access to the supportive structure that helped past generations to survive hard times. As a forthcoming study by the Joint Center for Political Studies shows, these changes have had an adverse effect on the poverty status of black chil-dren, with consequences that are likely to endanger not only this gener-ation but the one that will follow.

Some social science analysts, such as Charles Murray, have argued that the Great Society programs were the cause of the decline in marriage and the increase in dependence on government by reducing the family's role in providing economic support and changing individual values toward work and responsibility. Other policy analysts, such as William J. Wilson, have put forth the hypothesis that the policies have had unintended consequences. Civil rights laws opened opportunities for some members of the community in terms of increased access to high wage jobs and better quality housing that led to their movement out of the traditional black community and the increased isolation and concentration of low income people.

The chapters in this volume prove that the cause and effect relationships are much more complicated than implied by the dichotomous views expressed above. While evidence is presented showing that the values of those on public assistance are not systematically different from those who are economically independent (but not necessarily well-to-do), some of the current problems of the black community are not the result of successful public policies but of inadequate or flawed policies. In other cases, policies to increase economic well-being have been swamped by larger economic trends that were not managed properly by the federal government. Other chapters in the book show that the very success of some programs, such as integration of institutions, has led to the demise of some of the pillars of the black community. And access to new types of employment (such as in the police force) has served to place additional stresses on the family.

But change is not a new phenomenon. James Stewart points to Du Bois's analysis of the effects of industrialization and urbanization on the postbellum black family as an indication that family disruption is not unique to the 1980s. The solution, then, can be sought in examining the frameworks for analysis that were developed by early black sociologists such as Du Bois and Frazier. Moreover, development of appropriate intervention strategies should not be dependent on only one cultural and societal view of the family or the community and the responsibilities of these institutions. Rather, an alternative or multicultural approach, enlightened by cross-national studies, is most likely to lead us to the development of the correct set of private and public support mechanisms for the black family and for black children—the future of the black community.

Margaret C. Simms
Joint Center for
Political Studies

INTRODUCTION AND CONTEXT

Harold E. Cheatham and James B. Stewart

The papers in this volume are an outgrowth of a conference held at Penn State University in November 1985 entitled "The Black Family: Contemporary Issues and Concerns."

Dialogue stimulated by the conference reinforced the need for research and writing that contributes to the emerging objective, scientific, and rigorously derived body of knowledge about black families—knowledge now being utilized to reconceptualize these families. A consistent theme among the papers is the questioning of utility of existing research paradigms and challenging of the traditional perspectives (e.g., pathology premise) about black families. Much of that research is inconclusive and contradictory but nonetheless has, by repetition, gained legitimacy and has affected the course of political debate and, as well, the development of public policy regarding black families.

Through rigorous empirically grounded discussions, this volume provides alternative models derived from more comprehensive observations of the range of characteristics exhibited by black families. The models have greater explanatory power for the study of black families by transcending perspectives that have led to research focused on single constructs (e.g., matriarchy) or theoretical approaches (e.g., deficit model).

As the development of the volume proceeded, we replaced the construct "black family" with "black families" to accurately reflect the diversity and complexity of family structure among African-Americans as documented in the work of Andrew Billingsley. Also, several papers in this volume were not presented at the conference but were invited as original, unpublished papers to achieve a comprehensive, interdisciplinary profile. The volume is designed to explicate both the general patterns of response to various external, macro constraints (i.e., economic systems) and the internal dynamics of black families functioning at the micro level (i.e., interpersonal relationships).

This volume consists of complementary presentations by established and emerging scholars in the disciplines of economics, education, sociology, psychology, social welfare, counseling, health education, family studies, and religious ethics. The papers build on the considerable contributions of scholars such as Billingsley, McAdoo, and Nobles, among others, whose pathbreaking research and theoretical formulations have advanced substantially understanding of the characteristics and functioning of black families.

A distinctive feature of this volume is that, relative to black families, it provides knowledge of the research process from conceptualization to implications. Issues related to theory development and methodology are addressed in Part I by Stewart, who compares the scholarship of two giants, W.E.B. Du Bois and E. Franklin Frazier, whose pioneering works set the course for modern scholarship on the subject of black families.

The parts of this book examining ecological perspectives, family form and functioning, intracultural perspectives, and stress, coping, and social support report the results of empirical inquiry. Part II, "Ecological Perspectives," begins with a chapter by Poole, who examines the critical linkage between the black church and black families. Also in this section, Rice, Leigh, and Hill provide assessments of the impact of public policy on the quality of life of black families.

Black family form and functioning, as affected by a variety of exogenous and endogenous factors, is addressed in chapters by Spencer, Cazenave and Smith, and Williams in Part III. Stress, coping, and social support is the focus of Part IV, in which chapters by Myers, Johnson, and Benjamin and Stewart examine resources used by black families to contend with adversity. Part V, "Intracultural Perspectives," continues the theme of Part III, with special focus on similarities and differences among families of African descent in St. Vincent and Nigeria and among West Indians, in the United States. This section emphasizes that our use of the term *black families* is not constrained by geographical considerations. It is responsive to E. Franklin Frazier's concern that African-American families be studied from a comparative perspective with reference to families of African descent in other societies.

Part VI, "Policy and Social Service Delivery Systems," brings the research process full circle, illustrating the important links among theory, research methods, and substantive issues and, further, how those links translate into developing intervention programs appropriate for black families. Contributors to this section are Gibbs, Solomon, and Cheatham.

In the concluding section the co-editors, Cheatham and Stewart, provide a retrospective and integrated discussion of the contents of this volume consistent with our initial goal of contributing to that scholarship that guides the reconceptualization of black families.

I

Theoretical and Methodological Perspectives

INTRODUCTION

One of the major objectives of this volume is to integrate perspectives from various disciplines to enhance collective understanding of black families. Attempts to use an interdisciplinary approach to the study of specific topics often fall short. This problem arises for a variety of reasons. Among them are the difficulty of creating intellectually coherent interdisciplinary theories and the values of the modern academy that emphasize specialized training within circumscribed disciplinary boundaries.

This set of circumstances, unfortunately, creates artifical barriers to the study of black families. To address this problem we propose, to borrow a phrase from the lone chapter in this section, to go "back to basics." In the context of this project, going "back to basics" entails the detailed examination of authentic historical precedents for the study of black families that can inform contemporary interdisciplinary approaches. Many scholars have identified the writings of W.E.B. Du Bois and E. Franklin Frazier as the classic works on black families. Unfortunately, their scholarship has been misrepresented and in many cases obscured. Stewart resurrects the analyses of these two giants and subjects it to detailed scrutiny, using tools of analysis adapted from the philosophy of science.

Stewart's analysis identifies a "disciplinary matrix," common to the works of both analysts, which, he argues, can provide the foundation for contemporary studies. He asserts that this common approach has the following characteristics: (a) use of a historical evolutionary perspective that links contemporary status and functions with historical conditions and constraints, (b) use of sophisticated concepts of race, class, and culture that instate the uniqueness of African-American people, (c) use of an ecological model to examine cross-sectional family status and functioning, treating black families as systems interacting both with other societal systems and the physical environment, and (d) use of synthesis of qualitative and quantitative data to describe and model complex social interactions.

The various chapters in this volume collectively provide a synthesis and extension of Du Bois's and Frazier's approaches to the study of black families. As an example, the chapter examining the black church highlights a community system identified by both scholars as critical in shaping the environment in the black family functions. Du Bois, in fact, argued that the black church preceded the family as an institution in black communities. The remaining chapters in Part II identify critical external subsystems that affect the viability of black families.

Parts III and IV move beyond the weaknesses of the methodologies of Du Bois and Frazier by combining these scholars' macro-ecological framework with detailed examination of internal family dynamics. As noted in Stewart's analysis, Frazier pursued the study of black families as a means of understanding broad patterns of race relations in cross-cultural perspective. The articles in Part 5 are consistent with Frazier's interests, examining various issues addressed in other sections while using black families in St. Vincent and Nigeria, and West Indian families living in the United States.

The precedent for systematically connecting detailed studies of black families to the process of developing interventions designed to improve their circumstances was established in Du Bois's "The American Negro Family." That study included both the findings of the research conducted by Du Bois and the proceedings of a conference held involving scholars and help-providers called to translate the research findings into programmatic interventions. Part 6 represents our effort to present research, theory, and practice for intervention and service delivery with black families.

By integrating the processes of research and intervention modeling we hope to serve the interests of a broad range of professionals working to improve the lives of black families.

1

BACK TO BASICS: THE SIGNIFICANCE OF DU BOIS'S AND FRAZIER'S CONTRIBUTIONS FOR CONTEMPORARY RESEARCH ON BLACK FAMILIES

James B. Stewart

Research paradigms used by W.E.B. Du Bois and E. Franklin Frazier to study black families are analyzed. The examination is focused on clarifying issues at stake in contemporary debates about what sets of theories and research designs are appropriate to generate fruitful insights about black families. Commonalities identified in the work of Du Bois and Frazier proposed for resurrection in contemporary studies include (a) examination of how historical developments condition contemporary family structure and functioning and (b) use of an ecological perspective that treats black families as systems interacting with other societal systems. It is argued that synthesizing the paradigms of Du Bois and Frazier and those found in contemporary Afrocentric scholarship can significantly enhance the utility of future research on black families.

INTRODUCTION

This analysis explores the foundations of contemporary debates about black families via a comparison of the research paradigms employed by W. E. B. Du Bois and E. Franklin Frazier. Important dimensions of Du Bois's and Frazier's analytical frameworks are notably absent in most modern studies. Examples include the examination of the extent to which historical developments condition family structure and the treatment of the family as an institution in constant interaction with other societal institutions. More generally, what might be called the macro perspective advanced by Du Bois and Frazier has been increasingly supplanted by a more micro orientation that examines the functioning of individual families using sophisticated empirical techniques.

A thorough understanding of the work of Du Bois and Frazier can facilitate a synthesis of the macro and micro approaches. To accomplish this, it is first critical to deconstruct the scientific approach to study of black families. In the second section of this chapter, the concept of a "research paradigm" is used to demystify the so-called scientific method and its application to the study of black families. In so doing, emphasis is placed on how model development is influenced by ideology and values and the limitations of empirical techniques to generate reliable information.

The theoretical models used by Du Bois and others including their summary assessments of the future of black families is the focus of the third section. The comparison in the fourth section of theories and empirical techniques indicates that the forces hypothesized as affecting black families were similar; however, the relative explanatory power assigned to different factors varies substantially. These differences do not result from differences in empirical methods used by the two scholars.

These findings motivate the examination of the ideology and values that Du Bois and Frazier brought to their research. Important differences in critical values and ideology are identified. In particular, Du Bois brought an earlier version of what is now termed Afrocentric values and ideology to the study of black families. Frazier's appreciation of the need for an Afrocentric perspective only evolved long after his major work on black families had been completed. This discussion constitutes the fifth section. The concluding section undertakes a reconciliation of the value/ideology conflicts. The extent to which an adapted variant of Du Bois's and Frazier's research paradigms serves contemporary research is explored.

RESEARCH PARADIGMS AND BLACK FAMILIES: AN OVERVIEW

General Characteristics of Research Paradigms

The term *research paradigm* refers to the specific application of the scientific method within a particular area of inquiry. This term was popularized by Thomas Kuhn and was later replaced by the concept of a disciplinary matrix.[1] Other philosophers and sociologists have also generated important critiques of the institution of science.[2]

For Kuhn, a disciplinary matrix is comprised of four components. One component is the metaphysical part of paradigms, which involves beliefs in particular models.[3] Important differences between Du Bois's and Frazier's beliefs in particular models and, more generally, their metaphysical beliefs, have not been fully appreciated.

The values shared by practitioners constitute a second component of a disciplinary matrix. Micro order values are those beliefs about the nature of the scientific enterprise that guide the behaviors and judgments of practitioners. An example of micro order values is predictive power as a test of credibility and degree of compatibility with existing theories. A prime example of macro order value is the belief about how scientists and the institution of science should relate to other institutions. To illustrate, Kuhn suggests that on this issue scientists may disagree as to whether ''science should or need not be socially useful. . . .''[4] Du Bois and Frazier differed in their view of how the scientific study of black families was to be undertaken and how the results should affect public policy.

A third component of a disciplinary matrix is symbolic generalizations, or the translation of key concepts into shorthand symbols understood by practitioners in the field. This symbolic reductionism enables mathematical manipulation of the symbols through equation systems that allow testable hypotheses to be generated. For current purposes, this component can be extended to include observational language used to relate theoretical constructs to observable phenomena, measurement conventions, and methods of analysis. Both Du Bois and Frazier charged that sociology had increasingly developed a commitment to symbolic reductionism and was driven by the desire and opportunities to refine empirical techniques rather than by theoretical developments.

The political importance of symbolic reductionism is first to gain credibility within the larger scientific establishment and second to create a status difference between folk knowledge and the professional judgment of trained practitioners. This status difference enables scientists to make a claim on resources to support research. Frazier's work exhibits more symbolic generalization than that of Du Bois, and Du Bois was committed to broader based participation by laypersons in addition to professionals in the process of data collection and reporting.

The final component of disciplinary matrices is termed *exemplars*. Exemplars are ''the concrete problem-solutions that students encounter from the start of their scientific education, whether in laboratories, on examinations, or at the ends of chapters in science texts.''[5] The ability to generate exemplars is one of the indicators that an area of inquiry has ''matured.''

Although Kuhn's framework was specifically developed to explain normal scientific advances and scientific revolutions in the natural and physical sciences, it is generally applicable to the social and behavioral sciences because these enterprises have been preoccupied with mimicking the "value free" image of the natural and physical sciences. Yet, the thrust of Kuhn's argument is that even in the so-called hard sciences, world views and values significantly affect the enterprise. In the case of "scientific revolutions," the specific focus of Kuhn's inquiry, even the shared values of scientists and the other aspects of the culture of science common to practitioners do not prevent disintegration of normal patterns.

In the social and behavioral sciences the probability is greater than in the natural and physical sciences that ideological predispositions, political views, and differences in socialization can influence scientific activity. These influences may affect the conceptualization of a research problem, definition of the appropriate unit of analysis, decisions about what factors should be controlled for in the research and what influences can be ignored, how the research is to be conducted, the interpretation of results, and/or some combination of these.[6] These problems are compounded by the limited ability to conduct the equivalent of "laboratory experiments." Further, in the social and behavioral sciences the development of symbolic generalizations and their manipulation is less important than the language used to describe a given phenomenon or set of interactions. Terms thought to be "objective" by some can easily be attacked as "value laden" by others.

Finally, studies that span long periods of time are hampered by unevenness in the quality of data for different time periods. The tendency to cite early research uncritically as authority runs the risk of producing flawed exemplars, thereby blurring the line between supposition and fact.

Research Paradigms and Research on Black Families

The study of families has now achieved quasi-disciplinary status reflected in the existence of departmental academic units and professional journals focusing specifically on the family as the unit of analysis. Within this developmental context, research examining black families is typically undertaken within a comparative framework. Understanding the evolution of this pattern is of special importance.

The emergence and evolution of "disciplines" had a fundamental effect on both the research of Du Bois and Frazier and the extent to which their work has influenced contemporary research. Du Bois's major writings about black families preceded both the emergence of sociology as an academic discipline and the more recent development of a "family" research establishment discussed above. In contrast, the work of Frazier was shaped significantly by the sociological establishment and his approach to the study of black families was conditioned by the emergence of competing schools of thought within the discipline. For both Du Bois and Frazier the study of black families was to be undertaken as a part of a broader investigation of the black experience.

Du Bois advocated the equivalent of a macro level panel approach to the study of the black experience.[7] He proposed a research design in which ten topics, one of which was the black family, would be studied in succession, one annually, for a century. The systems approach of Du Bois was reflected in the choices of other topics to be examined. To illustrate, the black church was identified as a key research focus. Du Bois argued that the black church preceded the emergence of the black family in the United States and, in fact, provided the means for the stabilization of the family. Thus the analysis by Poole[8] is foursquare within the Du Bois tradition. Other topics included mortality patterns among blacks and the social and physical conditions of blacks in cities. Contemporary analyses of the health status (Rice and Myers)[9] and housing status (Leigh)[10] of blacks also directly extend the Du Bois tradition.

Du Bois believed that this approach would produce ". . . a continuous record on the condition and development of a group of 10 to 20 millions of men—a body of sociological material unsurpassed in human annals."[11] Central to Du Bois's approach was insistence that the research design focus on in-depth analysis of the black experience rather than on comparative research: ". . . the careful exhaustive study of the isolated group, then, is the ideal of the sociologist of the 20th century—from that may come . . . at last careful, cautious generalization and formulation."[12]

In Du Bois's view this approach was warranted because the relative isolation of black Americans necessitated the examination of unique adaptive patterns and detailed characteristics of the linkage among subsystems: ". . . never in the history of the modern world has there been presented . . . so rare an opportunity to observe and measure and study the evolution of a great branch of the human race as is given to Americans in the study of the American Negro. . . . By reason of color and color prejudice the group is isolated—by reason of incentive to change, the changes are rapid and kaleidoscopic; by reason of the peculiar environment, the action and reaction of social forces are seen and can be measured with more than usual ease."[13]

Frazier's interest in black families was functionally related to his broader concern with race relations, not simply in the United States but worldwide. As he noted: ". . . my work in sociology falls into two major fields of interest: *Race and Culture Contacts* and *The Family*. This has been owing partly to the fact that I have felt that the most fruitful approach to the study of *Race and Culture Contacts,* especially those aspects as regards acculturation and assimilation, was through the study of the family."[14]

For both scholars, the direct link between research on families to a larger research agenda meant that there would be much less concern with detailed study of the formation and functioning of individual families than is found in contemporary research. A first step in the process of exploring how these two research traditions can be synthesized is through a more detailed scrutiny of their research paradigms.

THE RESEARCH PARADIGMS OF DU BOIS AND FRAZIER—THEORIES, MODELS, EXEMPLARS

Du Bois and Frazier use several longitudinal models, each distinctly associated with particular time periods. Each model successively builds on the scholars' previous models of the origins and evolution of black families. The periodization that circumscribes each model reflects the conventional wisdom about important historical junctures, e.g., the preslavery experience in Africa, slavery, the rural experience after the Civil War, and the early period of industrialization. The model of the family presented for each period is embedded in a systems framework that provides overarching theoretical coherence, connecting submodels and exemplars across time.

As noted previously, for both scholars the family is an institution that interacts with other institutions forming a social network. The necessary connecting threads among models across time are theories of how social forces altered black families through forced and voluntary adaptations. Black families are treated as continually undergoing change through their interaction with other institutions that themselves are also constantly subjected to forces that induce changes. Du Bois and Frazier both saw industrialization as the major force shaping the family in what was for them the modern era. They disagreed to some extent about patterns of adaptation and the capability and desirability of resisting the forces of change in the different eras. In the latest period examined by both, each used the ideal monogamous two-parent family as a standard of evaluation. Thus, the monogamous two-parent family served simultaneously as model, exemplar, and constellation of values.

Described below are the models of black families associated with each of the periods that Du Bois and Frazier identified as critical.

African Origins and African-American Families

The least developed components of the theoretical formulations of Du Bois and Frazier are the treatment of traditional African families and the discussion of the transition from traditional African families to African-American families during the slavery era. In the case of African families, both scholars rely on what are best described as exemplars rather than models or empirical data. Frazier, in fact, pays only lip service to African families. This is due, in part, to his effort to discount the phenomenon of African retentions as having a significant impact on the behavior and values of African-American families during slavery, a position held by Herskovits.[15] Frazier argued, in fact, that ". . . as regards the Negro family, there is no reliable evidence that African culture has had any influence on its development."[16]

Although Du Bois did incorporate material about traditional African families gleaned from several available secondary sources, unfortunately, the works upon which he drew could hardly qualify as objective analyses. To Du Bois's credit, he was able to dissect information that could be usefully integrated into the broader study from works that many modern scholars would characterize as racist interpretations of African culture. The nature of his sources contributed to his inability, despite courageous attempts, to effectively describe the connecting threads between African families and African-American families in any of the sections of the study. To illustrate, one of his most interesting exemplars is a graphic entitled "Evolution of the Negro Home." Several housing types are depicted, including traditional African huts, slave cabins, urban tenements, and single-family dwellings occupied by working class, middle class, and upper class blacks. The supporting narrative, however, unfortunately fails to demonstrate an evolutionary connection among the various housing types.[17]

Models of Families during Slavery

The models and exemplars of African-American families during slavery employed by both scholars are also flawed, although less so than is the case in the treatment of traditional African families. As an example, both scholars correctly point to the imbalance in the sex ratio as a critical constraint on family formation. Equally useful is their shared view that efforts by African-Americans to adopt the values, mores, and patterns of familial organization and functioning that were developing among white

Americans were necessarily distorted by the institution of slavery. A third important theoretical contribution of Du Bois and Frazier is the emphasis on early patterns of class differentiation among black families conditioned by slavery. Their analyses fall short, however, because there is an explicit supposition that the destruction of African traditions left in its wake a group of barbarians incapable of regulating sexual relations and establishing viable familial forms without the forced imposition of alien European control. This interpretation has been rendered obsolete by the more recent work of various scholars.[18]

For Du Bois and Frazier, although slavery constituted the ultimate human indignity, once it had occurred, the forced introduction of Western mores and values was seen as a positive development militating against social anarchy. Frazier pushes this idea further than Du Bois does, but it is present in the analyses of both. To illustrate, Du Bois argued ". . . on the whole it is fair to say that while to some extent European family morals were taught the small select body of house servants and artisans, both by precept and example, the great body of field hands were raped of their own sex customs and provided with no binding new ones. Slavery gave the monogamic family ideal to slaves, but it compelled and desired only the most imperfect practice of its most ordinary morals."[19]

Frazier combined the idea of destruction of traditional morality with the model of the slave mother as the source of intergenerational stability. Thus he notes: "Only the bond between the mother and her child continually resisted the disruptive effect of economic interests that were often inimical to family life among slaves. Consequently, under all conditions of slavery, the Negro mother remained the most dependable and important figure in the family."[20]

For both scholars, free black families during slavery provided a source of optimism regarding future developments. Du Bois assigned a special leadership role to this group in his classic conceptualization of the "Talented Tenth," later modified to reflect his greater realization of the erosion of caste.[21] Frazier, who viewed free black families during slavery as an ideal type, produced the conclusion: "It was among this class that family traditions became firmly established before the Civil War."[22]

Black Families in Postbellum America

Positing the existence of two models of black families during slavery would be expected to produce a similar bifurcation in the examination of the postbellum period. Frazier, in fact, did identify two streams of development or models in the postbellum period. One model described families that had achieved a fair degree of organization during slavery. "In these families the authority of the father was firmly established, and the woman in the role of mother and wife fitted into the pattern of the patriarchal household. Moreover, in assuming the responsibilities of his new status, the father became the chief, if not the sole breadwinner."[23]

The second model, which Frazier saw as more typical, involved the breakup of ". . . the loose ties that had held men and women together in a nominal marriage relation during slavery."[24] The process of family formation was de-emphasized in this model and a matriarchial family structure was projected as inevitable as "[o]ften the woman with family ties, whether she had been without a husband during slavery or was deserted when freedom came, became responsible for the maintenance of the family group."[25]

It is this model of the black family that has been resurrected and applied to describe more contemporary social patterns by Moynihan and his protégés. This extension has been made possible because Frazier also used the same models to describe Black families in northern urban America during the industrial period.

Black Families in Industrializing America

In describing the urbanization of blacks in the late nineteenth and early twentieth centuries, Frazier argued that it would be difficult to maintain family organization in an urban setting without substantial economic and cultural resources. Frazier further maintained that ". . . the most significant element in the new social structure of Negro life is the black industrial proletariat. As the Negro has become an industrial worker and received adequate compensation the father has become the chief breadwinner and assumed a responsible place in his family."[26]

Du Bois saw the proletarianization of African-Americans in industrial America differently. He argued that economic conditions were influencing the distribution of labor across gender in two ways; ". . . low wages and a rising economic standard is postponing marriage to an age dangerously late for a folk in the Negro's present moral development [and] present economic demand draws the [N]egro women to the city and keeps the men in the country, causing a dangerous disproportion of the sexes. . . ."[27]

The differences in Du Bois's and Frazier's views of the impact of industrialization and urbanization on black families reflect differences in their perceptions of the ideal model toward which family patterns should be evolving. For Frazier, the ideal pattern involved the progressive assimilation of the mores, values, and folkways of the majority culture. The assimilation process was juxtaposed to a pattern of progressive disintegration that accelerated with the end of slavery. In Frazier's words: "When one views in retrospect the waste of human life, the immorality, delinquency, desertions, and broken homes which have been involved in the development of Negro family life in the United States . . . the Negro has found within the patterns of the white man's culture a purpose in life and a significance for his strivings which have involved sacrifices for his children and the curbing of individual desires and impulses indicates that he has become assimilated to a new mode of life."[28]

Du Bois did not view the wholesale assimilation of the culture of the larger society as the ideal developmental path for black families. In discussing sexual mores, Du Bois argued:

> The Negro attitude in these matters is in many respects healthier and more reasonable. Their sexual passions are strong and frank, but they are, despite example and temptation, only to a limited degree perverted or merely commercial. The Negro motherlove and family instinct is strong, and it regards the family as a means, not an end, and although the end in the present Negro mind is usually personal happiness rather than social order, yet even here radical reformers of divorce courts have something to learn.[29]

The increasing availability of empirical data sharpened the ability of both Frazier and Du Bois to refine their analyses of black families in industrial America in contrast to earlier periods. To illustrate, both Frazier's and Du Bois's use of slave narratives as a data base is unreliable for the development of generalizations, if for no other reason than the fact that an individual's capacity to prepare such a narrative presupposes a certain degree of assimilation. Du Bois was more sensitive to this problem than Frazier, who wrote:

> For past American conditions the chief printed sources of information must be sought for in the vast literature of slavery. It is difficult to get a clear picture of the family relations of slaves, between the Southern apologist and his picture of cabin life, with idyllic devotion and careless toil, and that of the abolitionist with his tale of family disruption and cruelty, adultery and illegitimate mulattoes.

Between these pictures the student must steer carefully to find a reasonable statement of the average truth.[30]

Du Bois's assessment of the developmental trajectory of black families based on empirical studies was highly optimistic. To illustrate, in discussing family formation, composition, and dissolution Du Bois noted:

> In these statistics we have striking evidence of the needs of the Negro American home. The broken families indicated by the abnormal number of widowed and separated, and the late age of marriage, show sexual irregularity and economic pressure. These things all go to prove not the disintegration of Negro family life but the distance which integration has gone and has yet to go. Fifty years ago family statistics of nine-tenths of the Negroes would have been impossible. Twenty-five years ago they would have been far worse than today, and while there is no perceptible change of moment in the statistics of 1890 and 1900, most of the tendencies are in the right direction, and a healthier home life is in prospect.[31]

In general, Du Bois used descriptive statistics in making assessments. In contrast, as described below, Frazier's data and empirical analyses were connected to a particular analytical framework.

DATA AND EMPIRICAL METHODS

One of the significant aspects of Du Bois's methodology is the simultaneous collection of broad ranging micro level data in different communities that illustrated the interactions of the social forces that had been theoretically or intuitively identified as important influences on family functioning and adaptation.

The Philadelphia Negro and *The Negro American Family* are noteworthy as examples of Du Bois's use of empirical techniques in studying black families. As noted by Rudwick, *The Philadelphia Negro*

> . . . was more than the obvious model for the surveys of Negroes in New York and Boston by Ovington, Haynes, and Daniels in the period before World War I. His pioneering work also bears important similarities to such later studies as Johnson's *The Negro In Chicago,* Frazier's *Negro Youth At The Crossways,* Davis and Gardener's *Deep South,* and Drake and Cayton's *Black Metropolis.* In

their holistic approach to the study of black urban communities, in their attention to the importance of social class, and in their painstaking scholarship and quest for scientific knowledge, their likeness to Du Bois is evident.[32]

The survey method developed by Du Bois in producing *The Philadelphia Negro* was the operationalization of his belief ". . . that the student of the social problems affecting ethnic minorities must go beyond the group itself. He must specially notice the environment: the physical environment of city, sections and house, the far mightier social environment— the surrounding world of custom, wish, whim, and thought which envelops this group and powerfully influences its social development."[33] The type of data collected to "test" their models of family dynamics and the process of data collection itself were directly tied to the structure of the theoretical models.

Du Bois and Frazier exhibited a special interest in the precise spatial configuration of individual communities. In Du Bois's case, this approach is most evident in *The Philadelphia Negro*. Both scholars expanded upon this focus and used a variety of data types to present a more holistic feature. For Du Bois, this approach is especially evident in *The Negro American Family*. That study contains a variety of empirical data taken from census publications and special government reports examining various issues, including family budgets, expenditures on necessity, conjugal conditions, divorce and illegitimacy rates, etcetera. In addition, detailed ethnographic surveys of 13 "higher type" families were undertaken and presented. Du Bois admitted that these studies of Negro families were included to focus on the emergence of stable families in the urban North.[34]

To study black families, Frazier adapted the human ecology model developed by the Chicago Sociological School. That model is based on the theory that the process of urban expansion could be measured by rates of change in poverty, home ownership, and other variable conditions for unit areas along the main thoroughfares radiating from the center of the city. The model requires the segmentation of a geographical space into zones with differing physical characteristics. Frazier's goal was to test the general hypothesis that ". . . the problem of family disorganization and reorganization of Negro family life are part of the processes of selection and segregation of those elements in the Negro population which have become emancipated from the traditional status of the masses."[35] The linkage to his general models described previously is evident.

Frazier used this empirical approach to produce cross-sectional case studies of black communities in particular cities, specifically Chicago and New York. The interpretations of the empirical data collected and analyzed in these studies were later integrated with quotations from personal documents from earlier periods to produce largely narrative treatises on black families and the "Negro" in the United States that, like those of Du Bois, subordinated the presentation of empirical data to support interpretative narrative.

To summarize the results of the comparison of the research paradigms of Du Bois and Frazier to this point, it should first be noted that the work of both can be legitimately criticized for employing simplistic models of internal family functioning. This weakness stems from their principal concern with the structural and associational aspects of social life. The specific models and metaphors used by Du Bois and Frazier in their analyses of both historical and contemporary developments were very similar, generally structured as longitudinal systems models describing relationships among institutions and social forces over time. Both attempted to validate their various models by combining quantitative and qualitative data. Frazier's research design emphasized cross-sectional replication, while Du Bois strongly advocated longitudinal replication. The data used to examine black families in the preindustrial period were similar. Frazier was able to use these data to perform empirical research in the tradition of evolving techniques.

Despite the similarities, Du Bois's and Frazier's evaluations of the relative strength of various forces affecting black families differ, as do their interpretation of the developmental trajectory of black families. This anomaly underscores the need to explore other components of Kuhn's disciplinary matrix to locate the sources of the differences. Two possible sources of difference are explored in the next section: (a) the macro and micro values related to the nature of science and its relationship to other institutions and (b) the "metaphysical" or "ideological" component of the disciplinary matrix.

VALUES AND IDEOLOGY

Micro-Order Values

Frazier reassessed his earlier fascination with the ecological model at a later point in his career. He cautioned that ". . . the relations which are revealed between phenomena in ecological studies are not explanations of social phenomena but indicate the selection and segregation of certain elements in the population."[36] The implication of Frazier's caveat is that ". . . ecological studies are not a substitute for sociological studies but supplement studies of human social life. For a complete understanding of social phenomena it is necessary to investigate the social organization and culture of a community and the attitudes of the people who constitute the community."[37]

The belief held by both Frazier and Du Bois that sound theorizing should take precedence over concern with data collection and data analysis was informed by similar micro order values. To illustrate, Frazier noted:

> The question of methods and techniques in sociological research just as in other fields of scientific inquiry is inseparable from the conceptual organization of the discipline. . . . In so many so-called sociological studies this simple fact is forgotten and virtuosity in the use of methods and techniques becomes an end in itself. . . . Many statistical studies lack sociological significance because they fail to show any organic relationship among the elements which they utilize for analysis.[38]

Frazier used this point to offer guidelines for the pursuit of sociological research examining peoples of African descent: ". . . the first task in sociological study is to define or formulate a problem in terms of the concepts of the discipline. Then the problem of methods and techniques resolves itself into one of utilizing the appropriate methods and tools. . . . The conceptual tools of sociological research—whether labelled by old or new verbal symbols—will become more precise as they are utilized to reveal significant relationships between social phenomena."[39]

Du Bois offered a similar critique in examining the limits of sociology; "If sociology describes and classifies more fully, realistically, and accurately than the other social sciences, let it describe only that which is susceptible of full and realistic classification. . . . Change and movement have to be further explained; but the sociologist, even the sociologist who has conceived a meaningful-causal system, dare not be too clear that it is man who causes movement and change; that would so constrict the validity of sociology."[40]

Du Bois and Frazier shared values about the nature of scientific research and decried vulgar empiricism. However, differences in macro order values and ideology produced fundamental differences in their assessments of black families as discussed below.

Ideology and Macro-Order Values

Two early articles that preceded Frazier's major work on black families provide interesting clues about the ideological underpinnings of Frazier's approach to the study of black families.[41] Frazier indicated that he ". . . emphasized the problem of family disorganization because I feel it lies at the basis of many of the Negro's problems."[42] Frazier argued that black families suffer especially from social "ignorance," i.e., ". . . lack of traditions, knowledge, and ideals which all people acquire by living in the social and physical environment to which they have become adapted."[43]

The emphasis in Frazier's models on sexual mores stemmed from his efforts to discredit the racist analyses of the "instinct psychology" school, which according to him was ". . . often called upon to support the belief that the sex instinct in the Negro broke through institutionalized sex controls."[44] The method of historical cultural analysis was advocated by Frazier as an alternative framework. He claims, in fact, ". . . any study of the Negro family which possesses value must study it historically and apply the method of cultural analysis."[45]

Unfortunately, Frazier's conceptualization of "culture" was problematic. Although, according to Frazier, the method of cultural analysis ". . . takes into account all the factors, psychological, social and economic, which determine the character of any group. . .,"[46] when he applied this method to the black experience he concluded that blacks don't have a culture! Thus, he argued that studying black families from this perspective would reveal that: ". . . it would not present the unique characteristics which a family group like the Chinese, where the family is based upon blood, land, law and religion, and is the 'practical unit of social control in the village,' would present if placed in the American social environment."[47]

Not only does Frazier argue that African-American families did not have a historical cultural core, he further maintained that family adaptations among African-Americans had no impact on the larger society: "Generally when two different cultures come into contact, each modifies the other. But in the case of the Negro in America it meant the total destruction of the African social heritage. Therefore in the case of the family group the Negro has not introduced new patterns of behavior; but has failed to conform to the patterns about him."[48]

In contrast, Du Bois believed that the African connection had not been totally severed. He argued that the attempt to connect current conditions to the African past was ". . . not because Negro-Americans are Africans, or can trace an unbroken social history from Africa, but because there is a distinct nexus between Africa and America which, though broken and perverted, is nevertheless not to be neglected by the careful student."[49]

Du Bois saw the experience of black women in the labor market as a precursor of developments in the larger society rather than as an incomplete adaptation. He saw an America unprepared for the economic emancipation of women:

> The family group, however, which is the ideal of the culture to which these folk have been born, is not based on the idea of an economically independent working mother. Rather its ideal harks back to the sheltered harem with the mother emerging at first as nurse and homemaker, while the man remains the sole breadwinner. Thus the Negro woman more than the women of any other group in America is the protagonist in the fight for an economically independent womanhood in modern countries. Her fight has not been willing or for the most part conscious but it has, nevertheless, been curiously effective in its influence on the working world.[50]

Additional perspectives on the sources of the different ideologies of Du Bois and Frazier can be gleaned from a selective examination of biographical information. Edwards argues that "Frazier's early interest in race problems was combined with an interest in socialism. At Howard he had been a member of the Intercollegiate Socialist Society."[51] It will be recalled that Frazier saw the emergence of an urban black proletariat as the most significant twentieth-century development pointing to possible advances for black families. Writing in retrospect about his early attraction to socialism, Frazier wrote: ". . . it appears to me that during this period I was developing an objective outlook on racial and other social problems which was divorced in a sense from my reactions to these problems as a person and as a member of society."[52] This "objectification" of the "race problem" was consistent with his supposedly dispassionate "scientific" approach to the study of black families.

Interestingly, although Du Bois also subscribed to a socialist ideology, his response to sociopolitical developments was quite different. In recalling his decision to abandon academe and pure research to become editor of the NAACP organ, *Crisis,* Du Bois observed:

> Gradually and with increasing clarity, my whole attitude toward the social sciences began to change: in the study of human beings and

their actions, there could be no . . . rift between theory and practice, between pure and applied science, as was possible in the study
of sticks and stones. The studies which I had been conducting at
Atlanta I saw as fatally handicapped. . . . I saw before me a problem that could not and would not await the last word of science, but
demanded immediate action to prevent social death.[53]

Thus Du Bois sought greater, rather than less, attachment to the group
he studied. Even in the structure of the Atlanta conferences, Du Bois
attempted to establish forums for the direct sharing of academic research
with practitioners involved in efforts to improve the status of black Americans. In fact, *The Negro American Family* ends with commentaries by a
social worker and a religious leader. The involvement of the church was
seen by Du Bois, along with adult basic education, as keys to strengthening black families. In contrast, Frazier avoided direct involvement in
social change efforts. He became the pure intellectual who, according to
Edwards, ". . . conceived his roles as that of an intellectual, not a policy
maker. This is why he refused offers in which he would be expected to
play the role of race relations expert or race relations advisor."[54]

Frazier's theories were also strongly influenced by his intense ideological commitment to racial integration. Edwards argues that Frazier
". . . thought that the only hope for the Negro American was full integration into American society. To achieve such equality the Negro must
be able to compete. . . ."[55] Du Bois, although also an integrationist,
recognized more than Frazier the need for the maintenance of a self-
development option. At various stages of his career he subordinated his
basic commitment to integration and openly advocated a nationalist agenda.
This was one reason that he was removed as editor of the *Crisis* in the
early 1930s.[56]

Edward's observation that although Frazier ". . . would be opposed to
the separatist objective of . . . Black Power advocates [he] would have
subscribed, however, to programs, short of complete separation, designed to produce in the Negro a sense of racial identity and self-
respect."[57] Frazier wrote in 1962:

The African intellectual recognizes what colonialism has done to the
African and he sets as his first task the mental, moral, and spiritual
rehabilitation of the African. . . . But the American Negro intellectual, seduced by dreams of final assimilation, has never regarded
this as his primary task. . . . I am referring to his failure to dig down

into the experience of the Negro and bring about a transvaluation of that experience so that the Negro could have a new self-image or new conception of himself. It was the responsibility of the Negro intellectual to provide a positive identification through history, literature, art music and the drama.
The truth of the matter is that for most Negro intellectuals, the integration of the Negro means just the opposite, the emptying of his life of meaningful content and ridding him of all Negro identification. For them, integration and eventual assimilation means the annihilation of the Negro—physically, culturally, and spiritually. . . . But even in the North where Negroes will achieve greater integration, I can not envision any assimilation in the foreseeable future . . . if the Negro is ever assimilated into American society his heritage should become a part of the American heritage, and it should be recognized as the contribution of the Negro as one recognizes the contributions of the English, Irish, Germans and other people. . . . But this can be achieved only if the Negro intellectual and artist frees himself from his desire to conform and only if he overcomes his inferiority complex.[58]

What we see, then, is Frazier's shift toward an Afrocentric focus that places his ideological position close to that of Du Bois. This convergence suggests the direction for synthesizing the combined legacy of Du Bois and Frazier to guide contemporary research.

TOWARD A RESURRECTION OF DU BOIS AND FRAZIER

The school of thought that is the legitimate heir to the Afrocentric approach to the study of black families has built on the work of Andrew Billingsley.[59] In the spirit of Du Bois and Frazier, Billingsley has characterized black families as a social subsystem mutually interacting with subsystems in the black community and in the wider society. Three critical patterns of interaction are identified:

(a) interactions with external subsystems including social forces and institutional policies associated with the domains of economics, politics, education, health, welfare, law, culture, religion, and the media;
(b) interactions with external subsystems in the black community, such as schools, churches, peer groups, social clubs, black businesses, neighborhood associations, etcetera;

(c) interactions within and among internal subsystems in families, such as intrahousehold interactions involving husbands and wives, parents and children, siblings, other relatives, and nonrelatives.

The third set of interactions constitutes Billingsley's major extension of the work of Du Bois and Frazier. A complex typology of family types is introduced that include 32 variants of nuclear, extended, and augmented households that can be found among blacks. Patterns of functioning are hypothesized to differ across types and to change within families as members pass through stages of the life-cycle. This theoretical framework overcomes one of the principal weaknesses of the approaches of Du Bois and Frazier, the absence of sophisticated models of internal family dynamics.

Allen has further extended the Du Bois–Frazier tradition by introducing developmental concepts into the ecological approach of Billingsley.[60] The developmental model is designed to describe the dynamic process by which family members move through the life-cycle. A series of different developmental stages is hypothesized. During each stage, families are confronted by differing demands and resource support. Black families are seen as developing coping strategies in responses to blocked opportunities.

Important strides have also been made in eliminating the weaknesses in the historical record of black families and the interpretation of that historical record that plagued both Du Bois and Frazier. The work of Sudkaharsa and Nobles has contributed to a dramatic reassessment of the significance of the African legacy for black families in America.[61] The research of Blassingame, Gutman, and Genovese has contributed to the slow emergence of a truer picture of the slave family than was possible for either Frazier or Du Bois to produce.[62] In a similar vein, Karenga, Nobles, and Kunjufu are providing an important counterweight to the persisting ideology that treats African-American families as unassimilated white families.[63] The analyses of Austin,[64] Millett,[65] and Okpala[66] provide the basis for comparative research on the development of black families in Africa and the African diaspora that complement an Afrocentric as opposed to Eurocentric perspective.

While the developments described above are encouraging, a more concerted effort to synthesize the older and newer Afrocentric approaches to the study of black families is needed. Careful analysis of the work of Du Bois and Frazier should facilitate the development of new insights regarding patterns of unwed motherhood in contemporary black America.

Both Du Bois and Frazier linked this phenomenon in the early twentieth century to the broader processes of industrialization and urbanization and their impacts on sex ratios and related variables. It should be possible to adapt this model to examine the process of de-industrialization that is currently disproportionately affecting African-Americans and the lives of black families.

In addition, while the use of sophisticated quantitative techniques can undeniably enhance the collective understanding of social forces and their impacts upon black families, the critiques of Frazier and Du Bois indicate the need for caution and diversification. Continuing refinement of ethnographic research techniques, media impact studies, oral histories, and other approaches to qualitative data may be more critical for producing the type of data necessary to inform meaningful efforts to promote change than further advances in statistical empirical research.

Second, the theoretical models employed by both Du Bois and Frazier locate race as a factor affecting the social conditions of African-American families simultaneously, independent of, and interacting with the phenomena of class and caste. Neither quantitative nor qualitative research that ignores these complex patterns of interaction will advance the state of collective understanding. One approach to recognizing the independent influence of race in empirical studies while simultaneously controlling for the class aspects of observed patterns is demonstrated in the Benjamin and Stewart[67] chapter in this volume.

Third, the cultural-historical approach of Du Bois and Frazier challenges contemporary researchers to develop a clearer understanding of how cyclical changes in socioeconomic systems produce derivative cyclical changes in the conditions and functioning of African-American families. This issue is related to the interaction between unwed motherhood and industrial change suggested above. To illustrate, Hill has documented how changes in family composition occur during recessionary and expansionary periods.[68]

Fourth, the comparison of Du Bois's emphasis on a direct link between research and structured intervention is reflected in the last section of this volume. In addition, the chapters examining social policy and the development of black families in part 2 describe the macro constraints on micro intervention strategies in a manner consistent with the Du Bois/Frazier systems approach.

Finally, there is an important lesson to be learned from the fact that this particular analysis is necessary at all. The systematic submergence of the tradition of Du Bois and Frazier is not simply a historical accident. Care must be taken to preserve the current efforts to foster continued development of an Afrocentric disciplinary matrix through collective effort by an identifiable group of committed scholar activists. Those scholars need to know how the institution of science functions and how specific approaches come to dominate others. Kuhn's study of scientific revolutions is pivotal as he reminds us that: "Scientific knowledge, like language, is intrinsically the common property of a group or else nothing at all. To understand it we shall need to know the special characteristics of the groups that create and use it."[69]

A generation of scholar activists who have a vested interest in the development of black families as part and parcel of the elevation of peoples of African descent must be produced so that the often cited dictum of Du Bois that the problem of the twentieth century is the problem of the "color line" will not have to be updated to describe the next century.

NOTES

1. Thomas Kuhn, *The Structure of Scientific Revolutions,* 2nd edition (Chicago: University of Chicago Press, 1970).

2. See for example, Diana Crane, *Invisible Colleges: Diffusion of Knowledge in Scientific Communities* (Chicago: University of Chicago Press, 1972) and Stephen Toulmin, *Human Understanding,* Vol. 2 (Princeton: Princeton University Press, 1972).

3. Kuhn, (1970), p. 184.

4. Ibid., p. 185.

5. Ibid., p. 192.

6. See for example D.P. Warwick, "The Politics and Ethics of Cross-cultural Research," in H.C. Triandis and W.W. Lambert, eds., *Handbook of Cross-cultural Psychology,* Vol. 1 (Boston: Allyn-Bacon, 1980), pp. 319-371.

7. W.E.B. Du Bois, "The Atlanta Conferences," *Voice of the Negro,* Vol. 1 (March 1904), pp. 85–90.

8. Thomas Poole, "Black Families and the Black Church: A Socio-historical Perspective," in H.E. Cheatham and J.B. Stewart, eds., *Black Families: Interdisciplinary Perspectives* (New Brunswick: Transaction, 1990).

9. Mitchell Rice, "Black Hospitals: Institutional Impacts on Black Family Development," in Cheatham and Stewart (1990), and Barbee Myers, "Hypertension as a Manifestation of the Stress Experienced by Black families," in Cheatham and Stewart 1990.

10. Wilhelmina Leigh, "Federal Government Policies and the Housing Quotient of Black American Families," in Cheatham and Stewart (1989).

11. Du Bois, p. 85.

12. Ibid., p. 88.

13. Ibid., pp. 86, 89.

14. Howard W. Odum, *American Sociology: The Story of Sociology in the United States through 1950* (New York: Longmans, Green and Company, 1951), p. 238.

15. See Melville Herskovits, *The Myth of the Negro Past* (Boston: Beacon Press, 1958).

16. E. Franklin Frazier, *The Negro Family in the United States* (Chicago 1939: rev. and abridged ed., University of Chicago Press, 1966), p. 8.

17. W.E.B. Du Bois, *The Negro American Family* (report of a social study made principally by the college class of 1909 and 1910 of Atlanta University, under the patronage of the trustees of the John F. Slater Fund; together with the *Proceedings of the 13th Annual Conference for the Study of the Negro Problems*) (Atlanta: Atlanta University Press, 1908), pp. 42-96.

18. See for example John Blassingame, *The Slave Community, Plantation Life in the Antebellum South* (New York: Oxford University Press, 1972); Eugene Genovese, *Roll, Jordan, Roll, the World the Slaves Made* (New York: Pantheon Books, 1974); Herbert Gutman, *The Black Family in Slavery and Freedom, 1750-1925* (New York: Pantheon Books, 1976); Melville Herskovits, *The Myth of the Negro Past* (Boston: Beacon Press, 1958); and Niara Sudarkasa, "Interpreting the African Heritage in Afro-American Family Organization," in Harriette McAdoo, ed., *Black Families* (Beverly Hills: Sage, 1981), pp. 37-53.

19. Du Bois (1908), p. 21.

20. Frazier (1966), p. 32.

21. The original articulation of the "Talented Tenth" appeared in W.E.B. Du Bois, "The Talented Tenth," in *The Negro Problem: A Series of Articles by Representative American Negroes Today, Contributions by Booker T. Washington, W.E.B. Du Bois, et al.* (New York: James Pott and Company, 1903), pp. 33-75. The best statement of his refined view is found in W.E.B. Du Bois, "The Talented Tenth Memorial Address," *Boule Journal*, Vol. 15, no. 1 (October 1948), pp. 3-13.

22. Frazier (1966), p. 362.

23. Ibid., p. 88.

24. Ibid., p. 88.

25. Ibid., p. 88.

26. Ibid., p. 366.

27. Du Bois (1908), p. 36.

28. Frazier (1966), p. 367.

29. Du Bois (1908), p. 42.

30. Ibid., p. 9.

31. Ibid., p. 31.

32. Elliott Rudwick, "W.E.B. Du Bois as Sociologist," in James E. Blackwell and Morris Janowitz, eds., *Black Sociologists, Historical and Contemporary Perspectives*. (Chicago: University of Chicago Press, 1974), p. 50.

33. W.E.B. Du Bois, (1899) *The Philadelphia Negro: A Social Study*, p. 5. Philadelphia: University of Pennsylvania.

34. Du Bois (1908), p. 134.

35. E. Franklin Frazier, "The Negro Family in Chicago," in *E. Franklin Frazier on Race Relations*, ed., G. Franklin Edwards (Chicago: University of Chicago Press, 1968), p. 121.

36. Frazier (1968), p. 137.

37. Ibid., pp. 137-138.

38. E. Franklin Frazier, "Theoretical Structure of Sociology and Sociological Research," in Franklin (1968), pp. 27-28.

39. Ibid.

40. Rushton Coulburn and W.E.B. Du Bois, "Mr. Sorokin's Systems," *Journal of Modern History*, Vol. 14 (1942), pp. 511-512.

41. E. Franklin Frazier, "Three Scourges of the Negro Family," *Opportunity*, Vol. 4 (July 1926), pp. 210-213, 234, and E. Franklin Frazier, "Is the Negro Family a Unique Sociological Unit?," *Opportunity*, Vol. 5 (June 1927), pp. 165-168.

42. Frazier (1926), p. 212.

43. Ibid., p. 210.

44. Frazier (1927), p. 165.

45. Ibid., p. 165.

46. Ibid., pp. 165-166.

47. Ibid., p. 166.

48. Ibid., p. 166.

49. Du Bois (1908), p. 9.

50. W.E.B. Du Bois, *The Gift of Black Folk: The Negro in the Making of America* (1924; reprint, New York: Washington Square Press, 1970), p. 142.

51. G. Franklin Edwards, introduction to Frazier (1968), p. x.

52. Odum (1951), p. 234.

53. W.E.B. Du Bois, "My Evovling Program for Negro Freedom," in Rayford W. Logan, ed., *What the Negro Wants* (Chapel Hill: University of North Carolina Press, 1944), pp. 56-57.

54. Edwards (1968), p. xx.

55. Ibid., p. xx.

56. See for example W.E.B. Du Bois, "A Negro Nation within the Nation," *Current History*, Vol. 42 (June 1935), pp. 265–270. Du Bois's public advocacy of communism and oppostion to U.S. imperialism in Liberia also conributed to his removal from his N.A.A.C.P. office.

57. Edwards (1968), p. xx.

58. E. Franklin Frazier, "The Failure of the Negro Intellectual," *Negro Digest* (February 1962), pp. 35-36.

59. Andrew Billingsley, *Black Families in White America* (Englewood Cliffs: Prentice-Hall, 1968).

60. Walter Allen, "The Search for Applicable Theories of Black Family Life," *Journal of Marriage and the Family* (February 1978), pp. 117-129.

61. Sudkaharsa (1981) and Wade Nobles, "Toward an Empirical and Theoretical Framework for Defining Black Families," *Journal of Marriage and the Family* (November 1978), pp. 679-688.

62. See Herskovits (1958).

63. Nobles (1978); Maulana Karenga, *Introduction to Black Studies.* (Los Angeles: Kawaida Publications, 1982); Jawanza Kunjufu, *Developing Positive Self-Images and Discipline in Black Children* (Chicago: African-American Images, 1984).

64. Roy L. Austin, "Family Environment, Educational Aspirations and Performance in St. Vincent," in Cheatham and Stewart (1990).

65. Robert Millette, "West Indian Families in the United States: The Boundaries of Conjugal Relations," in Cheatham and Stewart (1990).

66. Amon O. Okpala, "Child-Care and Female Employment in Urban Nigeria," in Cheatham and Stewart (1990).

67. Lois Benjamin and James B. Stewart, "Values, Beliefs and Welfare Recipiency: Is There a Connection," in Cheatham and Stewart (1990).

68. Robert Hill, *Black Families in the 1974-75 Depression* (Washington, DC: National Urban League Research Department, 1975).

69. Kuhn (1970), p. 210.

Part II

Ecological Perspectives

INTRODUCTION

Despite staggering odds, black families have met and overcome and even conquered considerable adversity, which inheres in the structure of U.S. society. In this section the authors address ecological factors of a predominantly Eurocentric society and demonstrate the effects on black families that result from structural discrimination in housing, medical care, and social and economic policies.

The resilience of these families is demonstrated in the first chapter in this section, where Poole examines the role of the black church in its capacities first as conservator and transmitter of values and second as guardian of a wider social agenda, namely uplifting the race. Poole addresses Christianity both as a tool used to legitimize enslavement of peoples and as the conduit through which slaves became evangelized. It is out of the peculiar institution of slavery, Poole notes, that the task of the black church after emancipation was born. He contends that the church was the only arena of African-American life in which true liberty was enjoyed. Institutions developed in the black church, then and now, foster the well-being of black families. Poole traces the history of the black church through to its current reemergence with a contemporary statement of its role in the life of black families and black communities.

Rice's chapter addresses the rise of black hospitals in response to racially discriminatory policies that precluded adequate health care delivery to black Americans. Ironically, he notes the same policies and practices account for the demise of the institutions that numbered more than 150 at the turn of the twentieth century, a number that exceeded 400 during the century. Rice traces the history of blacks' response to hospital segregation from the pre-Civil War period through to the 1957 Imhotep Conference called to address this issue and propose resolutions. He concludes that integration and the advent of Medicare and Medicaid are two of the most significant factors in the decline of black hospitals. He suggests that the revitalization of these hospitals lies in mergers, alliances, and diversification and development of specialties that reduce competition among these institutions. While no chapter in this volume addresses black collegiate institutions, there is a curious parallel in the history of black colleges' rise and demise attributable to the same ecological factors that Rice points out here as implicated in the history of black hospitals.

Leigh, using the concept of the "housing quotient," then examines the condition of housing, access to housing, and federal housing policies and programs as these affect black families. She provides this analysis through comparisons of available data for black and white families with the same socioeconomic characteristics. Leigh concludes that blacks have a less effective demand for housing due to their smaller proportion of married households and therefore might live in lesser quality houses than households of other groups. Using crowdedness—number of persons per room—as a measure of internal living conditions, she reports a considerable racial differential. Further, Leigh reports inequality of ownership and of access by blacks to the existing, available housing and little relief of these situations through federal programs. Although blacks are served by all federal programs, these programs fall considerably short of their prescribed potential to ameliorate blacks' housing conditions.

In the final chapter in this section Hill addresses the effects of economic forces and structural discrimination on black families' stability. Continuing the theme of the chapters by Rice and Leigh, Hill argues persuasively that social forces and policies result in disporportionate adverse effects on the functioning of low and middle income black families. Hill contends that black families were negatively affected in the 1980s by major economic trends, which included recessions, pervasive inflation, and industrial and population shifts. Economic policies likewise, he notes, have negatively affected these families. Hill's conclusion is that race is still the significant factor in blacks' social and economic condition and assessments that conclude otherwise have failed to consider the role of institutionalized racism as manifested in structural or unintended discrimination. He presents evidence that is at the base of each negative effect. Finally, he asks: ". . . are there actions that can be taken to counteract these adverse effects?"; "are these societal forces beyond our control?"; and "since negative consequences were not intended, is there moral or legal obligation to correct those inequities?" The answers that his analysis forces are *yes, no,* and *yes,* respectively.

2

BLACK FAMILIES AND THE BLACK CHURCH: A SOCIOHISTORICAL PERSPECTIVE

Thomas G. Poole

The purpose of this chapter is to examine the relationship between the church and the family in African-American life by providing a socio-historical account of the black church's role in family maintenance and value transmission. It argues that the church's unique status in African-American society and culture has been utilized to foster family well-being. These efforts, it will be shown, have been difficult to assess, in part because they have been subsumed into the larger and more general mission of the development and "uplifting" of the race.

RELIGION AND THE BLACK FAMILY IN SLAVERY

The history of slavery in the United States is inextricably bound to the slaveholders' and traders' practice of Christianity. These two groups had convinced themselves that the slave trade was justified because it led to the Christianization and civilization of the Africans. This justification, coupled with the hope that Christianity would make the slaves more docile and obedient, resulted in the manipulation and distortion of the Christian faith for the purpose of endorsing slavery. As Richard Wright observed: "The apex of white racial ideology was reached when it was assumed that white dominion was a God-given right."[1]

The claim to missionary involvement left the slaveholders no option but to introduce the Africans to Christianity. Initially both slaves and free blacks were evangelized and allowed limited participation in white churches. They were segregated from the white congregation during services, made to sit in the gallery or in "Negro pews" or to stand or sit along the back wall of the sanctuary. In time blacks broke away from the white churches. Free blacks in the North and South organized and established independent congregations and denominations. Likewise some groups of slaves began to meet on their own on the plantations, often in secret. These slave churches, which E. Franklin Frazier termed the "invisible institution," were often pastored by a slave preacher—one who stood out among the slaves for his or her knowledge of the Bible, leadership skills, and ability to read and sing.[2] These black religious institutions set about the task of fostering the spiritual development of the African-Americans.

Due to the variety of ways in which the slave might have participated in organized religion, it is difficult to ascertain the impact of any one religious organization on the slave family. However, it can be said that the facet of the slave experience that most disturbed the conscience of the white churches was family life.

The survival of the black family through the period of slavery was accomplished against the odds. Eugene D. Genovese (and Cheatham in "Empowering Black Families" in this volume) maintains that black families emerged from slavery with a more stable foundation and a stronger set of family values than one is often led to believe.[3] This is true, despite the fact that the slave system gave little regard to the well-being of slave families. While family life was fostered on some plantations, the general brutality of slavery conspired against family stability.

There were a number of factors that contributed to this systemic discouragement. First, the slave marriage was given no civil recognition as a legal and binding contract. Marriage for slaves was under the whimsical jurisdiction of the individual slaveholders. Second, in the eyes of most owners the slave family had little social significance. Husbands, wives, and children were first and foremost slaves, who were permitted to care for their own families and homes after they tended to their owner's family, home, and fields. Finally, there was little overriding concern for the unity of the slave family. Barter and economic considerations often led to the forced separation of family members. For example, James Oakes has documented the sale of three tracts of land in North Carolina for which the owner would "readily take either tobacco, hogs, negroes, or money."[4] Oakes also cites a party in Williamsburg, Virginia, at which the hostess entertained her guests by raffling off "a likely young Virginia Negro Woman, fit for House Business, and her child."[5] Further, Oakes notes that the transfer of slaves was seen as a way to pay taxes and settle debts.

It was this pervasive disregard for family unity that most disturbed the conscience of white Christians. Those churches that enrolled slave members were especially forced to deal with the issue of families that had been broken by the slave trade. The white preachers taught their enslaved parishioners to respect the marriage relationship, and they often urged slaveholders to prevent the disintegration of slave families. However, the continued breakup of the slave family forced the white churches into a desperate casuistry.

What was the marital status of the slave according to the church? Was a remarried slave, who had been separated from his or her original spouse, guilty of adultery? If this constituted adultery, should the guilty slave be allowed to remain in the church? Each church had to answer these questions for itself. The response of the Welsh Neck Baptist Church of South Carolina is one indication of the white church's acquiescence to slavery's attack upon the family. "Servants, separated by their owners & removed to too great a distance to visit each other, may be considered as virtually dead to each other; & therefore at liberty to take a second Companion, in the life time of the first, as the act of separation was not their voluntary choice; but the will of those, who had legal control over them."[6]

There is ample evidence that the slaves had a much higher regard for family life and the sanctity of marriage than was encouraged by many of the slaveholders. This was reflected in their attitude toward the wedding ceremony. Many times slave weddings were presided over by the wedding ceremony. Many times slave weddings were presided over by the slaveholder; the ritual was finalized by the couple's jumping over a broomstick. This alternative cermony might have been instituted, in part, to avoid the obvious hypocrisy of a Christian service. Yet many slaves appear to have preferred a religious service conducted by a member of the white clergy or by a slave preacher. It was more dignified and lent a sense of seriousness and sanctity to the event. Albert J. Raboteau reports that Minerva Davis boasted that her parents' master arranged for "a white preacher to read out of a book to them. They didn't jump over no broom. . . ."[7] When the service was conducted by slave preachers it sometimes included public recognition of the tenuous nature of the marriage bond. Kenneth M. Stampp found that it was the practice of a slave preacher in Kentucky to unite couples with the injunction "until death or *distance* do you part."[8] Furthermore, the testimonies of former slaves reveal that many couples chose to be "remarried" after Emancipation, when they could have a religious service and their union would be legally recognized.

This brief account of the difficulties the black family faced during slavery was presented in order to set the context for the task that was to be undertaken by the black church after Emancipation. After slavery the black church came to consist of those independent black congregations and denominations that were previously formed by free African-Americans, to which was added the liberated slaves who had practiced Christianity either in the churches of their masters or in the "invisible institution" of the slave church. One aspect of the church's responsibility was the clarification of family values by bringing them into conformity with biblical norms and social mores and articulating them within the framework of Christian theology.

THE BLACK CHURCH AFTER EMANCIPATION

Just as the advent of slavery destroyed the social network of the traditional African family and tribe, so too Emancipation disrupted the black family patterns that had developed in the environment of the plantation. It was through the institutional church that African-American life became structured and organized. For this reason it is nearly impossible to overstate the social significance of the black church between the end of the Civil War and World War I.

Given the proliferation of Black Codes throughout the South during Reconstruction, the eventual abandonment of Reconstruction, and the routine segregation of the North, the church was the only arena of African-American life in which true liberty was enjoyed. Only in the black church could the former slave find the opportunity for economic cooperation and education; only there could African-Americans exercise political power, leadership skills, and self-determination. In addition, as a spiritual organism the church served as the reservoir of the emerging African-American culture and the primary channel through which it was transmitted. For these reasons Frazier has referred to the black church after Emancipation as "a nation within a nation."[9]

Theological adjustments were necessary in the post-Civil War church. The "invisible institution" had come into being because the slaves had perceived the hypocrisy in the masters' practice of Christianity. In response the slave church developed a theology of hope and liberation that spoke directly to the severity of the slaves' existential condition. The circumstances of chattel slavery did not allow for the luxury of theological speculation regarding abstract doctrines such as the Trinity or the divinity of Jesus. Rather, the theology of the slave church consisted of the simple yet profound expression of the deep longing for freedom. Nowhere was this more evident than in the themes of the spirituals and field songs such as the traditional hymn "Oh, Freedom": "And before I'd be a slave, I'll be buried in my grave, And go home to my Lord, and be free."

After Emancipation the church assumed that it could move beyond the fight for survival and enter into the dual mission of "uplifting" the race from the degradation of slavery and advancing the race into full participation in American society. It was believed that these goals represented two sides of the same coin—a more meaningful participation in society would result, in part, from the white realization that African-Americans were capable of such participation. In other words, the black church was convinced that white America needed to be educated as to the African-Americans' ability to govern democratic institutions and contribute to the political and economic aspects of the commonwealth.[10]

One aspect of the "uplifting" of the race centered on the development of family values that would conform with the norms of white society. Within the nuclear family the church labored to establish stable monogamous marriage patterns that, under ideal conditions, were to be patriarchal in nature. Ample biblical testimony pointed to the man as the head of the family.

Perhaps of more significance was the development of the nuclear family within the context of emerging black communities that tended to revolve around the church. The corporate church itself was considered an extended family, a phenomenon that interestingly reflected the preservation of the African tribal heritage and the extended slave family. According to this model "the pastor functions as . . . male parent. The first lady . . . functions as female parent. The governing board of deacons, elders, or presbyters functions as the older adults in the consanguineal [sic] unit, and the membership at large functions as the siblings."[11] So long as men governed the extended family of the church "whatever control it attempted to exercise tended to confirm the man's interest and authority in the family."[12] Thus the church functioned as an agent of social control with respect to the black family. It sought to bring the nuclear family into conformity with the patriarchal practice of white America by means of both theological teachings and its own exemplary life as an extended family.

The black church also initiated several specific programs designed to foster the well-being of the nuclear family. Every major black denomination instituted Christian education programs and youth associations with the intent of ministering to the young people's spiritual needs while enhancing their leadership capabilities. Youth catechisms were written to aid parents and teachers in the task of instructing African-American youth as to the tenets of the Christian faith, including specific lessons on the nature of Christian marriage and family life.[13] Furthermore, the church, while functioning as an extended family, urged the family to function as an "extended church" by conducting family devotional services. In the African Methodist Episcopal Zion Church, for example, these were to consist of prayer and Scripture reading designed to remind the family members that they share "as fully as the most lofty of earth the fatherhood of God and the brotherhood of man."[14]

Another contribution to the progress of the race, which had implications for family life, was the church's advocacy of education. The slaveholders' intent to dominate every aspect of the slaves' lives led to severe restrictions on literacy. The church, being the center of African-American social life and community organization, took up the task of reversing this situation after Emancipation. Education in the black church had two foci. First, it became increasingly important that the clergy be educated. The uneducated preacher came under attack from a number of African-American leaders, including Booker T. Washington, author William Wells Brown, and the African Methodist Episcopal Church's Bishop Daniel Alexander Payne. An educated clergy was believed to be necessary not only to prevent the misinterpretation of the Christian message and the misinforming of the people, but to advance the black church as a serious and vital social institution within white society.

The second focus concerned the laity. While there was some disagreement as to the value of an education, most ministers felt that formal academic training was essential to the "uplifting" of the race. Education, it was assumed, would lead to a more sophisticated understanding of the demands of Christian discipleship, and this, in turn, would give rise to moral progress. The acquisition of knowledge was seen as a primary component in the guarantee of freedom. A more serious debate centered on the nature of one's formal training. Some insisted that a classical liberal arts education would best equip the African-American to enter the professional strata of American society. Others maintained that African-Americans needed to be trained as skilled laborers who could then enter industry and agriculture and make a contribution to the economic well-being of the nation. In fact, the black church encouraged and provided both kinds of education.[15] Not only did the churches establish elementary and secondary schools, but beginning with Wilberforce University in 1863 (rechartered by the African Methodist Episcopal Church) black denominations, sometimes joining with white denominations, founded a number of colleges and universities that provided theological, classical, and scientific training. Many of these institutions remain in operation today.

The final aspect of the church's ministry to black families between Emancipation and World War I was the encouragement of economic cooperation. This development is reflected in the numerous benevolent societies that arose, especially in the rural South (though northern, urban, and antebellum societies were not uncommon). The benevolent society ministered to the freed slaves who were suddenly on their own with no resources. Specifically they were designed to meet the crises of sickness and death and to provide aid for widows and fatherless children. These societies became established in the church as an institutionalized expression of Christian love.

We can conclude that the black church engaged in a number of programs that directly or indirectly affected the family life of African-Americans. The values reflected in the church's teaching and lifestyle attempted to reinforce the notion of stable monogamous relationships within patriarchal families. The result of these efforts is difficult to measure, in part because the overriding concern for the ''uplift'' and advancement of the race overshadowed the success or failure of any one particular program. Every program must be judged by the degree to which the race was advanced in white society. Therefore one must assess the total agenda of the church in this period.

Despite the many positive contributions made by the black churches between Emancipation and World War I, the goal of moving the race into the mainstream of American society was unfulfilled. Indeed, the end of Reconstruction signaled the beginning of a period of retrenchment that the church was unable to alter significantly. I will briefly review three of the theories proposed to account for this failure.

First, it can be said that the church underestimated the nature and cause of racism. As indicated earlier, the church's agenda was set, in part, by the belief that white people misunderstood African-American people. The church assumed that when white society came to realize that African-Americans were capable people—serious, educated, skilled, patriotic—they would be welcomed into the white world as full and equal partners. The problem with white people, in other words, was ignorance. Rather than demanding equality, freedom, and justice as that which was owed to African-Americans as human beings, the black church accepted the responsibility of proving to whites that African-Americans deserved to be treated with dignity.

The refusal to regard racism as an intentional and systematic attack upon blackness led to a preoccupation with bogus issues. For example, in his 1899 Presidential Address to the National Baptist Convention, Elias C. Morris denied that there was racial conflict in the country. Instead he pointed to a general disregard for law and order, which in his estimate threatened the very fabric of American society. He announced, "Those who are inclined to the opinion that there is a great 'Race Problem' confronting us, are asked to look beyond racial lines for a moment and behold the civil strife in many of the States of the Union."[16] Morris believed that those who detected racial conflict must "modify their opinion as to a race problem and agree that a serious law and order problem confronts the people of this country."[17] This tendency to apologize for and rationalize the racist acts and attitudes of white America contributed to the failure of the black church's social goals.

A second reason for the church's lack of success was the inherent discrepancy in its social mission. I have pointed out that the black church understood its obligation as being twofold—to uplift the race from the dehumanizing effects of slavery and to advance the race into full participation in American society. Many church leaders thought of the latter as the inevitable result of the former. Peter J. Paris has argued that this assumption turned the church's strategy into a self-contradiction. The black church came into existence to provide a forum for the free practice of Christianity, which had been denied to blacks in white churches. That is to say racism necessitated the founding of the black church and mandated the separate development of the African-American. Yet the black church remained committed to a social vision in which race would not be a determining factor in the enjoyment of freedom, equality, and justice. The uplifting of the race, though important in its own right, was seen as a necessary step in the nation's transformation from a racist society to an egalitarian society. So the black church, born of racism, worked toward the realization of a social ideal that was not shared by the society it sought to join. Furthermore, it pursued the goal by fostering progress for the race through education, family life, economic cooperation, and other programs from which African-Americans were systematically excluded in white society.[18] The result was, in essence, a program of separate development for the purpose of integration.

A third factor in the black church's limited success was its acceptance of the agenda of the white church. Rather than defining those areas of particular importance to African-Americans, the black church accepted the causes and projects that the white church deemed necessary—

moralizing on topics such as sexual promiscuity, dancing, smoking, and drinking, erecting large and costly buildings, and engaging in foreign missions (albeit to Africa and the Caribbean). In accepting these standards the black church moderated its challenge of the status quo and functioned in such a way as to establish an organization that paralleled the white church's ministry to white America.

Taken together these theories reveal the extent to which the black church "baptized" the philosophy of Booker T. Washington. It was Washington who had announced in his Atlanta Exposition Address that progress for African-Americans would result from the gradual increase in the white understanding that blacks could contribute to the welfare of the country. "No race that has anything to contribute to the markets of the world is long in any degree ostracized."[19] This, he noted elsewhere, was "a great human law which cannot be permanently nullified."[20] Washington's solution called for the training of African-Americans in industrial skills, which would demonstrate the economic importance of the race and thereby foster the gradual enlightenment of white society.

Washington's perspective did not go unchallenged. W.E.B. Du Bois, Frederick Douglass, and Pan-African ministers such as Edward Wilmont Blyden and Henry McNeal Turner offered differing philosophies that attracted considerable attention in the church between Emancipation and World War I. In the end, Washington's thought won out with the African-American clergy because, as Wilmore has reasoned, "it was consonant with the ethics of the white Christianity by which they were increasingly influenced."[21] Washington's gradualism seemed to match the lifestyle that Jesus demonstrated—the patient, loving, nonviolent, suffering servant. So the church tended to take on an accommodation-oriented mindset that, by following the lead of the white church, gave rise to what Wilmore has termed "bourgeoisification."[22]

We can conclude that the period between Emancipation and World War I witnessed the rise of the church as the single most important and influential social institution in African-American life. It served as the primary means by which the freed slaves organized their communities and attempted to bring family life into conformity with white America. Its ordained ministers were considered, by blacks and whites, to be the chief spokespersons for the African-American community. At the same time it held to a number of misconceptions about the nature of racism and these, in turn, led to what Paris has described as a deficient strategy for the overall advancement of the race.

THE BLACK CHURCH IN THE TWENTIETH CENTURY

The Great Migration and World War I mark the advent of a new era in the history of the African-American people and the United States. In 1915 rural southern blacks began to stream into the urban industrial areas of the North hoping that, as the United States began to activate its war industry, Booker T. Washington's philosophy would be proven accurate. To the contrary, the black work force was greeted by low wages, impoverished living conditions, and the dehumanization of oppressive racism. Moreover, when African-American troops were sent to Europe to defend democratic principles that they did not enjoy at home, they encountered segregation from the white troops, lower wages than those given to white soldiers, racial violence perpetrated by their white comrades, and a European citizenry that had been warned by white American soldiers of the inordinate sexual impulses of African-American men. They returned home to new forms of racial violence: the resurgence of the Ku Klux Klan, the July 4, 1917, attack on East St. Louis, Missouri, and the events of 1919 in which scores of African-Americans were killed in a variety of urban race wars.

The persistence of these conditions led African-Americans to question the significance of the black church and the relevance of its agenda for the advancement and "uplifting" of the race. The southern migrants could not find in sophisticated northern churches the spirit of the folk religion they had practiced at home. This disenchantment gave rise to the storefront churches and a number of black sects and cults. Others left the black church in favor of new religious or nationalist movements such as Noble Drew Ali's Moorish Science Temple, Elijah Muhammad's Lost-Found Nation of Islam, and the Universal Negro Improvement Association of Marcus Garvey. The establishment of the National Association for the Advancement of Colored People (1909) and the National Urban League (1911) and the political organizing of people such as William Monroe Trotter and Ida B. Wells-Barnett indicated that growing numbers of people no longer saw the church as the only vehicle by which progress could be pursued. Still others, a portion of the small black middle class, marked their new status by leaving the black church for white religious organizations.

These emerging alternatives to the black church were both the cause and the consequence of its waning influence in this century. They indicate a dissatisfaction with the church's social agenda that led to escalating criticism and distrust. The study of black urban life in Chicago between

1935 and 1940 conducted by St. Clair Drake and Horace R. Cayton demonstrated a growing attitude among African-Americans that the church had become hypocritical. It revealed a disapproval of the emphasis placed on money and a popular suspicion that funds were being used dishonestly; people perceived the church to be "racketeering on people's emotions."[23] Similarly, Johnson's survey of the rural South (also 1935–1940) showed that African-American youth harbored a feeling of skepticism with regard to the clergy. It denoted a criticism of the church that focused on hypocrisy, stereotyped sermons, and a double moral code.[24]

Manning Marable's comparative analysis of U.S. Census data documents the quantitative decline in the black church during the 1900s. In 1890 there were 12,159 black ministers in the United States. The number peaked in 1910 at 17,495. In 1970 the total was 12,850—a net gain of slightly less than 700 ministers in eighty years. At the same time other professions showed tremendous growth. The number of teachers, for example, grew from 14,100 in 1890 to 235,436 in 1970. The number of doctors expanded from 909 to 6,106 during that same period. The increase of new professional opportunities means that the church's monopoly on the African-American talent pool has been broken. This problem is compounded by the fact that the African-American population has grown. In 1890 there were 1.62 African-American clergy per thousand African-Americans. By 1979 that ratio had shrunk to .53 per thousand. This comparison makes it easy to see that the criticism of the black church in this century and the church's failure to enhance the social position of the African-American people are tied in a cyclical relationship to numerical decline.[25]

Paradoxically, the black church continues to be the single most important organization in African-American life. Its prominence as the ethical center of the community stems from its status as the oldest social institution in African-American history. It remains, as C. Eric Lincoln once declared, "the spiritual face of the Black community."[26] This is so because the church continues to be one of the few organizations that is owned and governed by and is accountable to African-Americans.

Lincoln maintains that the black church has entered into a new era that is marked by the simultaneous continuation and transformation of its theology, social agenda, self-identity, and worldview. This transformation has been brought about by the success of the civil rights movement, the popularity of the Black Power movement, and the articulation of black theology. While it is true that a large portion of the black church failed to support these developments initially, it is also true that the church could not hide from their influence. With their help "the Black Church has broken free from the chrysalis of accommodation" and it has been mobilized and empowered to "tell the good news of its self-liberation."[27]

This emerging church is already showing signs of a renewed ministry to the African-American family. For example, the following 1978 resolution of the Progressive National Baptist Convention articulates the intention that is presently shared by the major black denominations:

> WHEREAS, American Black family life is beset by disorganization, plagued by economic pressures, and overwhelmed by the daily problems of racism in the struggle for survival, and WHEREAS, some of these problems manifest themselves in poor inter-familial communication, under achievement and delinquency [sic] behavior amongst children, alcoholism, wife and husband abuse, child abuse and neglect, drug abuse, and collapse of the family unit;
>
> BE IT RESOLVED that our churches establish and conduct regular family life programs, conferences, and seminars for the education and edification of PNBC families and youths.[28]

Increasingly theologians are directing their attention to the need for family ministry. J. Deotis Roberts, for instance, has pointed to the church and family as the co-holders of the key to the future. Wisely, he has warned that the black church cannot minister to the family according to the agenda of the white church, for the African-American family encounters peculiar problems with which white families, even those in the lower socioeconomic classes, are not confronted. Similarly the black family ought not to become preoccupied with white family issues that are not crucial to its own welfare. Roberts urges the church to become proactive in its ministry to the family, especially with respect to those issues that are germane to the African-American condition. He suggests that this might lead to an investigation into the nature of motherhood and "wifehood," the sense of responsible fathering, and the liberation and holistic development of children. The contribution of the black church in this analysis must include the insistence that these problems be studied with an eye on the racist society in which they arise.[29]

Henry H. Mitchell and Nicholas Cooper Lewter identify the home as the ideal network through which the church can provide the "preventative maintenance" of unconditional love and enlightened care. Rather than waiting to aid the person in crisis, the church must minister to and in the environment of the home, where many crises originate. This effort to break "the grip of the vicious cycle of the shortage of love" will require a family spiritual discipline similar to the family devotions of an earlier time.[30] In this respect, the church, which has never lost its identity as an extended family, will have to nurture the nuclear family in order to remake it into an organism of trust, love, faith, and shared values.

Wallace Charles Smith has gone so far as to develop a sample curriculum for black family enrichment that is based on the following four goals: (a) to heighten self-image by the recognition that all persons are created in the image of God, (b) to familiarize African-American Christians with resources and methods that enhance family enrichment, (c) to develop skills that foster family enrichment, and (d) to heighten the awareness of African-American Christians as to the problems facing the black family. Smith is convinced that no effective family ministry can take place apart from the recognition that African-Americans, as a whole, comprise a suffering and disadvantaged community in the United States. This reality mandates that family enrichment include a plan for social mobilization designed to help African-Americans reach equality with whites in the areas of economic development, health care, housing, jobs, and education. That is, the church must fight the historic tendency to concentrate on spiritual development alone. Smith calls for a national effort on the part of the church and proposes a four-pronged attack to family enrichment—preaching, Christian education, counseling, and community organizing.[31]

In addition to theologians, social scientists are suggesting some ways in which the black church can use its traditional role in the community to enhance the health of African-American families. Wade W. Nobles and Lawford L. Goddard, for example, call for the church to make every effort to affect public policy on behalf of African-American families. Among needed reforms they recommend advocacy for financial incentives for the internal support patterns found in African-American families, participation in educational curriculum development at the state and local level, the demand for accurate treatment of African-American family life in textbooks and the media, and the demand for an evaluation of the current criminal justice system. They also urge the black church to serve as an agent of community development by providing the following: a link with the business and corporate world in order to generate funds for the community; economic and emotional support for those families that have members in prison; nutrition, education, and food cooperatives;

youth employment opportunities; and a forum for the community's discussion of legislative issues that affect the African-American community. Finally, they suggest that the church might develop archives, support computer-based retrieval systems, republish classic works, and support independent research centers.[32]

This movement forces the observation that the black church is beginning to focus on the issues related to black family life with a new seriousness and vigor. Whether or not these programs will be effective remains to be seen. Regardless, the contemporary church continues to operate within the historical paradox. Its future as an institution is not in doubt. Indeed, it is assured by the existential needs of the African-American people. At the same time, it is not clear that the church will emerge as a principal actor in their social, political, and economic liberation. Ministry to the family may well be the first step toward a revitalized social relevance and, subsequently, a renewed understanding of the church as a necessary agent in the process of change.

CONCLUSION

Throughout its history the black church has been the most important and influential social institution in African-American life. This remains true despite the fact that the church has periodically pursued an ill-conceived agenda that has hindered its effort to uplift and advance the race. Its ministry to the family must be seen within this context.

While serving as the primary transmitter of values to the family, particularly in the period immediately following Emancipation, the church's ministry to the black family has been hampered by an accommodation-oriented mindset patterned after the priorities of the white church. If the church has indeed been transformed by the events of the 1960s—the civil rights movement, Black Power, and black theology—the resulting perspective will focus family ministry on the issues that are pertinent to African-Americans.

NOTES

1. Richard Wright, introduction to St. Clair Drake and Horace R. Cayton, eds., *Black Metropolis: A Study of Negro Life in a Northern City*, Vol. 1 (New York: Harper and Row, 1962), p. xxi.

2. E. Franklin Frazier, *The Negro Church in America* (New York: Schocken Books, 1974), p. 23ff.

3. See Eugene D. Genovese, *Roll, Jordan, Roll: The World the Slaves Made* (New York: Pantheon Books, 1972), pp. 450-458.

4. James Oakes, *The Ruling Race: A History of American Slaveholders* (New York: Vintage Books, 1983), 26.

5. Ibid., pp. 26–27.

6. Albert J. Raboteau, *Slave Religion: The "Invisible Institution" in the Antebellum South* (New York: Oxford University Press, 1978), p. 187.

7. Ibid., p. 229.

8. Kenneth M. Stampp, *The Peculiar Institution: Slavery in the Antebellum South* (New York: Vintage Books, 1956), p. 344. Emphasis in original.

9. Frazier, (1951), p. 35ff.

10. This thesis is elaborated in Peter J. Paris, *The Social Teaching of the Black Churches* (Philadelphia: Fortress Press, 1985).

11. Wallace Charles Smith, *The Church in the Life of the Black Family* (Valley Forge: Judson Press, 1985), p. 74.

12. E. Franklin Frazier, *The Negro Family in America* (New York: Dryden Press, 1951), p. 134.

13. E. g., Samuel B. Schieffelin, *Milk for Babies & Children's Bread* (Philadelphia: African Methodist Episcopal Church, 1875).

14. William J. Walls, *The African Methodist Episcopal Zion Church: Reality of the Black Church* (Charlotte: A.M.E. Zion Publishing House, 1974), p. 115.

15. Edward L. Wheeler, *Uplifting the Race: The Black Minister in the New South 1865-1902* (Lanham, MD: University Press of America, 1986), p. 97ff.

16. Elias C. Morris, "1899 Presidential Address to the National Baptist Convention," in Milton C. Sernett, ed., *Afro-American Religious History: A Documentary Witness* (Durham, NC: Duke University Press, 1985), p. 277.

17. Ibid., p. 277.

18. Paris (1985), p. 83ff.

19. Booker T. Washington, *Up from Slavery* (New York: Dell Publishing, 1965), p. 158.

20. Ibid., p. 197.

21. Gayraud S. Wilmore, *Black Religion and Black Radicalism: An Interpretation of the Religious History of the Afro-American People,* 2d rev. edition (Maryknoll, NY: Orbis Books, 1983), 140.

22. Ibid., p. 152.

23. St. Clair Drake and Horace R. Cayton, *Black Metropolis: A Study of Negro Life in a Northern City,* Vol. 2 (New York: Harper and Row, 1962), p. 419.

24. Charles S. Johnson, *Growing Up in the Black Belt: Negro Youth in the Rural South* (New York: Schocken Books, 1967), p. 146ff.

25. Manning Marable, *How Capitalism Underdeveloped Black America* (Boston: South End Press, 1983), p. 195ff.

26. C. Eric Lincoln, *The Black Church since Frazier* (New York: Schocken Books, 1974), p. 115.

27. Ibid., p. 134.

28. Personal correspondence from C. J. Malloy, Jr., 16 October 1986.

29. J. Deotis Roberts has written extensively on the black church and the black family, e.g., *Roots of a Black Future: Family and Church* (Philadelphia: Fortress Press, 1980) and "The Black Church's Ministry to Families: Priestly Ministry," in his *Black Theology Today: Liberation and Contextualization* (New York: Edwin Mellen Press, 1983).

30. Henry H. Mitchell and Nicholas Cooper Lewter, *Soul Theology: The Heart of American Black Culture* (San Francisco: Harper and Row, 1986), p. 168.

31. Smith, (1985) p. 85ff.

32. Wade W. Nobles and Lawford L. Goddard, ''Black Family Life: A Theoretical and Policy Implication Literature Review,'' in Aminifu R. Harvey, ed., *The Black Family: An Afro-centric Perspective* (New York: United Church of Christ Commission for Racial Justice, 1985), pp. 25-89.

3

BLACK HOSPITALS: INSTITUTIONAL IMPACTS ON BLACK FAMILIES

Mitchell F. Rice

Evidence is that the slave infant mortality rate was "fantastic" and that only a modicum of health care was provided to ensure that slaves were functional. Following the "War between the States," black hospitals were founded to provide black families with health care that otherwise was unavailable or inadequate. This movement also led to the need to train more black medical doctors. From the 1891 founding of Provident Hospital and Training School (Chicago), which was to become the premier black hospital, generally these hospitals thrived until the advent of court-ordered desegregation and federally subsidized medical care. Of approximately 400 known black hospitals, only about 30 exist today. The negative effects of both segregation and integration on health care delivery to black families, as indexed in the rise and decline of black hospitals, are discussed in this chapter. Strategies to prevent the further decline and to reinstate these hospitals are also discussed.

INTRODUCTION

At the turn of the twentieth century a large number of black, racially identifiable hospitals served as the focal point of health care for a large majority of the black population. Discriminatory policies had denied blacks access to white hospitals. Further, research has shown that since the slavery era blacks have been the recipients of "second-class medicine."[1] One account of slave health status shows that blacks in 1850 had a life expectancy of only 21.4 years and slave infant mortality was "fantastic." In fact, Kenneth Stampp observes that slave infant mortality widened considerably the life expectancy rates between whites and blacks and the overall disparity in life expectancy rates between whites and blacks was greater because "slave deaths were unreported more often than Whites."[2] Numerous other accounts of slave health status indicate that blacks received only the modicum of health care necessary to maintain their functional status as slaves.[3]

When official federal government life expectancy data became available for the first time at the turn of the twentieth century, whites outlived blacks by nearly 15 years.[4] At that time significant disparities also existed (and continue to exist) between blacks and whites in the areas of infant and maternal mortality.[5] The need for hospitals to provide health and emergency care services to the black population was quite obvious and remains so.[6]

Wesley points out that since the Civil War about 500 hospitals have existed specifically for the purpose of providing health care to blacks.[7] In the early 1900s there were some 200 black hospitals with a combined bed capacity of about 10,000 beds.[8] Most black hospitals were located in the South. In recent years the number of black hospitals has declined to 26, or about one-eighth of the total that had existed in the early 1900s. Rice notes that black hospitals constitute less than .5 percent of the approximately 7,000 hospitals that exist today in the United States.[9] Despite their longevity and historically significant role in serving the health care needs of the black community, the existence of hospitals that exclusively served blacks is unknown to most individuals in both black and white communities.

Why do so few black hospitals remain? What circumstances and/or conditions have led to their virtual demise? This chapter is concerned with these questions. It briefly discusses the impact of segregation and integration on the rise and eventual decline of black hospitals and suggests strategies necessary for the future survival of black hospitals. The conclusion suggests that black hospitals can play a vital role in improving the health status of blacks by providing relevant, client-specific health care.

SEGREGATION, INTEGRATION, AND BLACK HOSPITALS

Segregation and the Rise of Black Hospitals

From the Civil War period to the 1960s hospitals owned and operated by black community interests provided a significant amount of health care to black Americans. The first black hospitals were dedicated to providing care to blacks whose access to white hospitals was severely restricted, if not nonexistent, because of segregation policies. Research indicates that prior to the Civil War hospital care was virtually nonexistent for blacks. The first American hospital, built on Manhattan Island in 1658 for sick soldiers, did provide care to West Indian blacks, and the Colored Orphan Asylum (New York City, 1836) treated blacks.[10] Only one hospital, the Georgia Infirmary (chartered in December 1982), was founded before the Civil War to care for blacks.[11]

A few of the first black hospitals after the Civil War were founded in the public sector. Many of these hospitals were operated by the Bureau of Freedmen, Refugees and Abandoned Lands.[12] Freedmen's Hospital in Washington, D.C. (now Howard University Hospital), began operating in 1863. The federal government sponsored the hospital in an attempt to deal with a number of diseases that were widespread among the black population in the District of Columbia.[13] Friedman notes that this was the first of more than 150 black hospitals that came into existence by the turn of the twentieth century.[14]

From the early 1900s to the 1950s black hospitals or those serving a large black constituency were founded in major cities throughout the East, South, and Midwest, such as Chicago, New Orleans, Miami, Washington, D.C., Detroit, Atlanta, Baltimore, Dallas, Kansas City, Missouri, St. Louis, and New York. Some other smaller cities having black hospitals during this time period were Flint, Michigan; Nashville, Tennessee; Roanoke, Virginia; Evanston, Illinois; Selma, Alabama; Montgomery, Alabama; Tuskegee, Alabama; Greensboro, North Carolina; and Richmond, Virginia.

With a small but growing number of black medical graduates starting professional practices, there existed a growing need for hospitals as a place for both additional training and to treat black patients. Prior to the creation of Howard University School of Medicine, blacks received formal training at a few white schools (in 1860 nine northern medical schools admitted blacks) or were trained abroad.[15] The first black to receive an American medical degree in 1847 graduated from Rusk Medical College in Chicago.[16] Prior to this time, however, a number of blacks did engage in medical practice and the "healing art."[17]

During the Reconstruction and post-Reconstruction era eight black medical schools were opened: Howard University Medical School (Washington D.C., 1868), six years after the founding of Freedman's Hospital); Meharry Medical College (Nashville, Tennessee, 1876); Leonard (Shaw) Medical College (Raleigh, North Carolina, 1882–1915); Louisville National Medical College (Kentucky, 1887–1910); Flint Medical College (New Orleans, Louisiana, 1889–1911); the Medical Department of the University of West Tennessee (1900–1923); and Chattanooga National Medical College (Tennessee, 1902). Of these, only Howard and Meharry have survived. Howard admitted both black and white students while Meharry admitted only blacks. George Hubbard Hospital of Meharry Medical College, however, did not open it doors until 1918.[18] With only two hospitals and the need for many more, the "Negro medical ghetto" began to develop.[19]

Most of the early black hospitals were owned by private black physicians; 10 percent were owned by the government, and about 30 percent were church-affiliated and owned.[20] Provident Medical Center in Chicago (initially named Provident Hospital and Training School) was founded in 1891 through the community leadership of Dr. Daniel Hale Williams, who approached the black community about the feasibility of a hospital "where Blacks could be treated with dignity and study the medical profession."[21] Provident Medical Center was to later become a premier black hospital. It was the first black hospital to provide postgraduate courses for minority physicians, the first black hospital to be approved by the American College of Surgeons for full graduate training in surgery, and the site of the first successful open heart surgery, performed in 1893 by Dr. Daniel Hale Williams.[22]

During the first few decades of the twentieth century Provident Hospital, Freedman's Hospital (Howard University), and George W. Hubbard Hospital (Meharry Medical School) were among the best nationally known black hospitals. The Tuskegee Institute Hospital and Nurse's Training School in Alabama (founded in 1892 and becoming John A. Andrews Hospital in 1912) was perhaps the most well-known black hospital in the Deep South. Other hospitals founded by black doctors or private black groups include the Home Infirmary (Clarksville, Tennessee), Red Cross Hospital (Lexington, Kentucky), McDonough Memorial Hospital (New York City), Douglas Hospital (Kansas City, Kansas), Douglass Memorial Hospital (Philadelphia), Whittaker Memorial Hospital (Newport News, Virginia), and Mound Bayou Community Hospital (Mississippi). Douglass Hospital was established by Dr. Nathan Francis Mossell in 1895. Whittaker Memorial Hospital was founded in 1908 by four black physicians as a four-bed facility. As of June 1985 it had expanded to 126 beds and was renamed the Newport News Community Hospital.[23] Mound Bayou Community Hospital was founded in 1941 in the all-black town of Mound Bayou, Mississippi, by a black fraternal order in order to provide health care to the community. The hospital closed in 1983.[24]

The Black Community's Response to Continuing Hospital Segregation

As a response to the continuing problem of hospital segregation, the

first Imhotep National Conference on Hospital Integration was held March
8–9, 1957, in Washington, D.C., sponsored by the National Medical
Association, the Medico-Chirurgical Society of the District of Columbia,
and the National Association for the Advancement of Colored People
(N.A.A.C.P.). The stated purposes of the conference included the following:

> To bring together representatives of all interests among hospitals,
> the public, the healing professions, and government agencies, which
> are concerned with this problem.
>
> To provide a complete, comprehensive situation throughout the coun-
> try as it exists today through first-hand presentations from various
> regions.[25]

Imhotep was chosen as the conference name for two reasons: First, as
a reminder that a dark skin was associated with distinction in medicine
before that of any other color, this served to emphasize the dignity of the
approach to the problem. Second, because the name meant, "He Who
Cometh in Peace," the sponsoring organization came in peace in a time
of emotional tension.[26] The meeting was attended by two hundred dele-
gates representing 16 constituent societies of the National Medical Association and N.A.A.C.P. and four branches of the National Urban League
and various medical and hospital societies. The first conference was
devoted to identifying the various forms of hospital discrimination and
acquainting the attendees with the forms of discrimination.

Dr. W. Montague Cobb, a longtime civil rights physician, served as
chairman of the conference. One of its first actions was to vote unanimously to seek an amendment to the Hill-Burton Act deleting provisions
for racial segregation. The conference also voted unanimously to "work
continuously and vigorously, in the spirit of amity until racial discrimination has been eliminated from all hospitals in the United States."[27]
Prominent speakers at the conference included Representative Barratt
O'Hara (Illinois), Congresswoman Florence P. Dwyer (New Jersey), Roy
Wilkins (N.A.A.C.P. executive secretary), Dr. Robert S. Jason (dean of
Howard University College of Medicine), Dr. T.R.M. Howard (president
of the National Medical Association), and Dr. Edward C. Mazique (president of the Medico-Chirurgical Society).[28]

The second conference was held in Chicago in May 1958. The meeting
focused on hospital discriminatory techniques in one major city. The third

conference, held in Washington, D.C., in May 1959, focused on the means of dealing with hospital discrimination and the attitudes of white professional personnel.[29]

Three additional annual Imhotep conferences were held, the last of which was the 1963 conference in Atlanta, Georgia. The conference was discontinued after the passage of the Civil Rights Act of 1964. At the 1962 conference, President Kennedy sent a special letter of greeting to the attendees advising them that the U.S. attorney general had intervened in a federal court case to support the argument that the segregation clause (separate but equal provision) in the Hill-Burton Act was unconstitutional. President Kennedy also sent a letter to the 1963 conference pointing out that the effort of the Imhotep Conference was "perfectly in tune with that of the federal government."[30]

Invitations requesting representatives to attend the conference were sent to those organizations representing the predominantly white professional and hospital power structure. It would seem that conference leaders believed that having official representation from the white professional and hospital power structure in attendance would bring an end to hospital segregation. These organizations, however, only sent observers (not high-ranking officials) or no one at all. The American Hospital Association and the American Medical Association had observers in attendance at the first conference. Other organizations in attendance were the U.S. Public Health Service; the National Health Council; the National Association of Social Workers; the District of Columbia Hill-Burton Advisory Council; the University of Pittsburgh; the Physicians Forum, the National AFL-CIO, New York; Hampton Institute; and others including a number of hospital representatives. The American Medical Association sent an observer to the 1959 conference. The American Nurses Association sent observers to the 1957 and 1963 conferences.[31]

Ironically, when the U.S. Department of Health, Education and Welfare convened a conference on the elimination of hospital discrimination in July 1964 (supported by President Johnson) all organizations that did not officially attend the Imhotep conferences were well represented at this conference. This included such organizations as the Federal Hospital Council, the American Hospital Association, the American Medical Association, the American Dental Association, and the American Nurses Association. The National Medical Association and the National Dental Association (both all black organizations) were represented at the conference.[32]

To the dismay of the attendees, who were expecting an appearance by

President Johnson, associate special counsel to the president Hobart Taylor (a black) represented the president and urged all those in attendance to support what would be explained to them. Taylor's appearance, perhaps more than his words, was in itself a powerful message to the assembled hospital power structure of the country. Department of Health, Education and Welfare (DHEW) secretary Anthony J. Celebreeze said that President Johnson expected hospitals to comply with the Civil Rights Act of 1964 and compliance would avoid needless controversy and litigation. This 1964 DHEW conference was termed the eighth Imhotep Conference by Dr. W. Montague Cobb, who conceived and organized the first Imhotep Conference.[33]

Integration and Black Hospitals

Until 1964 the black hospital was the primary source of hospital care for the black community. It was at this time that the ''separate but equal'' language in the federal Hill-Burton Hospital Construction Survey Act of 1946 (P.L. 79-725) was found unconstitutional. The legislation provided federal funding for the modernization and construction of hospitals nationwide and required the delivery of ''adequate hospital facilities or color, . . . *but an exception shall be made in cases where separate hospital facilities are provided for separate population groups*'' (emphasis added). For the first seventeen years following the legislation, the ''separate but equal'' provision allowed federal funds to support a racially separate hospital system.[34]

In 1962 in the case of *Simkins v. Moses H. Cone Memorial Hospital,* a group of black physicians and dentists, along with several of their black patients, challenged the separate but equal provision at Moses H. Cone Hospital and Wesley Long Community Hospital, both in Greensboro, North Carolina. Neither hospital had permitted privileges to black practitioners, and Cone Memorial rarely admitted black patients. Both hospitals had received sizable Hill-Burton grants. Cone Memorial had received $462,000 in 1954 and $807,950 in 1960. Long Community had received $1,617,150 in 1954 and $66,000 and $265,000 in 1961.

The black plaintiffs alleged that they were being denied equal protection of the law under the Fifth and Fourteenth Amendments of the Constitution. The U.S. District Court disagreed on the grounds that private hospitals were not instrumentalities of the federal government. Upon appeal, the Fourth Circuit reversed on the rationale that receipt of Hill-Burton funds by hospitals represented the ''necessary'' degree of federal and state involvement and participation. The separate but equal provision in the Hill-Burton legislation was declared unconstitutional. Congress amended the legislation to reflect the court's decision with the passage of the Civil Rights Act of 1964.[35]

Title VI of the Civil Rights Act of 1964 makes specific reference to nondiscrimination prohibitions when a program or activity receives federal financial assistance. Because of the Title VI provision, U.S. Surgeon General William H. Stewart on March 4, 1964, notified all hospital administrators that in order to be eligible to receive federal financial assistance or to participate in a federally assisted program, a hospital must be in compliance with Title VI.[36] Sampson and Friedman have argued that the Title VI provision has been responsible for the demise of a large number of black hospitals.[37]

THE DECLINE OF BLACK HOSPITALS

According to Nathaniel Wesley, Jr., a noted authority on black hospitals, more than 400 hospitals have been identified during the twentieth century as having been established, by black and white founders, to serve a black population.[38] By 1984 there were 32 black hospitals around the country, a decrease from 40 in 1983. Seven of the hospitals had closed or discontinued in-patient services in 1983.[39] At the end of 1988 there were only 26 black hospitals in the United States. Table 3.1 provides a listing of the 26 black hospitals. Several of the hospitals are now under management or ownership by private for-profit hospital chains or nonprofit entities. For example, Martland Hospital (Newark, New Jersey), Richmond Community Hospital (Virginia), and Whittaker Memorial Hopital (Newport News, Virginia) are under management by the Hospital Corporation of America—a private for-profit hospital chain. Detroit Receiving Hospital (Michigan), L. Richardson Memorial Hospital (Greensboro, North Carolina), and Memphis Regional Medical Center (Tennessee) are managed by nonprofit organizations.[40]

Cook County Hospital (Chicago) and Kings County Hospital (Brooklyn, New York) are the largest black public hospitals. Based on data from the American Hospital Association for the year 1982, these two hospitals have over 1,200 beds and employ more than 5,500 full-time employees. Their budgets exceed $172 million.[41] Jackson Park Hospital (Chicago) and Provident Hospital (Baltimore) were the largest private nonteaching

TABLE 3.1
Black Hospitals, 1988

Name	Location
Bethany Hospital**	Chicago
Charity Hospital of Louisiana***	New Orleans
Cook County Hospital***	Chicago
Cuyahoga County Hospital***	Cleveland
D.C. General Hospital***	District of Columbia
Detroit Receiving Hospital***	Detroit
George W. Hubbard Hospital of Meharry Medical College*	Nashville, TN
Harlem Hospital Center***	New York City
Howard University Hospital*	District of Columbia
Hughes-Spalding Community Hospital*	Atlanta
Jackson Park Hospital**	Chicago
Kings County Hospital Center***	Brooklyn, NY
King-Drew Medical Center***	Los Angeles
L. Richardson Memorial Hospital	Greensboro, NC
Memphis Hospitals*** (Regional Medical Center)	Memphis
Norfolk Community Hospitals*	Norfolk, VA
North General Hospital**	New York City
Richmond Community Hospital*	Richmond, VA
Riverside General Hospital*	Houston
Roseland Community Hospital**	Chicago
Southwest Community Hospital**	Atlanta
Southwest Detroit Hospital*	Detroit
St. Bernard Hospital**	Chicago
University Hospital (CMDN)***	Newark
Westland Medical Center***	Westland, MI
Whittaker Memorial Hospital (Newport News General Hospital,* effective 1985)	Newport News, VA

Source: Derived from Nathaniel Wesley, Jr., *1984 Black Hospitals Listing and Selected Commentary* (Washington, D.C.: Howard University, 1984), pp. 17–20; Frank D. Roylance, "Black Hospitals in Critical Conditions." *Baltimore Evening Sun,* September 23–26, 1985, four-part series; and Nathaniel R. Wesley, Jr., and Julie Benton Lynk, "Institutional Survival: Barriers to the Survival of Black and Other Health Care Facilities and Institutions Suring Predominantly Black Populations," paper presented at the Harlem Hospital Centennial National Health Conference, April 22–23, 1988, New York City.

  *Traditional black private hospitals   = 9
 **Transitional black hospitals   = 6
***Traditional black public hospitals   = 11
                          N = 26

black hospitals. Jackson Park Hospital in 1984 employed some 725 full-time employees and had a budget of approximately $55 million while Provident Hospital had about 1,000 full-time employees and a budget of more than $34 million.[42]

Between 1961 and 1988, 71 black hospitals have either closed, merged, converted, or consolidated (see table 3.2). The most common action was closure. Fifty-seven of these hospitals actually closed, representing an average of about two closures per year over the 27-year period. The years 1967 and 1983 seemed to have been banner years for black hospital closings. Nine hospitals closed in 1967, and 9 hospitals closed in 1983 (see Table 2). Since 1983 18 black hospitals have closed. Forest Avenue Hospital in Dallas, Texas, closed in 1984, and Flint-Goodridge Hospital at Dillard University in New Orleans closed in May 1985.[43] Provident Hospital (Baltimore) merged with Lutheran Hospital (Baltimore) in mid-1985. The consolidation agreement that officially took effect on July 1, 1986, means the end of Provident Hospital. The hospital had been under severe financial strain in recent years.[44] Fairview Medical Center in Montgomery, Alabama, closed in 1986. The Hospital of Englewood in Chicago, Illinois is the latest black hospital to close. The hospital closed in 1988. The most prominent black hospitals to close recently are Provident Hospital in Chicago and John A. Andrews Hospital in Tuskegee, Alabama. Both hospitals closed in 1987. Provident had provided service since 1891 and John A. Andrews since 1892.[45]

INTEGRATION, MEDICARE/MEDICAID, AND THE DECLINE OF BLACK HOSPITALS

Several explanations exist as to why black hospitals have closed. Two of the most important explanations are: (a) integration and its resultant attitudinal changes among the middle class black population regarding health care and (2) the advent of Medicare/Medicaid programs.

Integration

Integration has served as a double-edged sword for black hospitals: "Black hospitals were built to serve Blacks because Black patients and medical staff could not use segregated facilities run by whites."[46] Roylance points out that in 1960 in Baltimore, Maryland, only 1,000 of the estimated 5,200 beds were open to blacks. Provident Hospital, Baltimore's major black hospital, in 1960 was a 137-bed facility and was described as "grossly inadequate" to serve the needs of the city's black population. Although some beds were available to blacks at other hospitals in the city, according to Roylance; "Most private hospitals either excluded Blacks or relegated them to a fixed number of beds in segregated wards."[47]

TABLE 3.2
Black Hospital Closings and Transitions,* 1961–1988

Name	Location	Year Founded	Year Closed
St. Agnes Hospital	Raleigh, NC	1896	1961
Pinkston Clinic Hospital	Dallas, TX	1927	1961
Parkside Hospital	Detroit, MI	1918	1963
Brewster Hospital	Jacksonville, AL	1930	1963
Provident Hospital	Ft. Lauderdale, FL	1938	1964
McRae Memorial Sanitarium	Alexander, AR	1931	1965
Holy Family Hospital	Ensley, AL	1946	1965
Mercy Hospital	Wilson, NC	1930	1965
Good Shepherd Hospital	New Bern, NC	1937	1966
Good Samaritan Hospital	Charlotte, NC	1881	1966
Shaw Memorial Hospital	Oxford, NC	1953	1967
Hunter Clinic Hospital	Marlin, TX	1923	1967
St. Martin Porres Hospital	Mobile, AL	1950	1967
Jefferson Co. TB Hospital	Beaumont, TX	1924	1967
Moton Memorial Hospital	Tulsa, OK	1931	1967
Community Hospital	Wilmington, NC	1920	1967
Jubilee Hospital	Henderson, NC	1911	1967
Gaston Co. Negro Hospital	Gastonia, NC	1911	1967
People's Hospital	St. Louis, MO	1984	1967
St. Phillips Hospital	Richmond, VA	—	1968 (Merger)
St. Mary's Infirmary	St. Louis, MO	1877	1969
Dr. E.R. Noble Clinic Hospital	Rosedale, MS	1918	1970
Collins Chapel Hospital	Memphis, TN	1909	1971
Fla. A & M Univ. Hospital	Tallahassee, FL	1911	1972
Mercy-Douglass Hospital (1895–1948)	Philadelphia	1895	1973
Good Samaritan Waverly Hospital	Columbia, SC	1910	1974
Kate Biting Reynolds Memorial Hospital	Winston-Salem, NC	1938	1974 (consolidation)
E.H. Crump Hospital	Memphis, TN	1897	1974 (consolidation)
Burton Mercy Hospital	Detroit, MI	1939	1974 (merger)
Boulevard General Hospital	Detroit, MI	1933	1974 (merger)
Whitney M. Young Jr. Hospital	Los Angeles, CA	—	1975
Hancock Memorial Hospital	Sparta, GA	—	1975
Red Cross Hospital	Louisville, KY	1899	1975
Yazoo Clinic Hospital	Yazoo City, MS	1940	1975
Lincoln Hospital	Durham, NC	1901	1976 (consolidation)
Mercy General Hospital	Detroit, MI	1918	1976
Morrisania City Hospital	Bronx, NY	1929	1976
Highland Park Gen. Hospital	Highland Pk, MI	1920	1976

TABLE 3.2 (Continued)
Black Hospital Closings and Transitions,* 1961–1988

Name	Location	Year Founded	Year Closed
McClendon-Banks Mem. Hosp	Charleston, SC	1959	1977
Douglass Hospital	Kansas City, MO	1898	1977
St. Joseph Hospital	Kansas City, MO	1874	1977 (consolidation)
Forest City Hospital	Cleveland, OH	1957	1977
Tabernacle Community Hospital	Chicago, IL	1910	1977
West Adams Community Hospital	Los Angeles, CA	—	1978 (consolidation)
Arthur C. Logan Hospital	New York, NY	1862	1978
Burrell Memorial Hospital	Roanoke, VA	1915	1979
Homer G. Phillips Hospital	St. Louis, MO	1937	1979
Sydenham Hospital	New York, NY	1927	1980 (conversion)
Detroit Receiving Hospital	Detroit, MI	1915	1980 (conversion)
Morningside Hospital	Los Angeles, CA	1958	1980
Lockwood Hospital	Houston, TX	1957	1981
Community Hospital of Evanston	Evanston, IL	1930	1981 (conversion)
Clement Atkinson Mem. Hospital	Coatesville, PA	1937	1981
Jackson Hospital	Terrell, TX	—	1983
Kessler Hospital	Dallas, TX	—	1983
Riverside Adventist Hospital	Nashville, TN	1927	1983
Cumberland Hospital	Brooklyn, NY	1922	1983
Good Samaritan Hospital and Nursing Home	Selma, AL	1944	1983
Flint General Hospital	Flint, MI	1932	1983
Christian Hospital	Miami, FL	1918	1983
Mound Bayou Community Hosp.	Mound Bayou, MS	1942	1983
MLK Jr. Memorial Hospital	Kansas City, Mo	1918	1983
Forest Avenue Hospital	Dallas, TX	1966	1984
Flint-Goodridge Hospital	New Orleans, LA	1932	1985
Provident Hospital	Baltimore, MD	1894	1986 (merged)
Fairview Medical Center	Montgomery, AL	1951	1986
Provident Hospital	Chicago, IL	1891	1987
John A. Andrews Hospital	Tuskegee, AL	1912	1987
Milton Community Hospital	River Rouge, MI	1938	1987
The Hospital of Englewood	Chicago, IL	—	1988

Source: See Table 3.1
N = 71
Note: Hospitals were either closed, converted, merged, consolidated, or sold to private nonprofit or profit organizations.

Attitudes of the Black Community

Integration has also led to changes in the attitudes of the black community to include both black physicians and black patients. Black physicians, who once were denied practice and admitting privileges, suddenly had access to white facilities. Since many black hospitals are inadequately equipped, many black physicians and their patients willingly use white hospitals because of access to better equipment, library resources, and physical structures,[48] not to mention their sense of a right to practice in modern, well-appointed facilities. Once they have access to white facilities, black physicians admit black patients who are able to pay or who are insured through commercial insurance programs. Black and white physicians because of hospital policy of for-profit/proprietary hospitals admit their indigent patients to black, charity, or public hospitals. Further, the black middle class has sought out the white hospital and the patients left behind are the poor, the elderly, the penniless, and Medicaid recipients. Moreover, some blacks hold the attitude "that something is better because it's white."[49] Thus, "being 'black' can stigmatize a hospital among many Blacks, just as it does among many whites."[50]

Medicare and Medicaid

The advent of the Medicare/Medicaid programs has made black hospitals and black patients both victims and beneficiaries. André Lee notes that: "while on the one hand these programs have enabled black patients the access to white institutions, they simultaneously diminished the use of these [black] hospitals by black physicians and their patients—both assistance and self pay patients."[51] It is ironic then that while Medicare/Medicaid programs provided health coverage to a large number of uninsured persons, these same programs now serve as a basis for denial of hospital services by a large number of hospitals, especially for-profit ones.[52] Limited government reimbursement schedules under these programs do not allow hospitals to keep charges above costs. As a result, for-profit /proprietary hospitals attempt to limit the number of Medicare/Medicaid patients they serve because it is an economic disincentive.[53] Public hospitals then bear the burden of providing care to Medicare/Medicaid recipients as well as those patients who are uninsured. In California in 1979 Medicare and Medical (Medicaid) reimbursed hospitals 4 and 18 percent less than their costs, respectively. In county hospitals the patient care revenues received were 27 percent less than their costs.[54]

Public hospitals are thus put at a severe financial disadvantage in serving Medicare/Medicaid recipients because of reimbursement schedules that are set below the cost of actually providing the service and because care is not readily accessible to the poor from private for-profit hospitals. In many cities and countries the public hospital is the only department that operates in the red. Stated another way, local governments find it difficult to match their principal source of revenue (the property tax) against their most increasing expenditure (hospital costs).

Local governments because of fiscal pressures have become unwilling to continue to subsidize the costs of their hospitals. Public hospitals with a large black consistency such as Homer G. Phillips Hospital in St. Louis and Philadelphia General Hospital have been closed as a result of government action. Charity Hospital in New Orleans, D.C. General Hospital in Washington, D.C., and Boston City Hospital, all public hospitals, were so inadequately funded that they lost their accreditation by the Joint Commission on Accreditation of Hospitals.[55] Each of these hospitals served a large black population. Further, California's public hospital system has shrunk from 65 hospitals operated by 49 counties (out of a total of 58 counties) in 1964 to 37 hospitals in 29 counties in 1982 to 31 hospitals in 1985.[56] The 34 closed hospitals provided care to a large black and other minority population. Cook County Hospital in Chicago, which provides services to a largely black and poor clientele, has been on the brink of closure several times. Other public hospitals have followed a similar course.

Further, many of the few remaining black hospitals are in financial stress. Patients of black hospitals are typically minorities and poor individuals who either cannot pay for care or are Medicare/Medicaid recipients. Provident Hospital (Baltimore) in 1984, at the time struggling to remain financially solvent, had the third highest percentage of charity cases and bad debts of its total budget of all 52 hospitals in Maryland.[57] Howard University Hospital in Washington, D.C., in 1984 provided $25 million in charity care, a quarter of the charity care provided in the metropolitan D.C. area.[58]

A small body of research now exists that argues that the higher a hospital's charity care and/or Medicaid patients, the more likely it is to have financial stress. For example, Feder, Hadley, and Mullner, after analyzing data from 1,125 respondent hospitals, conclude that "the probability of financial stress was two times larger for hospitals heavily involved in serving the poor than for other hospitals."[59] In California a report by the California Hospital Association notes that Medi-Cal (California's Medicaid Program) may be dangerous to a hospital's fiscal health.[60] The report specifically points out that "the more income a hospital gets from Medi-Cal, the more its financial health seems to deteriorate." Friedman observes that a Medicaid percentage of 50 percent or more means financial trouble for a black hospital. This is especially the case for the small black hospital. As Friedman notes, "the size of the facility is important; if the hospital is larger, the survival time is longer, because it has more resources."[61]

CONCLUSION

This chapter has briefly discussed the impact of segregation and integration on the rise and decline of the black hospital. Segregation promoted the development and growth of the black hospital from the slavery period through the mid-1960s. In the mid-1960s court action and federal integration policy along with the advent of Medicare/Medicaid programs opened the once closed doors of white hospitals to black doctors and black patients. These activities seem to be largely responsible for the decline of the black hospital. Yet, one may ask, "So what? Are services and care not available to black from other hospitals? Why should the decline of the black hospital be an important issue in the black community?"

Public hospitals, which constitute about one-third of the community hospitals in the United States and are the principal health resource available to the black community, have been *declining* in number.[62] As pointed out, previously local governments are reducing their capacity to support public hospitals because in many instances public hospitals are becoming too expensive to fund and operate.[63] At the same time, a large number of public hospitals are being sold or leased to private for-profit or proprietary chains and hospital care is increasingly being provided by these chains. As was noted earlier, private for-profit hospitals limit or consider it fiscally imprudent to serve the poor and Medicare/Medicaid recipients. Further, private for-profit hospital are rapidly growing in number. In 1984 the four largest for-profit chains (Hospital Corporation of America, American Medical International, Inc., Humana, Inc., and National Medical Enterprises, Inc.) owned 709 hospitals with 105,000 beds, managed another 250 hospitals with nearly 32,000 beds, and owned 11 primary provider organizations, 58 psychiatric hospitals, and 20 health maintenance organizations.[64] It is estimated that by the year 1990 30 percent of all acute care hospitals will be proprietary.[65]

Further, blacks, like every other minority group, need institutions they can call their own; a hospital is perhaps one of the most serviceable institutions a minority group can have. The symbolic functions of a hospital for the black community are important. To name a few, a black hospital constitutes a resource for leadership, a focal point for community interests, devotion, and need, and at least one assurance of having arrived in the American political/economic system.

How are the few remaining black hospitals to survive? What survival strategies are necessary? According to Roylance, "developing specialty areas" is the key to black hospital survival. This is necessary to attract patients of all colors. Specialties may include such areas as geriatric medicine (Hubbard Hospital of Meharry Medical School), outpatient facility (Flint General Hospital), and a community-based alcoholism and drug addiction facility (Sydenham Hospital and Kirkwood General Hospital). Another alternative is for specialty black hospitals to become the counterpart of major well-known specialty white hospitals—remain nearly separate but becoming truly equal—and develop national or regional appeal to black doctors and prospective black patients because of their specialty services. This is to say that a specialty black hospital has to become the first choice of a very large number of blacks needing medical service.[66]

Further, if black hospitals can develop *separate* specialty areas they may be able to attract different segments of the black community and thus reduce competition among themselves for patients from the black community at large. Another strategy may involve mergers or alliances with other institutions. This may be most applicable in communities where more than one small black hospital exists. In 1974 Boulevard General and Burton Mercy hospitals merged to form Southwest Detroit Hospital. Cook County Hospital formed an alliance to buy a small number of beds and to refer patients with certain diagnoses to Provident Hospital (Chicago).[67] Ultimately, black hospitals must take these and other actions if they are to survive into the twenty-first century.

NOTES

1. See for example Mitchell F. Rice, "On Assessing Black Health Status: An Historical Overview," *Urban League Review*, Vol. 9 (Winter 1985/86): 6-12; H.N. Rabinowitz, "From Exclusion to Segregation: Health and Welfare Services for Southern Blacks, 1865-1890." *Social Service Review* (September 1974): 327–354; Todd Savitt, *Medicine and Slavery: The Diseases and Health Care of Blacks in Antebellum, Virginia* (Urbana: University of Illinois Press, 1982); E.H. Beardsley, *A History of Neglect: Health Care for*

Blacks and Millworkers in the Twentieth Century South (Knoxville: University of Tennessee Press, 1987); and Mitchell F. Rice and Woodrow Jones, Jr., "Black Health Inequities and the American Health Care System," *Health Policy and Education,* Vol. 3 (1982), pp. 195–214.

2. Kenneth M. Stampp, *The Peculiar Institution: Slavery and the Antebellum South* (New York: Knopf, 1956), pp. 317-318.

3. See for example F. Swados, "Negro Health on the Antebellum Plantations," *Bulletin of the History of Medicine* 10 (1941): 460-472; C.S. Sydnor, "Life Span of Mississippi Slaves," *American Historical Review* 35 (1930): pp. 566-574; M.C. Mitchell, "Health and the Medical Profession in the Lower South, 1845-1860," *Journal of Southern History* 10 (1944): 424-446; W.D. Postell, *The Health of Slaves on Southern Plantations* (Baton Rouge: Louisiana State University Press, 1951); and A.S. Lee and E.S. Lee, "The Health of Slaves and the Health of Freedmen: A Savannah Study," *Phylon*, Vol. 38 (June 1977): 170-180.

4. See U.S. Department of Health and Human Services, Public Health Service, *Health and Prevention Profile, United States, 1983* (Washington, DC: Government Printing Office, 1983).

5. See U.S. Department of Health, Education and Welfare, *Health Status of Minorities and Low-Income Groups* (Washington, DC: Government Printing Office, 1979), and U.S. Department of Health and Human Services, Public Health Service, *Health and the Disadvantaged, Chartbook II* (Washington, DC: Government Printing Office, 1980).

6. Inner-city hospitals, especially those serving a black constituency, are closing or relocating to the suburbs with increasing frequency. See Mitchell F. Rice, "Inner-City Hospital Closures/Relocations: Race, Income Status and Legal Issues," *Social Science and Medicine* 24, 1 (1987): 889-896.

7. Nathaniel Wesley, Jr., *1984 Black Hospitals Listing and Selected Commentary* (Washington, DC: Howard University, 1984).

8. See André L. Lee, "Black Community Hospitals: A Quest for Survival," *Urban Health* (March 1984): 46-47.

9. Mitchell F Rice, "The Urban Public Hospital: Its Importance to the Black Community," *Urban League Review 9* (Winter 1985/86): 64-70.

10. See "Integration Battlefront: Title VI and Hospitals," *Journal of the National Medical Association* 58 (May 1966): 212-215.

11. See H. Hewes, "Georgia Infirmary, First Hospital in the United States Founded for Negroes." *Negro History Bulletin* (October 1945): 2, 23.

12. See H. Morais, *The History of the Negro in Medicine* (New York: Publishers Company, 1967), especially pp. 50-51.

13. For a detailed discussion of the history of Freedman's Hospital see T. Holt, C. Parker-Smith, and R. Penn-Terborg, *A Special Mission: The Story of Freedman's Hospital* (Washington, DC: Howard University, 1975).

14. E. Friedman, "Private Black Hospitals: A Long Tradition Facing Change," *Hospitals* 52 (July 1, 1978): 63-68.

15. See Louis Sullivan, "The Education of Black Health Professionals." *Phylon* 38 (June 1971): 181-193, and Morais, (1967), pp. 26-34.

16. See Max Seham, *Blacks and American Medical Care* (Minneapolis: University of Minnesota Press, 1973).

17. See Morais, pp. 21-26.

18. For a brief discussion of these schools see ibid., pp. 60-70.

19. See National Association for the Advancement of Colored People, *Profile of the Negro Medical Ghetto* (pamphlet, 1947).

20. See Julius Rosenwald Fund, *Negro Hospitals: A Compilation of Available Statistics* (Chicago: Julius Rosenwald Fund, February 1931). By 1983 a large majority of black hospitals were church-related. See "Black Community's Crisis of Care Hits Hospitals and Consumers," *Hospitals,* 51, 6 (March 1977): 70-73.

21. See Editor, "Provident-Chicago Celebrates 95th Anniversary," *NRW Report* (June 1986): 3-5.

22. Ibid.

23. See Editor, "Whittaker Opens New Facility, Changes Name," *NRW Report* (December 1985): 2.

24. See "Letters to the Editor," *Bolivar Commercial,* November 3, 1983, and "Mound Bayou Hospital Leaves Void for the Area," *Atlanta Daily World* October 23, 1983. For a reprint of these articles see Wesley (1984), pp. 67-70.

25. See "The Black American in Medicine," *Journal of the National Medical Association,* supplement 73 (December 1981): 1197.

26. Ibid.

27. Along the NAACP Battlefront, *Crisis* (April 1957): 219-220. The Hill-Burton Act was enacted by Congress in 1946 to build new and modernize existing hospitals across the nation. The legislation contained a separate but equal provision specifically inserted by southern Congressmen to maintain separate hospital facilities. See following pp. 8-9.

28. Ibid., p. 219.

29. Ibid.

30. "The Black American in Medicine," p. 1198.

31. Ibid.

32. Ibid., pp. 1198-1199.

33. Ibid.

34. See O.R. Ewing, "The President's Health Program and the Negro," *Journal of Negro Education* 18 (1949): pp. 436-443 and U.S. Commission on Civil Rights, *Equal Opportunity in Hospitals and Health Facilities: Civil Rights Under the Hill-Burton Program* (Washington, DC: Government Printing Office, 1965).

35. For a discussion of the Hill-Burton program and various court cases see Woodrow Jones, Jr., and Mitchell F. Rice, "Health Care Civil Rights and the Black Community," *Policy Studies Review* Vol. 3 (August 1983): 114-119 and Mitchell F. Rice and Woodrow Jones, Jr., "Health Care, Public Policy and the Courts: Black Health Status as a Civil Rights Issue," *Health Policy* 5 (1985): 207-221.

36. See "Integration Battlefront," pp. 213-214.

37. C. C. Sampson, "Death of the Black Community Hospitals: Fact or Fiction," *Journal of the National Medical Association* (March 1974): 165-168, and Friedman, pp. 63-68.

38. Wesley (1984).

39. Ibid.

40. Ibid.

41. Ibid., pp. 22-23.

42. Ibid., p. 32.

43. See F.D. Roylance, "Provident Survives While Others Shut Down," *Baltimore Evening Sun,* September 23, 1985, pp. A1, A4.

44. See Editor, "Court Approves Merger of Provident Hospital and Lutheran in Baltimore," *NRW Report* (August 1986): 1.

45. Defining a black hospital is not an easy task. While there have been many racially identifiable black hospitals during the segregation era, in the present era according to Wesley and Lynk: "For some reason there is reluctance to attach a racially or ethnically oriented description to most inner city hospitals." Black hospitals can be classified into

three categories: traditional black hospitals, transitional black hospitals, and transient hospitals. Transitional and transient hospitals were originally founded to serve a white clientele; however, due to ownerships changes or changes in racial composition of the community surrounding the hospital they now serve a majority black constituency. See Nathaniel R. Wesley, Jr., and Julie Benton Lynk, "Barriers to the Survival of Black and Other Health Care Facilities and Institutions Serving Predominantly Black Populations," paper presented at the Harlem Hospital Centennial National Health Conference, April 22-23, 1988, New York City.

46. See R.C. Lokeman, "Many Black Hospitals Face Critical Times," *Kansas City Star* (December 7, 1983).

47. See Roylance (1985).

48. See Lee (1984), p. 47.

49. Quote of Nathaniel Wesley, Jr., cited in Friedman (1978), p. 64.

50. See F.D. Roylance, "Provident Seeking Allegiance of Blacks," *Baltimore Evening Sun* September 24, 1985, pp. A1, A4.

51. Lee (1984) p. 46.

52. See E.R. Brown, "Public Hospitals on the Brink: Their Problems and Their Options," *Journal of Health Politics, Policy and Law* (Winter 1983): 927-944. See also G. Dallek, "The Continuing Plight Hospitals," *Clearinghouse Review,* (June 1982): 97-101.

53. On these points see M. Rice, (1985/86), pp. 64-70, and National Health Law Program, "For-Profit Hospitals and the Poor," *Clearinghouse Review* 17 (December 1983): 860-867.

54. See Brown (1983) pp. 935-936.

55. See J.G. Haughton, "Municipal Hospitals: Their Relevance to the Black Community," *Urban League Review* 4 (Summer 1977): 25-28.

56. See Brown (1983) pp. 933-935, and G. Dallek, "Health Care for America's Poor: Separate and Unequal," *Clearinghouse Review,* special issue 20 (Summer 1986); 361-371.

57. See Roylance, "Provident Seeking Allegiance of Blacks," pp. A1, A4.

58. Ibid.

59. J. Feder Hadley, and R. Mullner, "Poor People and Poor Hospitals: Implications for Public Policy," *Journal of Health Politics, Policy and Law* (Summer 1984), pp. 237-250.

60. "Warning: Medi-Cal May Be Dangerous to Your Health," *CHA Insight* (September 3, 1980): 2-5.

61. Friedman, (1978), p. 68.

62. See Rice (1985/86).

63. See ibid. and D.H. Hitt and R.B. Sullivan, "Multi-Institutional Arrangements: Ownership Issues Confront County Hospitals," *Hospitals* (July 16, 1985): 69-84.

64. See S. Martin and J. Gooderis, "Policy and Structural Change in the Health Care Industry," *Antitrust Bulletin* (Winter 1985): 949-974.

65. See National Health Law Program (1983).

66. F. D. Roylance "Developing Specialty Areas Key to Survival," *Baltimore Evening Sun,* (September 26, 1985). pp. A1, A4.

67. Ibid.

4

FEDERAL GOVERNMENT POLICIES AND THE "HOUSING QUOTIENT" OF BLACK AMERICAN FAMILIES

Wilhelmina A. Leigh

The "housing quotient"—the condition of and access to housing—is defined for black American families and is examined in conjunction with the major relevant federal policies and programs. Policies considered include fair housing and the national urban policy. Programs examined include public housing and rental assistance. The lack of data constrains the completeness of the analysis, although certain programs seem to enroll blacks in disproportion to the rest of the population. The paper concludes that blacks currently are served by all federal programs, even though many programs historically have failed to live up to their potential to assist blacks.

This article examines the operation of federal government policies and programs with respect to the "housing quotient"—the condition of and access to housing—of black Americans.[1] Federal housing programs and policies, beginning with public housing established in the 1930s, up to and including the Section 8 voucher program authorized in 1983, all have had an impact upon black families and will continue to. Available information suggests, however, that some of these policies and programs may not have performed up to their potential for assisting eligible black families.

The next three sections cover the condition of housing, the access to housing, and federal housing policies and programs, respectively. The second section compares the condition of housing—measured by structural quality and internal living conditions—consumed by black and white households and families with the same socioeconomic characteristics. The third section discusses access to housing and covers two broad categories—access without discrimination based on race, family composition, or welfare status, and access to housing by ability to afford it. Access to the unit and location of choice come under the former while access to ownership falls under the latter. The fourth section details how some of the major federal government programs and policies have affected the "housing quotient" of blacks.

CONDITION OF HOUSING

Households and Families

Because data on housing conditions are available for households rather than for families, this section first examines the differences between households and families to determine how to modify interpretations of our findings.

The Census Bureau defines a family as a subgroup of households with two or more persons related by blood, marriage, or adoption. Since families often include children, one might expect them to be more concerned than nonfamily households about yard space, unit size, access to excellent schools, and quality of the overall environment.

The percentage distributions of households and family types by race since 1960 reveal that white households and families reflect the pattern of all races, with family households a solid majority of all households and married couples the majority of all family households.[2] The proportion of family households and the proportion that married couples are of these households have decreased over time, however, for all races, including whites. In 1960, for the entire population, family households were 85 percent of all households, but by 1984, they were 73 percent. Married couples decreased from 74 percent of family households in 1960 to 59 percent in 1984. White married couples dropped from 76 percent to 61 percent of family households over the same period.

The picture differs for black Americans. The percentage that family households were of all households declined from 83 to 73 between 1960 and 1984. Over the same period, the share of married couples, out of all family households, declined from 61 to 37 percent. At the same time, the proportion of female-headed households rose from 19 percent to 31 percent of family households, an increase from 2 to 3 times greater than the comparable figure for whites.

How do these differences in the distributions of black and white households affect the condition of housing occupied? One can't say precisely. Although one might expect family households, in general, to have greater demand for higher quality units than nonfamily households, incomes would determine the effectiveness of this demand (i.e., the ability of households to obtain the desired housing). Among all races, as among blacks, and among whites in 1983, married couples had the highest median incomes—$27,329, $21,893, and $27,736, respectively—and therefore the greatest effective demand.[3]

Since a smaller proportion of black households than households of other races are married couples, collectively blacks would have less effective demand and therefore might live in housing of lesser quality than households of other racial groups. In general, when examining data on the condition of housing, one should be aware that the households with greatest incomes—male-headed family households and married couples—are most likely to live in housing in good condition. Female-headed family households and single person nonfamily households are most likely to experience a diminished quality of life, as reflected by the condition of their housing.

Parameters of Housing Condition

Do blacks and whites with the same socioeconomic characteristics consume different quantities of housing? Straszheim and Kain and Quigley found that blacks consume smaller quantities of housing attributes than do whites with similar incomes and life-cycle characteristics.[4] Barton Smith found that in Houston in 1977 blacks consumed less housing quality than whites with similar socioeconomic characteristics.[5] These and other research findings support the notion that race as well as socioeconomic characteristics influences the condition of housing consumed.[6]

How does the structural quality of housing consumed by blacks and whites compare? Although it is the most objective parameter with which to assess a racial differential, structural quality has not been easy to define or to measure consistently.[7] Of the many possible proxies for structural quality, an overall condition measure is used with separate measures of plumbing adequacy and bathroom access.[8] Sizable differences between black households and households of all races are found using these measures.

In 1950, 69 percent of nonwhites lived in sound units and 32 percent lived in dilapidated ones. By 1960, only 55 percent of nonwhites lived in sound units, 28 percent lived in deteriorating units, and 17 percent lived in dilapidated units. Among households of all races, 91 percent in 1950 and 83 percent in 1960 were reported to live in sound units. In 1960, 13 percent lived in deteriorating units and 4 percent lived in dilapidated units, a halving of the percent living in dilapidated units in 1950.

Plumbing adequacy shows similar trends to overall housing condition. Each decade between 1960 and 1980, black renters lacking some or all plumbing decreased by at least 10 percentage points, while the percentage of renters of all races in similar circumstances nearly halved. Among owners, blacks lacking some or all plumbing decreased from 25 percent (1960) to 14 percent (1970) to 5 percent (1980). For households of all races, the comparable figures at least halved each decade. (See Table 1).

Sharing or having no bathroom facilities characterized 68 percent of nonwhite renters and 59 percent of nonwhite owners in 1950. For all races, the 1950 figures were 34 and 26 percent for renters and owners, respectively. By 1960, 45 percent of black renters and 21 percent of renters of all races were still disadvantaged. By 1980, 8 percent of black renters and 4 percent of renters of all races shared or had no bathroom facilities; among owners, only 5 percent of blacks and 2 percent of all races were similarly disadvantaged. (See Table 1).

How do internal living conditions differ by race? Internal living conditions are most often measured by crowdedness within units—the number of persons per room, with 1.00 as the standard. This measure has shown considerable improvement for the population generally and now affects only certain subgroups. In 1946, ten percent of the nation's households lived in overcrowded accommodations.[9] By 1975 the proportion of overcrowded units had declined to 5 percent. However, the rate among black households remains twice as high as the rate among all households.

Renters experienced worse crowding than owners from 1940 to the 1980s. Forty-two percent of nonwhite renter households in 1940 lived with 1.01 or more persons per room while only 25 percent of households of all races did likewise, a gap of 17 percentage points. By 1950, the gap was 19 percentage points. In 1960, the gap was 17 percentage points again, falling to 11 percentage points in 1970 and 4 percentage points in 1980. (See Table 1).

Thus, as measured by crowdedness, a considerable racial differential in internal living conditions appears.

ACCESS TO HOUSING

Housing access for blacks and whites includes access to a location (a suitable environment or a unit of choice) and access to ownership.[10] The

TABLE 1
Measures of Housing Adequacy by Race, 1940 to 1983 a/ b/

	1940	1950	1960	1970	1973	1975	1977	1979	1980	1983
STRUCTURAL QUALITY										
Lacks Some or All Plumbing (Renters)										
Nonwhites	N/A	N/A	28.6	17.6	11.3	10.0	9.1	7.3	7.1	5.3
All Races	N/A	N/A	16.3	7.9	5.8	4.8	4.2	3.6	3.6	2.9
Lacks Some or All Plumbing (Owners)										
Nonwhites	N/A	N/A	24.9	14.4	9.5	7.0	5.5	4.9	4.9	4.4
All Races	N/A	N/A	8.9	4.2	2.3	1.8	1.4	1.4	1.5	1.4
Shared or No Bath (Renters)										
Nonwhites	N/A	67.5	44.6	19.2	11.9	10.8	9.5	7.9	7.5	5.8
All Races	45.5	34.3	21.3	9.2	6.8	6.7	4.9	4.3	4.3	3.6
Shared or No Bath (Owners)										
Nonwhites	N/A	59.4	34.6	15.3	9.8	7.2	5.4	5.2	5.1	4.7
All Races	40.1	25.5	10.6	4.8	2.9	2.0	1.7	1.7	1.7	1.7
INTERNAL CONDITIONS										
Crowded (Renters) c/										
Nonwhites	42.4	40.8	32.9	22.2	14.5	13.2	11.9	10.2	10.0	9.0
All Races	24.9	21.6	16.1	10.6	7.0	6.7	6.2	5.8	6.2	5.6
Crowded (Owners) c/										
Nonwhites	32.0	24.9	21.0	15.5	11.5	10.9	9.2	8.5	7.9	5.8
All Races	14.2	10.9	8.7	6.4	4.8	4.0	3.4	3.1	3.1	2.3
EXTERNAL CONDITIONS										
Overall Opinion of Neighborhood Excellent or Good										
Nonwhites	N/A	N/A	N/A	N/A	65.2	69.5	58.4	59.6	N/A	N/A
All Races	N/A	N/A	N/A	N/A	86.1	82.2	81.4	81.0	N/A	N/A

SOURCES: Census Bureau Reports, Annual American Housing Survey, and Statistical Abstract of the United States.

N/A means not available.

a. Figures are percentages indicating (by race) the proportion of units so characterized.

b. Nonwhites reflects primarily blacks. In 1940 and 1950, however, blacks cannot be isolated from nonwhites as they can in later years. All races includes nonwhites.

c. Crowded is defined as 1.01 or more persons per room.

two categories are not mutually exclusive and the issue of access to ownership is part of the broader issue of affordability, both for renters and owners.

Access to Location

What is the importance of having access to the location or unit or environment of choice? Proponents of the suburbanization of blacks (or the choice of a unit located in the suburbs, presumably with a suitable living environment) favor it because of the associated potential increase in access to jobs.[11] Suburban or not, residence choice often determines the school attended, and education can affect future economic well-being for a family. This section examines patterns by race in access to existing housing, to newly constructed housing, to suitable living environments, and to market information.

Do blacks and whites have equal access to the existing housing stock? In 1980, although the metropolitan areas of the United States were 13 percent black, their central city populations were 22 percent black and their suburban populations were only 6 percent black.[12] Surveys of the residential preferences of blacks and whites indicate that blacks would prefer to live in integrated neighborhoods rather than in the segregated central city ghettoes they populate.[13] The difference between the actual and the preferred distributions of blacks throughout metropolitan areas suggests a negative response to the question of equal access.

Sorensen, Taeuber, and Hollingsworth[14] used a dissimilarity index to measure the percentage of the black population that would have to move for the proportion of blacks on each block to equal the proportion of blacks in the city overall. The index enabled them to evaluate the extent to which black households are distributed throughout each of 109 metropolitan areas as compared to their proportion in these areas between 1940 and 1970. The mean dissimilarity index for 28 of these localities— those with the largest black populations in 1980—remained close to 90 over the years 1940 through 1970, but had decreased to 81 in 1980. Other researchers, Bianchi, Farley, and Spain also found that the high level of residential racial segregation in metro areas lessened but did not disappear between 1960 and 1977.[15] The dissimilarity index and other measures continue to reflect inequality of access by blacks to the existing housing stock.

Do black and white families have equal access to newly constructed housing? Data suggest that the answer to this question is "no." Between 1970 and 1976, households moving into newly constructed units were younger and more affluent than average and often included children. Although black households on average tend to be younger and to include children, their incomes and locations—not in the suburbs where most new construction takes place—generally preclude them from residing in newly constructed units. Between 1970 and 1976, the rate at which blacks occupied new housing was 72 percent of the white rate.[16] Nationwide in 1976, 11 percent of black households but 16 percent of white households resided in newly constructed houses. Within the central cities, 7 percent of blacks and 11 percent of whites lived in newly constructed units, while in the suburbs, 18 percent of blacks and 19 percent of whites did likewise.

Do blacks and whites have equal access to suitable living environments? Some of the most commonly cited measures of a suitable living environment are quality of schools, services, police protection, and desire to move from or remain in current neighborhood. The 1978 Survey of the Quality of Community Life reported several differences by race in assessments of local amenities. While blacks and whites were close when ranking schools excellent or pretty good—59 percent of blacks and 63 percent of whites—they were far apart when evaluating neighborhood crime. Sixty-nine percent of blacks but only 29 percent of whites felt it was a serious problem.[17]

When external neighborhood conditions are assessed by the percentages holding "overall opinion of neighborhood—excellent or good," the figures varied quite a bit by race and over time between 1973 and 1979. For blacks the figures declined from 65 percent to 60 percent and for whites from 86 percent to 81 percent. These surveys indicate that smaller percentages of blacks than of whites (or all races) perceived their living environments as suitable. (See Table 1).

Do blacks and whites have equal access to market information? The use of testers in many housing markets suggests the answer is "no."[18] Testers reveal that blacks and Hispanics receive less information about available housing than whites in both the rental and sales markets of many cities. In the 1977 nationwide Housing Market Practices Survey, agents were found to discriminate against blacks on several aspects of rental unit availability: whether a unit was available, date of apartment availability, number of units available, number of units offered for inspection, and length of waiting list for an apartment. Real estate sales agents discriminated against blacks when supplying the following information: whether housing was available in the requested price range and neighborhood, number of houses offered as serious possibilities, and number of houses offered for inspection.

Access to Ownership

The rate of homeownership has been deemed the single most meaningful statistic to sum up overall housing conditions.[19] In addition, homeownership, compared to renting, generally is associated with more amenities (both within the dwelling unit and its environment), pride in one's residence, and a certain degree of social status.

Access to homeownership is determined by the treatment of blacks in the real estate market as well as by the ability of blacks to afford it. The issue of ability to afford also could mask a differential in price paid by blacks and whites for comparable units. This section raises such issues and discusses actual and expected ownership rates, as well as the affordability question for renters.

Do similar black and white families pay the same for housing of comparable size, quality, and neighborhood amenity? Although existing research does not allow an unequivocal response to this question, substantial evidence suggests that blacks pay more than similar whites for comparable housing.[20] In addition, black households consume substantially less dwelling quality, neighborhood quality, and exterior space than white households of identical size, composition, and labor market attachment.[21]

What is the probability of ownership for blacks and whites? After controlling for household characteristics, blacks are much less likely to own than are whites with similar life-cycle and socioeconomic characteristics.[22] In 1975 in both St. Louis city and county, black households were 9 percentage points less likely to own than white households after controlling for the influences of age, education, income, job stability, and life cycle.[23] In addition, black movers were less likely to become home buyers than white movers with similar incomes, household sizes, composition, and labor force attachment.[24] Using a different data set, between 1974 and 1978, Silberman, Yochum, and Ihlanfeldt found a decrease in the racial differential in ownership for all households and a further diminution in it for newly formed households.[25]

Homeownership data since the 1940s substantiate the expectation of lower ownership rates for black families than for white families. In 1940, 24 percent of nonwhites but 44 percent of households of all races—20 percentage points more—owned their homes. By 1950, the gap was still 20 percentage points, but 35 percent of blacks and 55 percent of all races owned. In 1960, the gap was 24 percentage points although ownership had increased for both population groups. In 1970, the gap had declined to 21 percentage points, while by 1980 it had returned to its 1940 and 1950 levels of 20 percentage points. In 1980, 44 percent of blacks and 64 percent of all races were owners.

To what extent is the ownership gap between the races due to differences in affordability? Using the most common measures of affordability for both owned and rented units, black households and households of all races face roughly comparable burdens due to shelter costs.[26] (Affordability is often discussed using rent-to-income ratios for tenants and value-to-income ratios for owners.[27]) Between 1970 and 1977, median gross rent as a percent of income among nonwhites ranged from 20 percent to 27 percent, while the comparable range for all races was from 20 percent to 25 percent. Similarly, between 1970 and 1977, the median home value-to-income ratio for nonwhites ranged from 1.5 to 2.0; for all races it ranged from 1.8 to 2.3.

While median gross rent as a percent of income and the median home value-to-income ratios were close during the 1970s for the two racial groups of interest, numerical gaps between median gross rents, median house values, and median household incomes both in constant and current dollars are sizable. Median gross rents for nonwhites rose from $89 in 1970 to $150 in 1977, while for all races this figure increased from $108 to $184. At the same time, median house value for nonwhites increased from $10,700 to $23,900 and for all races from $17,100 to $36,900. Current dollar median household income for nonwhites rose from $6,516 to $8,422 and for all races from $8,734 to $13,572 between 1970 and 1977. These increases translate into 1984 constant dollar income gaps for both years of more than $8,000.

Thus, while there is little difference in the ability to afford ownership between blacks and whites, the units owned by the two groups appear to differ.

FEDERAL HOUSING POLICIES AND PROGRAMS

This section briefly describes federal housing policies and programs and then cites available examples of their effect on the condition of and access to housing by black families. Lack of information limits the comprehensiveness of our discussion of the relationship between federal government policy and the condition of and access to housing for black families.

Federal Policies

Although the 1932 Hoover Committee was the first national body[28] to examine housing conditions, the objective stated in the 1949 Housing Act of a decent home and a suitable living environment for every American family has become for most people the first federal reckoning on housing conditions and needs. The riots and urban disorders of the 1960s which highlighted the many aspects of racial inequality in this country and contributed to passage of the 1968 Civil Rights Act[29] retained the national focus on the housing conditions of black families. The Kerner Commission report[30] on the riots suggested measures to ameliorate the following housing conditions for blacks—substandard, old, and overcrowded structures, the necessity to pay higher rents for poorer quality housing, and discrimination in housing code enforcement.

Since 1968, federal policy statements have noted the need to improve the quality of life for blacks. One of the four broad goals of the 1978 Urban and Regional Policy Group Report[31] was to provide improved housing, job opportunities, and community services to the urban poor, minorities, and women. The national urban policy articulated in 1980[32] includes as policy IV "to expand opportunity for those disadvantaged by discrimination and low income." The President's Commission on Housing in 1981 reaffirmed the following principles for national policy—to recognize the continuing role of government to address the housing needs of the poor and to assure maximum freedom of housing choice.

Federal Programs

Federal housing assistance has three major elements: low-rent public housing, mortgage insurance, and rental assistance payments.[33] The 1937 Housing Act established the first of these—low-rent public housing—that allowed the federal government to fund the construction of public housing projects throughout the nation. Through the Department of Housing and Urban Development (HUD), the federal government funds the construction of public housing units, which are operated and managed by local housing authorities (LHAs) or public housing authorities (PHAs).[34]

Since its establishment in 1934, the Federal Housing Administration (FHA), now an entity within HUD, has provided mortgage insurance, guaranteeing private lenders the repayment of their mortgage loans in case individual borrowers or multifamily developers default.[35] Mortgage insurance programs for developers of multifamily projects include incentives for the construction of certain types of projects or to serve certain types of households.

Section 8, established in 1974, is perhaps the best known of the programs in which the federal government makes partial rent payments to private landlords on behalf of eligible lower-income tenants. Originally, Section 8 units could be newly constructed, substantially rehabilitated, moderately rehabilitated, or existing, but in 1983, the new construction and substantial rehabilitation programs were repealed, except for funds earmarked to assist the elderly. A Section 8 voucher demonstration program, authorized in 1983, was made a permanent program by the 1987 Housing and Community Development Act.

Under the Section 8 program, HUD pays a landlord the difference between 30 percent of tenant income and the maximum unit rent or fair market rent (FMR) established by HUD for a given size standard unit in a given locality.[36] A Section 8 tenant may lease a unit that rents for more than the FMR only in the voucher subprogram.

For a voucher recipient, HUD pays the difference between 30 percent of income and a payment standard (usually equal to the area FMR) which may be greater than, less than, or equal to the dwelling's rent. If a unit's rent exceeds the payment standard, the tenant is responsible for that portion of the rent in excess of the standard. One objective of the voucher demonstration program was to provide tenants added incentive to lease units with rents less than the FMR by allowing them to pay less than 30 percent of income in those cases. Another objective was to sever the connection between the FMR and the overall rent levels of area apartments. Under the Section 8 program in many areas the market rents had become identical to the FMRs, and the Section 8 program was alleged to contribute to rent inflation.

Federal Impact on Housing Condition

The efficacy of modernization programs aimed at improving the condition of low-rent public housing is uncertain. The existing modernization program, the Comprehensive Improvement Assistance Program (CIAP), which provides federal aid to LHA/PHAs to finance capital improvements in low-rent public housing, is being examined in a forthcoming study for the Department of HUD.

The Section 8 program provides financial assistance to lower-income renter households that occupy standard quality dwellings. The dropout rate for minority group[37] households suggests that even with a Certificate of Family Participation, they may not obtain standard and affordable units. In 1982, in the Section 8 program, 72 percent of minority versus 52 percent of nonminority enrollees failed to become recipients within 60 days, the period before the certificate expires.[38] Part of this dropout rate may be due to discrimination that has limited the choices of minority households and made it nearly impossible to find units in some markets.

Federal Impact on Access to Housing

Access to a location, a suitable living environment, or a unit of choice is affected by siting decisions for federally subsidized housing. Suburban communities—and perhaps all communities—prefer elderly housing to family housing. Low-rent public housing is still being located primarily in minority areas or in areas undergoing racial transition, despite federal policies of spatial deconcentration and numerous court cases.[39] In addition, because of the sizable minority enrollment in public housing—minorities occupy 59 percent of all units—after siting a large project, the proportion of minority residents in that area greatly increases.[40] The siting and occupancy patterns for public housing have done little to improve access to the integrated neighborhoods and suitable environments that blacks prefer.

Minority group households benefit only minimally from newly constructed housing, such as that provided by the Section 8 new construction program, before its repeal in 1983. To the extent that Section 8 new construction placed units in predominantly white suburbs that were hostile to blacks (or that blacks were unwilling to move to), then blacks seldom obtained housing through this program. Eighty percent of the residents of Section 8 new construction projects are elderly, with minorities only 11 percent of these elderly—that is, minority elderly are 8.8 percent of all new construction beneficiaries. In total, 15 percent of the recipients of housing assistance under the Section 8 new construction program are minority.[41]

The Section 8 existing and housing voucher programs, which require households to seek units in the private market for which they will receive federal subsidies, do not solve entirely for blacks and other minority groups the problem of access to units and locations of choice. In the Section 8 existing-housing program, minority groups, such as black Americans, with larger than average families, often are unable to find units large enough to accommodate their families at rents less than the maximum FMRs. Even in the voucher program, which eliminates maximum rents as a constraint on the size of the available pool of rental units, large households still encounter difficulties finding units of the necessary sizes.[42]

Federal Impact on Access to Ownership and on Affordability

Ownership The Federal Housing Administration (FHA) and the Veterans Administration (VA) insure privately written home mortgage loans to encourage lenders to fund home purchases. In its early years, the FHA was alleged to have redlined many minority or racially mixed neighborhoods and to have made it virtually impossible to get loans for homes there. More recently, the FHA has been accused of encouraging the displacement of lower-income and minority households because the borrowers it now funds for the formerly redlined areas are upper-income households.

The Section 235 program was enacted in 1968 to enable low- and moderate-income households to become owners. HUD insures mortgages and makes monthly payments to lenders to reduce the interest rate for the new homeowner to as low as 4 percent. The program has been both "revised" and "restructured" to correct for the problems of shoddy appraisals and families not fulfilling the responsibilities of homeownership. HUD now owns many of the defaulted and foreclosed homes assisted under that program.

In addition, the Section 235 mortgage insurance program, was found to have exacerbated residential racial segregation in several ways.[43] First, new Section 235 housing was in most instances located in suburban areas, and nearly all of it was purchased by white families. Second, if minorities purchased new Section 235 housing, the housing was located in subdivisions occupied exclusively by minorities. Finally, in a survey of four metropolitan areas, most of the existing Section 235 housing was found in ghetto areas or changing central city neighborhoods, and nearly all of it was purchased by minority families.

Affordability The Section 8 program, on the other hand, enhances shelter affordability for blacks because it lowers rental payments to 30 percent of income for those families able to qualify and to find units to live in. Section 8 rental assistance could lessen the rent burden for sizable numbers of black households, since roughly 50 percent of all black households paid more than 30 percent of their incomes for rent in 1983.

SUMMARY AND CONCLUSIONS

Despite improvements between the 1940s and the 1980s in the "housing quotient" of black families — as measured by structural quality, internal conditions, and external conditions — sizable gaps, relative to other races, remain. In addition, examples of federal housing policies and programs with the potential to improve the condition of and access to housing for black families suggest that obstacles may remain to the achievement of this potential.

Black families that include married couples, with their higher relative incomes, are the most likely to improve their "housing quotient." On the other hand, because of their incomes, they may be ineligible as participants in federal housing programs.

Notable racial differentials exist both in the quantity and quality of housing consumed, and in the crowdedness of dwellings. Blacks also have less access than whites to the newly constructed and to the existing stocks of housing. Blacks lack equality of access to suitable living environments and to market information as well. The probability of ownership is less among blacks than among whites, and black families often pay more than similar white families for comparable housing. The gap in actual ownership rates between blacks and whites reflects not only lower family and household incomes for blacks but also the differences in the quality of the units purchased by blacks.

Although federal housing programs from public housing (the earliest) to the Section 8 voucher program (the latest) all have enrolled black families, housing market discrimination continues to operate in this country — despite legislation and lawsuits — and proscribes whatever increased access federal housing assistance might offer black families. Programs that do not involve relocation to the suburbs, either in federally developed units or in the private market, are most likely to assist the large numbers of black families who will continue to enroll in federal programs.

The ability of federal housing policies and programs to improve the "housing quotient" of black families in general is indeterminate. Data are scant, and it is very difficult to control for all the factors necessary to examine this issue fully. Although a framework of federal programs is in place that could ameliorate the condition of and access to housing by black families, relative to families of all races, available program data confirm the existence of continuing racial differentials.

NOTES

1. Principal Analyst, U.S. Congressional Budget Office (CBO). This analysis is the author's own and should not be attributed to the CBO.

2. Note that "all races" includes blacks, whites, and all other races, most notably Hispanics in recent years. Comparisons often are made between all races and any one or more of the racial groups that constitute "all races."

3. Incomes for 1983 are reported in the text because the most recent housing data are from that year. The most recent income data are for 1985, when median incomes of married couple households were $31,161, $24,685, and $31,660 for all races, blacks, and whites, respectively. See *1988 Statistical Abstract of the U.S.* (Washington, DC: GPO, 1988).

4. See Mahlon Straszheim, *An Econometric Model of the Urban Housing Market* (New York: National Bureau of Economic Research, 1975); and John Kain and John Quigley, *Housing Markets and Racial Discrimination: A Microeconomic Analysis* (New York: Columbia University Press, 1975).

5. See Barton Smith, "Racial Composition as a Neighborhood Amenity," in *The Economics of Urban Amenities*, edited by Douglas B. Diamond Jr. and George S. Tolley (New York: Academic Press, 1982), p. 184. Smith defines housing quality both in terms of the age of housing and of a single hedonic weighted variable of several attributes.

6. For citations of some of the many articles on this subject, see John Yinger, "Prejudice and Discrimination in the Urban Housing Market," in *Current Issues in Urban Economics*, edited by Peter Mieszkowski and Mahlon Straszheim (Baltimore: Johns Hopkins University Press, 1979), p. 458.

7. The 1940 Census of Housing classified units as either having or lacking essential plumbing and as either needing or not needing major repairs to approximate structural quality. In 1950, the Census replaced the category "needing major repairs" with the two categories, sound and dilapidated. The 1960 Census of Housing added a third category, deteriorating, to the two defined in 1950, to cover what they found to be a gray area. Because a 1962 evaluation of the 1960 Census of Housing found that most units would be classified differently on the three measures if resurveyed, the Census Bureau dropped these condition proxies from the 1970 Census.

Since 1973, the Annual Housing Survey — now the American Housing Survey — has provided a variety of indicators of housing condition: plumbing (lacks or shares complete), kitchen (lacks or shares complete), sewage, heating type, maintenance (leaking roof, cracks or holes in wall or ceiling, holes in floor, broken plaster or peeling paint), condition of public hall, toilet access, and electrical condition. See U.S. Department of Commerce, Bureau of the Census, *The Annual (American) Housing Survey* (Washington, DC: U.S. Government Printing Office, selected years).

8. For a discussion of possible measures of structural quality see U.S., President's Commission on Housing, *Report* (Washington, D.C., 1982), p. 7 and Richard Clemmer and John Simonson, "Trends in Substandard Housing 1940 to 1980," *AREUEA Journal* 10 (Winter 1983), pp. 442-464.

9. See U.S., President's Commission on Housing, *Report*, p. xviii.

10. See Kain and Quigley, *Housing Markets and Racial Discrimination: A Microeconomic Analysis*, chapters 2 and 8, for a discussion of housing as a bundle of attributes with location and environmental quality among them.

11. See Ibid., pp. 87-91, for a discussion in favor of suburbanization of blacks. See also Anthony Downs, *Opening Up the Suburbs: An Urban Strategy for America* (New Haven, CT: Yale University Press, 1973) and Paul Peterson, ed., *The New Urban Reality* (Washington, DC: Brookings Institution, 1985). For arguments against black suburbanization, see George M. von Furstenberg, *et al.*, eds., *Patterns of Racial Discrimination Volume I: Housing* (Lexington, MA: Lexington Books, 1974).

12. *Statistical Abstract of the United States 1986*, Table 22, p. 19.

13. For a discussion of surveys of blacks' residential preferences, see John Yinger, "Prejudice and Discrimination in the Urban Housing Market," p. 432 and Thomas Pettigrew, "Attitudes on Race and Housing: A Social-Psychological View," in *Segregation in Residential Areas: Papers on Racial and Socioeconomic Factors in Choice of Housing*, edited by Amos H. Hawley and Vincent P. Rock (Washington, D.C.: National Academy of Sciences, 1973), pp. 21-84. See also Wilhelmina A. Leigh, "The Social Preference for Fair Housing—During the Civil Rights Movement and Since," *American Economic Review* 78 (May 1988), pp. 156-162.

14. See Annemette Sorensen, Karl Taeuber, and Leslie Hollingsworth Jr., "Indexes of Racial Residential Segregation for 109 Cities in the United States, 1940 to 1970," *Sociological Focus* 8 (April 1975), pp. 125-133; and Karl Taeuber, "Appendix," in *A Decent Home: A Report on the Continued Failure of the Federal Government to Provide Equal Housing Opportunity*, Citizens Commission on Civil Rights (Washington, DC, 1983), pp. 1-7. Then see Norman R. Cloutier, "The Measurement and Modeling of Segregation: A Survey of Recent Empirical Research," *Regional Science Perspectives* 14 (1984), pp. 15-32, for an evaluation of the dissimilarity index in this usage.

15. See Suzanne M. Bianchi, Reynolds Farley, and Daphne Spain, "Racial Inequalities in Housing: An Examination of Recent Trends," *Demography* 19 (February 1982), pp. 37-51.

16. See Donald C. Dahmann, "Racial Differences in Housing Consumption During the 1970s: Insights from a Components of Inventory Change Analysis," *Urban Geography* 4 (1983), pp. 203-222.

17. See *The 1978 HUD Survey on the Quality of Community Life: A Data Book* (Washington, DC: U.S. Department of Housing and Urban Development).

18. Testers are white and minority group persons given similar socioeconomic information to use when sent separately on the same day to selected real estate agents and rental companies to inquire about available properties. A comparison of results from these paired visits indicates the behavior patterns of agents toward potential owners/renters of different races. See Harriet Newburger, *Recent Evidence on Discrimination in Housing* (Washington, D.C.: HUD, 1984), pp. 8 and 12.

19. *FHA Homes, 1967: Data for States and Selected Areas on Characteristics of FHA Operations Under Section 203* (Washington, D.C.: FHA, Division of Research and Statistics, Statistics Section, 1967), quoted in Kain and Quigley, *Housing Markets and Racial Discrimination: A Microeconomic Analysis*, p. 118.

20. For evidence on this issue, see A. Thomas King and Peter Mieszkowski, "Racial Discrimination, Segregation, and the Price of Housing," *Journal of Political Economy* 81 (May/June 1973), pp. 590-605; John Yinger, "The Black-White Price Differential in Housing: Some Further Evidence," *Land Economics* 54 (May 1978), pp. 187-206; Robert Schafer, "Racial Discrimination in the Boston Housing Market," *Journal of Urban Economics* 6 (April 1979), pp. 176-196; and John Yinger, "Prejudice and Discrimination in the Urban Housing Market," p. 463.

21. Kain and Quigley, *Housing Markets and Racial Discrimination: A Microeconomic Analysis*, pp., 255 and 282.

22. For citations of work supporting this, see John Yinger, "Prejudice and Discrimination in the Urban Housing Market," p. 458.

23. See Kain and Quigley, *Housing Markets and Racial Discrimination: A Microeconomic Analysis*, p. 137.

24. Ibid., pp. 7 and 145. When expected black ownership rates based on the 1960 Census of Housing were computed by multiplying the matrix for white households of ownership rates (by income and family size) and the distribution of black households (by income and family size), in all 18 of the SMSAs considered, the actual rate for blacks was less than the expected, with the gap ranging from 10 to 28 percentage points.

25. See Jonathan Silberman, Gilbert Yochum, and Keith Ihlanfeldt, "Racial Differentials in Home Purchase: The Evidence from Newly-Formed Households," *Economic Inquiry* 20 (1982), pp. 443-457.

26. See H. James Brown and John Yinger, *Home Ownership and Housing Affordability in the United States: 1963-1985* (Cambridge, MA: Joint Center for Housing Studies of the M.I.T. and Harvard University, 1986) for recent affordability statistics but without race detail. See Wilhelmina A. Leigh, *Shelter Affordability for Blacks: Crisis or Clamor?* (New Brunswick, NJ: Transaction Books, 1982) for affordability comparisons by race for 1978.

27. Some challenge the use of rent-to-income and value-to-income ratios to reflect affordability. (See U.S., President's Commission on Housing, *Report*, pp. 9 + .) They criticize the rent-to-income ratio specifically because this ratio can increase if income falls simply because higher income renters become owners and leave mainly lower income households as renters. The rent-to-income ratio can increase also if rents rise, reflecting improved unit quality. Instead of looking at the rent-to-income ratio, they suggest looking at trends in rents and in incomes separately.

28. See J.M. Gries and J. Ford, eds., *Home Ownership, Income, and Types of Dwellings*, IV, *Report on the President's Conference on Home Building and Home Ownership* (Washington, D.C.: National Capital Press, 1932).

29. The 1968 Civil Rights Act only makes racially motivated discrimination in the housing market illegal; it does not outlaw residential racial segregation.

30. See Otto Kerner (chairman), *Report of the National Advisory Commission on Civil Disorders* (New York: Bantam Books, 1968).

31. See U.S., President's Urban and Regional Policy Group, *A New Partnership to Conserve America's Communities* (Washington, D.C.: U.S. Department of Housing and Urban Development, 1978), p. III-2.

32. See *President's National Urban Policy Report: Executive Summary* (Washington, D.C.: U.S. Department of Housing and Urban Development, 1980).

33. For a discussion of major federal housing programs, see John C. Weicher, "Urban Housing Policy," in *Current Issues in Urban Economics*, edited by Peter Mieszkowski and Mahlon Straszheim (Baltimore: Johns Hopkins University Press, 1979), pp. 469-508. See also *Programs of HUD 1985/1986* (Washington, DC: U.S. Department of Housing and Urban Development, 1986).

34. PHAs are one type of LHAs.

35. Since 1934, homeowner mortgage insurance has been available in the Section 203 program, while mortgage insurance for developers has been available in the Section 207 program.

36. When the Section 8 program was established in 1974, the percent of income paid by tenants toward rent was 25 percent. The 1981 Omnibus Budget Reconciliation Act increased the required percentage to 30—from the date of legislative enactment for new tenants, and phased in by one percent each year for current tenants, reaching 30 percent in 1986.

37. Minority group refers to groups other than whites—blacks, Hispanics, and other nonwhites.

38. U.S., President's Commission on Housing, *Report*, p. 41. Upon request, in hardship situations, households may be granted an extension of 60 additional days to find a unit.

39. In the 1968 Gautreaux case in Chicago, the U.S. Supreme Court provided a landmark decision by concurring with the district court that the Chicago Housing Authority had deliberately segregated low-rent public housing by its choice of project locations. The federal policy of spatial deconcentration grew out of this case. In addition, HUD was prohibited from constructing high-rise buildings for families unless extenuating circumstances existed.

Another example is provided by the court case *U.S. v. Yonkers Board of Education*, 1985, N.Y. (624 F. Supp. 1276). Although the city of Yonkers had received $20 million in Community Development Block Grant funds in 1980, conditioned on its agreement to provide 200 units of scattered site housing in East Yonkers (an area with few minorities), this housing has yet to be built. Despite a court order, the freezing of all other development in the city, and the levying of fines, ground has yet to be broken for this housing.

40. U.S., President's Commission on Housing, *Report*, p. 41.

41. Ibid., p. 20.

42. HUD overestimated the number of households it could assist with its funds in the voucher demonstration because it underestimated the average family size among enrollees for the new program.

43. See *President's National Urban Policy Report* (Washington, D.C.: U.S. Department of Housing and Urban Development, 1978), p. 69 for discussion of a 1971 report by the U.S. Commission on Civil Rights on the FHA Section 235 program.

5

ECONOMIC FORCES, STRUCTURAL DISCRIMINATION AND BLACK FAMILY INSTABILITY

Robert B. Hill

The social and economic gains achieved by black families during the 1960s were severely eroded during the seventies and eighties. Unemployment, poverty, single-parent families, out-of-wedlock births, and adolescent pregnancies soared to alarming levels. According to the thesis of the declining significance of race, this crisis is mainly concentrated among the black "underclass" and it is broad societal trends, not racism, that is mainly responsible for their increased deprivation. We contend that this thesis fails to assess the role of institutionalized racism as it is manifested in "unintended" or "structural" discrimination, i.e., the disproportionate adverse effects of economic trends and policies on the functioning of low-income and middle-income black families. Moreover, we argue that social forces or policies that have racially disparate adverse effects are "discriminatory" by result, whether intended or not. The major economic trends that affected black families adversely during the seventies and eighties were: back-to-back recessions, double-digit inflation, and industrial and population shifts. The key economic policies that undermined black family stability have been: anti-inflation fiscal and monetary policies, trade policies, plant closings, social welfare, block grants, and federal per capita formulas for allocating funds to states and local areas that have not been corrected for the census undercount.

The economic gains achieved by black families during the sixties were severely eroded during the seventies and eighties. In 1969, only 28,000 or 5.6 percent of black women heading families were unemployed, but by 1987, ten times as many (286,000) of them were jobless, with unemployment rates of 16.5 percent. At the same time, the number of unemployed black husbands almost tripled (from 84,000 to 209,000), while their jobless rate more than doubled from 2.9 percent to 7.0 percent.

This economic instability in two-parent black families was accompanied by record-level rates of divorce and separation. Consequently, between 1969 and 1987, the proportion of black families headed by women spiraled from 28 percent to 42 percent, while the proportion of black children living with one parent rose from 46 percent to 54 percent. Thus, 43 percent of black children lived in poor families by 1986, compared to 40 percent in 1969.[1]

What are the reasons for the marked erosion in the social and economic stability of black families? Unfortunately, the quality of the national dialogue about the black family crisis has not progressed much farther than it was twenty years ago. The "deficit model," a perspective popularized by the 1965 Moynihan Report, continues to be the predominant explanation offered by conservatives and liberals today.[2]

This perspective, also known as the "blaming the victim" syndrome, attributes the social ills afflicting minority and low-income families to internal rather than to external factors. According to this view, joblessness, poverty, and welfare among black families are primarily caused by "underclass" cultural values and life-styles as manifested by: lack of a work ethic, low educational attainment, poor work skills and high rates of one-parent families and teenage pregnancies.[3]

According to proponents of the deficit perspective, "underclass" values and life-styles have taken on a "self-perpetuating" life of their own "without assistance from the white world."[4] Thus, remedies for these problems must be sought within the black, and not white, community. In short, change must be sought within the "culture" of the black poor and not within societal institutions or by combatting racism.

Wilson's notion of the declining significance of race also exonerates racism of major culpability for the deprivation of low-income black families. According to this thesis, the destabilization of black families is mainly concentrated among the black "underclass," while the black middle-class is reputed to have continued its upward mobility. Since the "unstinting" progress of middle-class blacks is construed as reflecting a significant decline in racism, Wilson contends that class is a more important determinant of black life-chances today than race.[5]

A major deficiency in Wilson's analysis is its failure to examine the role of institutionalized racism and its various contemporary forms. More specifically, Wilson fails to assess the "unintended" adverse effects of institutional structures and policies on the structure and functioning of black families. Moreover, while civil rights leaders and black scholars attribute many problems in the black community to institutional racism, this concept is rarely defined and operationalized systematically.

Although the adverse impact of structural unemployment on black workers has been widely documented, most economic analysts have not viewed its disparate effects on blacks as a form of institutional discrimination. We shall argue that social forces or policies that have racially disproportionate effects are discriminatory by result, whether intended or not. Thus, we will attempt to demonstrate that the current crisis among black families cannot be adequately understood without examining the role of structural discrimination, i.e., the disparate adverse consequences of societal trends and policies that may not have been explicitly designed to have racially discriminatory effects.[6]

FORMS OF INSTITUTIONAL RACISM

Prejudice and Discrimination

Before describing how key economic trends and policies structurally discriminate against black families, it is important to clarify several concepts related to individual and institutional racism. For our purposes, racism is operationally defined as any attitude, action or institutional structure that subordinates blacks relative to whites. The two basic dimensions of racism are prejudice and discrimination. Although prejudice and discrimination are often used interchangeably, they differ substantively from each other. Prejudice involves negative attitudes or beliefs about racial or ethnic groups, while discrimination involves negative treatment of them.[7]

Prejudice and discrimination may be manifested by individuals or institutions. Individual prejudice refers to negative racial or ethnic attitudes by individuals or groups, while individual discrimination refers to negative treatment of racial or ethnic minorities by individuals or groups. On the other hand, institutional prejudice (or "cultural racism") refers to norms, values, beliefs or behaviors of the dominant society that are deemed superior to the norms, values and behavioral patterns of racial and ethnic minorities.[8] The stereotypical portrayal of black families, based on the deficit model, by the media, policymakers and social scientists is an example of institutionalized prejudice.[9]

Institutional Discrimination

Institutionalized discrimination (or "institutional subordination") refers to laws, regulations, policies and informal practices of organizations or institutions that result in differential adverse treatment or subordination of racial and ethnic minorities.[10] Over forty years ago, Merton identified "unprejudiced discrimination" as a form of racism that has been neglected by scholars.[11] Institutional racism and discrimination, as Carmichael and Hamilton perceptively observed, can be unintended as well as intended.[12]

A major impediment to the development of viable strategies to counteract institutional racism has been the failure of many black leaders and scholars to recognize or acknowledge the role of "unintentional" or "structural" discrimination. Several social scientists, however, have underscored the declining significance of intentions as the overriding criterion for determining racism or discrimination. For example, Downs observes:

> Racism can occur even if the people causing it have no intention of subordinating others because of color, or are totally unaware of doing so. Admittedly, this implication is sure to be extremely controversial. Most Americans believe racism is bad. But how can anyone be "guilty" of doing something bad when he does not realize he is doing it? Racism can be a matter of *result* rather than *intention* because many institutional structures in America that most whites do not recognize as subordinating others because of color actually injure minority group members far more than deliberate racism.[13]

Similarly, Pettigrew notes:

> Institutional racism avidly supports individual racism . . . racist institutions need not be headed by racists or designed with racist intentions to limit black choices. Indeed, it makes little difference to black Americans what the formal intentions are, for the restrictive consequences are the same.[14]

Intentional Discrimination

Overt and Covert Discrimination: It is important to carefully distinguish unintentional discrimination from intentional discrimination. Intentional institutionalized discrimination may be overt or covert. Overt discrimination refers to the deliberate mistreatment of minorities by organizations or institutions, based on *explicit* racial or ethnic criteria. Overt institutional discrimination has been manifested by slavery, the passage of the Black Codes after emancipation, and the imposition of "de jure" segregation in the North and South.

However, covert intentional discrimination refers to the deliberate mistreatment of minorities by organizations or institutions, based on nonracial criteria that are strongly correlated with race. Covert or subtle discrimination is also known as "patterned evasion," the deliberate use of proxies for race in order to deny equal opportunities to racial minorities. The "grandfather clause," literacy tests, and poll taxes are early examples of patterned evasions in the area of voting rights.[15]

More recently, numerous court cases have uncovered covert intentional institutional discrimination by local authorities in such circumstances as: (a) urban renewal that resulted in the differential dislocation of black families from their homes and communities; (b) redlining, i.e., the differential refusal by banks, insurance companies, etc. to grant home mortgage loans, commercial credit and insurance for fire, property and automobiles to minority families living in designated (or "red-lined") neighborhoods and communities; and (c) zoning, i.e., the differential denial of housing options to minority families due to zoning ordinances prohibiting low-income and multifamily dwellings in predominantly white communities.[16] However, it should be emphasized that not all instances of urban renewal or zoning are intentionally discriminatory.

Covert intentional discrimination is also manifested through: (a) dilatory tactics (such as tokenism, the formation of study commissions and laxity in complying with or enforcing civil rights laws or affirmative action guidelines), and (b) differential withholding from racial minorities of important information about program eligibility.

An example of the latter is reflected in the widespread lack of knowledge among low-income black families about an important welfare program for poor two-parent families—Aid to Families with Dependent Children of Unemployed Parents (AFDC–UP). Although the AFDC–UP program was established in 1961, most poor black families (as well as the American public) are not aware of the existence of a welfare program for poor two-parent families. The sharp underrepresentation of unemployed black fathers on the AFDC–UP rolls relative to unemployed white fathers suggests covert intentional discrimination by many local welfare agencies.[17]

Unintentional Discrimination

Technological Shifts: Unintentional or structural discrimination is often manifested by industrial trends that were not explicitly designed to have disparate adverse effects of black families, such as technological changes, economic cycles and population shifts. Technological changes refer to structural transformations in: (a) American industries, i.e., from agriculture to manufacturing or from manufacturing to services; (b) technology, i.e., automation, from low-tech to high-tech or from labor-intensive to capital-intensive; (c) sectors, i.e., from public to private, and (d) occupations, i.e., from farm to factory work, from factory to clerical work, from self-employed to salaried.

Frazier, for example, describes at length how the shift from an agricultural to a manufacturing economy had destabilizing effects on rural black families between 1865-1925.[18] Johnson provides an in-depth analysis of how specific changes in industrialization and technology undermined the economic well-being of blacks during that period.[19] And several scholars have identified technological change as a key source of structural unemployment among blacks and other minorities because of their disadvantaged educational and work skills.[20]

Periodic Recessions: Economic cycles that have had unintended adverse effects on black families are recessions and inflationary spirals. Wage-earners in black families have been disproportionately affected by recessions or "cyclical unemployment" because of: (a) the seniority principle of "last hired, first fired" and (b) their concentration in unskilled and semi-skilled jobs, which have the greatest vulnerability to economic slumps. As Frazier noted, black workers were laid off disproportionately during the depression of 1921 and the Great Depression of the 1930s.[21] Although black workers were also disparately affected by the eight slumps between 1948 and 1982, they were more severely impacted by the four most recent recessions—1970-71, 1974-75, 1980 and 1981-82.[22]

Moreover, contrary to popular belief, several studies have found that unemployment among black youth is also strongly related to business cycles.[23] Although numerous investigators have found a strong correlation between black unemployment and family instability, there appears to be a strong reluctance on the part of many economic analysts to assess systematically the impact of recent recessions on black family instability.

Double-digit Inflation: At the same time that black families were reeling from the effects of back-to-back recessions during the 1970s, however, they were also subjected to double-digit inflation. Although economic theory said it was impossible to have high levels of unemployment and inflation simultaneously, the U.S. economy, apparently, had not been informed of this "fact." Thus, economists had to coin a new term, "stagflation," to describe the combination of lagging productivity and rampant inflation.

Between 1969 and 1980, consumer prices soared at an unprecedented annual rate of 12 percent, compared to only three percent during the 1960s. However, the record-level unemployment caused by the devastating 1981-82 recession brought two-digit inflation down sharply. Thus, consumer prices increased at an annual rate of only four percent for the 27-month period ending in December 1983. And, by 1986, inflation was averaging less than three percent.

Although consumer prices increased annually at about two or three percent prior to the 1970s, there have been few systematic studies of the impact of inflation on black families. However, the few analyses that have been conducted reveal that black families are disparately impacted by the price inflation. For example, in his 1976 study of urban families, Caplovitz concluded that "inflation was primarily a problem of the less privileged groups in society"—the poor, retired, unskilled and semi-skilled workers and blacks and Hispanics.[24] His data revealed that the incomes of 75 percent of black families had fallen behind rising prices, compared to the incomes of 53 percent of white families.

Further corroborating findings about the disparate impact of inflation on black families can be found in several Census Bureau reports. For example, between 1969 and 1982, inflation eroded the purchasing power of black families by 14 percent, compared to only a five percent decline in white family income. In short, real income fell about three times as much among black than among white families between 1969 and 1982.[25]

Population Shifts: Two kinds of population shifts have had differential consequences for black families: migration (i.e., the movement of blacks from rural to urban areas and from the South to the North) and immigration (i.e., the movement of foreigners, such as Europeans, Hispanics and Asians to the United States.) In several works, Frazier describes in detail the destabilizing effects on black families of urbanization and the movement of blacks from the rural areas to towns and cities.[26]

Frazier identified several effects of the urban environment that undermined the stability of black families: pressures on breadwinners to travel long distances from their families in order to find work; pressures on wives to supplement the low wages of their husbands by going to work and leaving their children unattended; the diminished influence of religious institutions; and the lack of adequate facilities and services in such areas as housing, health and education. Consequently, Frazier concluded, it is not surprising that black families in cities are disproportionately characterized by high rates of family disruption, delinquency, crime, ill health, low educational attainment and overcrowding.[27] Immigration has always had an adverse effect on black workers and their families. During slavery, employment opportunities for free blacks in the North were related directly to the extent of competition for those jobs from newly-arriving foreigners.[28] And, after emancipation, numerous race riots broke out between immigrants and blacks over perceived or actual job competition. Immigrants also adopted restrictive labor union practices in order to eliminate blacks from certain jobs and industries. Thus, blacks made their greatest occupational advances—during both World Wars—when European immigration was curtailed.[29]

Several recent studies suggest that an increasing source of black unemployment may be competition from Hispanic and Asian immigrants. For example, between 1974 and 1977, 53 percent of the new jobs in the private sector went to white women, 26 percent went to white men, and 12 percent went to Hispanics, while blacks and Asians each obtained five percent of the new jobs.[30]

It is important to point out that although Asians are only one-fifth the number of blacks, they obtained an equal number of jobs to blacks; and while Hispanics are about half the number of blacks, they obtained more than twice as many jobs as blacks. Since most demographers predict that Asians and Hispanics will constitute the fastest-growing groups in the United States into the twenty-first century, the job competition between them and blacks will become more acute during the 1990s.[31]

Adverse Economic Policies

Black families were also negatively impacted by a broad range of economic policies during the 1970s and 1980s. Many of these policies were explicitly designed to adversely affect low-income and minority families. They include: the dismantling of major "War on Poverty" programs by the Nixon administration, the shifting of the tax burden to middle-income and working-class families, and the sharp budget cuts in programs for the poor by the Reagan administration.[32] But many other economic policies, while not designed or intended to have a disparate impact on black families, had those consequences, nevertheless. Such structurally discriminatory policies were in the areas of finance, trade, plant closings, federal aid to localities and social welfare.

Fiscal and Monetary Policies: The preceding section described how black families were destabilized by back-to-back recessions since 1970. But it is important to point out that those four recessions were not "natural disasters," like earthquakes or hurricanes, but were *induced* through government fiscal and monetary policies as strategies for combatting spiraling inflation. Traditionally, the Federal Reserve Board (the "Fed") tried to stem inflation by keeping interest rates within predetermined ranges, while permitting the money supply to expand more freely. But these restrictive fiscal policies induced the recessions of 1970-71 and 1974-75. Although consumer prices declined somewhat after the latter slump, they began to climb to two-digit levels toward the end of the seventies.

Consequently, Paul A. Volcker, Federal Reserve Board chairman, announced in October, 1979 that he was not going to fight inflation with traditional policies. Instead, he would set more restrictive targets on the money supply and permit interest rates to rise unfettered. The soaring interest rates that resulted led to the 1980 recession. And similar tight monetary policies also led to the 1981-82 recession—one of the most severe since the Great Depression. The back-to-back recessions that were induced by the Fed's fiscal and monetary policies had a disparate impact on black families.[33]

Trade Policies: Many government trade policies also have unintended adverse effects on black workers and their families. Several studies have revealed that the industries with the largest job losses due to imports have a higher representation of black workers than those industries that have gained jobs, most due to exports. Thus, black men have been disproportionately affected by imports in the auto, steel and rubber industries, while black women have been disproportionately affected by imports in the apparel industry.[34]

While blacks comprise only 7 percent of the work force in the twenty manufacturing industries that gained the largest number of jobs due to exports between 1964-75, blacks accounted for 11 percent of the work force in the twenty manufacturing industries that lost the largest number of jobs due to imports. Another study estimated that while blacks gained 229,000 jobs through exports in 1970, they lost 287,000 jobs because of imports—for a net loss of 58,000 jobs.[35] Clearly, more in-depth studies are needed to assess the extent to which U.S. trade policies have helped to undermine the economic well-being of black families.

Plant Closings: Black displaced workers are about twice as likely as white displaced workers to remain unemployed. Of the 5.1 million workers who lost jobs (they had held for at least three years) due to periodic recessions, technological shifts and plant closings between January 1979 and January 1984, 41 percent of black workers were still unemployed by

1984, compared to only 23 percent of white workers.[36] According to Bluestone and Harrison, private disinvestment policies related to plant closings and relocation have also disparately impacted wage-earners in black families:

> Blacks are especially hard-hit because they are increasingly concentrated within central cities and in those regions of the country where plant closings and economic dislocation have been most pronounced . . . Moreover, as the number of jobs grew rapidly in the south, whites moved in to take the overwhelming majority of them . . .[37]

Block Grants: Many governmental processes for allocating financial aid to states, cities and other local areas also have disparate effects on the economic well-being of black families. The transforming of categorical to block grants by the Nixon and Reagan administrations have had such consequences. Block grants differ from categorical grants in that the latter are designed to benefit specific categories of target populations, while the former pools monies for various target groups. Moreover, while categorical grants are distributed primarily on the basis of economic need, block grants are distributed at the discretion of the local authorities and are based more on political considerations.[38]

And, finally, while there is close federal oversight of categorical grants, there is very little federal monitoring of block grants since they are part of the government decentralization efforts. As might be expected, evaluations of the major Nixon block grants—CETA, Community Development Block Grant, and Title XX—revealed that blacks and low-income groups benefitted less from block grants than from categorical grants.[39]

Per Capita Formula Grants: Government formulas that allocate funds to local areas based mainly on population data structurally discriminate against black families because of the disproportionate census undercount of the black population. The Constitution mandates that a census be conducted every ten years in order to allocate seats in the House of Representatives. But the economic importance of the census has increased sharply, since over one hundred federal programs use census data to distribute billions of dollars in such areas as social welfare, education, and employment each year.[40]

Censuses conducted between 1790 and 1860 were "intentionally" discriminatory, since the government mandated a 40 percent black undercount, that is, only three slaves were counted for every five whites for purposes of political apportionment. By 1960 and 1970, the Census Bureau estimated that 8.0 percent and 7.7 percent, respectively, of all blacks were omitted, while 5.9 percent of blacks were missed in the 1980 census. As a result, central cities with large black populations are denied disproportionately their equitable share of grants-in-aid because of the undercount.[41]

Thus, the census undercount produces a perverse form of structural discrimination: inner-city areas with the greatest need for funds to serve their disadvantaged families are least likely to receive their fair share. More research is needed to determine the extent to which black families are affected by the census undercount in the allocation of funds for specific programs in such areas as housing, health, education, employment, child care and social services.[42]

Social Security Retirement Age Policies: Many social welfare policies have unintentional adverse effects on black families. In 1983, Congress enacted legislation to raise the eligible age for retirement at full Social Security benefits to ages 66 and 67 between the years 2000 and 2022. Since the overriding purpose of this policy change was to increase the solvency of the trust fund for all future retirees, it was racially neutral in intent.

Nevertheless, it will have disparate adverse impact on minorities with lower life expectancies than whites—most especially, black males, whose current life expectancy of 64 years prevents most of them from receiving full retirement benefits at age 65. Moreover, since the life expectancy for all blacks declined for two consecutive years (from 69.7 in 1984 to 69.5 and 69.4 in 1985 and 1986, respectively), this law will disproportionately affect blacks and their families throughout the 1990s.[43]

AFDC-UP Eligibility Criteria: Another example of a social welfare policy that has disparate adverse effects on black families is the AFDC–Unemployed Parent (AFDC–UP) program. Since its inception in 1961, AFDC–UP has comprised only about five percent of all families on the AFDC rolls because of very restrictive eligibility criteria. To qualify for AFDC–UP, unemployed breadwinners in poor families must: have a stable work history, be eligible for unemployment insurance, and have no UI disqualifications. Such criteria are structurally discriminatory to black workers, since they are more likely than white workers to have unstable work histories, to be ineligible for jobless benefits and to have UI disqualifications.[44]

Foster Care and Adoption: Numerous policies in the area of foster care and adoption structurally discriminate against black families. For example, for many agencies, potential adoptive parents must meet the following criteria: (a) consist of husband and wife, (b) be middle-class, (c) able to afford various agency fees, (d) have no children of their own, and (e) less than 55 years old.[45]

Since the black families that are most interested and available for adopting children are likely to be one-parent, low-income, with children of their own and over 55 years old, they are least likely to qualify as adoptive parents. Consequently, although black children in foster care are less likely than white children in foster care to have physical disabilities, black children are less likely to be adopted than white children.[46]

Liberal Welfare Benefits: According to many "conservative" scholars, welfare policies of "liberals" have had unintended adverse effects on black families by increasing, rather than decreasing, dependency.[47] For example, they argue that the "unavailability" of welfare to two-parent families encourages jobless black fathers to leave their families. Moreover, they contend that "attractive" income, housing and food benefits from welfare induce black teenagers to have children out-of-wedlock.[48]

The first assertion is partly contradicted by the fact that the twenty-five-year-old AFDC–UP program for poor two-parent families exists in about twenty-six northern states, where rates of family break-up have been as high, if not higher, than family dissolution in the remaining states without the AFDC–UP program.[49] The second contention is undermined by the sharp decline in the purchasing power of welfare benefits, since most states have not adjusted their grants for inflation since the mid-1970s.[50] It is important that careful analyses be undertaken to assess properly the unintended positive and negative effects of social welfare policies.[51]

Detecting Intentionality: It is crucial to distinguish between unintended adverse effects of structural discrimination that are acceptable and those that are unacceptable. For example, the differential impact on blacks of raising the eligible age for Social Security benefits may be unintended, but deemed tolerable in order to insure the solvency of the trust fund for future generations. Similarly, many legislators may consider the disproportionate effects on the poor of budget cuts in social programs to be a necessary and acceptable short-term evil for the long-term good of the American economy.

To the extent that specific policies have positive consequences for the majority of people affected, any negative side-effects for racial and ethnic minorities are likely to be ignored or tolerated. Furthermore, since most decisionmakers consider only intended harmful effects on racial minorities as racism or discrimination, they may not feel a moral or legal obligation to mitigate unintended side-effects.

The presumption of unintentionality for structurally discriminatory policies attempts to avoid prejudging the intentions of decisionmakers. Thus, the black community should establish a new litmus test to determine the actual intentions of policymakers: the extent to which they are willing to eliminate, modify or cushion the disparate adverse effects of societal trends and policies *after* they have been made aware of their inequitable consequences. For those who refuse to alter those inequities, it may be confidently inferred that those "unintended" adverse effects were in fact "intended and acceptable." In short, those recalcitrants may now be reclassified as intentional discriminators or racists.

Unintentional Benevolence

Although our primary focus is on societal factors that have disparate negative impact on black families, it is essential to point out that forces in the larger society may have unintended positive effects as well. We have already noted that some catastrophes, such as world wars, accelerated the occupational mobility of blacks due to war-time labor shortages. Moreover, industrialization and urbanization also had some positive consequences, especially in raising sharply the occupational and earnings levels of wage-earners in black families as they moved from farm to factory work or from operatives to higher-paying clerical and technical jobs.[52]

Government programs that have had unintended disparate favorable effects on blacks include the G.I. Bill, Guaranteed Student Loans, the All-Volunteer Army, Medicare and Social Security cost-of-living adjustments (COLA's.) For example, the sharp decline in poverty among the black elderly during the 1970s was due, in part, to the institution of COLA's that kept Social Security pensions abreast with spiraling inflation. As a result, some black aged had higher and more stable income during retirement than throughout their years in the labor force.[53]

Intentional Benevolence

This analysis would not be complete without some reference to "intentional institutional benevolence," that is, policies, practices and actions of institutions and organizations that are designed to have disparate

FIGURE 1
A Typology of Intentional and Unintentional Discrimination and Benevolence

	INTENTIONAL	UNINTENTIONAL
DISCRIMINATION	Slavery Black Codes De Jure Segregation Gerrymandering Redlining Zoning Urban Renewal	Recessions Inflation Automation Block Grants Census Undercount Foster Care Policies Tax Policies Standardized Tests
BENEVOLENCE	School busing Set-asides Pell Grants Job Corps Head Start Affirmative Action Indian Child Welfare Act	World Wars Urbanization Industrialization G.I. Bill Student Loans All-Volunteer Army Health Programs Social Security

favorable effects on members of minority and low-income families. Examples of deliberate benevolence include: school busing, set-aside programs for minority businesses, Pell grants, scholarships for low-income students, Job Corps, Head Start, Medicaid, and affirmative action.[54]

In sum, societal trends and policies may manifest themselves in four patterns: intentional discrimination, unintentional discrimination, intentional benevolence and unintentional benevolence. These forms with accompanying examples are depicted in the typology in Figure 1.

POLICY IMPLICATIONS

We contend that institutional racism has contributed significantly to the erosion of the social and economic well-being of black families over the past two decades. More specifically, we argue that the sharp increases in unemployment, poverty and one-parent families among blacks were due, in large part, to the structurally discriminatory effects of major economic forces and policies. In short, black families are being subjected increasingly to discrimination by structural proxies.

The major economic trends that have adversely impacted black families are: back-to-back recessions, double-digit inflation, technological changes, and immigration. And the major economic policies that have had negative effects on black families are: fiscal and monetary strategies to fight inflation, plant closings, imports, foster care, and the increasing use of block grants and per capita formulas for allocating funds to localities that are not corrected for the census undercount.

Are there any actions that can be taken to counteract the adverse effects of structural discrimination on black families? Are these societal forces beyond our control? Since the negative consequences of those economic trends and policies were not intended, is there any moral or legal obligation to correct those inequities?

Social scientists lag significantly behind the legal profession in assessing various strategies for combatting structural or "unintentional" discrimination. For example, in the area of voting rights, the courts have made it clear that all forms of electoral processes (such as at-large elections, runoff primaries and multimember districts) that have disparate adverse effects on minorities are discriminatory and unconstitutional—even if they were not designed to have such impact.

Moreover, the U.S. Congress overwhelmingly inserted the "effects" standard in its renewal of the Voting Rights Act in 1982 to ensure that consequences and not intent would be the overriding criterion for determining the constitutionality of particular electoral processes. Similarly, in *Griggs v. Duke Power Co.* (1971), the U.S. Supreme Court declared that the company's employment tests, which had an unintended adverse impact on the hiring and promotion of minority workers, violated the Constitution. Important legal strides have also occurred in combatting housing policies that have had unintended adverse effects on racial minorities.

In short, the courts have made it clear that malicious intent is not necessary to declare many forms of structural arrangements racially discriminatory.[55] Thus, we contend that it is possible to mount successful challenges to structural discrimination in many other areas that adversely impact black families by placing greater emphasis on "positive" proxies that lead to unintentional benevolence.

The Earned Income Tax Credit (EITC) is an example of a positive proxy against structural discrimination in the area of tax policies. Many advocates of the working poor convinced Congress that some action was needed to offset the regressive impact of spiraling Social Security payroll taxes. Working poor families were often paying more social security taxes than income taxes. And they were often paying at higher effective tax rates than wealthy individuals and corporations.[56]

Thus, the EITC was enacted as a refundable tax credit in 1975 to refund a portion of the payroll tax to poor families. Moreover, the Welfare Reform Act of 1986, not only raised the income thresholds of the EITC, but also removed about four million working poor families (one-fourth of whom are black) from the income tax rolls.[57] Advocates for the poor must ensure that such positive tax reforms are not eroded by deficit-reduction policies and tax increases during the 1990s.

In the area of foster care and adoption, the black community should seek a functional equivalent to the Indian Child Welfare Act (1978), which ensures that native American children in need of foster care or adoption are placed within their extended families or tribes. Concerted efforts by blacks could obtain comparable changes to guarantee that the highest priority will be given to placing black children with kin. For example, if current federal policies were reversed to provide the highest reimbursements for children placed with relatives, the number of qualified kin eligible to be foster or adoptive parents would soar dramatically.

Numerous other examples could be cited of possible strategies for combatting the negative effects of structural discrimination on black families. However, it is clear that the social and economic well-being of black families will not be enhanced until multipronged strategies are used to eliminate all forms of institutionalized racism and discrimination.[58]

NOTES

1. Robert B. Hill, "Critical Issues for Black Families by the Year 2000," *The State of Black America, 1989* (New York: National Urban League, 1989), pp. 41-61.

2. Lee Rainwater and William L. Yancey, eds., *The Moynihan Report and the Politics of Controversy* (Cambridge, Mass.: MIT Press, 1967); George Gilder, *Wealth and Poverty* (New York: Basic Books, 1981).

3. Ken Auletta, *The Underclass* (New York: Vintage Books, 1982); Charles Murray, *Losing Ground* (New York: Basic Books, 1984).

4. Rainwater and Yancey, *op. cit.*, p. 93.

5. William J. Wilson, *The Declining Significance of Race* (Chicago: University of Chicago Press, 1978); William J. Wilson, *The Truly Disadvantaged* (Chicago: University of Chicago Press, 1987).

6. Robert B. Hill, "Structural Discrimination: The Unintended Consequences of Institutional Processes," in Hubert J. O'Gorman, ed., *Surveying Social Life: Papers in Honor of Herbert H. Hyman* (Wesleyan University Press, 1988), pp. 353-375.

7. Robert B. Hill, "Intergroup Relations," *Encyclopedia of Social Work-18th Edition*, Vol. 1 (National Association of Social Workers, 1987), pp. 944-957.

8. James M. Jones, *Prejudice and Racism* (Reading, Mass: Addison-Wesley, 1972).

9. Examples of the deficit model in the news media include: the December 5-9, 1983 series on black families in the *Baltimore Evening Sun;* the November 20-21, 1983 series in the *New York Times;* and the CBS-TV documentary, "The Vanishing Family" by Bill Moyers in January 1986.

10. Richard M. Burkey, *Racial Discrimination and Public Policy in the United States* (Lexington, Mass: D.C. Heath and Co., 1971).

11. Robert K. Merton, "Discrimination and the American Creed," in R.M. MacIver, ed., *Discrimination and the National Welfare* (New York: Harper, 1948), pp. 99-126.

12. One of the first works to use the term "institutional racism" was Stokeley Carmichael and Charles Hamilton, *Black Power* (New York: Vintage Books, 1967).

13. Anthony Downs, "Racism in America and How to Combat It," in A. Downs, *Urban Problems and Prospects* (Chicago: Markham Publishing Co., 1970), p. 78; Robert Friedman, "Institutional Racism: How to Discriminate Without Really Trying," in Thomas F. Pettigrew, ed., *Racial Discrimination in the U.S.* (New York: Harper & Row, 1975), pp. 384-407.

14. Thomas F. Pettigrew, "Racism and the Mental Health of White Americans," in Charles V. Willie, et.al., (eds.) *Racism and Mental Health: Essays* (Pittsburgh: University of Pittsburgh Press, 1973), p. 275.

15. C. Vann Woodward, *The Strange Career of Jim Crow* (New York: Oxford University Press, 1955).

16. Dorothy K. Newman, et.al., *Protest, Politics and Prosperity: Black Americans and White Institutions, 1940-75* (New York: Pantheon, 1978); Charles Sackrey, *The Political Economy of Urban Poverty* (New York: W.W. Norton & Co., 1973).

17. Robert B. Hill, "The Impact of the AFDC-UP Program on Black Families," Prepared for the Black Family Impact Analysis Program of the Baltimore Urban League (May 1987).

18. E. Franklin Frazier, "Family Disorganization Among Negroes," *Opportunity*, Vol. 9, No. 7 (July 1931), pp. 204-207.

19. Charles S. Johnson, "The New Frontier of Negro Labor," *Opportunity*, Vol. 10, No. 6 (June 1932), pp. 168-173.

20. A. Philip Randolph, "The Economic Crisis of the Negro," *Opportunity*, Vol. 9, No. 5 (May 1931), pp. 145-149; Charles C. Killingsworth, "Structural Unemployment in the United States," in Jack Stieber, ed., *Employment Problems of Automation and Advanced Technology* (New York: St. Martin's Press, 1986), pp. 128-156.

21. E. Franklin Frazier, *The Negro in the U.S.* (New York: Macmillan, 1957).

22. Robert B. Hill, *Black Families in the 1974-75 Depression* (Washington, D.C.: National Urban League Research Development, 1975).

23. Charles L. Betsey, et.al., *Youth Employment and Training Programs: The YEDPA Years* (Washington, D.C.: National Research Council, 1985), Chapter 2.

24. David Caplovitz, "Making Ends Meet: How Families Cope With Inflation and Recession," *The Annals*, Vol. 456 (1976), pp. 88-98.

25. U.S. Bureau of the Census, "Money Income of Households, Families, and Persons in the U.S.: 1982," *Current Population Reports*, Series P-60, No. 142 (February 1984).

26. E. Franklin Frazier, *The Negro Family in the United States* (Chicago: Univerity of Chicago Press, 1939).

27. E. Franklin Frazier, "Three Scourges of the Negro Family," *Opportunity*, Vol. 4, No. 43 (July 1926), pp. 210-213; 234.

28. St. Clair Duke and Horace R. Cayton, *Black Metropolis*, Vols. 1 & 2 (New York: Harper & Row, 1945).

29. Frazier, *Negro in the U.S.*, op. cit.

30. Robert B. Hill, *The Widening Economic Gap* (Washington, D.C.: National Urban League Research Department, 1979).

31. U.S. Census Bureau, "Projections of the Hispanic Population," *Current Population Reports*, Series P-25, No. 995 (November 1986).

32. Robert B. Hill, "Public Policies and Black Progress," *Centerboard*, Spring (1986), pp. 24-34.

33. Robert B. Hill, "Income, Earnings and Incidence of Poverty," in Harry A. Ploski and James Williams, eds., *The Negro Almanac: A Reference Work on the Afro-American*, 4th edition (New York: John Wiley & Sons, 1982), pp. 645-678.

34. A. Philip Randolph, *op. cit.;* Manning Marable, *How Capitalism Underdeveloped Black America* (Boston: South End Press, 1983).

35. National Commission for Employment Policy, *Trade and Employment*, Special Report No. 30 (Washington, D.C.: November 1978).

36. U.S. Bureau of Labor Statistics, "Displaced Workers, 1979-83," *BLS Bulletin 2240* (July 1985).

37. Barry Bluestone and Bennett Harrison, *The Deindustrialization of America* (New York: Basic Books, 1982), pp. 54-55.

38. Coalition on Block Grants and Human Needs, *Civil Rights Implications of the Block Grants* (Washington, D.C., 1983); John L. Palmer and Isabel V. Sawhill, eds., *The Reagan Record* (Cambridge, Mass: Ballinger Publishing Co., 1984).

39. William Mirengoff and Lester Rindler, *CETA: Manpower Programs Under Local Control* (Washington, D.C.: National Academy of Sciences, 1978); Children's Defense Fund, *A Children's Defense Budget: An Analysis of the President's FY 1985 Budget and Children* (Washington, D.C., 1984).

40. Robert B. Hill, "The Synthetic Method: Its Feasibility for Deriving the Census Undercount for States and Local Areas," in U.S. Census Bureau, *Conference on Census Undercount: Proceedings of the 1980 Conference* (Washington, D.C.: Department of Commerce, July 1980), pp. 129-141.

41. Illinois Council for Black Studies, *Black People and the 1980 Census.* Volume 1, "Proceedings for a Conference on the Population Undercount," (Chicago: Chicago Center for Afro-American Studies and Research, 1980).

42. Herrington J. Bryce, "The Impact of the Undercount on State and Local Government Transfers," in *Conference on Census Undercount*, op. cit., pp. 112-124.

43. Currently, about one-third of black men and 15 percent of black women workers are likely to die before retirement, compared to one-fourth of white men and ten percent of white women workers. See U.S. Bureau of Labor Statistics, *Worklife Estimates: Effects of Race and Education* (Washington, D.C., February 1986).

44. Hill, "Impact of AFDC-UP on Black Families," op. cit.

45. Andrew Bilingsley and Jeanne M. Giovannoni, *Children of the Storm* (New York: Harcourt, Brace and Jovanovich, 1970).

46. Robert B. Hill, *Informal Adoption Among Black Families* (Washington, D.C.: National Urban League Research Department, 1977).

47. Walter E. Williams, *The State Against Blacks* (New York: McGraw-Hill, 1982); Gilder, op. cit.; Murray, op. cit.

48. Murray, op. cit.

49. Robert B. Hill, *Economic Policies and Black Progress* (Washington, D.C.: National Urban League Research Department, 1981).

50. Wilson, *The Truly Disadvantaged*, op. cit.

51. William A. Darity, Jr. and Samuel L. Myers, Jr., "Does Welfare Dependency Cause Female Headship?: The Case of the Black Family," *Journal of Marriage and the Family* (November 1984), pp. 765-779; Williams, op. cit.

52. Frazier, *The Negro in the U.S.*, op. cit.

53. Robert B. Hill, "Income Maintenance Programs and the Minority Elderly," in R.L. McNeely and John L. Cohen, eds., *Aging in Minority Groups* (Beverly Hills, Calif: Sage Publications, 1983), pp. 195-211.

54. Sar A. Levitan, *Programs in Aid of the Poor for the 1980's.* (Baltimore, MD: The Johns Hopkins University Press, 1980).

55. Harold J. Sullivan, "Formula for Failure: A Critique of the Intent Requirement in School Segregation Litigation," *Journal of Negro Education*, Vol. 52, No. 3 (Summer 1983), pp. 270-289; Lino A. Graglia, "From Prohibiting Segregation to Requiring Integration," in Walter G. Stephan and Joe R. Feagin, eds., *School Desegregation* (New York: Plenum Press, 1980), pp. 69-96.

56. Center on Budget and Policy Priorities, *Falling Behind: A Report on How Blacks Have Fared Under the Reagan Policies* (Washington, D.C., October 1984); Center on Budget and Policy Priorities, *End Results: The Impact of Federal Policies Since 1980 on Low-Income Americans* (Washington, D.C.: Interfaith Action for Economic Justice, September 1984).

57. Hill, "Critical Issues for Black Families by the Year 2000," op. cit.

58. Theodore Cross, *The Black Power Imperative* (New York: Faulkner, 1984).

Part III

Family Form and Functioning

INTRODUCTION

In this section we shift our attention from a focus on sociosctructural issues and black families to internal dynamics of black family development and functioning. The treatment continues, however, in the tradition of the ecological models advocated by Du Bois, Frazier, and Billingsley. One of the concerns of both Du Bois and Frazier was the role of values and coping mechanisms in shaping patterns of family formation and functioning.

The chapters in this section examine this issue from two critical perspectives. First, the process by which values are transmitted between generations is examined in the context of stresses produced in black families' interaction with other societal subsystems. Second, the extent to which values affect responses of black males and females to demographic constraints imposed on black families' formation by the shortage of black males is explored.

Spencer's analysis examines whether stress produced by the Atlanta child murders affected parental values, beliefs, and child-rearing strategies. Spencer examines the extent to which observed patterns differed depending on the availability of socioeconomic resources. Consistent with the ecological framework, she finds that the additional stress resulting from the Atlanta child murders was a much less important contributor to adverse child-rearing outcomes than was daily stress resulting from ongoing "socioeconomic or caste status-related stress." She also finds that single-parenting undermines optimum child development outcomes as a result of restricted access to socioeconomic resources. At the same time, Spencer emphasizes that similarities persist in "espoused child rearing values and beliefs . . . among African-American parents independent of economic resources." She concludes the analysis with a discussion of ways in which some black parents have been successful in neutralizing the effects of continuing stress on parenting, including involvement in the black church.

Slaughter and Dilworth-Anderson examine the special adaptations required to neutralize the stress resulting from caring for victims of childhood sickle cell anemia. The chapter describes the extended kin relations used by female-headed, nuclear, and multigenerational black families to care for middle school-aged black children with sickle cell disease. The ecological perspective is evidenced by the finding that upon learning that their child had sickle cell disease all but one of the families studied were "confronted with the problem of educating themselves and other extended families members about the disease, as they were victims of not knowing about an essential aspect of their sociocultural heritage and of not having available trusted supportive community institutions and groups around them to help them solve their problems."

Cazenave and Smith explore the effects of negative stereotypes about black men and women on relationships. Their discussion begins with an analysis of the sociohistorical etiology of negative stereotypes about black males and females. The analysis of the empirical data suggests significant patterns of acceptance of negative stereotypes by both black men and women. Consistent with the ecological model, the authors find that respondents who hold negative stereotypes about black men or black women are less likely to report being adversely affected by racism and tend to report that blacks don't take advantage of available opportunities. Drawing upon the sociohistorical insights and the patterns that emerge from their data, Cazenave and Smith conclude with suggestions for cultivating more positive perceptions, within black men and women, about black male-female relationships.

Williams addresses the issue of the scarcity of black males—an issue with which Du Bois grappled. Through a careful presentation of existing empirical evidence the reality of the worsening sex ratio is documented. Williams evaluates a particular strategy for dealing with problems emanating from the declining pool of available black marriageable men and black women's desires for conjugal bonds, i.e., polygyny. He concludes, through an extended discussion of the changes in mating patterns and values which blacks have experienced across time that polygyny is not a viable or a desirable strategy for ameliorating the problem.

6

PARENTAL VALUES TRANSMISSION: IMPLICATIONS FOR THE DEVELOPMENT OF AFRICAN-AMERICAN CHILDREN

Margaret Beale Spencer

Data from African-American children and their parents were obtained at two different time periods separated by three years. There were two major patterns of findings. First, an extreme level of environmental stress was associated with fewer adverse outcomes than the ongoing or mundane level of socioeconomic or caste status-related stress. Second, single-parenting efforts often exacerbate optimum child development outcomes, since single-parenting efforts were correlated with lower socioeconomic status. Social class differences emerged as a significant factor affecting the parent's ability to identify and utilize available child-rearing resources. An important social class-related conclusion was that similarities in espoused child-rearing values and beliefs exist among African-American parents independent of economic resources. The assumed effect of ''different values'' is the often touted explanation for the adverse life-course outcomes of many economically disadvantaged persons. However, the findings suggest many similarities in child-rearing values across social class lines.

INTRODUCTION

As used by cultural anthropologists, the term *enculturation* refers to the specific ways in which human infants and children learn to become adult members of a particular society. Human infants, according to cultural anthropologists, develop into competent or efficacious adults only through being reared in a *human* and *humane* society. Enculturation plays a salient role in the process. Each infant grows into a particular kind of human—rather than simply as human. Accordingly, *becoming human* reflects (a) a complex interaction between universal human capacities and culturally varying *child-rearing* practices, (b) individual heredity, and (c) the common experiences patterned by the culture.[1] There remains little research on the content of child-rearing practices, strategies, and processes for oppressed minority group families.

The experiences created by the majority (Caucasian) American culture for minorities (vis-à-vis social policies) result in discontinuities between *what* is (a) expected (in the long run), (b) recognized as important, and (c) reinforced for African-Americans versus concomitant expectations, perceptions, and reinforcements made available to non-minority group citizens. Further, and much more consequential as regards individual group members' motivation, the evaluations and analyses of inconsistencies, successes, and failures as outcomes for each group are applied differently. In fact, recent research contributions and theoretical statements by Ogbu, Garbarino, and Muga illustrate the point.[2] Together their perspectives propose the following: (a) each suggests very different ecosystem or environmental experiences for African-American children and youth versus those for nonminority youth; (b) each interprets the environment as a potential or actual source of stress and risk; and (c) each suggests the critical role of the nation's economic history and its fluctuations for understanding current experiences of race and ethnicity along with associated expectations, constraints, and supports for minorities, in particular.

We introduce the term *castelike minorities* to emphasize the structural groups in the United States. In stratification, people are *assigned* to their particular groups by birth—e.g., according to skin color. The individual generally has few opportunities or options to escape the derogation associated with the designation or stratification. Unlike castelike minorities, immigrant minorities usually enter the host society more or less voluntarily. Although initially lacking power and a clear comprehension of the depreciated value associated with their status, the relevant ''other'' for evaluating current experiences is ''the homeland.'' Autonomous minorities, according to Ogbu, do not experience stratification, although they may experience some prejudice.[3] Importantly, their separateness is not based on a degraded, specialized economic or political status. Although the concept of castelike minorities is helpful, at least for the North American situation, there *is* significant *diversity* of outcomes within groups that would *not* be expected for the traditional caste situation.[4] The issues of social class diversity and skin color variation make the traditional assumptions by Ogbu less than reliable when applied to the unique American situation of race-inspired oppression.[5]

Until the latter part of the 1970s, few researchers studied the *develop-*

mental processes of African-American children's group identity formation, associated *parental strategies* employed for the rearing of competent children, and the specific parental values that required transmission. Instead, at least up until that point, the literature continued to abound with assumptions that lacked both a developmental perspective and general empirical validation for the assumptions concerning the group identity construct.[6] Our research findings suggest the importance of linking parental child-rearing strategies to social class and child outcomes.

The present study's goal has several component sections: (a) to delineate differences in behavioral problems and competencies as a function of one's proximity to a major stressor (the Atlanta child murders), (b) to determine the relationship between socioeconomic status and behavioral outcomes, and (c) to examine differences in parental values, beliefs, and child-rearing strategies as a function of the availability of socioeconomic resources.

The background for the study is supported by several premises that guide our interpretation of research findings on parental child-rearing beliefs and values.

First, as viewed by Garbarino and Wynn, the *status* of American childhood and youth is coupled with or linked to at-risk conditions that undermine its optimum development and exists independent of socioeconomic stratification.[7]

Second, the fact of minority status only exacerbates or worsens the at-risk status of children. More specifically, as supported by Pierce's research and clinical observations, minority children live under conditions of daily or mundane levels of stress.[8] According to Muga and Baron, much of the mundane or daily stress experienced is exacerbated by economic constraints and policies that generate institutionalized stress for all minorities—especially the historically oppressed groups (African-Americans, American Indians, and Hispanic Americans).[9]

Third, Jordan suggests that, in its structuring of the family microsystem, parenting may play a buffering role in mediating against adverse effects of mundane or daily forms of stress.[10]

BACKGROUND

The basic issue of child and youth placement in society or, in fact, their "nonfittedness" remains an unvarying age-old problem. Phillippe Aries, a historian, had documented the vulnerable status of children of medieval

Europe.[11] Pomeroy identified similarly vulnerable conditions of children living between 500 B.C. and 350 B.C. who experienced direct forms of child abuse.[12] The practice of infanticide was not uncommon during this period.

Lerner, a more recent policy theorist, has used adult/child biblical dilemmas to further document the entrenched lack of value placed on children.[13] When coupled with the previous observations and the current infant mortality rate of minority infants, it may be suggested that American children and youth are reared in an insensitive — often openly hostile — society. In fact, Chestang introduces the term *social inconsistency* for describing the discontinuity between word, deed, and legislative promise experienced by minority group members.[14] Almost fifty years of race preference research (i.e., group identity findings) suggests that adverse conditions have not significantly changed for African-American children who continue to cope with the issues of color and race as imposed by socializing institutions and practices.[15] There may have been changes in the form of racism experienced, although the content and consequences of oppressive conditions have remained virtually unchanged. More specifically, the often unavoidable societal exposure of minority status children and youth to direct and subliminal forms of discrimination results in at-risk and stressful ecosystem experiences.[16] Socioeconomic status-related discrimination is often linked with caste experiences. For Wilson, behavioral outcomes are often linked to housing segregation patterns.[17]

Although not approached generally as a source of environmental stress, low socioeconomic status (i.e., impoverishment) should be considered as a source of unchanging or mundane stress. Several other relationships are apparent. For example, the transmission of cultural values has implications for child outcomes. Positive group-identity values transmitted by parents are associated with greater intellectual performance for children. Although the relation is salient for both lower and middle income families, the issues appear worsened by socioeconomic disadvantage.[18]

For a two-year period the city of Atlanta's environment was life-threatening for children. The corpses of neighborhood children served as concrete unavoidable evidence. Twenty-nine black youths and physically immature young adults were abducted and murdered between the spring of 1979 and summer of 1981 in the metropolitan area. Except for two girls, the victims were males. The publicity surrounding the crisis was international in scope and subsided following the apprehension and subsequent conviction of a local resident. In fact, under "normative" conditions, the childhood and adolescent years of minorities should be considered a period of externally (racism-related) derived stress. Potentially, the combined experiences of race and economic disadvantaged conditions place children at greater risk for possible psychopathology or behavioral problems, less competent-appearing cognitive performance, and less than optimum life-course developments. Given caste-determined economic conditions, the predicted course of development for African-American youth in North America is for untoward or problematic outcomes unless societal, community and parental level interventions are introduced.

This research begins the process of illuminating the *content* of cultural value transmission and specific parenting strategies in African-American families. It is proposed that these contents and strategies are linked with children's more general group identity processes and competencies. Further, and most important, the ability of parents to *effectively parent*, which includes mediating or buffering against adverse environmental effects, is linked to socioeconomic status (which also has implications for or is linked with single-parenting).

THE STUDY

Sample

Assessed were 384 children living in a large southern metropolitan area and attending either preschool or public primary schools. The children were equally divided by gender and socioeconomic status. The design both replicated and extended earlier research by the author.[19] Children were either 3-, 5-, 7-, or 9-year-olds who attended full-day predominately African-American programs at their respective schools. The goal of the research was to examine developmental variables of hypothesized importance for competence formation. A multimethod multiple measure, cross-sectional design was implemented. In addition, a subsample of 45 parents were interviewed for assessing their beliefs and perceptions in several areas of child rearing: parenting goals supported, parental strategies employed, beliefs concerning gender role development, perceptions of the child's school and its administration, cultural beliefs/values, perceptions of children's life chances, evidences of child-rearing support, and, finally, perceptions of empowerment.

The youth victimization crisis of Atlanta suggested the need to replicate and extend the previous (Time 1 [T1]) research for delineating the effects of the crisis as an acute stressor on children's perceptions and coping skills. More specifically, the longitudinal research effort or follow-up study concerned itself with African-American children's ability to cope with an exotic life-course event type stress: the murders of mostly male, poor African-American children and youth living in a southern metropolitan area. During the follow-up phase at the end of the crisis (i.e., Time 2 [T2]), approximately 150 children and their parents (i.e., *mothers*) were contacted anew and again tested and interviewed. At the follow-up (T2), the sample of children ranged from 6 to 12 years of age. All were reassessed on many of the original instruments and rating scales along with some replacements and additions for the early adolescents.

Many of the topical areas and questions asked of the parents in the initial 45-member pilot or T1 interview were asked again in the extensive follow-up. However, more questions concerning cultural beliefs, the specifics of child-rearing strategies employed, and demographic information were included. Parents also completed the Achenbach and Edelbrock child symptomatology and behavioral competence checklist.[20] The purpose of the epidemiological rating form was to determine whether or not Atlanta parents would discern *more clinical symptoms* and *fewer behavioral competencies* (i.e., induced by the stress). Other sites where parental ratings were obtained (although no interview data were collected) were Nashville, Tennessee; Washington, D.C.; Chicago, Illinois, and Philadelphia, Pennsylvania.

Measures and Interview Protocols

The Child Behavioral Checklist (CBCL) developed by Achenbach and Edelbrock was designed (a) to provide prevalence data on behavioral problems and competencies, (b) to identify differences related to demographic variables, and (c) to compare clinically referred and demographically similar nonreferred children.[21] The Child Behavior Checklist (CBCL)was used to obtain data and includes 20 social competence items and 118 behavioral problems. From the behavioral competency information several competence subscales were derived and then combined to obtain scales for activity, social, and school competence in addition to a total behavioral competence score.

Demographic data were also included on the rating form, which supported the construction of a socioeconomic index for assessing the family's socioeconomic status. Socioeconomic status was determined by employment category (census classification), family income, and educational status. Achenbach and Edelbrock report good psychometric properties for the scales that included referred and non-clinically referred 4-to 16-year-olds who varied by social class and race.[22] The interclass correlation coefficients were .952 for behavior problems and .996 for social competence.

FINDINGS

Mundane and Exotic Contributions to Stress

Socioeconomic Effects. Previous research has consistently linked socioeconomic status to single-parenting.[23] For our sample of Atlanta parents, 45 percent were married; the remaining 55 percent were single parents due to divorce ($N = 15$), separation ($N = 20$), becoming widowed ($N = 6$), or "other" ($N = 14$)—usually never having been married. The chi square for marital status by socioeconomic status was significant (χ^2 [4, $N = 100$] = 38.74, $p < .0001$). Being married was associated with middle income status while being unmarried was associated with lower income status. Similarly, having 12 years or less of schooling was associated with lower socioeconomic status: (χ^2 [6, $N = 100$] = 55.3, $p < .0001$). Similarly, father's education, along with child's maternal grandparents' education level, was associated with the family's current socioeconomic status. However, there was no association between the child's parental grandparents' attained educational level and the family's current socioeconomic status. Consistent with previous theorizing in the area of human development, which stresses the "trend-setting" role of the mother for the family, it is the child's *mother and her own parents' economic and educational status* that are salient. That is, the data support the human development research perspective, which suggests that the mother's structuring of the familial environment has the most salient implications for the child's development.

Having more children residing at home was associated with lower socioeconomic status (χ^2 [5, $N = 96$] = 12.35, $p = .03$). Given the cost of rearing children, the relationship was consistent. The linkage between parental education, marital status, and socioeconomic status was not surprising. However, less often discussed and certainly more rarely reported as "a counter *intuitive*" or unexpected finding is the apparent *independence* between parental educational values (i.e., minimum education *expected* of children from parental reports) and socioeconomic status. That is, there were no differences obtained by social class for the minimum education or minimum number of years of schooling expected of children in the future (χ^2 [4, $N = 100$] = 1.09. $p > .89$).

All parents, independent of social class or economic resources, *expected* an equally high number of completed years of schooling.

Exotic Stress Effects. There was little effect due to city of residence and the manifestation of behavioral symptoms.[24] In fact, a nonsignificant correlation between the CBCL and city/noncity was obtained. Only the activity scale demonstrated a significant relationship with the city/noncity variable: $r(350) = .19$, p .001. On the other hand, the difference across sites by SES was startling. For the entire sample, independent of site, there was a significant difference for SES and CBCL (r [344]$= -.17$, $p = .001$). Lower income children manifested more behavioral symptoms as indicated by parental ratings. A similar trend was apparent for observed competence.

Behavioral competence on each of the three scales indicated significantly more rated competence for middle income children ($p = .001$) for the activity, social, and school competence scales. The pattern was more apparent for the Atlanta sample since more demographic information was available for them. The highest correlation was between annual income and the CBCL: lower income children show a greater frequency of behavioral problems ($r =$ [83] $-.43$, $p<.001$). In addition, more symptoms were associated with children of mothers and fathers with less education. Further, the prevalence of behavioral symptoms was associated with highest education obtained for the child's *maternal* grandparents. Again, the more education the fewer manifested behavioral symptoms reported. The relationship was not significant for the CBCL and the *paternal* grandparental level of education.

In sum, the greater the presence of economic resources and educational attainments of family members across generations, the more frequent the reports of manifest competence and the less prevalent the reports of behavioral symptoms.

Major Parenting Findings by Three Levels of Social Class (Lower, Modest, Middle)

General Child-Rearing Information Resources. There were significant differences in parental help seeking behavior regarding child-rearing information. Middle income (MI) parents obtained a higher mean frequency when asked about the various *sources* of information. In fact, 85 percent of lower income (LI) parents could list only one source of information, while 50 percent of the middle income respondents were able to mention two or more. There were also SES differences in the source reported by parents seeking information. Middle income respondents more often mention spouse ($p = .04$) and medical sources (trend level, $p = .1$). More importantly, MI parents mentioned literature as a child-rearing source significantly more often ($p = .001$). There were no significant differences in the infrequent use of either friends or religion.

Significant differences emerged in the salience of the source named. Middle income parents rated "self" as extremely or most important more often than did lower income parents. Similarly, MI parents were twice as likely to rate the medical community as very or extremely important for child-rearing information when compared with medical resource use for lower income mothers (χ^2 [4, $N = 100$] = 10, $p = .04$). Likewise, literature was rated as "very" to "extremely" important for MI parents versus LI respondents (χ^2 [4, $N = 100$] = 14.04, $p < .01$).

There were no SES differences in the number of roles that the father should play in the rearing of children. However, there were differences in the content of the roles. For example, MI respondents more often reported that the role of the father was equal to that of the mother (χ^2 [2, $N = 99$] = 12.72, $p = .002$).

Differences by social class for the sheer number of maternal roles identified were not significant. Interestingly, although not significant, there was a trend for the lowest and highest SES groups to list more maternal roles. The significant difference was due to the variation in respondent listing of the maternal role, "supplying of material needs" as important. The two lowest SES groups indicated a specific role for the mother significantly more often than did the highest SES group (χ^2 [2, $N = 100$] = 8.7, $p = .01$). No differences in the frequency of listings for the maternal roles "modeling" and "morality teacher" by social class were apparent. To state it differently, independent of social class, parents were consistent in their suggestion of "modeling" and "moral teacher" as two important roles for the child's mother.

No SES differences were apparent in the perception of the child's grandparents as generally important. Similarly, independent of social class, grandparents were *neither* perceived as a source of financial assistance nor historical reference (i.e., as the repository of the culture). The one SES difference obtained was for the identification of grandparents as a source for *emotional assistance*. The lowest and highest SES groups showed a similar trend for grandparental use. However, the modest socioeconomic status group identified the grandparents as an emotional assistance resource almost twice as often as did the two other groups (χ^2 [2, $N = 99$] = 5.9, $p = .05$).

Although both SES groups showed little difference in their moderate ratings of friends as resources (or for television, which was rated as unimportant by both groups), there was an unexpected trend for religion to be rated as only moderately important for LI respondents although of extreme importance for more MI respondents (i.e., both modest income and middle income).

The Transmission of Specific Values. The previous SES findings are important when considered along with the family's church attendance data. There were no differences by social class for the rated importance of church attendance. Independent of social class, all respondents classified church attendance as very important. Interesting variations in the use of the church as an information resource were obtained.

Lower income respondents reported only a moderate importance for religion in child-rearing as compared to its extreme importance for the modest and middle income samples. However, when *directly asked,* there were no SES differences for those who responded that church attendance affects child-rearing. There was also no SES difference in the additional function of religion for promoting and fostering prayers and devotion. The only remaining social class differences, which were not surprising, were those responsible for variations in who, or the actual family members, attending church. For LI families, mother/children groupings were more often reported to attend church together as opposed to total family groups (i.e., including father) reported for MI families. (The relationship was consistent with the findings of greater father-absence among LI families).

The data suggested that religious values were present and used for family prayer and devotion, although there were differences in the extended or additional use of the religious community for child-rearing support. There were *negligible* SES differences in reported values by social class in other areas of family functioning. There were quite significant differences apparent in the use of the religious community for the identification and utilization of resources for supporting child-rearing efforts.

When asked about the values that were reinforced with their children in the course of child-rearing, MI parents usually were able to articulate a larger number of values reinforced (χ^2 [4, $N=99$] $= 10.41$, $p = .03$). However, there were few differences or trends in the *quality* or *content* of values reinforced. All parents, independent of SES, listed personal values (i.e., being good, kind, etcetera), racial pride (although *infrequently* reported on the whole), moral values (highly represented by *all* parents) with some differences for education. The modest SES grouping showed a pattern to reinforce educational values more often (χ^2 [2, $N = 99$] = 7.2, $p = .09$). It may be that this midplacement or "modest SES" parenting group *can see* a middle class life style "on the horizon" and in response places more emphasis on education with their children "to get them over the top." Independent of what actually happens in the classroom, all parents rated the child's "self-discipline" as important. That is, although there exist popular beliefs of teachers concerning the behavior of caste status or minority children in the classroom (along with assumed parental expectations), *good behavior* and the importance of getting *at least* a basic level of education are also valued by minority parents across social classes. The finding is consistent with the previously reported finding of no difference by SES for minimal amount of schooling expected.

When asked about the specific forms of discipline that they used when their children misbehaved, there were no differences in the number of discipline techniques offered. They included reasoning, corporal punishment, and loss of privileges. Only the latter, loss of privileges, demonstrated significant differences in use by SES (χ^2 [2, $N = 100$] = 8.6, $p = .01$). Higher SES members (i.e., MI parents) more often reported using this method. Although not significant, modest and middle income parents slightly more often mentioned corporal punishment.

There was consistency in the number of punishable acts identified across SES groups. Differences by SES emerged, however, in the *number* of discipline informational sources perceived as available by SES (χ^2 [2, $N = 80$] = 7.43, $p = .02$). More economically advantaged groups (i.e., modest and middle) were able to articulate *more* discrete sources of discipline-centered child-rearing sources. There were no differences by social class in the identification of internal sources of discipline information, or the use of literature or friends. There was a trend, however, for higher SES families to identify the medical community as a resource. The one significant difference in source of discipline information was the use of the child's maternal grandparents. Higher SES respondents mentioned the use of grandparents significantly more often (χ^2 [2, $N = 80$] = 10.5, $p = .005$).

Associated with the issues of value enculturation and the expectations for disciplined behavior, there were interesting similarities in the methods reinforced for handling conflict with "others" generally, with siblings, with individuals of the opposite gender, and with white children, specifically. First, there were significant differences in the number of ways listed as acceptable to handle others' aggressive behaviors (χ^2 [2,

$N = 100] = 12.3, p = .002$). Middle income parents were able to articulate *more* methods for handling insults, although there were similarities in the content. For example, there were no differences by socioeconomic status in the frequency with which "ignore," "refer to adult," and "reciprocate" were used. However, there was a pattern for MI respondents to suggest "reasoning with the other" more often than did LI respondents (χ^2 2, $N = 100 = 8.6, p = .01$).

There were significant differences in the number of solutions to conflict when the individual to be retaliated against was a sibling (χ^2 [2,$N = 89] = 8.59, p = .01$), a child of the opposite gender (χ^2 $N = 100] = 10.22. p = .006$), or a white child ($\chi^2$ [2, $N = 98] = 12.38$, $p = .022$). In all cases, the MI parents reported a greater variety of methods reinforced in their children for handling conflict. When in conflict with a sibling, the method of "stop and make-up" ($p = .055$) was suggested more often for lower and modest income parents, although "reasoning" with the sibling was more often suggested by MI parents ($p = .03$).

In retaliation against a child of the opposite sex, both middle and lower income respondents reported an almost equal frequency in use of "ignoring," although the modest SES group used "ignoring" most often in cross-gender conflicts. When in conflict with white children, although MI parents suggest more methods to resolve conflicts, there were no differences in the frequency of the specific methods listed by social class.

Most interesting was the more frequent use of reasoning as a method for resolving conflict by social class. When there were differences in the proposed methods for handling conflict, the use of reasoning to resolve conflict (i.e., for the situations "retaliation against *others [generally]*" and "retaliation against siblings [specifically]*") was the trend reported more often by MI respondents. The implications are important, since it is generally suggested by the socialization literature that more inductive approaches are associated with better outcomes for personality and moral behavior.[25]

The Transmission of Cultural Values. As noted in the introduction, the literature is consistent in its reporting of racial attitude, preference, and color connotation findings: young children, irrespective of ethnicity, gender, and social class, learn the negative evaluations associated with the color black and African-American persons and learn the positive attributes associated with the color white and Caucasian persons.[26]

Research during the previous several decades shows this pattern for young preschool cognitively egocentric children. Another pattern emerges, however, during the early and middle school years. At best, inferred is a pattern of neutrality or no preference for young black children. On the other hand, most apparent is the consistent pattern of white preference for Caucasian children. Research by this writer demonstrates that for African-American children, Afrocentric responses are associated with improved performance on standardized tests. In addition, parental cultural value transmission, as a consequence of specific child-rearing practices, patterns, and beliefs, is associated with children's cultural values.[27] One may conclude that, for the most part, unless there is some parental or other microsystem-level intervention, the expected cultural value orientation obtained by black children is race dissonance: white-preferred cultural values and attitudes are expected for black children although an own-group orientation is expected for white children independent of chronological age and social class.[28]

For the current study there were specific parental responses that were consistent independent of social class, which together suggests a pattern of race-related stress experienced by caste-minority group children generally. There were no differences by social class in the frequency of racial incidents experienced. Similarly, there were few variations in parental response to racial incidents. Parents reported either ignoring "the child report," interpreting the incident to the child as a sign of ignorance by the other, or doing nothing. The implications from these data for black child protection, cultural advocacy, and the development of trust (versus *mistrust*) are clear.

Similar to the precrisis (Time 1) data reported, there were no SES differences in the parents' own racial identification.[29] For the most part, all identified themselves as black (as opposed to Negro). There was a significant difference in the reasons offered for the self-categorization of racial identity. Higher SES respondents indicated an identification based upon their upbringing. On the other hand, LI SES respondents more often indicated "no reason" or offered responses that were not applicable to the question posed (χ^2 [8, N, = 15.3, $p = .05$).

When asked about specific problems that might be associated with the rearing of a black child, there were no differences in the number of problems expected or experienced. In fact, most respondents (i.e., 60–65 percent of sample) could not (or resisted reducing experiences to a single example) list one problem. For those individuals who responded, there was a predictive trend for the low and modest status groups to list economic problems as most pressing (χ^2 [2, $N = 98$] $= 5.4$, $p = .07$). Similarly, when asked, "When you talk about Black culture/race—what do you tell your child?,'' for the total sample there were no differences by social class for the number of different ''teachings'' or specific content of racial knowledge communicated. Issues raised or notions shared involved concerns about equality, race differences, history, or in some cases (25 percent) —*no* discussion at all. When specifically asked whether teaching the child about race is important, there were no differences by SES. Approximately 25 percent clearly stated that race is *not important*.

Respondents were also asked whether or not their children experienced *advantages* as a *black* child. No differences by SES were found. About 50 percent of those reporting said that there were *no* advantages or that they ''didn't know.'' More middle class respondents offered vague or tentative responses, although not significant. There were no SES differences in the frequency of disadvantages noted that were associated with being an African-American. Although the low-socioeconomic group more often reported ''none,'' about 50 percent of the sample generally could not list any disadvantages. Those disadvantages *that were* listed included differences in quality of schooling available (white schools better), limited jobs, and discrimination. Although the listing of any given disadvantage was not significantly different by SES, LI respondents listed discrimination *least frequently* of all.

Parents were also asked whether or not they felt that the disadvantages had changed significantly from the period when they were growing up as children. There were no significant differences in the perceptions of improvements or deteriorated conditions. Although not significant, there was a trend for the *lowest* and *highest* SES groups to believe that improvements had been made in the area of educational opportunities. The finding was consistent with general responses to another set of questions concerning their children's education. The lowest and highest SES groups (although not significant) responded as most satisfied with their child's school situation. Again, it may well be that the modest SES grouping was more critical since, in addition to perceptions of helplessness and hopelessness, they were also seeing the possibility of real or potential SES gains (i.e., hopefulness or perceptions of hope). Accordingly, modest SES parents were critical of social structures that might further block or impede access to perceived *screens of opportunities* for economic improvements or real gains.

SUMMARY AND CONCLUSION

There were two major patterns of findings. *First,* comparatively speaking, an extreme or acute level of environmental stress was associated with fewer behavioral problems or diminished behavioral competencies when compared with the experiences of ongoing, mundane, or daily levels of *socioeconomic or caste status*-related stress. *Second,* single-parenting efforts often exacerbated or undermined optimum child development outcomes, since single-parenting efforts were correlated with lower socioeconomic status. Social class differences emerged as a significant factor affecting the parent's ability to identify and utilize available child rearing resources. Equally important was the observation that there were many similarities in espoused child-rearing values and beliefs independent of the availability of economic resources.

The patterns of findings for the stress reactivity data and the parental interview data together suggested intriguing interpretations and developmental implications for black children and their adaptational processes.[30]

As noted initially, the processes of socialization involve the manner by which the parent as the primary or most immediate agent of socialization (a) *makes meaning* or inferences from the various levels of the ecosystem (e.g., perceptions of the school, social structures, and associated social policies), (b) *translates* that meaning into specific parental attitudes, opinions, values, and goals, and finally (c) *transforms* those general beliefs into specific child-rearing strategies. The specific child-rearing strategies, ideally, should enhance specific behavioral outcomes and the enculturation of or internalization by the child of specific success-oriented behavioral patterns. In sum, it was expected that success or competence orientations toward the world evolve from specific life-course experiences both in the family and as a consequence of being a part of a specific minority group.

The findings suggested that the daily *life experiences* of minorities are more stressful than generally acknowledged. That is, given the magnitude and consensus of trauma associated with the Atlanta youth murders, there were *no differences* between that stress and the daily experiences of children living in other cities at the time of the Atlanta murders.[31] The finding of no differences, in and of itself, is stress-producing for that "legion of hopefuls" who believed that the civil rights era of the 1960s resulted in significant, long-term (in fact, permanent) institutionalized changes for people of color living in the United States. The data suggested that there have been, perhaps, *superficial* alterations of "deep structure" tensions as experienced by minorities.

The "first blush" analysis or interpretation was consistent with socioeconomic status findings as a main effect. That is, the general undermining effects of lower socioeconomic status have been consistently stated when discussing the general plight of the nation's "so-called under-class." However, less well understood or, in fact, recognized has been the penchant for social class and caste membership experiences "to deaden" or "to anesthetize" one's reactivity to exotic, extreme, or life-course type stress. Until the availability of the current data set, empirical findings have been unavailable that explored and/or substantiated the theoretical musing of more clinically oriented scholars such as Pierce or Carter.[32]

Pierce's formulation suggested that minorities suffer daily and varied forms of disrespect that results in persistent mundane levels of stress that subsequently inures them against the impacts of life-course or exotic level stress.[33] These data offer empirical validation for Pierce's clinical observations concerning the relationships between exotic and mundane stress. However, the findings also explore the apparent *price* of *adaptation* to mundane stress levels.

As noted in the introduction, the consistent pattern of group identity findings (i.e., race dissonance findings for African-American children and consistent own-group preferences for white children) suggested that desegregation efforts were inadequate to address the complexity and the depth of institutionalized racism. Although stress is associated with deprivational conditions that are directly related to economic deficits, however, the more crippling effects may also be associated with a defensive altering of the child's perceptional experiences and the behavioral modes that are adopted to enhance one's coping efforts. The analogous case for parents was the consistent *pattern* of psychological *denial,* which perhaps reflects a distortion of perceptual processes and an adaptational strategy.

In the case of adaptive modes of coping used by minority group youth, perceptual distortions of reality and adaptive behavioral modes specific to certain microsystems (e.g., the school and male/female interpersonal [sexual] relations) may preserve mental health in the *short run* (e.g, drop-out/push-out statistics; early commitments to sexual intimacy thus early pregnancy or unwillingness /inability to control sexual libidinal drives; or inability/unwillingness to inhibit [aggressive] libidinal drives that maintain high rates of black-on-black crime and suicides). Such short-term defenses have long-term or life-course implications. Negative consequences and affects include the following: (a) the potentially compromised psychological health and adult status of the individual youth, (b) the African-American family's viability, (c) the nature of black male-female relationships, and (d) the future survival of the group (or cultural unit).

These adaptational practices might well be directly related to the parental child-rearing orientations found. For example, it was salient that, independent of SES, there were no differences in the *number* of roles that parents felt fathers should play in the rearing of black children. However, what varied was the content or what those roles should be. The issue has important implications for gender-role development, since both social learning theorists and role theorists see specific functions for the father in child development. That is, the father both reinforces the female for appropriate feminine behavior (i.e., as a "safe male" he plays the role "of husband" to the daughter) and teaches his son to be a man.

Similarly, independent of SES, there was consistency in the number of listings for the maternal role. However, it was clear that LI mothers and modest income mothers believe that supplying the child with *material needs* is *very important*. Perhaps these mothers need to evolve an understanding that supplying the child with *time* may be of greater importance. However, their pursuit of economic viability would make "the sharing of time" a value *less* likely identified in light of perceived more immediate economic needs. The consistent finding that values concerning discipline and morality were important independent of SES was predictable from a general knowledge of the black community. More important was the finding that there were significant differences by SES in parental identification and utilization of child-rearing information and perceived resources. In general, it would appear that parents have many of the "success-oriented" values, hopes, and aspirations for their children.[34] They appear to vary or to differ in their ability to operationalize these hopes, aspirations, and values into *differentiated child-rearing strategies*. Clearly, the preoccupation with "making ends meet" is a disorienting reality that undermines "priority-setting" processes for ensuring the hoped for product: healthy, hopeful, high-aspirational, and competent youth.

Carter's analysis of current African-American family life suggests a need for the black family to recommit itself to its acknowledged strengths.[35] This should occur while also developing additional assets: the black family's historical use of religious faith and the community's historical interdependence. Carter notes that a new reoperationalization of goals should include the need to be whole, wholesome, and holy. By "wholeness" Carter is referring to psychological wholeness that is based upon an intact and firm identity. Black people have to *know* who they are and to accept and revere their cultural connectedness with the past. With regard to the needed "interdependence," the role of grandparenting in supporting the connections between the present and the past is vitally important. For this study, grandparents had rather restricted roles, independent of socioeconomic status and resources. From a life span perspective, additional research needs to address alterations in the specifics of the grandparental roles and the implications for family viability.

Behavioral *wholesomeness,* according to Carter, requires a confrontive approach to issues that undermine and destroy the group. The African-American family and its members—particularly its males—remain under siege.[36] The race dissonance literature demonstrated the institutionalized and reinforced negative racial values and images that continue to abound both in concrete and subliminal forms. The proposed (confrontive) posture *runs counter* to the consistent use of denial as a defense mechanism for ensuring short-term adaptations to mundane or daily sources of caste- and class-related stress.

The findings indicated that African-American families continue to use the church both as symbolic of their religious faith and as a general (emotional and spiritual) resource, although in an incomplete manner. That is, the black church is *not* used consistently as a specific source of child-rearing information and support. For assisting children and families to become maximally viable, psychologically whole, and behaviorally wholesome, more research on the identification of value transmission processes will have to be initiated, strengths identified, more informational sources introduced, and programs of support implemented.

NOTES

The research report was funded by grants from the NIMH (PHS-1-Rol-MH31106) and the Spencer Foundation (Chicago, IL). The author is especially grateful to the project coordinator, Ms. Dena Swanson, and Dr. Fleta Jackson, who served as project director during a portion of the second phase, and to the other research assistants. Most of all, sincere gratitude is extended to the children and their parents who agreed to participate during a period of severe training.

1. S. Nanda, *Cultural Anthropology* (New York NY: D. Van Nostrand, 1980).

2. J. Garbarino, *Children and Families in the Social Environment* (New York: Aldine Press, 1982); D. Muga, "Academic Sub-Cultural Theory and the Problematic of Ethnicity: A Tentative Critique," *Journal of Ethnic Studies,* Vol. 12 no. 1 (1984), 1–51; and J. Ogbu, "A Cultural Ecology of Competence Among Innercity Blacks," in M.B. Spencer, G.K. Brookins, and W.R. Allen, eds., *Beginnings: The Social and Affective Development of Black Children* (Hillsdale, NJ: Erlbaum, 1985).

3. J. Ogbu, "Crossing Cultural Boundaries: A Comparative Perspective on Minority Education," *Race, Class, Socialization and the Life Cycle* (symposium presentation in honor of Allison Davis, John Dewey Professor Emeritus, University of Chicago, 1983).

4. H.T. Trueba, "Culturally Based Explanations of Minority Students' Academic Achievements," *Anthropology and Education Quarterly* Vol. 19, no. 3 (1988), pp. 270–287.

5. Ogbu (1983), (1985).

6. M.B. Spencer, "Self Concept Development," in D.T. Slaughter, ed., *Perspectives on Black Child Development: New Directions for Child Development* (San Francisco, CA: Jossey-Bass, 1988).

7. J. Garbarino (1982) and E. Wynn, "Behind the Discipline Problem: Youth Suicide as a Measure of Alienation," *Phi Delta Kappan,* 1978, pp. 307-315.

8. C. Pierce, "Treatment of Colored Ethnic Groups in the U.S.A." (symposium presentation at Howard University Hospital, Washington, DC, March 29, 1980).

9. H.M. Baron, "The Demand for Black Labor," *Radical America,* Vol. 5, no. 2 (1971), pp. 1-46, and D. Muga, "Academic Sub-Cultural Theory and the Problematic of Ethnicity: A Tentative Critique," *Journal of Ethnic Studies,* Vol. 12, no. 1 (1984), pp. 1-52.

10. D. Jordan, "Developmental Universals and Their Implications for Parent Competence," in M. Fantini and R. Cardeanas, eds., *Parenting in a Multicultural Society* (New York: Longmans, 1980).

11. P. Aries, *Centuries of Childhood* (London: Jonathan Cape, 1962).

12. S.B. Pomeroy, *Goddesses, Whores, Wives, and Slaves,* (New York: Schoken Boules, 1976).

13. B. Lerner, "Children's Rights in the United States," Lecture #4 in the International Lecture Series for the Year of the Child, sponsored by St. Patrick's College (Dublin, Ireland, 1979).

14. L.W. Chestang, *Character Development in a Hostile Environment,* Occasional Paper No. 3 Series (Chicago: University of Chicago, 1972).

15. M.B. Spencer (1988).

16. M.B. Spencer, "Cultural Cognition and Social Cognition as Identity Factors in Black Children's Personal-Social Growth," in Spencer, Brookins, and Allen, (1985) and M.B. Spencer, S.R. Kim, and S. Marshall, "Double Stratification and Psychological Risk: Adaptational Processes and School Experiences of Black Children," *Journal of Negro Education,* Vol. 56, no. 1 (1987), p. 77-86.

17. W.J. Wilson, *The Truly Disadvantaged,* (Chicago: University of Chicago, 1988).

18. M. Spencer, "Children's Cultural Values and Parental Child-Rearing Strategies," *Developmental Review,* Vol. 4 (1983), pp. 351-370.

19. M.B. Spencer and F.D. Horowitz, "Racial Attitudes and Color Concept—Attitude Modification in Black and Caucasian Preschool Children," *Development Psychology,* Vol. 9 (1973), pp. 246-254.

20. T. Achenbach and C. Edelbrock, "Behavioral Problems and Competencies Reported by Parents of Normal and Disturbed Children Aged 4-16," *Monographs of the Society for Research in Child Development,* Serial #188 (1981).

21. Ibid.

22. Ibid.

23. J.A. Ladner, "Teenage Pregnancy: The Implications for Black Americans," in James D. Williams, ed., *The State of Black America, 1986* (New York: National Urban League, 1986).

24. M.B. Spencer, "Risk and Resilience: How Black Children Cope with Stress," *Journal of Social Sciences,* Vol. 71 (1986), pp. 22-26.

25. D. Baumrind, "Current Patterns of Parental Authority," *Developmental Psychology Monographs,* Vol. 4 (1971), pp. 99-103, and L. Odom, J. Seeman, and J.R.A. Newbrough, "A Study of Family Communication Patterns and Personality Integration in Children," *Child Psychiatry and Human Development,* Vol. 1 (1971), pp. 275-285.

26. Spencer (1985) and Spencer (1988).

27. Spencer (1983), pp. 351-370.

28. M.B. Spencer (1985).

29. Spencer (1983), pp. 351-370.

30. Spencer (1986), pp. 22-26.

31. Ibid., pp. 22-26.

32. Pierce and M. Carter, "Personal Communication," (1980).

33. Pierce (1980).

34. D.T. Slaughter and D. Johnson, *Visible Now: Blacks in Private School* (Westport, CT: Greenwood Press, 1988).

35. M. Carter, personal communication, 1985.

36. J.D. McGhee, "*Running the Gauntlet: Black Men in America,*" unpublished report (National Urban League, 1984).

7

SICKLE CELL ANEMIA, CHILD COMPETENCE, AND EXTENDED FAMILY LIFE

Diana T. Slaughter and Peggye Dilworth-Anderson

Chronic illness poses a special adaptational situation for the family as a whole and for all individual family members, including the developing child. In this chapter, childhood sickle cell anemia is conceptualized as a particular form of stress to which the black extended family adapts. Successful adaptation is assumed to be indicated by overt behavioral manifestations of child competence during the middle childhood years. The chapter describes the extended kin relations used, more or less successfully, by three types of urban families to cope with caring for middle school-aged black children with sickle cell disease: (a) female-headed, single-parent families, with highly restricted extended kin contact; (b) nuclear families, generally natural mother and father families, with restricted extended kin contact; and (c) multigenerational families, frequently spanning more than one household, with extensive kin contact.

INTRODUCTION

As a form of continuing stress in the family, chronic illness poses a special adaptational situation for the family as a whole and for all individual family members, including the developing child. In this chapter,[1] childhood sickle cell anemia is conceptualized as a particular form of stress to which the black extended family adapts. Successful adaptation is assumed to be indicated by overt behavioral manifestations of child competence during the middle childhood years.

Throughout the study, the competence motivational model, initially elaborated by White, is the psychological perspective guiding the design and interpretation of obtained data.[2] Competence motivation was posited by White to be a neurophysiologically based drive stimulating competency-oriented, or positive coping, behaviors. This motivational perspective assumes that human organisms continually strive to experience a sense of personal efficacy. Existing social relations will be marshaled, as resource-fully and effectively as possible, toward this goal. The person's felt cumulative experiences of efficacy or inefficacy comprise his or her sense of competence or positive self-concept.[3]

The purpose of this chapter is to describe the extended kin relations used, more or less successfully, by three types of urban families to cope with caring for middle school-aged black children with sickle cell disease: (a) female-headed single-parent families, with highly restricted extended kin contact; (b) nuclear families, generally natural mother and father families, with restricted extended kin contact; and (c) multigenerational families, frequently spanning more than one household, with extensive kin contact.

The three types of families were inductively identified during a larger study using two criteria: (a) the primary caregiver's identified secondary caregiver(s) and (b) if intergenerational relations were invoked to assist in child care.[4] Female-headed single-parent families are those in which few or no adult secondary caregivers are regularly involved in helping the primary caregiver rear the child. If intergenerational relations are invoked for child care, the secondary caregiver is considerably *younger* than the primary caregiver. Mother-father families are those in which, whether or not the parents share the same household, they clearly share co-parenting roles and typically in which contact with other extended kin is not heavily depended upon for child care. Multigenerational families are those in which, whether or not father is present, other more senior (i.e., to pri-mary caregiver) adult kin are regularly involved in the child's care. These senior adults may or may not share the child's household. Intergenera-tional relations are often invoked because secondaries are usually con-siderably *older* than the primary caregiver.

Each of these familial types has its own distinctive adaptive coping style, relative to management of the child's disease, and each has its own particular set of strengths and vulnerabilities. Possibly, individual paren-tal coping strategies initiated at the time of diagnosis during infancy and early childhood helped to established the kind of caregiving systems structures found embracing the children during middle childhood.

BACKGROUND

Defining Sickle Cell Anemia: A Chronic Stressor

Sickle cell anemia is an inherited disease for which there is currently no known cure.[5] Chronic illness in the form of sickle cell disease usually results only when two persons who possess the trait produce a child. Because the gene for sickle cell trait is recessive, when both parents are genetically positive for the trait each one of the children born to them has a 25 percent chance of being afflicted with the disease.

As for clinical symptoms, red blood cells containing Hemoglobin *S* do not live as long as normal red cells. Normal cells live about 120 days, Hemoglobin *S* cells anywhere from 6 to 30 days. Therefore, there are fewer red blood cells in the body and tissues receive only a marginal supply of oxygen. Physical problems develop. Individuals experience muscle fatigue more readily, and the heart works harder to adequately support bodily tissues. Because blood circulation is poorer than normal, various ulcers may develop, particularly around leg joints and ankles. During infancy in particular, parents may notice swelling of the fingers, hands, and feet of their children. Even worse, the resultant "sickle" shape of the cells may create blockages in the blood vessels or capillaries, causing severe pain episodes that concentrate in the abdomen, chest, and joints and can last anywhere from several hours, to days, to longer than a week. The pain episodes are currently unpredictable. Incidence rates, severity, and duration of pain vary greatly between individuals. Pain episodes are the most commonly reported symptom of this disease. They may be severe enough to require hospitalization, where narcotics and fluids to prevent dehydration are administered. Some children may be repeatedly incapacitated over two- to three-week intervals during any given year. A fortunate few may experience pain episodes for the first time later in life (e.g., early adolesence), if at all.

Over time, because the percentage of sickle hemoglobin in the red blood cells is so high (at least 80 percent, according to Whitten and Nishiura), all major bodily organs may be affected. Children seem underweight and of small bone size for their chronological ages (skeletal system); sexual maturity is delayed (urogenital system); the heart enlarges and develops a murmur; the skin and white of the eyes become jaundiced, and other symptoms of liver dysfunction, including gallstones, may develop; even cerebrovascular accidents or "strokes" (neurological system) can occur. Afflicted children and adults experience a reduced resistance to infections (e.g., pneumonia, hepatitis), particularly infections associated with the repeated transfusions that are necessary to counter anemia.[6] Beginning in the first year of life, sickle cell disease is a chronic, often severely debilitating illness that particularly afflicts developing black children.

The Emergence of Competence in Children

White argued that persistent, enduring behavioral patterns emerge in early childhood that appear to be independent of physiological drives.[7] Human behavior cannot be explained solely in terms of approaches toward pleasurable, and avoidance of painful, intrapsychic experiences. The behavioral patterns observed by White appeared to have as a unifying core the child's own efforts to explore, manipulate, and act upon its environment to produce intended effects. Effects that are both intended and achieved, White argued, produce a "feeling of efficacy."[8]

White reserved the concept of "sense of competence" to refer to the feeling engendered by the person's own history of efficacies and inefficacies. He stated: "Competence means fitness or ability. The competence of an organism means its fitness or ability to carry on those transactions with the environment which result in its maintaining itself, growing, and flourishing."[9]

For Brewster-Smith, the core of the competent self is the perception of oneself as causal in social relations.[10] The competent self accepts responsibility when intended effects are not achieved, is attracted to perceived moderate challenges from the environment, and generally expects positive outcomes from efforts. The competent self is rarely despairing, self-doubting, passive, dependent, or fatalistic; rather it is hopeful, confident, active, independent, and trusting. The competent self exhibits considerable resiliency under stress and of course has high self-esteem. The etiology of the competent self is found in two sources of feedback: (a) direct feedback received by the person from objects as to the effects of its own actions and (b) indirect feedback from the reflected appraisals of significant others. Emerging competence is a function of the child's actions on its environment and the responses received as a consequence of those actions. Kohlberg has argued that it is not the responses but the affirmation experienced as a result of those responses that is most reinforcing to the developing child.[11]

In the developmental literature, middle school-aged children are often described as uniquely oriented toward mastery and competence.[12] Among children between roughly 5 and 11, the significant psychological environment broadens to include not just immediate family and extended kin, but other adults (e.g, teachers, neighbors, group leaders, and coaches) and, most important, peers. Children appraise themselves according to whether they experience successful interactions with these newer significant others. Role modeling in the family and in the broader community assumes new importance. Children deliberately select persons to imitate and repeatedly strive to organize and regulate their own behaviors so as to accurately approximate the behaviors of persons they respect and admire.[13] They have achieved sufficient self-definition to be acutely aware of how they measure up to valued others' expectations. The competence motive extends to adultlike environmental objects and experiences. Middle school-aged children typically want to know how objects function/work in the real world and particularly, how to make them work. Usually they are vested in successful competition, whether in academics, sports and games, or other leisure-time activities. Finally, these children continue to experience sustained and differentiated physical growth, a growth that, toward the end of this life segment, escalates rapidly as children enter puberty. Each child struggles to master perceived environmental demands with the ever-changing capabilities and assets inherited as a unique biological being. Effective self-regulation—that is, the sense of being in control of oneself—is contingent upon the middle school-aged child's ability to self-consciously integrate his/her diverse psychological processes toward increasingly self-selected, sustained periods of purposive, goal-directed behavior.

Of course, families potentially provide the cognitive, social, and emotional bases for children's eventual competence. Further, the familial home environment provides the immediate ecological context, including community, in which the child will strive to challenge and prove itself. Given the symptomatology associated with sickle cell disease, clearly the families of afflicted children confront special challenges in rearing psychologically healthy youth. Some families, regardless of family structure, cope better than others.

Impact of Children Upon Families

Few family-focused studies of children with sickle cell disease have been conducted. We just concluded such a study of families with middle school-aged black children.

Martin and Martin define the black extended family as a "multigenerational, independent kinship system which is welded together by a sense of obligation to relatives; organized around a 'family base' household, and generally guided by a dominant family figure. . . ."[14] Further, they suggest that the family extends across geographical boundaries to connect family networks and has a built-in mutual aid system for the welfare of its members and the maintenance of the family as a whole.

Using their definition, we predicted that families with viable (close ties, frequent, open communication) extended kin networks would be more successful in coping with rearing children with sickle cell disease. We also predicted that individual family members with higher levels of self-esteem would report that their families more effectively cope with children with sickle cell disease than do family members with lower levels of esteem. Coping effectively could enhance esteem, and higher esteem could generate more effective coping strategies.

METHOD AND PROCEDURES

In the overall study, each adult member of the sick child's household was separately interviewed, as well as, if possible, a member of the grandparent generation. Similar open-ended questions and personality inventories were administered to each adult. The sick child and, if available, any close-aged sibling in the age range of all study children were also separately interviewed and administered three standard measures of self-concept. Finally, a socialization interview was administered jointly to the child's primary and secondary caregivers by a trained clinical interviewer. The interviewer later supplemented obtained data with clinical observations of the couple. In the 34 sample families, a total of 76 adults and 51 children were interviewed. Other details regarding the methods and procedures of the overall study have been described elsewhere.[15] In this chapter, we confine our discussion to a description and an analysis of the role of extended kin in child care in the identified family types as perceived primarily by the child's mother. Additional information from the joint interview with mother and her designated secondary caregiver is also used.

Sample

Two different Chicago area hospitals were the source of a total of 34 families of children with sickle cell disease enrolled in this study. At hospital A, families of children ages 5.5 to 11.0 (i.e., middle childhood) were included. Nineteen families were recruited from hospital A and 15 families from hospital B. The 34 families contacted represented 71 percent of the eligible pool of families (N = 48) and approximately 10 percent of the estimated numbers of such children in this age group (5.5 – 11.5 years) in the metropolitan area.[16] The available sample may be slightly biased toward higher income levels. The greatest number of families not interviewed were those without phones or whose phones were disconnected during times when research contacts were initiated (n = 10 or 21 percent of eligible pool). However, since the majority of such families may seek the care of private physicians, the populations at both hospitals may be disproportionately overrepresented by lower middle to lower income families.[17] When they were employed, both mothers and fathers tended to work in either service occupations or as operators and laborers (U.S. Census occupational categories), rather than in executive, professional, or administrative positions.

Fathers were absent from 19 (55.9 percent) of the households in which the study children resided. These homes had significantly lower annual incomes, in comparison to father-present homes. In father-absent homes, the mean annual income for 1983 was between $5,000 and $9,000 per year; in father-present homes it was between $20,000 and $24,000 per year. Primary caregivers (mothers) averaged 33.4 years ($SD = 11.76$) of age and 12.4 years ($SD = 2.28$) of education. There were no significant mean age or educational attainment differences between the two groups of mothers, although mothers in father-present homes were more likely to have completed high school. At the time of child testing, children averaged 8.5 years, with an age range from 6 to 12 years. In the total sample, 21 children had been diagnosed as having the potential for the most severe form of the disease, while 13 others had various diagnoses, considered less severe.

Variables and Measures

Child Competence. A clinical assessment of the child's overall competence, relative to whether or not it seemed to be thriving as a middle school-aged child, was made according to several criteria. First, children scoring at or below the level of 85 percent of the 212 elementary school children in the norming sample of the Culture-Free Self Esteem Inventory (Form B) were identified. Second, those children scoring below the standard deviation cut-off of some normative data offered by Spencer on 33 northern black elementary school children on the Thomas Self Concept Values Test were identified.[18] Third, parents' discussions of these children's academic achievements and peer relations, as well as the child's own comments about school, and the child interviewer's comments about the child were examined.

Children's whose esteem scores were especially low and for whom at least one area (school or peer relations) was deemed less than optimal were classified as not thriving. There was a total of 12 such children: 6 children were members of single-parent, female-headed families, 4 were members of mother-father families, and 2 were members of multigenerational families. Of the 20 children perceived as "thriving" (or at least holding their own), 4 were members of single-parent families and 8 each belonged to mother-father and multigenerational families, respectively.

Clinical Variables. For purposes of this chapter, the domains of interest are: past and present support provided to the primary caregiver, those open-ended sections of the primary caregiver interview focusing on extended kin and community relationships, and those sections of the joint parent interview focusing on the parents' knowledge of and feelings about sickle cell disease.

Data Collection

All interviews and tests were verbally administered in the homes of respondents by black research team members selected and trained by the co-investigators. Adult interviewers were females, but child interviewers were both female and male.

Results

First, the extended kin relations of female-headed single-parent families in which children were judged to be thriving or not thriving will be compared and contrasted, to be followed by similar comparisons and contrasts for mother-father families and mutigenerational families.

Female-Headed, Single-Parent families

None of the ten primary caregivers in these families reported that they were aware that a child with sickle cell disease could be produced in their family. Six of the 10 primary caregivers reported that illnesses during the first year of life eventually culminated in an official medical diagnosis. Four reported that the disease was identified following tests made during a routine checkup and that they were subsequently notified in a letter from the hospital, after which they had consultation with a nurse. Nine families were informed within the first 15 months of the child's life; one was not officially notified until the child was 4.5 years old.

Since caregivers were unaware of the disease, its etiology, or its prevalence in black communities and, from their perspectives, were either notified quite precipitously or during a period of especially high stress (e.g., parts of the infant's body had swollen up and/or the child was obviously suffering from severe, unaccountable pain), they needed considerable support.

In this sample, the overwhelming majority of primary caregivers report that they turned to family members, including extended kin, for support following receipt of the child's diagnosis. However, the caregivers of many children in the female-headed single-parent families reported no adult family members to turn to for help in caregiving.

An inability to rely upon family members was especially characteristic of caregivers in this group whose children were not thriving in middle childhood. Three of the six caregivers reported having had no family member to turn to at the time of diagnosis, and two others reported one or two siblings. A sixth caregiver reported the child's father and three female relatives (mother, sister, sister-in-law) were helpful at the time of diagnosis, but that none is currently available. In contrast, two of the caregivers of children who are thriving now had early supports and they reported that these same supports continue. A third caregiver of a thriving child reported persistent support, then and now, from one sister and a male neighbor who is a good friend. However, Mrs. A., the fourth caregiver of a thriving child reported, "No one. I didn't have anyone . . . [Then and now] I help myself."

Two family-related factors appear to have contributed to the children being judged as "nonthrivers" in middle childhood. First, some caregivers experienced a continuing, diminished number of persons available to support them and the child's growth and development from infancy and early childhood to date, and second, many of their earlier supporters were, over time, lost to death or illnesses. In this sample, female-headed single-parent families whose children are not thriving had been especially deprived of social supports, related economic and social resources, and scientific information about the implications of the disease for the children's phychosocial development.

In contrast, children who are thriving in these families have caregivers who report frequent contacts with extended kin. The caregivers report borrowing or lending goods and services with their kinfolk, interactions that are rarely mentioned by families of nonthriving children, in a manner similar to that suggested by Stack.[19]

In addition, caregivers seem less reluctant to describe their needs. An interviewer commented about the mother to one such child in the B family, "Mrs. B. knows that she wants the best for S. and she gets the best she can get. Mrs. B. is blind but she doesn't let that stop her at all . . . . Told me she doesn't have time to sit around and feel sorry for herself . . . . S. didn't start school until last year [at age six]. Now he is in the second grade. Mrs. B. said: 'I talked to those teachers and explained the situation so they helped me to help S.' Mrs. B. also expressed the need for the [honorarium]. She said she wanted it to help out on S.'s Christmas things. . . .''

Finally, in some families, like the C. and D. families, teen siblings assume secondary caregiver roles with great dedication and compassion. In the C. family, the primary caregiver has ten children, the first six of whom are daughters. Living conditions are so poor that the mother reports that some siblings are actually envious when the study child has to stay overnight at the hospital. Despite extremely poor living conditions, the older daughters help the caregiver ensure that all children are clean. Mrs. C. stressed that all her children were independent and able to do for themselves (i.e., clean their rooms, cook, keep their clothes clean, etcetera), and it was clear from the interviews that she does not perceive the study child, nor any of her children, to be especially fragile or dependent.

In the D. family, the study child's teenage brother is frequently truant from school, has held several part-time jobs to bring money into the family, now primarily supported by public assistance, and has had brief encounters with local police authorities. When asked, "How do you get extra income for [child's] health care if you need to?" he commented; "Working at a restaurant. I'll find a way to get it or I will borrow it. I might do something bad [illegal], but I'll get the money." The well-being of the study child is purchased at cost to an older sibling.

Mother-Father Families

In this study, families with fathers available tend to have significantly higher incomes and therefore more financial security relative to the longer-term medical demands of the children's illness. Further, fathers, more than any other family members, are likely to share in the nurturant caregiving directly associated with the child's illness.[20] Unlike other kinfolk, fathers consistently engage in "mothering." Mothers in these families tend to have more education, including college attendance, in comparison with mothers in other families. Thus, despite jobs held, the families have middle class achievement aspirations and values for their children. However, despite the obvious signs of family stability and educational achievement, only 1 of the 13 couples was aware that they could produce a child with sickle cell disease.

With one exception, children in the mother-father families were diagnosed as having the disease by age 24 months. Following the child's diagnosis, mothers usually turned first to the children's father for emotional support and assistance. Many mothers also report talking with maternal kinfolk and a few with friends whom they had reason to believe would have practical knowledge of the disease. Fathers, however, tended to turn to their own kinfolk and friends for support. Together, the couples then sought and have continued to negotiate within the health care delivery system, as well as other institutions involved in caring for the children (e.g., schools). Of the three family types, the experiences of the mother-father families, whether the parents are living together or apart, are most similar to those generally discussed in the literature on chronic illness in childhood.[21]

In mother-father families, the scope of the father's role in relation to child care is particularly flexible and broad and the father's active role appears to be paralleled by a diminished influence of maternal relatives upon the primary caregiver.

There were many examples of the broader scope of the father's role in these families. Fathers frequently assumed major responsibility for negotiating with and informing hospital staff when the child is hospitalized. Fathers stated that they had had opportunities to express concern about "unnecessary surgery," excessive use of narcotics, or the inappropriate withholding of narcotics to both nurses and doctors. Fathers have taught themselves how to read their children's charts, have actively advised mothers on childbearing strategies to minimize the tendencies of children, especially male children, to "feel sorry for themselves" or be otherwise passive and dependent in relation to control of pain and the management of their illness. Mothers seem especially grateful to fathers for managing issues associated with the continuity of the child's care with medical personnel at various hospitals; this is especially important because children have usually, by these ages, had contact with several hospitals. Fathers in these families also broaden their roles to include significant nurturant, expressive dimensions. Mrs. E. had married since giving birth to the study child, and the new stepfather was able to help significantly with the stepdaughter. Mrs. E. commented, "Before marriage, I didn't know how to deal with R. . . . [If she's sick] he'll come in and get her and rub her. If she wakes up at 2 o'clock in the morning, he'll jump up. When I can't deal with it, he's there. He works with her. Since I've been married, I haven't dealt with her in a crisis, S. has. . . . It makes me feel complete [that] he's took on that [role]. I love her [and] that makes me love him.''

Generally, children in mother-father families were judged to be thriving in middle childhood. In four families, children were not thriving, and in one instance, extended kin patterns in relation to child care were implicated. In the F. family, the family, the mother and maternal grandmother, both deeply religious, maintained a close relationship. Rearing of the daughters seemed to be largely left to them, but rearing of the study child, a son, seemed to be largely left to the father, who was himself currently undergoing an extremely debilitating illness.

Inputs from extended maternal or paternal kin are diminished when the family lives some distance from members of one or both groups. Often, in the mother-father families, parents reported that members of their extended kin groups could not understand how the child's disease originated or cope with its consequences. The G. family, who had three sons, the eldest of whom had been born handicapped, had earlier found that extended family members could not easily cope with the child's problems. As a couple, they had drawn closer together to care for this child, as well as their third child, born with sickle cell disease. Even in this situation, however, the parents reported that the extended kin members had been personally supportive to them, if not active, regular caregivers to the children.

Multigenerational Families

Ten multigenerational families are identified in this study who reflect, to varying degrees, Martin and Martin's definition of black extended family functioning.[22] Six of these families share the same household with at least three generations living together. Only in three of these shared households are both parents of the sick child present. The other four families do not share a household with relatives but are involved in a connected kin network that provides a mutual aid system. Three of these four families have both parents present. At least 50 percent of the parents are unemployed, and only four parents have above a high school education. Among those who are working, the majority have blue collar jobs or are laborers.

Only one parent was aware that she could possibly produce a child with sickle cell disease. The other parents knew very little or nothing about sickle cell disease at the time they conceived their children. Therefore, incidents precipitating diagnosis of the disease were either through routine visits to the doctor or the child became ill, requiring medical care. At the time of diagnosis none of the families received support from community organizations or agencies. The hospital was the only institution that has provided, to varying degrees, support to these families, generally in the form of information/education and counseling.

From the extensive interviews with the sick child's primary and secondary caregivers who were the parents and/or grandparents, it became obvious that the extended family provided significant support. Although Martin and Martin assert that the black extended family can do little to help its members become full participants in urban society such as helping with employment, housing, and economics, the family is nevertheless a powerful mechanism for assuring psychosocial needs and for giving its members a sense of solidarity.[23] Our findings support those cited above in that all the multigenerational families studied were only able to provide very little economic assistance, but because of the enmeshed and embedded structure of these families, members provided one another with emotional support, a family identity, a sense of belonging and solidarity. Thus, the psychosocial characteristics of these multigenerational families in our study fostered provision of the primarily psychological support needed when caring for a child with sickle cell disease.

Given the strength of these families, we examined them more closely to determine the specific types of support they provide, who provides it, and what family patterns help determine their strong sense of familism that enables caring for a chronically ill child. To illustrate these points, 4 of the 10 multigenerational families are discussed. Each of the study children in these families is male. Two families live in a shared household with three generations present (Group A), and two (Group B) live in separate households. Only in Group A are there study children judged to be not thriving (Families H. and I.). In one case the father is present in the home, and in the other case he is not. Neither of the fathers is considered by the mother to be the child's secondary caregiver.

The H. family shares a multigenerational household including the sick child, his mother, maternal grandparents, and an uncle. The father is not present in the home. This family encourages interdependence but allows for individual growth and development of its members. The sick child and his mother receive a lot of support from the maternal grandmother.

Both grandparents, however, share in the co-parenting and health care of the child. Further, this family shares goods and services with one another and provides emotional support that fosters a high level of familism. Mrs. H. stated, "My family has been very supportive and understanding. They give a lot of love and care."

The I. family also shares a multigenerational household, which includes the sick child, both of his parents, paternal grandparents, and an aunt. The extended family provided significant support to both parents who are unemployed and on public aid. The mother indicated that the paternal grandmother, not the child's father, is the child's secondary caregiver. It is the secondary caregiver who functions in the co-parenting role with the mother and serves as her major source of support in caring for her sick child. The mother indicated that the grandmother provided emotional support and that she is consistently there during a crisis. Although Mrs. I. did not indicate that her husband was their child's secondary caregiver, she did state that he provides support, especially during times their son is hospitalized.

In general, Mrs. I. describes her multigenerational family as ". . . close, someone you can talk to, that's able to help you when they can." She further stated that her family ". . . lets me know that I am not alone in caring for my child. . . ."

The next two families, unlike those previously discussed, share extended family relations but do not share a single household. However, similar to the previous two families, fathers are not secondary caregivers, whether or not they are present in the child's home.

The J. family has both parents present in the home. Each parent has at least two years of college education, and both are employed in lower-level management jobs. They have six children who are cared for, to a great extent, by their maternal grandmother. Mrs. J. describes her extended family as close, with members who share feelings and have a strong religious faith in God. This family also shares goods and services, and members can rely on one another. Mrs. J. stated that the grandmother, not the child's father, is the secondary caregiver. The grandmother, according to her daughter, provides a range of support. She supports her daughter in whatever way is helpful to her family.

The K. family, unlike the one described above, has one parent, the mother, in the home with her two children. She is unemployed and receives public aid. The maternal grandmother provides significant support to Mrs. K's family. Therefore, the maternal grandmother, Mrs. K. stated, is her sick child's secondary caregiver. Although poor and unemployed herself, the grandmother provides Mrs. K. with emotional support, but little in the way of tangible goods. In fact, Mrs. K. indicated it was her mother who has provided her with consistent support since her child was diagnosed as having sickle cell disease.

Although much as been written about female-headed single-parent families and two-parent families, little is known of how multigenerational families affect child care and development. This is unfortunate because in this study, multigenerational families appear to be as effective as are mother-father families in coping with children who are chronically ill with sickle cell disease. We can only speculate that children not thriving in these contexts somehow get "lost" in the family. As the numbers of significant persons increase, it must be even more important for a child who is frequently sick to be able to have someone to whom he/she can express his/her most private feelings. Of course, it is also especially important that these family members work cooperatively with regard to the child's illness.

CONCLUSION

In conclusion, it is significant that we did not initiate this research by seeking to identify and describe pathology. Given the nature of this disease, it would have been very easy to focus on the deficits inherent to the children and the management "problems" created for their families. Instead, this paper has attempted to describe three different family types found to be caring for black children with sickle cell disease. Some strengths and weaknesses of each family type, as they emerged in this study, have also been highlighted. Within each family type that we inductively derived we also found children who, in their middle childhood years, were judged to be thriving and not thriving. We believe it is very probable that the obtained differences in child competence observed are associated with the noted sociopsychological differences in family functioning within family type. However, it is also possible that both the child and the family's well-being were substantially impacted by the quality of health care received between diagnosis and the time we saw family members in middle childhood. In future studies of the early development of similar children we hope to investigate this issue.

Our research demonstrates that the caregiving systems that contribute significantly to black children's developing competencies are not usefully described as merely "one" or "two-parent" households. From the perspective of available child care and psychosocial support to primary caregivers, many familial households in both categories are actually multi-generational units. Multigenerational families serve many functions for their individual members; usually, these functions only incidentally concern child care, as contrasted with the survival and well-being of the families as a whole. If communication between adult members of these families and children is poor, chronically ill children, ironically, may be especially vulnerable to feeling alone and isolated.

Importantly, all but 1 of our 34 families were, upon learning that their child had sickle cell disease, confronted with the problem of educating themselves and other extended family members about the disease, as they were victims of not knowing about an essential aspect of their sociocultural heritage and of not having available trusted supportive community institutions and groups around them to help them solve their problems. Our study shows that, in turning first and foremost to other close relatives, black primary caregivers coped especially well with what must have been, and continues to be, a singularly formidable challenge to parenthood in society today: rearing a psychologically healthy child who must daily cope with persistent, chronic illness. The role of those interested in tertiary prevention must surely be to attenuate the stresses associated with this caregiving and thus support the group most responsible for continuity of the child's health care, the family.

NOTES

1. An earlier draft of this chapter was presented at the annual meeting of the Groves Conference on Marriage and the Family, London, July 16–20, 1986. The research was supported by a grant from the March of Dimes Birth Defects Foundation. Supplemental support was provided by Northwestern University and by Northeastern Illinois University. Assistance was also provided by the University of Illinois Sickle Cell Center.

2. R. White, "Motivation Reconsidered: The Concept of Competence," in D. Fiske and S. Maddi, eds., *Functions of Varied Experience* (Homewood, IL: Dorsey Press, 1961), pp. 278–325, and R. White, "Competence and the Psychosexual Stages of Development," in S. Maddi, ed., *Perspectives on Personality: A Comparative Approach* (Boston, MA: Little, Brown and Company, 1971), pp. 272–307.

3. R. White (1971). Also see A. Bandura, "Self Efficacy Mechanism in Human Agency," *American Psychologist*, Vol. 37 (1982), pp. 122–147.

4. See D. Slaughter and P. Anderson, *Impact of Sickle Cell Anemic Children upon Black Extended Family Functioning*, proposal to the March of Dimes Birth Defects Foundation (1983), and P. Anderson and D. Slaughter, "The Impact of Sickle Cell Anemic Children Upon Black Extended Family Functioning: Some Theoretical and Methodological Concerns," in A. Hurtig and C. Viera, eds., *Understanding and Treating Sickle Cell Disease: Overview and Current Status,* (Champaign-Urbana: University of Illinois Press, 1986), pp. 114–130.

5. C. Whitten and E. Nishiura, "Sickle Cell Anemia," in N. Hobbs and J. Perrin, eds., *Issues in the Care of Children with Chronic Illness* (San Francisco, CA: Jossey-Bass, 1985), pp. 236–260.

6. Sickle cell disease primarily affects persons of African descent. However, it has been found among other peoples not usually identified with African biological ancestry. Many believe that over thousands of years gradual genetic mutation occurred in the form of biological adaptation to resist the devastating effects of malaria, since persons possessing the trait have been found more highly resistant to severe attacks of malaria and since prevalence of the trait is generally found in parts of the world where the incidence of malaria was once particularly high. See D. Wilkerson, "For Whose Benefit? Politics and Sickle Cell," *Black Scholar,* Vol. 5 (1974), pp. 26–30, for discussion of the preceding points. According to Whitten and Nishiura (1985), in the United States among black Americans ". . . sickle cell conditions occur . . . with a live birth frequency of approximately 8 percent for sickle cell trait and .2 percent for sickle cell anemia" (p. 237). About 50 to 60,000 persons in the United States have sickle cell disease, including cystic fibrosis and PKU. For example, cystic fibrosis occurs in 1 of 1–2,000 live births and PKU in 1 of 10,000 live births, but sickle cell disease occurs in 1 of 4–500 live births according to G. Travis, *Chronic Illness in Children* (Stanford, CA: Stanford University Press, 1976). Death rates are highly variable. Many persons live beyond age 60, but for most, given the improved medical treatment of symptoms, the average life span is between 25 and 45 years.

7. White (1961), White (1971).

8. White (1971).

9. White (1971), p. 275.

10. M. Brewster-Smith, "Competence and Socialization," in J. Clausen, ed., *Development During Middle Childhood: The Years from Six to Twelve* (Boston, MA: Little, Brown, and Company, 1968), pp. 270–320.

11. L. Kohlberg, "The Cognitive-Developmental Approach to Socialization," in D. Goslin, ed., *Handbook of Socialization Theory and Research* (Chicago: Rand McNally, 1969), pp. 347–480.

12. W. Collins, ed., *Development During Middle Childhood: The Years from Six to Twelve,* (Washington, DC: National Academy Press, 1984).

13. See White (1971) for the theoretical perspective that provides the foundation for this discussion. Also see Bandura (1982) for a more in-depth discussion of social learning theory that provides added information.

14. E. Martin and J. Martin, *The Black Extended Family,* (Chicago: University of Chicago Press, 1978), p. 1.

15. Slaughter and Anderson (1986).

16. Two families will not be discussed due to incomplete data. In the overall study, 76 adults and 51 children were individually interviewed. At the conclusion of all individual family interviews (i.e., primary and secondary caregivers, at least one grandparent if available, etcetera), primary and secondary caregivers were jointly interviewed. An average of three or four visits per family were required to complete the interviewing. Families received an honorarium for their participation.

17. Whitten and Nishiura (1985), pp. 252–253.

18. M. Spencer, "Cultural Cognition and Social Cognition as Meta-Identity Factors in Black Children's Personal-Social Development," paper presented at the Society for Research in Child Development (SRCD) Study Group, "Social and Affective Development of Minority Status Children," funded by the Foundation for Child Development and the Carnegie Foundation, Emory University, Atlanta, December 1980, and W. Thomas, *The Thomas Self Concept Test,* (Grand Rapids, MI: Educational Service Company, 1969).

19. C. Stack, *All Our Kin: Strategies for Survival in a Black Community,* (New York: Harper and Row, 1974).

20. D. Slaughter and P. Dilworth-Anderson, ''Care of Black Children with Sickle Cell Disease: Fathers, Maternal Support, and Esteem,'' *Family Relations,* Vol., 37 no. 3 (1988), pp. 281-287.

21. Travis (1976) and N. Hobbs, J. Perrin, and H. Ireys, *Chronically Ill Children and Their Families,* (San Francisco, CA: Jossey-Bass, 1985).

22. Martin and Martin (1978).

23. Ibid.

8

GENDER DIFFERENCES IN THE PERCEPTION OF BLACK MALE-FEMALE RELATIONSHIPS AND STEREOTYPES

Noel A. Cazenave and Rita Smith

The relationship between gender and the perception of black male-female relationships is analyzed with particular attention to the acceptance or rejection of negative stereotypes about black men and black women. While a sizable number of the 256 respondents summarize their history of male-female relationships in a way that is categorized as a positive evaluation, nearly a third provide essentially negative descriptions. Multiple regression analysis revealed that respondents who describe their past intimate relationships in a negative manner tend never to have been married or to be currently divorced and to accept negative stereotypes about black men. Respondents who hold negative stereotypes about black men or black women are generally more traditional in their views of gender roles and are less likely to report being adversely affected by racism and tend to report that blacks don't take advantage of available opportunities.

INTRODUCTION

Today, many black families are experiencing unprecedented structural changes.[1] The black divorce rate is more than twice as high as the alarmingly high divorce rate for Americans generally, and only 42 percent of black children currently live with both parents.[2] There is growing concern that if this alarming trend continues, the customary family resources that blacks have relied on in difficult social and economic times will no longer exist for those black families who need them most.

There is also concern that these structural changes reflect increased conflict and tension in marital relationships and an overall decline in the quality of black male-female relationships in general. Indeed, while there is now more attention being paid to the relationships of men and women of all races and socioeconomic status levels, the unique impact of racism and socioeconomic oppression on black male-female relationships has produced a gestalt reality that may differ from male-female relationships generally in American society. For black Americans, this issue, and the very concept "black male-female relationships," has a distinct history and meaning that merits special focus.

This issue was the subject of a widely read and controversial book. In *Black Macho and the Myth of the Superwoman* Wallace asserted that ". . . perhaps the last fifty years there has been a growing distrust, even hatred, between black men and black women."[3] Wallace's book sparked a resurgence of the debate as to whether or not black male-female relationships are a legitimate area of focus.[4]

Franklin attempted to move beyond the dispute as to whether black men and women have relationship problems *or* if these problems, to the extent that they do exist, are simply a direct result of white racism. He suggested that, accepting white racism as a given for most black Americans, what is needed is a model of black male-female relationships that can explain why some black males and black females experience significant relationship problems while others do not.[5] Elaborating on Franklin's observations, Jewell stated that it is the acceptance or rejection of negative stereotypes about black males and females that determines whether such relationship problems manifest themselves. Jewell sees such stereotypes as not only assigning a low value to potential relationship partners, but as serving as a basis of distrust and suspicion that bias their evaluations of all of the future actions of their partners, should such relationships develop.[6]

Even prior to the mid-and late 1970s' debates over black male-female relationships, an extensive body of literature existed that documented both popular and social science stereotypes about black men and black women. Cazenave discussed three major negative images regarding black women.[7] First, beginning in the 1960s and continuing into the 1970s, there was an extensive literature about the so-called black "matriarchy" and the perception that black women had too much control and power in their families.[8] A second issue was the notion of the social "castration" of black men and the alleged participation of black women in this process of "keeping the black man down."[9] Third and finally, with the most recent resurgence of the women's movement and affirmative action, concern was expressed that qualified black women, who have experienced the dual victimization of sexism and racism, are more in demand for educational and job opportunities than are black men.[10] Some black men have expressed resentment that black women currently seem to have more opportunities than they do.

There are also numerous negative stereotypes about black men. One of the earliest derogatory images of black men dates back to the overt racism of slavery and Jim Crow, in terms of which blacks generally (both men and women) were depicted as being shiftless, lazy, and irresponsible. Eventually this stereotype became more gender specific, and modern day variations of its theme are still replete in American social science. For example, in their often cited study of American families Blood and Wolfe reported a concentration of "inadequate husbands, . . . (the deviant cases where the husband has no excuse but laziness or irresponsibility for his failure to share in housekeeping chores) among working-class black families."[11] Schulz stated that low income black males have not been socialized to accept responsible familial roles and, instead, turn to the streets to achieve masculine status.[12] More recently, Franklin suggested that black males and females may differ in their views of appropriate strategies to deal with a racially hostile environment, with black women more inclined to stress individual initiative and responsibility and black males more likely to focus on the more externally oriented perspective of system blame.[13]

Another common stereotype with extensive historical roots concerns the black male's alleged sexual prowess. Hannerz reported that sexual conquests are common forms of masculine expression among low income black males.[14] In his study of black street corner men, Liebow stated that there is a popular "Theory of Manly Flaws," which rationalizes sexual promiscuity on the basis of it being a part of manly nature.[15] More recently Benjamin discussed a similar popular rationalization, "The Dog Theory," which she found to be common among the blacks she interviewed. This stereotype views men as being "dogs" by nature, and of course "dogs" can be expected to do anything, especially when it comes to their sexual conduct.[16]

Black men have also been stereotyped as inadequate providers. The extensive literature on father absence suggests that in many instances black men either will not or cannot adequately provide for their families.[17] Hare observed that the provider role has been a major challenge facing black men throughout their history in America.[18]

Finally, popular works by black women have portrayed black men as being exploitative of the women with whom they are intimately involved.[19]

There is also increasing empirical evidence that documents the concern of black Americans about the quality of their intimate heterosexual relationships.[20] The literature has evolved largely from impressionistic essays and continues through to research studies that delineate the precise nature of these complaints.

The stereotyping of black men and black women is a major issue identified by researchers as being essential to understanding black male-female relationships.[21] Walum hypothesized that a number of general stereotypes about black men and black women may fit a pattern that results in intolerable black male-female relationships. She theorized that because of policies originating from what she referred to as the white substructure affecting black male-female relationships, black women may be placed in a position where it appears that they receive advantages at the expense of black males. That, Walum suggested, leads to the view that black women are more competent and responsible than black men. This, in turn, results in black women having a lack of respect for black males, and this causes resentment by black males, which ultimately results in hostility and rage directed from them toward black women.[22]

It appears that many of the relationship problems men and women in this country face are related to the existence of negative stereotypes about members of the opposite sex and relationships with them.[23] If this is true, such relationships may be improved by understanding precisely what these stereotypes are, who holds them, and something about their social origins.

The existing research on stereotypes affecting black male-black female relationships reveals no clear pattern. For example, Turner and Turner found that black college students, generally, are no more likely to make derogatory evaluations of other blacks than white students make of other whites. At the same time, they did find a greater tendency among black students to view black men as being ''no good'' and for black females, specifically, to see black men as being irresponsible. However, the negative evaluations of black men are limited to work-related traits affecting their ability to function in the larger society, over which most have little control. They do not apply to the more expressive (i.e., noninstrumental) dimensions more directly under the influence of the black subculture.[24] In a replication of the Turner and Turner study, Smith and Millham found little gender stereotyping for either race and concluded that ''the image of the 'shiftless' black male and the heroic 'matriarchal' black female is simply not a viable or general stereotype within contemporary Black America.''[25] Finally, Jackson administered Sarbin's adjective word list to one hundred black female college students and found that while upper class black males are evaluated more favorably than lower class black males, both are evaluated favorably, and both groups of black males receive higher, more favorable ratings than white males at either class level.[26]

In brief, the existing literature on black male-female relationships is inconclusive as to the salience, the origins, and the dynamics of the acceptance of such negative and potentially damaging stereotypes. The goal of this paper is to explore the relationship between gender and the perception of stereotypes affecting black male-female relationships.

METHOD

Procedure

The 256 respondents were enrolled in courses sponsored by the Community Education Program of Temple University. These courses are offered at little or no cost. They are noncredit and there are no admittance requirements. The courses cover a wide range of topics related to black studies, General Equivalency Diploma preparation, and self-improvement. The repondents were all residents of the greater Philadelphia metropolitan area.

A questionnaire was administered to classes by two black men and two black women in March of 1982. This device consisted of 46 forced-choice and open-ended items on: male-female relationships, desired traits in an ideal man and in an ideal woman, internal-external life orientations, life satisfaction, perception of the salience of racism, common stereotypes about black men and about black women, and social background information.

The Respondents

More than two-thirds of the respondents are female. The respondents ranged in age from 14 to 68, with a median age of 30 years. Forty-seven percent were single; 21 percent were currently married; 23 percent were divorced or separated; 4 percent were widowed; and 6 percent cohabited with someone of the opposite sex to whom they were not married. Sixty percent of the respondents reported having children. Twelve percent had less than a high school education; 39 percent completed high school only; 29 percent had some college experience; 15 percent had a college degree;

and 6 percent had completed college and had begun or completed graduate or professional training. The majority of the respondents had family incomes of less than $17,000, with the median income being $16,033.

In brief, while these respondents show a great deal of diversity in their SES characteristics, on average they are most representative of the working and lower middle classes. Chi-square tests of statistical significance reveal no gender differences for any of the sociodemographic variables.

The sample, however, is characterized by, first, the large number of female respondents and, second, a self-selection bias based on the respondents' decisions to enroll in the community education program and to take courses concerned with, for the most part, black-related issues.

Despite its limitations, it is hoped that the present sample will provide some heuristic insights into the nature of these relationship concerns, even though its nonrepresentativeness does not allow conclusions to be drawn about their pervasiveness among black Americans.

RESULTS AND DISCUSSION

Gender Differences in the Perception of Male-Female Relationships

In their response to Michele Wallace's thesis that ". . . for perhaps the last fifty years there has been a growing distrust, even hatred, between black men and black women,"[27] a sizable minority of the respondents (42 percent [n = 76] for males and 48 percent [n = 161] for females) either agree or strongly agree, while rather large percentages (25 percent and 26 percent for males and females respectively) are undecided and only 34 percent of the male respondents and 26 percent of the female respondents disagree or strongly disagree.

To obtain the respondents' perceptions of their actual experiences in intimate relationships they were asked, "Based on your own experiences, how would you summarize your male-female relationships?" While the percentages of men and women providing a positive or average-fair characterization of their relationships are very similar (41 percent [n = 66] positive for men and 39 percent [n = 140] positive for women and 9 percent average-fair for both males and females), the male respondents are more likely to give answers that fit into the rather ambiguous "other" category (27 percent for males and 17 percent for females), and the female respondents are more likely to characterize their relationships as being essentially negative (35 percent for females compared to 23 percent for males).

Effects of Independent Variables. Of the major socioeconomic status, marital, family, and family of origin background related variables included in this analysis only marital status is statistically significant in its relationship to how both male and female respondents evaluate their past relationships.

Those respondents who are not currently married (i.e., those who are single, separated, divorced, or widowed) are much more likely to view their relationships in a negative manner than those who are currently married. While 79 percent of the male respondents (n = 65) who are currently married give a positive description of their relationships, only 31 percent of those who are not currently married do so. On the other hand, 7 percent of the currently married males give a negative view of their relationships compared to 28 percent of those who are not currently married. The percentages for the average or fair and the "other" categories are 0 percent and 14 percent for currently married males and 12 percent and 29 percent, respectively, for those male respondents who are not currently married. Chi-square analysis reveals statistically significant marital status differences for this item (X^2 (3) = 10.46, $p \leq .05$).

This relationship between marital status and the evaluation of intimate relationships is even stronger for the female respondents. Seventy-eight percent of the females who are married (n = 138) describe their relationships positively while 13 percent describe it negatively, compared to 27 percent and 43 percent of the not currently married females who gave positive and negative responses, respectively. The average or fair and "other" response categories are 6 percent and 3 percent for currently married females and 9 percent and 21 percent, respectively, for those who are not currently married [(X^2 (3) = 27.27, $p \leq .001$]).

These findings are not surprising, since individuals who have chosen to marry and to remain in such a relationship might be expected to have a more positive view of their relationships than those who have not married or who have experienced unsuccessful marriages.

Table 8.1 presents multiple regression analyses predicting the impact of gender, age, socioeconomic status variables, and family variables on respondents' descriptions of relationship experiences in a negative manner. Step 1 shows that gender, per se, is not a predictor of negative relationships. The same pattern persists when age is introduced in the next step. Step 3 reveals that respondents with low family income tend to give negative descriptions of relationships. However, this effect disappears in Step 4 when the family related variables are introduced. This suggests that the impact of family income may be indirect. That is, it may

TABLE 8.1
Regression Equation Predicting Respondents' Negative Relationships with Gender, Age, Socioeconomic Status Variables, and Family Variables[a]

Step #/ Independent Variables	Respondents' Negative Relationships		Step #/ Independent Variables	Respondents' Negative Relationships	
	Beta	Sig. Level		Beta	Sig. Level
Step 1:			*Step 4:*		
Gender (Male)	−.10	(.26)	Gender (Male)	−.13	(.11)
Adjusted R Square	.002		Age	−.003	(.98)
			Education (H.S. or less)	−.01	(.86)
Step 2:			Family Income	−.10	(.29)
Gender (Male)	−.11	(.23)	Married	−.12	(.24)
Age	−.14	(.12)	Divorced	.27	(.01)*
Adjusted R Square	.01		Never Married	.43	(.001)*
			Number of Children	.13	(.22)
Step 3:			Adjusted R Square	.17	
Gender (Male)	.09	(.28)			
Age	−.07	(.41)			
Education (H.S. or less)	.002	(.98)			
Family Income	−.24	(.01)*			
Adjusted R Square	.05				

[a] Pairwise deletion used. Ns for: Respondents' Negative Relationships = 169, Gender (Male) = 256, Age = 243, Education (H.S. or less) = 256, Family Income = 170, Married = 256, Divorced = 256, Never Married = 256, and Number of Children = 240.
    *sig. $< .05$

be indicative of the stronger family related variables. Again, the evidence seems to suggest that the nonmarried respondents (be they never married or divorced) are more likely to provide negative descriptions of the relationships they have been invovled in than those who are currently married.

Gender Differences in Responses to Stereotype Items

One of the earliest social science stereotypes about black women is that they constitute a matriarchy in that they hold excessive power in determining family matters. This view is not accepted by the respondents, however. Only slightly more than a fourth of the women and less than a fifth of the men agree or strongly agree with the statement: "Generally speaking, black women have too much control and power in their families."

While most of the female respondents do not accept the view that "many black women, without realizing it, have helped to keep the black man down because of their low regard for him,'' the majority of the black males agree with this statement. In brief, although there is no consensus as to the culpability or nonculpability of black women in helping to keep black men down, a majority of the male respondents accept this view.

The final stereotype item focussing on women is, ''Black women seem to have many more opportunities than black men.'' The majority of the female respondents and a majority of the male respondents either agree or strongly agree with this statement.

In brief, most of the respondents, regardless of their gender, do not feel that black women have too much control and power in their families. A sizable minority of all the female respondents and a majority of the male respondents report that black women have helped to keep black men down because of their low regard for him. A large minority of the respondents, of both genders, feel that the relationships between black men and black women are deteriorating, and finally, the majority of both males and females believe that black women today have more opportunities than do black men.

In conclusion, the following stereotypes about black women seem to be operative. Black women are blamed by most of the males and a large proportion of the females for helping to keep black men down, and there is a common perception that black women have more opportunities than do black men.

To allow assessment of the extent of the acceptance of stereotypes about black men, the respondents were asked to indicate to what degree they agree or disagree with the following assertions: ''Generally speaking, black men aren't as reliable, accountable, or responsible as they should be in their relationships with their women''; ''The problem with black men is that they are not usually satisfied with only one woman,'' ''Most black men don't use enough of their money in providing for their family's economic needs''; and ''Many black men tend to exploit black women.''

There are statistically significant gender differences for all of the items involving stereotypes about black men (see table 8.3). Two-thirds of the females agree or strongly agree with the statement about black male irresponsibility compared to slightly less than half of the male respondents. While a sizable majority of the females agree or strongly agree with the statement that black men are not satisfied with only one woman, only 40 percent of the males do so. Nearly half of the female respondents agree or strongly agree that black men don't use enough of their money

TABLE 8.2
Summary of Results of Stereotype Items about Black Women by Gender

Item	Gender and Percentage Differences	Likert Scale, Percent and (Number)					% Total	N Total
		Strongly Agree	Agree	Undecided	Disagree	Strongly Disagree		
Many Black Women	Male	17.3 (13)	36.0 (27)	16.0 (12)	18.7 (14)	12.0 (9)	100	(75)
Have Helped Keep	Female	20.6 (34)	20.6 (34)	17.0 (28)	20.6 (34)	21.2 (35)	100	(165)
Black Men Down	Percentage Differences[a]	-3.3	15.4	-1.0	-1.9	-9.2		(240)
		$X^2 = 7.60$, 4 d.f. $p \leq .11$						
Black Women Have	Male	4.0 (3)	13.3 (10)	20.0 (15)	38.7 (29)	24.0 (19)	100	(75)
Too Much Control	Female	10.6 (17)	16.8 (27)	11.8 (19)	32.3 (52)	28.6 (46)	100	(161)
in families	Percentages Differences	-6.6	-3.5	8.2	6.4	-4.6		(236)
		$X^2 = 6.37$, 4 d.f. $p \leq .17$						
Black Women	Male	23.7 (18)	32.9 (25)	14.5 (11)	19.7 (15)	9.2 (7)	100	(76)
Have More	Female	16.8 (27)	37.9 (61)	16.1 (26)	18.6 (30)	10.6 (17)	100	(161)
Opportunities	Percentage Differences	6.9	-5.0	-1.6	1.1	-1.4		(237)
		$X^2 = 1.87$, 4 d.f. $p \leq .76$						

[a] + = Male is greater.
    − = Female is greater.

TABLE 8.3
Summary of Results of Stereotype Items about Black Men by Gender

Item	Gender and Percentage Differences[a]	Likert Scale, Percent and Number					% Total	N Total
		Strongly Agree	Agree	Undecided	Disagree	Strongly Disagree		
Black Men Are Not Responsible	Male	16.0 (12)	32.0 (24)	16.0 (12)	20.0 (15)	16.0 (12)	100	(75)
	Female	32.3 (51)	34.8 (55)	9.5 (15)	19.6 (31)	3.6 (6)	100	(158)
	Percentage Differences[a]	−16.3	−2.8	6.5	.4	12.2		(233)
	$X^2 = 16.77$, 4 d.f. $p \leq .002$							
Black Men Are Not Satisfied with One Woman	Male	16.0 (12)	24.0 (18)	17.3 (13)	25.3 (19)	17.3 (13)	100	(75)
	Female	31.9 (53)	29.4 (48)	18.4 (30)	14.7 (24)	5.5 (9)	100	(163)
	Percentage Differences	−15.9	−5.4	−1.1	10.6	11.8		(238)
	$X^2 = 16.37$, 4 d.f. $p \leq .003$							
Black Men Don't Provide for Families	Male	10.5 (8)	27.6 (21)	19.7 (15)	23.7 (18)	18.4 (14)	100	(76)
	Female	25.8 (42)	22.1 (36)	23.9 (39)	22.1 (36)	6.1 (10)	100	(163)
	Percentage Differences	−15.3	5.5	−4.2	1.6	12.3		(239)
	$X^2 = 14.68$, 4 d.f. $p \leq .005$							
Many Black Men Exploit Black Women	Male	13.3 (10)	34.7 (26)	22.7 (17)	17.3 (13)	12.0 (9)	100	(75)
	Female	26.7 (43)	33.5 (54)	24.2 (39)	11.8 (19)	3.7 (6)	100	(161)
	Percentage Differences	−13.4	1.2	−1.5	5.5	8.3		(236)
	$X^2 = 10.81$, 4 d.f. $p \leq .03$							

[a] + = Male is greater.
− = Female is greater.

in providing for their families' needs, compared to 38 percent of the males. Finally, while a sizable majority of the females agree or strongly agree that black men tend to exploit black women, slightly fewer than half of the males do so.

Overall, for both gender groups, there appears to be greater acceptance of negative stereotypes about black men than there is for those concerning black women.

For each item there is a statistically significant gender difference in the acceptance of these assertions, with women being more likely to show support for them. This is consistent with the finding of the Rodgers-Rose study that ''. . . women were able to list more negative qualities disliked in males than vice versa.''[28] However, large numbers of men also accept these stereotypes, although for no item do a majority of the men concur with these views about black men.

Effects of Independent Variables. Table 8.4 predicts the respondents' negative descriptions of relationships with their perception of growing distrust between black men and women, stereotype items about black men and about black women, gender, age, socioeconomic variables, and family variables. Step 1 shows that the perception of growing distrust between black men and women is predictive of negative relationships. Step 2 indicates that the acceptance of negative stereotypes about black males is also associated with negative relationships. However, it also reveals a surprising finding—that respondents who accept negative stereotypes involving black women are more likely to view their relationships positively.

Since the items about black women are less personal and focus primarily on their position or attitudes relative to black males, it is possible that they do not reflect indictments against black women, per se, but instead are indicative of a perception that there are relationship concerns that must be worked on to ensure a viable relationship. Steps 3 and 4 show that neither gender nor age is a significant predictor.

As the earlier regression analysis revealed, Step 5 indicates that low family income predicts the respondents' negative description of relationships. At this stage of the equation only family income and the perception of growing distrust between black men and women are statistically significant. Finally, as in the earlier regression equation, Step 6 reveals the impact of marital status. When the family variables are introduced into the equation it is found that only single or divorced status and the acceptance of negative stereotypes about black males remain as predictors of negative descriptions of relationships.

TABLE 8.4
Regression Equation[a] Predicting Respondents' Negative Relationships with Perception of Growing Distrust between Black Men and Women, Gender Stereotypes,[b] Gender, Age, Socioeconomic Status Variables and Family Variables

Step #/ Independent Variables	Respondents' Negative Relationships		Step #/ Independent Variables	Respondents' Negative Relationships	
	Beta	Sig. Level		Beta	Sig. Level
Step 1:			*Step 5:*		
Growing Distrust	.18	(.04)*	Growing Distrust	.18	(.05)*
Adjusted R Square	.02		Black Male		
			Stereo. Scale	.23	(.06)
Step 2:			Black Female		
Growing Distrust	.19	(.03)*	Stereo. Scale	−.22	(.06)
Black Male			Gender (Male)	−.04	(.69)
Stereo. Scale	.30	(.01)*	Age	−.06	(.53)
			Education (H.S.)		
Black Female			or less)	.002	(.98)
Stereo. Scale	−.29	(.01)	Family Income	−.20	(.03)*
			Adjusted R Square	.06	
Step 3:			*Step 6:*		
Growing Distrust	.19	(.03)*	Growing Distrust	.14	(.09)
Black Male			Black Male		
Stereo. Scale	.29	(.02)*	Stereo. Scale	.28	(.01)*
Black Female			Black Female		
Stereo. Scale	−.29	(.02)*	Stereo. Scale	−.21	(.07)
Gender (Male)	−.03	(.74)	Gender (Male)	−.06	(.47)
Adjusted R Square	.06		Age	.01	(.94)
			Education (H.S.		
			or less)	−.01	(.86)
Step 4:			Family Income	−.04	(.64)
			Married	−.13	(.20)
Growing Distrust	.18	(.04)*	Divorced	.26	(.01)*
Black Male			Never Married	.45	(.001)*
Stereo. Scale	.28	(.02)*	Number of Children	.15	(.13)
Black Female			Adjusted R Square	.22	
Stereo. Scale	−.26	(.03)*			
Gender (Male)	−.03	(.70)			
Age	−.11	(.23)			
Adjusted R Square	.07				

[a] Pairwise deletion used. Ns for: Respondents' Negative Relationships = 169, Growing Distrust = 242, Black Male Stereo. Scale = 256, Black Female Stereo. Scale = 256, Gender (Male = 256, Age = 243, Education (H.S. or less) = 256, Family Income = 170, Married = 256, Divorced = 256, Never Married = 256, and Number of Children = 240.

[b] Black Male Stereotype Scale Items = Black men are not responsible in their relationships + Black men are not usually satisfied with only one woman + Black men don't provide adequately for their families + Many black men tend to exploit black women/4.

Black Female Stereotype Scale Items = Many black women have helped to keep black men down + Black women have too much power and control in their families + Black women have more opportunities than black men/4.

*sig. < .05

Correlation Coefficients for Stereotype Items

Using Kendall's Tau correlation coefficients it was found that stereotypes about black men are more accepted than those about black women (see tables 8.5 and 8.6).

Correlation Coefficients for Stereotype Items for Male Respondents. These correlations suggest a pattern that may help to explain more about the nature of the concerns of the black male and the black female respondents.

For the males, the only stereotype items concerning women that are significantly correlated are the feeling that black women have helped to keep black men down because of their low regard for them and the perception that black women have more opportunities than black men (see table 8.5). That is, while there does seem to be a tendency to link the perceived relatively high status of black women to the low status of black men, there is no statistically significant stereotyping pattern that involves all three items on black women.

For the male respondents there are more statistically significant correlations between the stereotype items for black men and black women than

TABLE 8.5
Kendall's Tau Correlation Matrix for Male Respondents on Stereotype Items

	Variables and Coefficients						
	Bwfault	Bwcont	Bwmoop	Bmnotres	Bmnotsat	Bmnoprov	Bmexplw
Bwfault		.11	.20*	.32**	.14	.12	.14
Bwcont			.13	.07	.23*	.08	.18
Bwmoop				.30**	.05	.004	.22
Bmnotres					.46***	.50***	.47***
Bmnotsat						.35**	.39***
Bmnoprov							.38***
Bmexplw							

Key:
   Bwfault = Many black women have helped to keep black men down.
   Bwcont = Black women have too much power and control in their families.
   Bwmoop = Black women have more opportunities than black men.
   Bmnotres = Black men are not responsible in their relationships.
   Bmnotsat = Black men are not usually satisfied with only one woman.
   Bmnoprov = Black men don't provide adequately for their families.
   Bmexplw = Many black men tend to exploit black women.
   *p ≤ .05
   **p ≤ .01
   ***p ≤ .001

among those for black women, per se. This suggests that these black males are more likely to view both black men and black women negatively rather than exhibit a set of negative stereotypes specific to black women.

However, the correlation coefficients for the male stereotype items suggest that the male respondents do accept a pattern of closely related negative stereotypes about black men. That is, those males who agree that black men are not responsible in their relationships are also likely to report that: black men are not usually satisfied with one woman, black men do not adequately provide for their families, and many black men tend to exploit black women. Those males who feel that black men are not satisfied with one woman are also likely to accept the views that: black men do not adequately provide for their families and many black men tend to exploit black women. Finally, those males who agree that black men do not adequately provide for their families also feel that many black men tend to exploit black women.

In an earlier study of middle class black males there was found a tendency for those respondents who held negative stereotypes about black women to be more traditional in their gender role ideologies and to report being affected less by racial discrimination.[29] This is also supported by the current study. Evidence of this more conservative trend for both gender based and race-related ideologies is supported by the following

TABLE 8.6
Kendall's Tau Correlation Matrix for Female Respondents on Stereotype Items

	Bwfault	Bwcont	Bwmoop	Bmnotres	Bmnotsat	Bmnoprov	Bmexplw
			Variables and Coefficients				
Bwfault		.35***	.31***	.10	.11	.16*	.16*
Bwcont			.33***	.23**	.23**	.18**	.14*
Bwmoop				.21**	.24**	.25***	.13*
Bmnotres					.38***	.47***	.44***
Bmnotsat						.54***	.43***
Bmnoprov							.47***
Bmexplw							

Key:
Bwfault = Many black women have helped to keep black men down.
Bwcont = Black women have too much power and control in their families.
Bwmoop = Black women have more opportunities than black men.
Bmnotres = Black men are not responsible in their relationships.
Bmnostat = Black men are not usually satisfied with only one woman.
Bmnoprov = Black men don't provide adequately for their families.
Bmexplw = Many black men tend to exploit black women.
   *p≤.05
  **p≤.01
 ***p≤.001

findings. Males in the present sample who accept the view that "some equality in marriage is a good thing, but by and large the husband ought to have the final say-so in family matters" are more likely to agree that: black women have helped to keep black men down ($r = .24$, $p \le .05$). black women have too much power and control in their families ($r = .38$, $p \le .001$), black women have more opportunities than black men ($r = .29$, $p \le .01$), and black men are not responsible in their relationships with women ($r = .28$, $p \le .01$).

In addition, the male respondents who report that they have been affected by racial discrimination "not at all" or "very little" as compared to "somewhat" or "a great deal" are more likely to feel that black women have helped to keep black men down ($r = .-21$, $p \le .05$). Similarly, those men who accept the view that "while black people may not have the same opportunities as whites, most haven't prepared themselves enough to make use of the opportunities they do have" are more likely to agree that: black women have helped to keep black men down ($r = .20$, $p \le .05$); black women have more opportunities than black men ($r = .40$, $p \le .001$); and many black men tend to exploit black women ($r = .23$, $p \le .05$).

Correlation Coefficients for Stereotype Items for Female Respondents. Female respondents who feel that black women have helped to keep black men down because of their low regard for them are also likely to report that black women have too much control and power in their families (see table 8.6). In addition, those female respondents who feel that black women have too much control and power in their families tend to feel that black women have more opportunities today than black men. These females appear to accept the view that black women have gained status and power to the detriment of black men.

As was the case for the male respondents, all the stereotype items concerning black men are correlated. The female respondents who report that black men are not responsible also tend to feel that: black men are not satisfied with one woman, black men do not adequately provide for their families, and many black men tend to exploit black women. Female respondents who report that black men are not satisfied with one woman are also likely to accept the view that black men do not adequately provide for their families and tend to feel that many black men exploit black women. That is, it appears that the concern about black men having involvements with more than one woman at a time is associated with their concern about black men not providing adequately for their families with the resources they do have and with a fear of an overall pattern of exploitation. This possibility is also supported by a positive correlation for female respondents between the belief that black men do not adequately provide for their families and the feeling that many black men tend to exploit black women. These findings support Walum's view that such stereotypes may reflect a logical pattern of beliefs about stereotyped objects and relationships.[30]

As was true for the respondents in a previous study of middle class black men and the male respondents in the present study, the female respondents who accept negative stereotypes about black women are more likely to accept traditional gender roles.[31] That is, those females who report that while some equality in marriage is a good thing, by and large the husband ought to have the final say-so also feel that: black women have helped to keep black men down ($r = .15$, $p \leq .05$), black women have too much power and control in their families ($r = .20$, $p \leq .01$), and black women have more opportunities than black men ($r = .16$), $p \leq .05$). The feeling that the husband should have the final say-so is also correlated with their acceptance of the views that black men are not satisfied with one woman ($r = .16$, $p \leq .05$) and that many black men tend to exploit black women ($r = .16$, $p \leq .05$).

Female respondents who accept the view that while black people may not have the same opportunities as whites, most haven't prepared themselves enough to make use of the opportunities they do have are likely to accept each of three stereotypes about black women and the four stereotypes about black men (see tables 8.5 and 8.6).

In brief, the female respondents are similar to their male counterparts in the close association between the acceptance of stereotypes about black women and black men and their acceptance of traditional gender roles. However, they differ from the males in that there is no significant correlation between the acceptance of these views and a tendency to report being affected less by racial discrimination, although these attitudes do tend to be associated with the view that blacks are not as prepared as they can be to take advantage of available opportunities.

While the present study cannot adequately test Walum's hypothesized sequencing of stereotypes affecting black male-female relationships, it does suggest that these types of stereotypes are closely correlated and should therefore be the subject of further research.

SUMMARY AND CONCLUSION

This survey of black males and black females of various SES levels and backgrounds found that a substantial minority view their male-female relationships as being essentially negative in nature.

Multiple regression analysis revealed that respondents who describe their intimate relationships in a negative manner tend never to have been married or to be currently divorced and to accept negative stereotypes about black men.

Overall, there is greater acceptance of negative stereotypes about black men than there is regarding black women. There appears to be a clearly identifiable pattern of negative views about black men for both the male and the female respondents.

Finally, there is also a tendency for both male and female respondents who hold negative stereotypes about black men or black women to be more traditional in their views of appropriate gender roles and to accept the belief that blacks have not prepared themselves to take advantage of available opportunities.

This research supports the popular impression among many blacks that their particular sociohistorical experience in America has resulted in stereotyping and communication problems that severely challenge their male-female relationships.

Research Implications

Research is needed to delineate the origin and sequencing of various commonly accepted stereotypes about black men and black women. Information on the nature and origin of these stereotype issues is essential to understanding black male-female relationships.

Studies are also needed that are based on more representative samples of black men and black women, as well as further research using both race and gender as variables. Research should be done periodically to determine whether these issues can best be treated as aspects of ''black male-female relationships'' or relationships between American men and women generally. Indeed, if Randall Collins is correct, as more and more American women enter into the labor force and become increasingly independent, there will be an increasing need to renegotiate traditional relationships.[32] The issue of the male-female relationships has already become a common source of concern for many Americans. Lessons learned from the experiences of black men and black women about the effect of stereotyping on male/female relationships may have much to offer.

Programmatic and Social Movement Implications

This research has important implications for changes that are needed at both the personal-interpersonal/programmatic and the societal/movement levels.

The findings on the acceptance of negative stereotypes suggest the need for workshops, seminars, and courses on black male-female relationships that prepare black adolescents and young adults to deal with concerns that may be especially salient for or unique to black Americans. For example, in most instances the negative stereotypes that are attributed to black men or women are personalized manifestations of social reality over which black Americans have little control (e.g., the historic necessity for relatively autonomous women who are employed outside of the home, the effect of affirmative action programs on the perceptions of opportunities available to black women, and the relative shortage of black men that may contribute to exploitative relationships). Such problems should be addressed realistically and not just as negative and pathological distortions. In other instances, the stereotypes themselves may be problematic and associated with low self-esteem and related anti-male, anti-female, or anti-black biases that are the appropriate targets of counseling and educational intervention.

While there is much that black churches, fraternal organizations, social workers, psychologists, educators, and others can do to improve communication and reduce stereotypes between black males and females, the ultimate solution to these problems requires more fundamental changes in American social structure.

Time may show that one of the greatest strategic mistakes of the Black Movement of the 1960s and early 1970s was the separation of political and domestic issues. Black women who raised relationships issues were often told, ''We don't have time to deal with domestic concerns, we are in the midst of the 'revolution.''' The assumption was that both issues could not be addressed simultaneously. The mistake may have been the acceptance of the view that, indeed, the personal and political are separable. This ''you can't juggle two balls at one time'' simplemindedness resulted in the conclusion that one of these issues (the domestic) could be placed on hold indefinitely while the other (the movement) progressed.

Unfortunately, the acceptance of this false dichotomy distorts the nature of intimate relationships and social movements and may result in the fragmentation and failure of both.

Psychologists have shown that if two laboratory rats are placed in a cage and an electric current is sent through the grid upon which they stand they will tend to strike out against that which is nearest and most similar, each other. This suggests that the issues related to black male-female relationships must be taken seriously and placed within their proper political-economic context. They cannot be allowed to become the latest social and status-related fad of the black middle classes (e.g, "Have you been to a black male-female relationship party lately?"). Indeed these relationships are inherently political and economic acts with significant consequences for the literal future of black Americans, our children.

The state of black children in America is precarious. Indeed, *most* are born into abject poverty. Here lies not only the urgency for improving black male-female relationships, but perhaps a hint as to an important solution. In today's complex and changing "Alice in Wonderland" world it is often necessary to solve problems through indirect and nonlinear strategies that transcend the mirrored images of reality. This may be especially true now as America recovers from a lengthy "Me generation" hangover. Perhaps it is time to be more "Other" related in our quests in ways that go beyond the apparent "realities" of black men, black women, or, indeed, relationships.

This may be best accomplished through the involvement of black men and women in political struggles that necessitate communication, break down stereotypes, and boost self-esteem. While gender-specific issues like the exploitation of black women by black men and the black male as "an endangered species" are important and must be addressed, perhaps the best strategy to ensure success in improving relationships can come from focus on the gender-shared products of those relationships, black children, and the appropriate battles that must be collectively waged against the racist, class elitist, and sexist systems that oppress them.

By engaging in movements for child advocacy, economic justice, and political empowerment of the poor, black men and women will not only improve their racial well-being, but enhance their self-esteem, boost their solidarity and forge values around the fulfillment of little dreams and a brighter future. In this way, all of our relationships are bound to be better.

NOTES

The authors would like to acknowledge the assistance of Cheryl Hardy and Sherman Curl in the administering and coding of the questionnaires. We would also like to express our gratitude for the helpful advice received from La Frances Rodgers-Rose during the planning stage of this research. Finally, we would like to thank the administrators, faculty, and students of the Temple University Pan-African Studies Community Education Program for their consent and cooperation. Without their help this research could not have been done.

1. N.A. Cazenave, "Race, Class, Ideology and Changing Black Family Structures and Processes," in M. Tryman, ed. *Institutional Racism and Blacks in America: Challenges, Choices, Change.* Vol. 1 (Lexington, MA: Ginn Press, 1985), pp. 35–36.

2. U.S. Bureau of the Census, *Population Profile of the United States: 1980,* Current Population Reports, Series P–20, no. 363. (Washington, DC: U.S. Government Printing Office, 1981).

3. M. Wallace, *Black Macho and the Myth of the Superwoman* (New York: Warner, 1978), p. 27.

4. R. Staples, "The Myth of Black Macho: A Response to Angry Black Feminists," *Black Scholar,* Vol. 10 (1979), pp. 24–33, "Special Forum on Black Male-Female Relationships," *Black Scholar,* Vol. 10 (1970), pp. 17–67.

5. C.W. Franklin, "White Racism as the Cause of Black Male-Female Conflict: A Critique," *Western Journal of Black Studies*, Vol. 4 (Spring 1980), pp. 42–49.

6. K.S. Jewell. "Black Male/Female Conflict: Internalization of Negative Definitions Transmitted Through Imagery," *Western Journal of Black Studies,* Vol. 7, No. 1 (1983), pp. 43–48.

7. N.A. Cazenave. "Black Male-Female Relationships: The Perceptions of 155 Middle-Class Black Men," *Family Relations,* Vol. 32 (1983), pp. 341–350.

8. R. Blood, Jr., and D.M. Wolfe, "Negro-White Differences in Blue Collor Marriages in a Northern Metropolis," *Social Forces,* Vol. 48 (1969), pp. 59–63; J.H. Bracey, Jr., A. Meier, and E. Rudwick, eds., *Black Matriarchy: Myth or Reality?* (Belmont, CA: Wadsworth, 1971); D.P. Moynihan, *The Negro Family: Case for National Action.* (Washington, DC: U.S. Department of Labor, 1965); R. Staples, "The Myth of the Black Matriarchy," *Black Scholar,* Vol. 1 (1970), pp. 9–16.

9. J.C. Bond and P. Peery, "Has the Black Man Been Castrated?," *Liberator,* Vol. 9 (1969), pp. 4–8; N. Hare, "The Frustrated Masculinity of the Negro Male," in R. Staples, ed., *The Black Family: Essays and Studies.* (Belmont, CA: Wadsworth, 1971), N. Hare. "Will the Real Black Man Please Stand Up?" *Black Scholar,* Vol. 2 (1971), pp. 32–35, R. Staples, "The Myth of the Impotent Black Male," *Black Scholar,* Vol. 2 (1971), pp. 2–9.

10. R. Staples, "Masculinity and Race: The Dual Dilemma of Black Men," *Journal of Social Issues* Vol. 34 (1978), pp. 168–183, Staples (1979); R. Staples, "Black Manhood in the 70s: A Critical Look Back," *Black Scholar* Vol. 12 (1981), pp. 2–9.

11. R. Blood and D.M. Wolfe, *Husbands and Wives: The Dynamics of Married Living* (New York: Free Press, 1960), p. 66.

12. D.A. Schulz, *Coming Up Black: Patterns of Ghetto Socialization.* (Englewood Cliffs, NJ: Prentice-Hall, 1969).

13. Franklin (1980).

14. U. Hannerz, *Soulside: Inquiries Into Ghetto Culture and Community* (New York: Columbia University Press, 1969).

15. E. Liebow, *Tally's Corner* (Boston: Little Brown, 1967).

16. L. Benjamin, "The Dog Theory: Black Male/Female Conflict," *Western Journal of Black Studies,* Vol. 7, no. 1 (1983), pp. 49–55.

17. N.A. Cazenave, "Middle-Income Black Fathers: An Analysis of the Provider Role," *Family Coordinator,* Vol. 28 (1979), pp. 583–593; N.A. Cazenave, "Black Men in America: The Quest for 'Manhood,'" in H. McAdoo, ed., *Black Families,* 1st ed. (Beverly Hills, CA: Sage, 1981).

18. Hare (1971).

19. N. Shange, *For Colored Girls Who Have Considered Suicide When the Rainbow Is Enuf: A Choreopoem* (New York: Macmillan, 1977); Wallace (1978); A. Walker. *The Color Purple* (New York: Harcourt Brace Jovanovich, 1982).

20. B.F. Turner and C.B. Turner, "Evaluations of Women and Men Among Black and White College Students," *Sociological Quarterly,* Vol. 15, (1974), pp. 442–456. L. B. Jackson, "The Attitudes of Black Females Toward Upper and Lower Class Black Males," *Journal of Black Psychology,* Vol. 1 (1975), pp. 53–64; L. Rodgers-Rose, "Dialectics of Black-Female Relationships," in L. Rodgers-Rose, ed., *The Black Woman* (Beverly Hills: Sage, 1980); R.L. Braithwaite, "Interpersonal Relationships Between Black Males and Black Females," in L.E. Gary, ed., *Black Men* (Beverly Hills Sage, 1981); Cazenave (1983); H. McAdoo, *Extended Family Support of Single Black Mothers,* final Report Submitted to N.I.M.H. (Rockville, MD: U.S. Department of Health and Human Services, 1983).

21. Turner and Turner. (1974); Jackson (1975); Rodgers-Rose (1980), Cazenave, (1983).

22. L.R. Walum *The Dynamics of Sex and Gender: A Sociological Perspective* (Chicago: Rand McNally, 1977).

23. Cazenave. (1983)

24. Turner and Turner. (1974).

25. L.E. Smith and J. Millham, "Sex Role Stereotypes Among Blacks and Whites," *Journal of Black Psychology,* Vol. 6 (1979), pp. 1–6.

26. Jackson (1975).

27. Wallace (1978), p. 27.

28. Rodgers-Rose (1980), p. 258.

29. Cazenave (1983).

30. Walum. (1977).

31. Cazenave (1983).

32. R. Collins. *Conflict Sociology* (New York: Academic Press, 1980).

9

POLYGAMY AND THE DECLINING MALE TO FEMALE RATIO IN BLACK COMMUNITIES: A SOCIAL INQUIRY

Michael W. Williams

The declining male to female ratio in black communities throughout the United States is a serious problem. It contributes to the drastic increase in the number of black single-parent female-headed households, creates a void in the life-cycle of thousands of black children, and increases the burden and concomitant stress level of thousands of black women who are saddled with the responsibility of caring for black children alone at rates unparalleled in U.S. history. This chapter critically examines one of the suggested solutions to this grave dilemma: polygamy.

INTRODUCTION

One of the most challenging problems facing the African-American community in the United States is the declining pool of available black men to serve as husbands and fathers within the context of the two-parent, monogamous family unit. The empirical dimensions of this crisis are staggering, as are most of its consequences. One reaction, among many, to this grave quandary is the recognition, promotion, or sanctioning of women sharing the extant pool of men in the black community, without regard to the conjugal status of the participants.

A recent illustration of this reaction is chronicled in Audrey B. Chapman's *Man Sharing, Dilemma or Choice: A Radical New Way of Relating to the Men in Your Life*. Chapman's main purpose in writing this book was to "ease the suffering and to cut down on the anger, guilt, and pain experienced by women who are man sharing or contemplating doing so."[1] Devoid of practically any empirical support for the countless assertions made throughout the book, Chapman offers a plethora of strategies, tactics, and justifications for women who have given up on the idea of settling down with just one man, in a monogamous relationship, for the more "realistic" alternative of "man sharing." Even casual sex between romantically uncommitted persons is strongly encouraged by Chapman as a way for women to meet their sexual-emotional needs.[2]

This attempt to sanction the existence of some form of polygyny in the black community in the United States is not new. Jacquelyne Jackson's groundbreaking and penetrating 1971 study in many ways served as the theoretical harbinger for those who promote this alternative family form. Unlike with Chapman's study, Jackson's examination is replete with persuasive empirical observations. Her major contribution was in demonstrating the exact demographical and historical dimensions of the black male population shortage. On the basis of these findings, while she relunctantly conceded that polygyny may be "a system appropriate in the absence of a sufficient supply of males,"[3] she seemed certain that "the legitimacy of polygyny could well benefit some females who are involved in 'playing at polygyny,' but who are denied legally any of the benefits to which they might otherwise be entitled."[4] Jackson concluded that further investigation into this question was necessary.

Such an investigation had to wait for the controversial 1976 study by Joseph Scott titled "Polygamy: A Futuristic Family Arrangement for African-Americans." Based on a sample of 22 black women living in Northwestern Indiana, Scott concluded that in most urban areas throughout the United States the male to female ratio imbalance is so great for the black community "that single women feel little hesitation about trying to attract the husbands of other women and establishing socio-sexual and even conjugal-type relationships with them."[5] However, Scott, like Chapman, provided practically no empirical evidence for such a broad-based conclusion. There are no references to attitudinal studies of black women in regards to marriage and the family, and one would necessarily question the generalizability of Scott's findings. Scott followed up his initial study a few years later with another one titled "Black Polygamous Family Formation: Case Studies of Legal Wives and Consensual 'Wives.'" In this study he strengthened his conceptual framework considerably. Scott's theoretical effort to defend the use of the term *polygamy* to describe certain types of man-sharing relations in the black community is admirable, if still problematic. However, the major flaw in this study parallels the problem of his previous one: the absence of any empirical evidence to validate his observation of the growth of polygyny in the black community in the United States.[6] In his later, 1986, effort, titled "From Teenage Parenthood to Polygamy: Case Studies in Black Polygamous Family Formation,'' Scott uses what appear to be the data collected in his original 1976 study.[7] Consequently, the same problems are recast, with too little attention given, this time, to describing what warrants the unmarried women in these relationships being considered, in his terms, ''consensual wives.''

The present social inquiry critically explores, for the first time, some of the implications of polygyny serving as a feasible, alternative family form to address the critically low male to female ratio in the black community. Proponents of polygyny in the United States have failed to consider the multiplicity of political, economic, social, ideological, and historical factors involved in the development of such an institution. Instead, they have reacted to the shortage of black men by speculating on the emergence of polygyny as a viable solution.

This inquiry begins with an examination of the empirical dimensions of the problem, followed by a historical account of the mating patterns of African-Americans from their traditional African background through to the contemporary American scene. On this empirical and historical basis, the current socioeconomic conditions facing the black community in the United States are examined in order to determine how practical and realistic it is to expect a polygynous family form to develop and meet the familial needs of the black community today and into the foreseeable future.

EMPIRICAL DIMENSIONS OF THE PROBLEM

According to recent U.S. Census Bureau statistics, there are 1.4 million more black females than there are black males in the United States. Not since 1820 has the population of black males in the United States outnumbered the population of black females. Beginning in 1840, when the black female population first outnumbered the black male population, by 7,672, which made the ratio 99.5 males to 100 females, the male to female ratio in the African-American community has been falling appreciably. Today the ratio is 90.0 to 100. However, for those black women considering marriage in the 25-55 age range, the male to female ratio is as low as 86.5 males per 100 females as compared to 100.5 for the whites in the same age range. Tables 9.1 and 9.2 below provide a more comprehensive account of these disparities.

What are the essential factors that help to explain this severe sex ratio imbalance in the African-American community? One of the most important factors is the extremely high homicide rate affecting African-

TABLE 9.1
Ratio of Males to Females by Age Group and Race: 1985

Age	Total	White	Black
All Ages	94.0	95.4	90.0
Under 14 yrs.	104.9	105.4	102.6
14–24 yrs.	102.2	102.8	97.4
25–44 yrs.	98.5	100.5	86.5
45–64 yrs.	91.5	92.8	81.6
65 yrs. and Over	67.8	67.7	67.0

Source: U.S. Bureau of the Census, U.S. Census of Population: Current Population Reports.

American males. As late as 1983, black males suffered from a homocide rate of 51.4 per 100,000 as compared to 8.6 for their white male counterparts and, more importantly, 11.3 for black women.[8] The homocide rate combined with the disproportionate number of deaths of black males from cancer, heart disorders, strokes, cirrhosis of the liver, and countless accidental causes[9] means a black male life expectancy almost ten years shorter than the United States average, as indicated in Table 9.3 below. The black male death rate is just as extreme relative to the U.S. popu-

TABLE 9.2
Black Population by Sex and Sex Ratio, 1820–1974

Year	Male	Female	Sex Ratio
1820	900,796	870,860	103.4
1840	1,432,988	1,440,660	99.5
1860	2,216,744	2,225,086	99.6
1890	3,735,603	3,753,073	99.5
1910	4,885,881	4,941,882	98.9
1930	5,855,669	6,035,474	97.0
1940	6,269,038	6,596,480	95.0
1950	7,269,170	7,757,505	93.7
1960	9,097,704	9,750,915	93.3
1970	10,748,316	11,831,973	90.8
1974	11,452,000	12,592,000	90.9

Source: U.S. Department of Commerce, Bureau of the Census, Historical Statistics of the United States: Colonial Times to 1970, House Document No. 93-78; and Current Population Reports, Special Studies Series P-23, No. 54; The Social and Economic Status of the Black Population in the United States, 1970, 1973, and 1974.

TABLE 9.3
Life Expectancy at Birth: 1985

Year	Total	White Male	White Female	Black Male	Black Female
1985	74.7	71.8	78.7	65.3	73.7

Source: U.S. National Center for Health Statistics, Vital Statistics of the U.S., annual.

lation in general and black women in particular.[10] Furthermore, as indicated in Table 9.4 below, the suicide rates for black males as compared to black females, at all ages, are exceedingly greater.

Although counted as part of the U.S. population, black men who are incarcerated are not really a part of the available pool of marriageable men. While making up approximately 6 percent of the U.S. population, black males make up slightly less than 50 percent of the U.S. prison population.[11] What is significant for this inquiry is the greater number of black men who are missing from the civilian population due to incarceration. In 1983, for example, there were 80,671 black male jail inmates as compared to the much smaller figure of 6,836 for black females; the median age for both groups was 26.9.[12] It is worth noting that in 1985 blacks and other nonwhite minorities accounted for 688 of the 903 prisoners, approximately 76 percent, sentenced to death.[13] The greater majority of these were black males.

As a result of the difficulty and frustration so many black males experience in trying to succeed in the civilian population, many decide to join the military establishment.[14] Consequently, while only making up 6 percent of the U.S. population, black males constitute 18 percent of the male Active Duty Forces in the military.[15] Black women have a much smaller participation rate. And although these men are of the marriageable age they are often not quite accessible to the black female civilian population. Moreover, in general, black males are more than twice as likely than black women to be institutionalized in some form or fashion.[16]

The growing number of black men who are attracted to nonblack women for potential mates further reduces the pool of available men for black women. As shown below in Table 9.5, in 1985 of all the black-white interracial married couples in the United States, the number of

TABLE 9.4
Black Male-Female Suicide Rates by Age: 1983
(Rates are per 100,000 population)

Age	Male	Female
All Ages	9.9	2.0
5-14 yrs.	.5	.6
15-24 yrs.	11.5	2.7
25-34 yrs.	19.1	2.9
35-44 yrs.	14.0	3.5
45-54 yrs.	12.1	3.0
55-64 yrs.	11.6	1.7
65 and over	14.2	1.4

Source: U.S. National Center for Health Statistics, Vital Statistics of the United States, annual.

TABLE 9.5
Interracial Married Couples: 1970-1985
(in thousands)

Item	1970	1980	1985	Item	1970	1980	1985
Total Married Couples	44,597	49,714	51,114	Other Interracial Married Couples	245	484	628
Interracial Married Couples All Black-White	310	651	792	Black Husband-Other Race	8	20	26
Married Couples Black Husband-	65	167	164	Black Wife-Other Race	4	14	3
White Wife	41	122	117	White Husband-Other Race	139	287	362
Black Wife-White Husband	24	45	47	White Wife-Other Race	94	163	237

Source: U.S. Bureau of the Census, Census of the Population.

black male-white female unions was more than double the number of black female-white male unions. In the same year, of all the *other* types of interracial married couples in the United States, the black male participation rate was more than eight times greater than the black female participation rate.

When the number of black men who are homosexual, already married, uninterested in marriage, and for other reasons unacceptable as mates are excluded from the official Census Bureau statistics, the male to female ratio in the African-American community, in real terms, declines even more. In fact, Staples has suggested that in practical terms, there may be no more than one black man for every five single black women in the United States.[17] Hence, as clearly demonstrated above, the declining male to female ratio in the African-American community is quite veritable. The debate, then, does not center around whether the problem exists. Instead, it centers around what must be done. Polygyny is one suggested solution. In order to determine its feasibility in the context of the contemporary social order of the United States, it is necessary to appreciate the history of mating patterns of the African-American community.

A BRIEF HISTORICAL SUMMARY OF BLACK MATING PATTERNS

Traditional Africa

It is generally agreed by students of Black Diasporan Studies that peoples of African descent who were taken from Africa were quite successful in retaining and making use of cultural patterns first cultivated in

Africa, not the least of which includes familial patterns.[18] Consequently, in order to understand the polygyny construct as it relates to the mating patterns of the African-American community in the United States, it is appropriate that the familial patterns of traditional Africa be explicated. And in elucidating these patterns, the discussion of polygyny is pivotal. This is because polygyny, although always practiced alongside monogamy in traditional Africa, was such a necessary and integral part of the institutional fabric of traditional African mating patterns. Such an approach would also provide a definitive understanding of the institutional characteristics of polygyny, thus isolating the significant socioeconomic and demographical variables germane to any discussion of this very ancient institution.

Several related factors operating in traditional African society accounted for the emergence of polygyny. A relatively low sex ratio was one significant factor. As traditional Africa was a nonindustrial, agrarian society, production was labor-intensive, and a relatively high birth rate was required from its women to ensure relatively stable population growth. In conjunction with this demand, the relative shortage of men at the socially approved marriageable age (at least ten years the female's senior) resulted in polygyny being practiced by those men who could afford it. Here it is important to note that men married late in traditional Africa to "prove" themselves acceptable to the older male-dominated community that had control over the marriageable young females. This "proof" was normally verified by their ability to produce (with the help from their kinfolk) a socially approved bride-price to deliver to their in-laws before marriage. Women married early, partially to reduce the chances of any out-of-wedlock pregnancy, a disgraceful occurrence in most of traditional Africa. The low sex ratio for those of marriageable age, then, resulted primarily from an increasing birth rate, coupled with a high mortality rate.[19] This meant, in both instances, the population size of older people would always be smaller than that of younger people.

Niara Sudarkasa explains why polygyny developed to cope with this relative shortage of marriageable age men: ". . . the premium which Africans placed on having children led women as well as men to place a high value on a system (namely polygyny) that afforded all women the possibility of motherhood within the context of family."[20] In other words, as a result of the relative male to female imbalance, a suitable set of attitudes and values was formed to sanction the institutional establishment of a system of co-wives that ensured the reproduction of the young within the economic context of the African extended family, the major production unit in traditional Africa. Furthermore, because African women would breast-feed their infants for a period not less than two years, while abstaining from sexual intercourse for fear of its adverse effects on their milk should conception occur, a conjugal system excluding the possibility of co-wives would have reduced the number of births significantly, thus unfavorably affecting production in the communal economy. In short, sanctioned polygyny played a very vital role in the traditional African society.

Two other important factors characteristic of the polygynous family in traditional Africa are worth mentioning. First, despite the occasional presence of rivalry and jealousy among the co-wives, it is certain that the normal mode of interaction between them was, more often than not, based on "affection, mutual respect and cooperation."[21] African marriages would not have been as stable as they were and African women would not have encouraged their husbands to take additional wives as often as they did if this were not the case. Second, it was required that men with plural wives treat them and their children impartially, without favoritism. Relatedly, siblings of different mothers but the same father were expected "to behave toward each other as if there were no differences in maternity."[22] What is significant here is not how remarkably close practice approximated the ideal, but rather that there was an attitudinal and value system in place to ensure the harmonious interaction among the polygynous family members. These were just some of the important factors that contributed to the emergence, development, and stability of polygyny, in particular, and the general mating patterns that African-Americans brought to the United States from Africa.[23]

Slave Experience

During slavery, a combination of factors contributed to the development of a unique pattern of black mating practices on the plantation. These factors included African and European cultural influences, the demands of the slave economy, and certain demographic variables. During the prenuptial period, black slaves drew heavily from their African traditional courtship practices, which "led to the evolution of unique courtship practices in the slave quarters."[24] As in Africa, those practices and rituals were characterized by the use of "metaphor, indirection, story-telling, poems, songs, riddles, and symbolic languages."[25] Their purpose was to ascertain the possibility of a romantic relationship being developed between a man and a woman, normally initiated by the former.

Another element characteristic of the prenuptial relations between black men and women during slavery was the prevalence of sexual intercourse. Blassingame argues that part of this pattern can be traced, again, to the African heritage, which had a view of sexual intercourse devoid of the negative and puritanical connotations given to it by Western European society. However, there were other, perhaps more powerful, forces that may have also contributed to this pattern of sexual behavior. Genovese explains that in North America "An early end to the slave trade, followed by a boom in cotton and plantation slavery, dictated a policy of encouraging slave births."[26] Gutman goes a bit further, demonstrating convincingly that the demands of the slave economy for more slaves (especially after the abolition of the slave trade in the United States) encouraged black men and women to engage in sexual intercourse. In other words, the slave labor force had to reproduce itself, so "the system put a high premium on females who began early to bear children, inside or [emphasis added] outside of marriage."[27] It is important to realize, however, that while the master saw the birth of another black child in primarily economic terms, the black slave community did not share this perception. In his very arduous studies of slave communities in the South, Gutman found that prenuptial intercourse and pregnancy were not "evidence of indiscriminate mating" but instead were more "compatible with settled marriage."[28] In fact, for black men and women contemplating marriage during slavery, having children quickly was one of the best ways to prevent being sold and separated and to secure their future together.[29] While there were perhaps other factors involved that help to explain this phenomenon of prenuptial sexual intercourse, those discussed above appear to be the most essential ones, as agreed upon by the leading scholars in this field.

Euro-Christian dogma, intensely promoted by white ministers, was another critical factor that contributed to the formation of black mating patterns during slavery. Although unable to undermine the exigencies of the slave economy that fostered prenuptial sexual intercourse between slaves, this dogma was greatly successful in eliminating the institution of polygyny in the black community and in establishing, at least in principle, the "sinfulness" of fornication and extramarital affairs from a Judeo-Christian perspective in the black community.[30] This point cannot be overemphasized when trying to understand the attitudes and values of African-Americans in regards to marriage and the family, particularly as they relate to the polygyny construct as explored in this chapter. These values began during slavery, under the constant prodding and careful tutelage of white churches.

> White churches continued to exercize moral oversight over the slaves after weddings. Frequently investigating charges of adultery and fornication, the churches tried to promote the development of Christian moral precepts in the quarters. Consequently, they often excommunicated or publicly criticized slaves for abandoning their mates, having premarital pregnancies, and engaging in extramarital sex. Since an overwhelming majority of the cases were brought to the attention of the church by the slave members, the increase in the charges of moral lapses between 1830 and 1860 represented the spread of Christian moral precepts in the quarters.[31]

Eventually, however, black churches, in principle, adhered to these doctrines just as strongly. For instance, Gutman reports: ". . . the Beaufort Baptist Church, most if not all of its members South Carolina slaves, published people guilty of adultery and fornication. To commit adultery meant suspension from the church for three months."[32]

Perhaps no less significant than the ideological factors that serve to explain the spread of monogamous unions within the slave community is one very important demographical factor: sex ratios. Unlike in parts of Latin America during slavery, in the antebellum South of North America the sex ratio among the slaves was nearly equal, regardless of age.[33] Consequently, during slavery there was no real basis on which polygyny, as an African custom, could reestablish itself in North America within the African-American community.

In sum, African-American mating patterns during slavery were shaped by traditional customs practiced in Africa, but these practices were significantly modified by new ideological, economic, and demographical factors peculiar to the slave experience in North America.

Post Slavery in the South

After slavery and for at least a half a century later, the great majority of African-Americans remained in the rural South. In fact, according to the 1910 census, 3 out of 4 lived in rural areas and 9 out of 10 lived in the South. Moreover, many studies reveal that very similar political, economic, and social forces that had shaped the life of blacks as slaves were also at work after slavery.[34] African-Americans remained as exploited laborers, a racially subservient caste whose primary function was to perform the most degrading and least economically rewarding work. For this reason, the black mating patterns that had taken shape during slavery did not undergo any radical alteration. There were no contravening forces that would have disrupted what had by then become tradition.

The assimilation of Euro-Christian religious doctrines by the black community continued unabated. Consequently, fornication and adultery were still considered sins. Nevertheless, prenuptial relations were still characterized by the prevalence of sexual intercourse,[35] despite the warnings of the black church. In fact, according to Frazier, "the discipline of the church did not appear as a very effective means of social control."[36] Indeed, both Frazier and Johnson, two keen observers of this period, explain that neither the woman or man received any social condemnation for producing children out of wedlock.[37] Instead, because of the labor-intensive character of their agrarian condition, the procreative potential of women was lauded. In such a situation, for numerous reasons, children were a genuine asset, particularly for single women.[38] And to this extent, as was the case under slavery, the nature of black female fertility in particular and black mating patterns in general was heavily conditioned by economic factors.

The character of black conjugal units during this period was also, at least partially, a consequence of important economic forces. As the South gradually began to industrialize after 1880, black men began to migrate from rural areas in search for temporary work in the sawmills, coal mines, lumber and turpentine camps, and railroad construction sites that were beginning to appear just outside of the burgeoning towns of the South. Such movement accounts for the minority of black families that were headed by single women in the South before mass migration.[39] Still, the great majority of African-American families in the towns and country of the South, even as late as the Second World War, were two-parent and relatively stable units, notwithstanding the regularity with which the black poor entered into common law marriages.[40]

As for the growing black middle class, mating patterns were considerably different from those described above. To the best that they were able, these families mirrored white middle class families. For instance, entering into a common law arrangement would have been unthinkable for a group so intent on demonstrating its dissimilarity with the black masses and its affinity with European-American ideals. This attitude was applicable to prenuptial relations as well. Powdermaker found evidence of this in her vivid study of life in a Mississippi town during the 1930s. In her discussion of prenuptial relations among males and females of the "Negro upperclass," she stated: "In such courtships the idea of sexual relations before marriage would be scandalous. It is considered essential that the girl be a virgin when she is married, and that the marriage be legal, usually with a church ceremony."[41]

If there was any mating pattern in which blacks across class lines converged, it was perhaps the frequency with which black men engaged in extramarital affairs. Women did so also, but it appears at a much lower frequency. Moreover, the black woman's tolerance level was much higher than her mate's; this was particularly true if the latter was making a significant financial contribution to the family and at the same time was relatively discreet in his philanderings.[42]

Post World War Two

Whereas in 1910 the overwhelming majority of African-Americans were residing in rural areas in the South, by a half a century later they were mainly an urban-based population. Almost three-fourths were then residing in the city, and about half lived outside the former slave states. As a corollary to, and in conjunction with, this dramatic residential shift, major economic, political, and social changes occurred in the black community in particular and the United States in general. Below is an attempt to summarize the effects these enormous changes had, and are continuing to have, on the evolution of black mating patterns since the Second World War.

On the whole, the urbanization process noted above seemed to have had an adverse effect on black mating patterns, particularly among the black poor. The factors are varied and somewhat complicated. The role of government assistance is one such factor. Prior to becoming city dwellers, blacks were forced to rely on themselves for economic survival. Although they were taken advantage of through various means, their precarious access to the soil usually assured their economic sustenance, even if this meant quite an impoverished existence. In the cities, however, many became dependent upon public assistance. Drake and Cayton found this dependency to be a factor in the great increase in out-of-wedlock births, because for black women seeking assistance "even illegitimate babies were an asset when confronting a case worker."[43] Hannerz likewise has partially attributed the large increase in male desertions, accompanying the urban migration, to this same phenomenon.[44]

For years states would not provide assistance to families if there was an "employable" male around, thus effectively undermining an already tenuous union between a poor black couple by giving the male a "legitimate" reason for not being around. Even today, states are not required to provide Aid to Families with Dependent Children (AFDC) for two-parent families with an unemployed male.

Relatedly, the economic frustrations experienced by millions of blacks in cities, and black men in particular, have also proven to be a seemingly insurmountable obstacle in the struggle to build viable relationships between black men and women. Without decent work, men simply do not settle down to raise families; and when there is not enough money to meet familial needs, couples, even if one or both are working, find it very difficult to stay together. Stack concluded: ". . . the most important single factor which affects interpersonal relationships between men and women in the Flats is unemployment, and the impossibility for men to secure jobs."[45]

Stack also uncovered a very interesting and ironic relationship between economic frustration, the extended family, and black mating patterns in the city. Even though one of the major purposes for the continuation of the black extended family in the city has been to mitigate the most onerous effects of economic deprivation, Stack found that this has occasionally disrupted the stability of black pair-bonding over the years also. In short, extended family members may work to terminate a relationship between a mate and one of their kinsmen if that relationship is causing a drain on the economic resources of the extended family network.[46] Stack's findings point to far-reaching and complicated effects that economic deprivation has continued to have on black mating patterns within the urban environment.

By the 1940s, as the conditions grew worse for the growing black underclass, the declining sex ratio in the black community was beginning to be felt. Cox was the first social scientist to recognize its influence on black mating patterns.[47] From 1940 to 1970, the ratio droped from 95.0 to 90.8. In addition to making it more difficult for women to find mates, it seemed to exacerbate the black male virility cult that grew to govern the sexual appetite of countless urban black males. In what Staples has coined the "Black Dating Game," many black males have learned to take advantage of their numerical scarcity and black women often end up tolerating more abuse than they would under different demographical circumstances. This abuse includes, ultimately, marital infidelity.[48] Additionally, in his classic study of the black underclass in New York City during the

1960s, Clark argued persuasively that this perverted definition of masculinity was another contributing factor to the increase in out-of-wedlock births among black teenagers: "The marginal young Negro male tends to identify his masculinity with the number of girls he can attract. The high incidence of illegitimacy among Negro young people reflects this pervasive fact. In his compensatory distortion of the male image, masculinity is, therefore, equated with alleged sexual prowess."[49] Other important causal factors include the ignorance and aimlessness associated with poverty, the sexual enticing messages provided by the mass media, peer pressure at school, and the familial shortcomings in the home.[50] One of the most serious characteristics of this crisis is that it seems to be almost self-perpetuating, i.e., the children of teenage mothers are most likely to become unwed mothers while still in their teens.[51]

As has been true with much of the description so far, middle and upper middle class blacks are not as victimized by the teenage preganancy dilemma as are their lower class brethren. This is due in part to their more stable economic condition, thus enabling them to avoid many of the tragic familial consequences associated with poverty. Clark's findings apparently are just as relevant today: "The consistently high illegitimacy rate among Negroes is not a reflection of less virture or greater promiscuity, but rather of the fact that the middle-class teenagers are taught the use of contraceptives and learn how to protect themselves from the hazards of pre-marital and illicit sexual contacts."[52]

However, during this postwar period there have been a number of circumstances from which middle and upper middle class blacks have been unable to escape, not the least of which has been the declining male to female ratio. Staples has demonstrated the frustrations that black college-educated females have been experiencing since the 1970s in trying to find mates with equal levels of education.[53] This has been very difficult given the greater number of black female college graduates relative to their black male counterparts. Relatedly, there is no evidence available to suggest that the mates of upwardly mobile black women have been any less attracted to the opportunities of marital infidelity afforded them than their counterparts of lower income black women.

Most of the contemporary social scientists who have studied African-American male-female relationships have concentrated on culture as one of the most important variables explaining the problems black men and women have been experiencing over the last few decades. The consensus among them seems to be that blacks have internalized the cultural roles of male and female as defined by the dominant culture of American society, and as a result, have been socialized into incompatibility.[54] Foremost among this cultural influence is, once again, the Judeo-Christianity of European civilization. Asante charges that the black church, as a result of its enthronement of this European theology, is one of the major culprits that has caused great damage to the relationship between black men and women.[55] This is, he argues, because Judeo-Christianity institutionalizes the role of the white male, promotes sexism, forces couples to stay together even after the relationship is, in effect, over, thus encouraging hypocrisy and infidelity, and requires blacks to become immersed into an alien experience, with its own alien rites of passage.[56] Regardless of the contestability of Asante's argument, the fact that Judeo-Christianity still weighs heavy on the minds of African-Americans is indubitable.

In sum, the relevant studies, collectively, point to the fact that black mating patterns are a product of a complicated combination of historical, economic, cultural, and demographical factors. However, the specific historical evolution of black mating patterns, as discussed above, does not lend any support to the possibility of a polygynous future for the black community in the United States.

POLYGYNY AND THE CURRENT REALITY OF BLACKS IN THE UNITED STATES

Undoubtedly, there is no single, absolute, or ideal family type that is the most appropriate for any and all groups of people, regardless of the socioeconomic conditions under which they live. Familial life, as an aspect of culture, continues to be an expression of a people's struggle to adapt, survive, and flourish in their physical and social milieu. There is ample anthropological evidence to support this conclusion. With this being the case, what are the current socioeconomic conditions facing the black community in the United States that will dispose of the feasibility of expecting a polygynous marriage form to meet the familial needs of the black community for today and in the foreseeable future?

Currently, there is only one major factor that could lend support for polygyny as an alternative marriage and family form within the black community. This, quite obviously, is the very low male to female ratio. However, as important as this factor may seem to be in providing a raison d'être for polygyny in the black community, several other factors seem to invalidate any such possibility for polygyny to take hold. (It should be remembered that even in traditional Africa there were other variables involved in the maintenance of polygyny besides the low sex ratio.) Below is a discussion of some of these factors.

Marriage and Family Values

One very important factor is the attitudinal orientation of blacks in the United States, especially black women, with regard to marriage and the family. The major studies done in this area demonstrate, conclusively, that blacks, across class lines, consider the mainstream (monogamous) marriage model to be the most acceptable type of conjugal unit. Two decades ago, Liebow found this to be the case with low income blacks, despite the frequency of extramarital affairs.[57] Hannerz found the same thing.[58] Concerning male-female relationships he insightfully concluded that: "No ghetto-specific model for a male-female Union has anything close to the normative validity which the mainstream model enjoys in the ghetto as well as outside it, and this makes it hard for couples to find a state of the union which is as morally satisfying to them."[59]

More recently, Heiss[60] and Myers[61] subjected this question to empirical investigation, which included the use of probability samples of black and/or white women across class lines. In Heiss's study, titled "Women's Values Regarding Marriage and the Family," his hypothesis that the attitudinal differences between black and white women pertaining to marriage and the family would be insignificant was clearly supported by the data. Without denying the quite discernible differences in the familial patterns of behavior between blacks and whites in the United States, Heiss's study concluded that "It seems extremely likely that much of the racial variance in family behavior is a function of situational and resource differences rather than attitude differences."[62]

In Myers's study titled "On Marital Relations: Perceptions of Black Women," one of her major concerns was uncovering the reasons for marital conflict. While there were different subgroups within her two randomly selected samples of black women in Michigan and Mississippi, what emerged, overall, as the single most consistent source of marital conflict was "suspicion of husband infidelity."[63] With some exception, it even proved more significant than other factors such as occupation and financial matters, disciplining children, and infrequency of sexual activity. These results too, strongly support the notion that black women consider the traditional Judeo-Christian monogamous unit the most satisfying form of conjugality. And if there are any lessons to be learned from the history of polygyny in traditional Africa, one would have to be the necessity of female compliance with an institution that so intimately affects their lives.

Economic Condition of Black Men

A second facto that is definitely an obstruction to the development of polygyny in the black community is the economically marginal status of black men. According to recent U.S. Bureau of Labor Statistics, black men have the highest unemployment rate in the United States; they have even surpassed the rate for black women for the first time in the 1980s. With an unemployment rate of 2½ times greater than that of their white counterparts, the official black male unemployment rate is 15.3 percent, as compared to 6.1 percent for white males.[64] This problem is especially acute for those young black males between the ages of 20 and 24, in which case the unemployment rate is 23.6 percent, and between the ages of 16 and 19, in which case the unemployment rate is an astonishing 41.0 percent.[65] (It is important to realize that many of these unemployed black males are already biological fathers.) For white males in the same two age categories, the much lower percentages are 9.7 and 16.6, respectively. Furthermore, whereas the 1985 median income for white men was $21,684.00, it was only $15,808.00 for black men.[66]

These figures strongly suggest that, collectively, the minority of black men of marriageable age are not in a stable position to make significant contributions to the economic sustenance of monogamous units and their children, not to mention polygynous units and their children. This, then, is another major impediment to the proposition of a viable polygynous alternative for the black community. After all, it has been empirically demonstrated that a significant amelioration of the economic misery of black men would significantly increase their numerical availability, [67] thus obviating the "need" for the polygynous alternative and eliminating the basis from which the advocates of polygyny argue.

Health Risks

A third impeding factor, which is only recently gaining serious, and well deserved, attention, is the prevalence in the African-American community of the Acquired Immune Deficiency Syndrome, the sexually transmitted disease commonly known as AIDS. A recent federal report indicated that blacks, who constitute approximately 12 percent of the U.S. population, account for 25 percent of the known AIDS cases in the United States and are more likely than whites to get this deadly disease.[68] Worse still, 58 percent of the 350 AIDS cases in children under 15 are black. These children acquire the disease, primarily, from their mothers before or during birth. In response to this crisis, Dr. Wayne Greaves, one of two Howard University Hospital staff members working on AIDS research and treatment, has warned that "it is a problem that Black women need to pay attention to."[69] He cautions that black women "should ask serious and searching questions before becoming intimate and should definitely limit their number of sexual partners and avoid casual sex."[70] Dr. Beny Prim, the director of the Addiction Research and Treatment Corporation in Brooklyn, New York, has buttressed Dr. Greaves's caveat with his own sobering observation: "It's the most serious problem facing the Black community at this juncture."[71]

While the AIDS epidemic in the African-American community certainly does not rule out the possibility of polygynous relationships taking shape, who, given the above revelation, could pursue such an arrangement today with factoring in the tremendous health risks involved? This question is particularly relevant if the studies are true that report a propensity for some black men to measure their virility by tallying the number of women with whom they can become sexually involved. At least, if the polygyny experiment is to be practiced, it seems that it should not take the very loose form suggested by Chapman, who treats the peril of AIDS with an amazing degree of calm.[72]

Legal Obstacles

Finally, in the absence of any legal support for a polygynous alternative in the United States, the nonmarried female participant in such a union is extremely vulnerable to abuse, with little or no protection from the state.[73] Moreover, expecting any legal reform in favor of polygyny to occur within the United States is quite unrealistic. This is so because of the tenacity with which a monogamous morality is adhered to by practically all segments of the U.S. population. The Mormons are one of the very few exceptions.[74] Perhaps the cause of polygyny would be advanced, and even laws amended to accommodate it, if the observers of this phenomenon, such as Scott, would provide some empirical evidence to substantiate the claim that it "is indeed a growing family form in the U.S."[75]

CONCLUSION

The low male to female ratio in the African-American community is a grave problem. On this there is little disagreement. However, the results of this social inquiry into the socioeconomic and historical forces operating in the black community do not lend credence to the notion that to cope with this dilemma polygyny will be or should be a family type adopted and sanctioned by the black community in the United States. There are no empirical findings to account for the existence of polygyny. Additionally, it requires quite a stretch of the sociological imagination, and consequently distortion of facts, to subsume under the conceptual label of polygyny the many types of romantic and temporal affairs between black men and their multiple partners. Most women, if not the majority of men as well, still regard this as "cheating." And while it is conceivable that people's attitudes and values on this subject could change, as well as the concomitant set of laws, the more fundamental question to be raised is whether or not this change would be feasible. If the abnormally low ratio of males to females in the black community is, as convincingly argued by many, a result of socially structured penury, then would it not be more appropriate to work at trying to eliminate the adverse economic conditions that have been empirically identified as causes of the severe sex ratio imbalance in the first place? Otherwise, the apologists for polygyny may fall into the trap of appearing to be advocating an adaption to the socioeconomic iniquities plaguing blacks in American society.

Still, because the consequences of this dilemma are so onerous, something must be done before the monumental task of dismantling the structures of inequality is complete. Below are a few possible suggestions deserving further study:

(a) Black women could seriously consider black men from Africa, the Caribbean, and other parts of the African world (who reside, often temporarily, in the United States) as part of the pool of available and acceptable black men with whom they could share their lives. These men are often eager to establish such unions. Furthermore, such a development would contribute to meeting the need for greater cooperation between peoples of African descent throughout the world. Although a considerable amount of cultural sensitivity will be required, the resultant cultural synthesis could be well worth the effort.

(b) Black women could relocate to parts of the United States where the shortage of black men is not as great. Logistically, black men would probably find it much easier to relocate than black women (and their children), but the likelihood of them doing so to achieve a greater sex ratio balance is quite slim.

(c) Upwardly mobile black women could consider establishing bonds with responsible and caring black men whose socioeconomic status is lower than their own. Although in order for such unions to succeed the degree of "class suicide" required of the women would probably be substantial, these bonds would certainly engender less value conflict than would an attempt to practice a surreptitious form of man-sharing bound to produce a huge amount of cognitive dissonance for participating women. Confining the search for available and acceptable black males within a given socioeconomic circumscription may serve only to exacerbate the problem of too few black males.

(d) In order to abate the harmful impact this problem is having on black youth, especially young black males, more responsible black men could take the initiative to serve, as some have done already, as positive role models or surrogate fathers for the myriads of fatherless black children. This arrangement could take place in the context of extended family formations or Big Brother type programs designed specifically for this purpose. In addition to filling a serious void in the life-cycle of so many black children, this effort could concurrently reduce the burden and concomitant stress level of thousands of black women, thus enhancing their ability to care for their children.

NOTES

1. Audrey Chapman, *Man Sharing, Dilemma or Choice: A Radical New Way of Relating to the Men in Your Life* (New York: William Morrow, 1986), p. 17.

2. Ibid., pp. 56–73, 128–143.

3. Jacquelyne Jackson, "But Where Are the Men?," *Black Scholar,* Vol. 4 (December 1971), p. 38.

4. Ibid., p. 38.

5. Joseph W. Scott, "Polygamy: A Futuristic Family Arrangement for African-Americans," *Black Books Bulletin,* Vol. 4, no. 2 (Summer 1976), p. 14.

6. Joseph W. Scott, "Black Polygamous Family Formation: Case Studies of Legal Wives and Consensual 'Wives,'" *Alternative Lifestyles,* Vol. 3, no. 1 (February 1980), pp. 41–64.

7. Joseph W. Scott, "From Teenage Parenthood to Polygamy: Case Studies in Black Polygamous Family Formation," *Western Journal of Black Studies,* Vol. 10, no. 4 Winter 1986), p. 172-179.

8. U.S. National Center for Health Statistics, *Vital Statistics of the U.S.,* annual, 1983.

9. Lawrence E. Gary, "Health Status," in L. Gary, ed., *Black Men* (Beverly Hills: Sage, 1981), p. 47-71.

10. U.S. National Center for Health Statistics, *Vital Statistics of the U.S.*, annual, 1986.

11. Robert Townsy, "The Incarceration of Black Men," in Gary (1981), p. 229-230.

12. U.S. Bureau of Justice Statistics, *Jail Inmates,* 1983.

13. U.S Bureau of Justice Statistics, *Capital Punishment,* annual, 1985.

14. Scott and Stewart have shown that this difficulty and frustration experienced by black males explains not only their disproportionate inclusion into the military, but also their general elimination from the U.S. population. See Joseph W. Scott and James B. Stewart, "The Institutional Decimation of Black American Males," *Western Journal of Black Studies,* Vol. 2 (1978), pp. 82-93.

15. U.S. Department of Defense, Office of the Deputy Assistant Secretary of Defense (Military Manpower and Personnel Policy), 1985.

16. U.S. Burau of the Census, *Census of Population,* Vol. 2 (PC80-2-4D), 1980.

17. Robert Staples, "Masculinity and Race: The Dual Dilemma of Black Men," *Journal of Social Issues,* Vol. 34, no. 1 (1978), pp. 169-183.

18. Niara Sudarkasa, "African and Afro-American Family Structure: A Comparison," *Black Scholar* (November/December 1980), pp. 37-60.

19. Eugene Hillman, *Polygamy Reconsidered: African Plural Marriage and the Christian Churches* (Maryknoll, NY: Orbis Books, 1975), 87-107, See also Vernon R. Dorjahn, "The Factor of Polygyny in African Demography," in W. Bascom and M. Herskovits, eds., *Continuity and Change in African Cultures* (Chicago, IL: University of Chicago, 1959), pp. 95-96, 105-109.

20. Sudarkasa (1980), p. 46.

21. Ibid. See also William Bascom, *The Yoruba of Southwestern Nigeria* (New York: Holt, Rinehart, and Winston, 1969), p. 64-65.

22. Sudarkasa (1980), p. 46.

23. For instance, the practice of arranged marriages and the patrilocality of the conjugal units are two other factors that characterized mating patterns throughout much of traditional Africa. However, they were not discussed in the interest of brevity because of the paucity of space. For further information on these and other related issues see Paul Bohannan and Philip Curtin, *Africa and Africans*, Rev. Ed., (New York: Natural History Press, 1971), pp. 101-118, and Colin M. Turnbull, *Man in Africa* (New York: Doubleday, 1977), pp. 37-41.

24. John W. Blassingame, *The Slave Community: Plantation Life in the Antebellum South,* Rev. and enlarged Ed. (New York: Oxford, 1979), p. 158.

25. Ibid., p. 157.

26. Eugene D. Genovese, *In Red and Black: Marxian Explorations in Southern and Afro-American History* (New York: Vintage, 1971), p. 87.

27. Herbert G. Gutman, *The Black Family in Slavery and Freedom 1750-1925* (New York: Vintage 1976), p. 75. See also Eugene D. Genovese, *Roll, Jordan, Roll: The World The Slaves Made* (New York: Panthenon, 1974), p. 464-466.

28. Gutman, (1976) p. 60,63.

29. Ibid., p. 75-76.

30. Blassingame (1979), p. 162-170; Gutman (1976), pp. 70-71.

31. Blassingame (1979) p. 170.

32. Gutman (1976), p. 70.

33. Blassingame (1979), pp. 149-150. See also Genovese (1971), p. 87.

34. August Meier and Elliot Rudwick, *From Plantation to the Ghetto* (New York: Hill and Wange, 1970), pp. 177-212; Harold M. Baron, "The Demand for Black Labor:

Historical Notes on the Political-Economy of Racism,'' *Radical America* , vol. 5 (March-April, 1971), pp. 1-46; Philip S. Foner, *Organized Labor and the Black Worker 1619-1973* (New York: Praeger 1974), pp. 120-128; James A. Geschwender, *Racial Stratification in America* (Dubuque, IO: William C. Brown, 1978), p. 153-171.

35. E. Franklin Frazier, *The Negro Family in the United States,* (Chicago: University of Chicago Press, 1966), pp. 89-101.

36. Ibid., p. 98.

37. Charles S. Johnson, *Shadow of the Plantation* (Chicago: University of Chicago Press, 1934), p. 49; Frazier (1966) pp. 93-95.

38. Johnson (1934), p. 66-67; Frazier (1966), pp. 94-95.

39. Jacqueline Jones, *Labor of Love, Labor of Sorrow: Black Women, Work, and the Family from Slavery to the Present* (New York: Basic Books, 1985), p. 92.

40. Johnson, (1934), p. 66. See also Hortense Powdermaker, *After Freedom: A Cultural Study of the Deep South* (New York: Antheneum, 1969), p. 153; Gutman (1976), p. 144.

41. Powdermaker (1969), p. 150.

42. Ibid., pp. 143-174.

43. St. Clair Drake and Horace R. Cayton, *Black Metropolis, Vol. II: A Study of Negro Life in a Negro City* (New York: Harcourt, Brace and World, 1962), p. 582.

44. Ulf Hannerz, *Soulside: Inquiries into Ghetto Cultures and Community* (New York: Columbia University Press, 1969), p. 75. See also Carol B. Stack, *All Our Kin: Strategies for Survival in a Black Community* (New York: Harper, 1974), p. 113.

45. Stack (1974), p. 112.

46. Ibid., pp. 113-115.

47. Oliver C. Cox, ''Sex Ratio and Marital Status Among Negroes,'' *American Sociological Review,* Vol. 5 (1940), pp. 937-947.

48. Robert Staples, ''The Black Dating Game,'' in R. Staples, ed., *The Black Family: Essays and Studies* (Belmont, CA: Wadsworth, 1978), pp. 65-66. See also by Staples, *Black Masculinity: The Black Male Role in American Society* San Francisco CA: Black Scholar Press, 1982), p. 103.

49. Kenneth B. Clark, *Dark Ghetto: Dilemmas of Social Power* (New York: Harper and Row, 1965), p. 71.

50. See ''Children Having Children: Teen Pregnancies are Corroding America's Social Fabric,'' *Time,* (December 9, 1985), p. 78-90; ''What Must Be Done About Children Having Children,'' *Ebony,* March 1985, pp. 76-84; ''The Black Family in Crisis: Teenage Pregnancy,'' *Essence,* April 1984), pp. 94-96, 144, 147.

51. See ''Children Having Children, p. 79.

52. Clark (1965), p. 71.

53. Staples, p. 103.

54. See Clyde W. Franklin II, ''Black Male-Black Female Conflict: Individually Caused and Culturally Nurtured,'' *Journal of Black Studies,* Vol. 15, no. 2 (December 1984), pp. 139-154; Ronald L. Braithwaite, ''Interpersonal Relations Between Black Males and Black Females,'' in Gary (1981), pp. 83-97; Molefi K. Asante, ''Black Male and Female Relations: An Afro-Centric Context,'' in Gary (1981), pp. 75-82; Delores P. Aldridge, ''Toward and Understanding of Black Male/Female Relationships,'' *Western Journal of Black Studies,* Vol. 8, no. 4, (Winter 1984), pp. 184-191.

55. Asante (1981), pp. 76-77.

56. Ibid., p. 76.

57. Elliott Liebow, *Tally's Corner: A Study of Negro Streetcorner Men* (Boston: Little, Brown and Co., 1967), pp. 103-136.

58. Hannerz (1969), pp. 70-104.

59. Ibid., p. 102.

60. Jerold Heiss, "Women's Values Regarding Marriage and the Family," in H. McAdoo, ed., *Black Families,* (Beverly Hills: Sage, 1981), pp. 186-198.

61. Lena Wright Myers, "On Marital Relations: Perceptions of Black Women," in L.F. Rodgers-Rose, ed., *The Black Woman* (Beverly Hills: Sage, 1980), pp. 161-172.

62. Heiss (1981), p. 197.

63. Myers (1980), p. 169.

64. U.S. Bureau of Labor Statistics, *Employment and Earnings,* monthly, 1985.

65. Ibid., p. 66.

66. Ibid., p. 66.

67. Scott and Stewart (1978), pp. 82-93.

68. Dorothy Gilliam, "Blacks and AIDS," *Washington Post,* November 3, 1986, p. D3; Don Colburn, "AIDS, the Growing Impact," *Health, Science and Society: A Weekly Journal of Medicine,* June 2, 1987, *Washington Post, p.* 12.

69. Gilliam (1986), p. D3.

70. Ibid., p. D3.

71. Ibid., p. D3.

72. Chapman (1986), pp. 148-149.

73. Susan J. MaCovsky, "Coping with Cohabitation," in R. Walsh and O. Pocs, eds., *Annual Editions: Marriage and Family 82/83,* (Guilford, CT: Dushkin, 1982), pp. 219-221; and Bernard Farber, *Family and Kinship in Modern Society* (Glenview, IL: Scott, Foresman and Company, 1973), pp. 83-113.

74. Gary L. Bunker and Davis Bitton, *The Mormans Graphic Image 1834-1914,* (Salt Lake City: University of Utah, 1983).

75. Scott (1986), p. 172.

Part IV

Health Outcomes and Economic Resources

INTRODUCTION

Comprehensive efforts are needed in examinations of how the functioning of black families is affected by (a) differential exposure to high risk health factors, (b) constraints on efforts to ameliorate the consequences of adverse health status, and (c) the interaction between attempts to mitigate economic subordination and health outcomes. Detailed research on these topics is especially critical, however, given the ecological constraint of black families' declining access to medical care, as documented in Rice's chapter (Part 2).

Myers's analysis examines the interrelationship of physiological and psychosocial risk factors and the prevalence of hypertension among black female college students and their parents. She finds, in part, that measures of socioeconomic status such as parents' education, annual income, and occupational status are highly correlated among hypertensive urban parents. This finding supports the need to utilize an ecological model in examining patterns of morbidity and mortality among black families.

The focus on stresses resulting from the interaction of black families with other societal subsystems is extended in Johnson's investigation. She uses a "Work-Family Tension Model" to analyze the interrelationship of job stressors, job strain, and marital strain among black police officers. Johnson finds that perceived job stressors such as differential treatment based on race are associated with job strain. In addition, job stressors and job strain influenced the level of marital interaction and the potential for separation and divorce.

The study by Stewart and Benjamin examines related issues and further supports an ecological approach to the study of black families. They utilize the construct of "self-efficacy" to analyze relationships between black and white women's values and beliefs and welfare recipiency and work attachment. The investigation compares the relative explanatory power of individual and structural explanations of welfare dependency. A direct connection to the other chapters results from a secondary focus on the linkage between self-reported illness and welfare dependency. Measures of values and beliefs were found to have little explanatory power in predicting receipt of public assistance. No linkage was found between receipt of public assistance and reporting of illnesses, but a linkage between sense of self-efficacy and reporting of illnesses was confirmed.

Collectively, these analyses bridge the gap between purely ecological and purely internal analyses of black families. Bridging this gap extends the Du Bois-Frazier tradition in ways that complement more contemporary approaches to the study of black families.

10

HYPERTENSION AS A MANIFESTATION OF THE STRESS EXPERIENCED BY BLACK FAMILIES

Barbee C. Myers

The interrelationship of physiological and psychosocial risk factors for hypertension among black female college students and their parents is examined. Among the students, measures of adiposity were most significantly related to blood pressure. A familial relationship between hypertensive parents and daughters was also observed. Measures of socioeconomic status such as parents' education, annual income, and occupational status were correlated among hypertensive urban parents. The implications these findings have for future risk of developing hypertension among students, as well as the psychosocial family dynamics of hypertensive parents, are discussed. Indications for future research are proposed.

Cerebrovascular disease (stroke) is the third leading cause of death in the United States among black Americans. Mortality rates are more than twice as high among blacks as whites. In 1981, age-adjusted mortality rates for stroke among individuals aged 35–74 years were 129 per 100,000 for black men, 50 for white men, 96 for black women, and 39 for white women.[1] It is known that the principal cause of stroke is hypertension (high blood pressure); therefore, this large racial differential in stroke mortality can be partially explained by the higher blood pressure levels among black Americans.[2] However, due to the lack of prospective or even retrospective studies among black populations, researchers are limited in making quantitative statements with respect to additional causes of the high racial differential in cerebrovascular mortality rates among black persons. Consequently, researchers have focused primarily on discerning the causes of the racial differential in hypertension among both black men and women when compared to their white counterparts.

Traditionally, biological risk factors, such as genetic predisposition and obesity, were examined to explain the greater prevalence of hypertension among blacks. Nonetheless, the basic physiology of blood pressure regulation is not fully understood and the resultant effect is that progress has been slow in terms of the development of comprehensive models to explain the racial and gender differences in susceptibility to hypertension.

In a review of large population and epidemiologic studies, Marmot and Winkelstein revealed that not all the traditional biological risk factors are valid predictors of cerebrovascular disease in every cultural setting.[3] Hence, one is led to conclude that despite the fact that much is known about the pathogenesis of cerebrovascular disease, much also remains unknown. Consequently, new factors should be sought to resolve some of the controversy relative to the racial difference in hypertension among blacks and whites. An exploration of psychosocial variables by numerous researchers revealed that the high rate of hypertension among blacks is thought to be the result of constant exposure to unavoidable behavioral stressors that severely tax the coping resources of persons of lower socioeconomic status.[4]

In this chapter, an attempt is made to provide as much factual material as possible in terms of the relationship between blood pressure and psychosocial variables previously implicated in initiating and/or sustaining hypertension among black Americans. Research findings related to the black family will be discussed, and when appropriate, mechanisms of action will be proposed. Suggestions for future research will also be offered. Because of the paucity of information regarding the causality of hypertension due to psychosocial factors, these research findings should be viewed as tentative hypotheses rather than firm conclusions. Nonetheless, the importance of such issues to the well-being of black Americans certainly warrants investigating major questions about the susceptibility to hypertension in black populations.

FAMILY ENVIRONMENT AND BLOOD PRESSURE IN BLACK FEMALE COLLEGE STUDENTS

In a research project conducted at Pennsylvania State University, 86 black female students were screened on the basis of cardiovascular risk factors. The twofold purposes of the project were to (a) assess the bivariate relationship between blood pressure and cardiovascular risk factors among college students and (b) assess the relationship between hypertension and socioeconomic status among parents of the black female college students. Students were selected from the University Park campus because Penn State is a predominantly white university with less than 5 percent black students.

The cardiovascular risk factor status of the students was assessed by measurement of physiological variables including age, body weight, and obesity. Psychosocial risk factors included measurement of anger frequency and measurement of the coronary prone behavior pattern. This coronary prone behavior pattern is also known as the Type A personality and is determined by the Jenkins Activity Survey (JAS). The questionnaire used is an adaptation of the JAS and is classified as Form C. The Educational and Counseling Psychology Department of the University of Tennessee, Knoxville, has documented the validity of the Jenkins Form C.[5]

The relationship between hypertension and socioeconomic status among parents of the black female college students was assessed by a questionnaire administered to the students. The students were asked to report on their parents' educational level, income, cigarette smoking status, hypertension history, and occupational status. Demographic characteristics of the families were explored to possibly further our understanding of the relationship between risk of hypertension and the impact of environmental surroundings for both the students and their parents. The current cardiovascular risk factor status of black female students matriculating at a predominantly white institution is discussed. Finally, hypotheses are proposed relative to the causality of the high prevalence of hypertension, in terms of environmental factors, among the black parents.

RESULTS

General Descriptive Statistics

Table 10.1 presents mean scores for continuous physiological and psychosocial variables among black female participants and their parents. The mean age of the students was 20 years, which corresponds with sophomore status at the university. The average blood pressure level of the participants was 110/74 mm Hg (normal blood pressure = 120/80 mm Hg). This reading is comparable to national values for resting blood pressures of black women in this age group. Two participants had high blood pressure, and two subjects were borderline hypertensive. It should

TABLE 10.1
Mean Scores for Continuous Physiological and Psychosocial Variables among Black Female Students and Parents

Variable	Statistic
Age (Years)	Mean = 20.0
	SD = 2.4
Systolic Blood Pressure	Mean = 110.0
	SD = 11.3
Diastolic Blood Pressure	Mean = 74.0
	SD = 7.7
Weight (pounds)	Mean = 140.0
	SD = 21.5
Height (inches)	Mean = 64.8
	SD = 2.4
Body Mass Index^2	Mean = 23.5
	SD = 3.1
Triceps + Subscapular SKF**	Mean = 35.0
	SD = 12.8
Jenkins Activity Survey	Mean = 48.0
	SD = 23.7
Weekly Anger Frequency	Mean = 3.7
	SD = 7.0
Father's Education (years)	Mean = 13.6
	SD = 2.6
Mother's Education (years)	Mean = 13.7
	SD = 3.1

**SKF = skinfolds.

be noted that though the mean blood pressure level was normal, black females have higher resting blood pressures than white females of similar ages.

The average weight of the participants was 140 pounds, and the average height was 64.8 inches. The black females weighted an average of 10 pounds more than the white females even though both groups were the same height. The measure of obesity used was the Durnin and Womersley equation for determination of body fat based on the sum of skinfold readings taken in the upper body regions. Based on this equation, 39 percent of the black females were obese. Surprisingly, when the students were asked how they perceived their present body weight, 62 percent felt they were "too heavy" or "much too heavy." Fifty-two percent were actually defined within the normal range of body fat, but only 31 percent felt they were "about right."

Only 16 percent of the black female students were current cigarette smokers. Of these smokers, the average number of cigarettes smoked per day was less than one-half a pack. Conversely, a much higher percentage were current users of the birth control pill (43 percent). Most of them started using the pill approximately at the time they entered college. Relative to weight gain, the average amount of weight gained since entering college at age 18 years was 10 pounds. This weight gain could be partially explained by the concurrent initiation of oral contraceptive use.

The coronary-prone behavior pattern or Type A lifestyle was measured by the JAS behavior rating scale. This behavior pattern is described as a hard-driving, aggressive, competitive, rushed style of life in which the person tends to suppress fatigue and is related to an increased risk of coronary heart disease. The Type B lifestyle is described as an easygoing, nonaggressive style of life in which the person is not pressured by a sense of time urgency. Type B persons tend to have a much lower risk of developing cardiovascular disease. The average JAS behavior rating score was 48 percent for black female subjects. This value was consistent with the previous, although scarce, research conducted with black women within this age group. White females scored higher and were more likely to have the Type A personality than black females. Only 19 percent of the black women were classified as Type A and 23 percent as Type B.

When the study participants were asked how many extremely angry or annoyed episodes they had experienced during the previous seven days, the average number per week was 3.7 times, and this was rated by them to be typical of an average week in terms of anger frequency.

With respect to the parents of the black female students, 93 percent were from large urban cities such as Philadelphia, Pittsburgh, and New York City. The average age of the black fathers was 48 years, and the black mothers were 45 years old. Twenty-eight percent of the students were from a single-parent home, and the average number of children for all families was 3.7 per family.

An equal percentage of fathers and mothers (34 percent) were hypertensive or had a history of hypertension. Four parents had died prematurely from a stroke or heart attack. Two black mothers had died at ages 35 and 36 and two black fathers at ages 40 to 48 years.

In terms of the educational level of parents, the mean number of years of education was similar for mothers and fathers (13.6 years). There was more variability within the educational level of the black mothers than black fathers. Ten percent of the mothers versus 6 percent of fathers had not completed high school. Within the families, every father who had not completed high school married someone who also had not done so. The mean number of years of education for parents not completing high school was 8.6 years for mothers and fathers. Of the approximately 50 percent who had more than a high school education, similar numbers had completed the equivalent of four years of college (38 percent of mothers and 37 percent of fathers). Finally, 11 percent of mothers had attained more than 16 years of education compared to 13 percent of fathers. Even though more fathers had some graduate education, the eight families with 16 or more years of education displayed interesting patterns. Of those eight families, the mothers had an average of 19.5 years of education and the fathers had an average of 16.3 years.

With respect to occupational status of parents, three categories were included.[6] "Blue collar" workers included those engaged in service occupations, fabricators, laborers, and operators. "White collar" workers included those engaged in technical, sales, administrative support, managerial, and professional occupations. The third category included homemakers, unemployed persons, and retired persons. Fifty-nine percent of fathers and 27 percent of mothers were blue collar workers. Thirty-one percent of fathers and 58 percent of mothers were white collar workers. Ten percent of fathers were retired or unemployed, and 15 percent of mothers were homemakers, retired, or unemployed.

The mean student-reported annual income for black families was $20–25,000 per year. Nearly one-fourth of the families were within this income category. Since 31 percent of black families had incomes less than $20,000 per year, a combined total of 56 percent of the families had incomes less than $25,000. Another 20 percent had incomes within the $45–55,000 range. Only two families had incomes in excess of $55,000 per year.

Pearson Correlation Coefficients

Table 10.2 presents Pearson Product Moment correlation coefficients for the bivariate association between blood pressure and physiological and environmental factors among the students and their parents. Among black female students, adiposity (as assessed by the sum of skinfolds) had the highest direct correlation to resting systolic blood pressure. (.36). Body weight followed second (.35), and body mass index (weight/height^2) was third (.30). None of the remaining variables had a significant association with systolic blood pressure among the subjects. Body weight had the strongest direct correlation to resting diastolic blood pressure (.34) and was followed by adiposity (.31) and height (.31). Body mass

TABLE 10.2
Pearson Correlation Coefficients for the Bivariate Association between Blood Pressure and Physiological and Environmental Factors among Black Female Students and Their Parents

Variable	Correlation Coefficient	
	Systolic BP	Diastolic BP
Age	.12	.01
Height (inches)	.16	.31**
Weight (pounds)	.35***	.34***
Body Mass Index^2	.30**	.19*
Triceps + Subscapular SKF	.36***	.31**
Present Cigarette Smoker	−.15	−.07
Oral Contraceptive User	−.06	−.19
JAS Behavior Rating Score	.12	.15
Weekly Anger Frequency	−.08	−.04
Father's Hypertension History	.15	.18*
Mother's Hypertension History	.12	.18*
Father's Edcation	−.13	−.13
Mother's Education	−.02	−.14
Father Smokes Cigarettes	−.00	−.01
Mother Smokes Cigarettes	−.04	−.02
Annual Family Income	−.11	−.11

*denotes $p < .05$.
**denotes $p < .01$.
***denotes $p < .001$.

index was also directly correlated with diastolic pressure (.19) but the strength of the association was weaker and less significant. None of the remaining variables had a significant correlation with diastolic pressure.

Seven familial influence variables were included in bivariate analyses of the blood pressure levels of the students. When fathers' and mothers' educational level, parents' history of hypertension, parents' cigarette smoking status, and annual family income were correlated with systolic and diastolic blood pressure, only having a hypertensive father or mother was directly associated with diastolic blood pressure of the daughter (.18).

Table 10.3 shows an intercorrelation coefficient matrix of environmental influence variables among parents of black female students. The variables included were parents' education, parents' history of hypertension, parents' cigarette smoking status, and annual family income. The strongest direct correlation was between father's and mother's educational level (.63). The second strongest direct correlation was between mother's educational level and annual family income (.43). Next was father's educational level and annual family income (.33). Father's educational level and father's hypertensive status were also directly correlated (.28).

TABLE 10.3
Intercorrelation Coefficient Matrix of Environmental Influence Variables among Parents of Black Female Students

Variables	Father Educ.	Mother Educ.	Father HTN#	Mother HTN#	Father smokes	Mother smokes	Annual Income
Father's Education	—	.63***	.28*	−.07	−.14	−.05	.33**
Mother's Education		—	.03	.11	−.24*	.08	.43***
Father Is Hypertensive*			—	−.09	−.04	.15	.09
Mother Is Hypertensive*				—	−.14	−.18	−.12
Father Smokes Cigarettes					—	.04	−.02
Mother Smokes Cigarettes						—	−.15
Annual Income							—

*denotes p<.05
**denotes p<.01
***denotes p<.001

Finally, mother's educational level was indirectly associated with the father being a cigarette smoker (-.24). None of the other variables had significant intercorrelation coefficients.

DISCUSSION AND SUMMARY

Current Risk Factor Status of Black Female Students

Numerous research studies support the strong relationship between blood pressure and body mass index found in this study. deCastro, Biesbroeck, Erikson, Farrell, Leong, Murphy, and Green studied hypertension in adolescents attending an inner city high school.[7] They found race, obesity, and muscle mass to be significantly correlated with hypertension. Goldring and associates studied blood pressure in a high school population and found body weight to be significantly related to blood pressure in females.[8] Harlan, Hall, Schmouder, and others computed blood pressure correlates with the data from the National Health Survey of 1971–1975. They found body mass index to be most significantly related to blood pressure among all racial groups.[9]

Data from the National Health and Nutrition Examination Survey (NHANES) of 1972–1975 revealed current users of oral contraceptives to have higher blood pressure levels.[10] The findings of this study are in direct contrast to the NHANES. Oral contraceptive use had no relationship to blood pressure level among black female college students in this study. These results are supported by two other studies involving black females.[11] Blumenstein and associates offer several suggestions to explain the results of these studies.[12] The reasons include possible differences in the characteristics of the study group, the composition of the oral contraceptive agents, the time of observation in each study, and most important, the mechanisms of blood pressure elevation in black women. According to Wilder the "law of initial values" may suggest that a higher baseline level of blood pressure in black females could mask the ability to detect other influences, such as those that could be imposed by oral contraceptives.[13] Friedman's prevalence data suggesting that no significant relationship may exist between oral contraceptive therapy and diastolic blood pressure in black females aged 25–35 years appears to be the only data lending support to the findings of those two studies and the current one.[14]

Since so few black students were smokers and of the smokers the number of cigarettes smoked was so few, the researcher expected to find no relationship between smoking and blood pressure. Similarly, since the mean JAS behavior rating score was below the fiftieth percentile, the researcher did not expect to find a significant relationship between Type A behavior rating and blood pressure.

Finally, of the behavioral and familial influence variables included, only having a hypertensive parent was directly associated with the diastolic level of the daughter (.18). Although the parents' educational level had fairly strong inverse correlations, the relationship was not significant.

Three important conclusions should be noted from these findings. First, the risk of developing cardiovascular disease for these black female students is greater than for white female students matriculating at Penn State University. The high prevalence of obesity among the participants presents a source of potential concern if the problem is not controlled. Second, among black women in this age category physiological measures have a stronger association with blood pressure than behavioral or familial environmental variables. The strong and significant association between parents' history of hypertension and the current blood pressure level of the students should not be ignored. Finally, further research studies, including a cross-validation of this study, need to be conducted to determine whether these trends are specific only to this population or if they are generalizable to other black females 18–24 years of age.

ENVIRONMENTAL CORRELATES OF HYPERTENSION AMONG BLACK PARENTS

Despite the relatively young age of the parents, 34 percent of them had hypertension and 5 percent died at very young ages from stroke or heart attack. The research hypothesis proposed to explain the high prevalence of hypertension is that social status and related sociocultural influences contribute to the observed pattern of elevated blood pressure and increased incidence of stroke in black populations. Low or high socioeconomic status may be related to hypertension risk due to an association with adverse risk factor distributions. The principal assumption is that a number of personal and societal variables unite to deter the progress of many employed blacks striving to attain some measure of security and upward mobility in their jobs.

The results of this study support the research hypothesis. Even with both parents working in most households, a large percentage of black families had incomes far below those of comparable white families (median income = $20–25,000 versus $40,000 per year, respectively). This is true in spite of the fact that black and white parents had an equal amount of education (13.6 years) and similar numbers of children (3.7). Though half the black parents had more than a high school education, interesting dynamics occurred within the families when mothers were compared to fathers. For instance, in the eight families where both parents had 16 or more years of education, the mothers had an average of three more years of education than did the fathers. Similarly, when the occupational status of the parents was assessed, 59 percent of the fathers were blue collar workers and only 27 percent of the mothers were categorized as thus. This suggests that even though mothers and fathers had similar levels of education, women more frequently had jobs reflective of their level of education.

An important observation is related to the struggle between black men and women within the household. Regardless of the fact that both parents were well educated in most instances, the black mother was generally better educated than the father. Since the mother's educational level had a stronger association with the annual family income than did the father's educational level, it appears that the mothers did in fact have jobs reflective of their level of education more frequently than did the fathers. It is possible that the higher educational level of the mothers in eight of the families and the higher income earned by mothers in most families could create stress within the household. This increased stress within the home could eventually affect the blood pressure levels of both parents.

In terms of explaining the significance of the association between father's educational level and his being hypertensive, a few observations seem relevant. Apparently the stress associated with a higher occupational status affects the risk of hypertension among black men. Not only is the black father exposed to stressors on the job, but having to cope with the additional pressure of the potentially higher income of the black mother could prove to be instrumental in causing hypertension. Furthermore, the family incomes are significantly lower than for white parents not living in the inner cities with a similar educational level. The implication is that urban blacks are underpaid for white collar jobs regardless of their high educational level. This may be part of the mechanism whereby hypertension is initiated at relatively early ages among well-educated black parents residing in urban communities. Apparently, even with both parents working in white collar jobs and having high levels of education, subsistence within the urban environment is stressful to the extent of causing hypertension in blacks at relatively young ages. And, rather than the association between hypertensive parents and higher blood pressure levels among daughters being mediated through genetic factors, the author contends that these environmental factors are more significant. This contention is based on the fact that the students resided in a stressful environment while at home with their parents in the inner city and moved to another stressful environment by choosing to matriculate at a predominantly white university.

Several investigators have researched the role of environmental stressors and increased risk of hypertension.[15] These researchers contend that inhabitants of inner-city areas are constantly exposed to an environment that is sharply different from suburban and rural areas. When factors such as education, recreation, and sanitary and service facilities are considered, suburban areas manifest performance rates that far exceed those characterized by urban areas. In addition to these factors, inhabitants of inner cities repeatedly exhibit higher divorce rates, crime rates, homicide rates, unemployment rates, and greater population density than do suburban and rural areas.

As a result of the adverse environmental characteristics of urban areas, Harburg and associates investigated the impact of living in high-stress areas versus low-stress areas of Detroit, Michigan.[16] They demonstrated that the average blood pressure levels were actually higher among both black men and women residing in high-stress areas of Detroit compared to those residing in low-stress areas. These high-stress areas exhibited higher crime and unemployment rates, and crowded living conditions were chronic features of the environment.

Studies of adolescents have also shown that black youths who reside in lower socioeconomic inner-city areas tend to have higher blood pressure levels when compared to those living in more affluent, economically stable environments.[17] Among these, Kotchen et al. reported that blood pressure levels were higher for both black male and female high school seniors from the inner-city area compared to black youths residing in suburban areas.[18] Hence, by late adolescence, racial and gender differences are apparent among blacks living in varying degrees of stressful areas.

Since hypertension among blacks appears to be more common in an urban environment, regardless of age, environmental factors may truly exert a stronger impact on initiating and sustaining hypertension among blacks than do genetic influences. A common denominator of hypertension and social class, income, housing, education, and occupation seems to be the occurrence of situations requiring frequent or continuous behavior adjustment. Joblessness, low income, lack of education, and crime seem to be important precursors of hypertension that are more prevalent in an urban environment. Most researchers contend that there are also more life-threatening events, anxiety, and competition in an urban environment than a rural one; thus hypertension would occur in such an environment more frequently, even among the well educated. If these are indeed the variables responsible for causing hypertension, then one would not only expect hypertension to be more prevalent in an urban environment, but that environmental factors would prove to be more influential in causing high blood pressure than would genetic predisposition.

Ostfeld and Shekelle contend that the psychological appraisal of threat from a stimulus coupled with the person's perceived ability to deal with the threat were probable chronic mediators of blood pressure levels.[19] The researchers provided a four-point framework representing characteristics of routine life situations deemed to be related to pressor responses. These are: (a) the outcome of the event is uncertain; (b) the possibility of bodily or psychological harm exists; (c) although running away or physical resistance may be considered and/or desired, neither would be allowed as appropriate responses; (d) the participant involved constantly feels compelled to maintain a vigilant mental attitude until resolution of the adverse situation is achieved. Objectively stated, their theoretical proposition is that a sustained pressor response occurs when the behavioral stressor appears to be uncontrollable yet neither fight nor flight are viable options. Inhabitants of inner cities are more frequently exposed to such situations and are more often found to be hypertensive than suburban or rural inhabitants.

INDICATIONS FOR FUTURE RESEARCH

Based on the information presented above, there are six major areas of concern for future research. In black populations, research findings support an inverse relationship between low socioeconomic status and hypertension risk. Nonetheless, additional research is needed with respect to black middle and upper class employed men and women.

A second major shortcoming of previous cross-sectional epidemiologic studies is that they state little more than the existence of an inverse association between environmental stressors and risk of hypertension. There is evidently a need to establish how, or if, psychosocial factors contribute to this inverse association.

Third, it is not clear why some persons chronically exposed to a low socioeconomic status environment develop hypertension when others do not. Adequate coping techniques have been implicated in this phenomenon. Harburg and associates examined the role that anger-coping styles may play in the relationship between extensive exposure to environmental stressors and hypertension risk in black men.[20] The researchers hypothesized that suppressed hostility may be implicated in the higher incidence of hypertension among blacks. *Suppressed hostility* refers to a process of coping by inhibiting negative attitudes in situations where the person is the target of appraised noxious stimuli from some source of power. In objective terms, suppressing hostility to noxious stimuli involves avoidance of displaying hostile feelings to the unjustified attack and feeling that the display of hostile feelings should arouse guilt. They found evidence that a tendency to suppress angry feelings or, alternatively, to vent such feelings without much reflection were associated with higher blood pressures. This suppressed hostility pattern (anger-in) was found to be associated with elevated diastolic blood pressure for all men. The anger-in coping style was related to both higher blood pressure levels and the number of actual hypertensives in all groups except black low-stress men.

In a subsequent report, Harburg, Blakelock, and Roeper reported that styles of coping with anger provocation according to social class and other such differences are related to blood pressure levels.[21] "Reflective coping" (a response pattern involving appropriate appraisal, constructive behavioral response, and vascular and neural deceleration) was contrasted with the anger-in-and anger-out coping styles (collectively termed *resentful coping*). The anger-out pattern was more typical among working class persons than among middle class persons, whereas anger-in did not vary across groups. The "reflective coping" style, which was consistently but moderately associated with lower blood pressure levels, was more prevalent among women.

Such studies stimulated the interest of researchers with regards to the association between general coping styles (not just anger coping styles) and hypertension risk among blacks. Some hypothesized that black Americans living in a high-stress environment and who also try to control situations through active coping may have higher blood pressure levels than blacks in similar situations who are more resigned about life.[22] James and associates further hypothesized that when actual coping resources are low, a strong predisposition to cope actively with environmental stressors might increase risk of hypertension among persons.[23] Conversely, when actual coping resources are available and the situation is more conducive to successfully coping, a person's high achievement motivation may actually decrease risk of developing high blood pressure.

The investigators tested this hypothesis in a sample of southern working class black men aged 17–60 years. They were administered the John Henry Active Coping Scale, which measures the degree to which a person believes he/she can control his/her environment through hard work and determination. The researchers hypothesized that men scoring below the median on educational level and at the same time scoring above the median on "John Henryism" would have higher blood pressure levels than other comparison groups. The hypothesis was found to be true. This hypothesis needs to be tested among black women and middle and upper class black men.

A fourth area of future research is related to the significance of the Type A personality in terms of increasing risk of hypertension. Numerous studies found a positive relationship between Type A behavior and risk of heart disease in whites. Such research is also needed among black populations, particularly black urban professionals. Waldron et al. caution that Type A behavior scores for blacks cannot necessarily be inferred from the data presented on whites.[24] They reported that participants in the Chicago Heart Association Detection in Industry study comprised the largest population group, containing substantial numbers of blacks and women, to take the JAS. Black women were found to be more Type B and white women were more frequently Type A; however, the prevalence of hypertension was higher among blacks. Myers also found black women to be more Type B though they had higher blood pressure levels.[25] Thus the relationship between the coronary prone behavior pattern and blood pressure may be different among black populations than among whites. Perhaps other types of psychosocial stressors are more significant precursors of hypertension than Type A behavior among blacks.

A fifth area for future research efforts should be the health status of single black mothers. The adverse health status typically characteristic of never-married and divorced/separated persons clearly justifies the need for a more vigorous approach toward answering major questions among single black mothers. According to the Bureau of the Census, almost 41 percent of the 6.4 million black families compared to 12 percent of white families were maintained by a woman.[26] Thirty-two percent of these black women had never married compared to 11 percent for white families. In 1981, the median income for families maintained by black women was $7,510, or about 38 percent of the median income of black married-couple families. By 1982, the combined divorce ratio for black men and women was more than twice that of whites (220 versus 107 per 1,000, respectively).

These statistics are certainly alarming. Yet, when one considers the adverse implications in terms of health-related variables, the picture becomes even bleaker. Verbrugge studied the relationship between marital status and health and reported that in America the mortality rates are higher for nonmarried persons.[27] Likewise, mortality rates are especially high for the formerly married. On a continuum from worst health status to best health status, the rank order would be divorced/separated, widowed, single people (probably without children), and married people. High rates of chronic conditions, such as cardiovascular and cerebrovascular disease, which limit social activity and affect an increased propensity toward disability, are characteristic of divorced and separated people in particular.

Never-married and divorced/separated mothers should be especially concerned because their responsibility for maintaining the household may limit their capability to take short-term actions or implement routine preventive practices. They frequently are unable to depend upon home care and attention when becoming ill or injured. There is no spouse to provide home support and income so that the mother can be allowed adequate recovery time. The potential significance of these untested hypotheses in the black households headed by females reflects the need for an aggressive approach toward answering major questions about the health status of the excessively high numbers of never-married and divorced/ separated black mothers. Last, many researchers contend that the simultaneous study of psychosocial and traditional biological risk factors should become the approved design for both epidemiological and behavioral studies of hypertensive and coronary heart disease. This design would further our understanding of the pathophysiologic mechanisms and would possibly provide insights for more-effective preventive programs. It is hypothesized that intervention should be implemented at the community level because more widespread benefits could be achieved than through the individually oriented treatment programs currently in effect. Regardless of the source of intervention, ultimately very little will be achieved by simply understanding the pathophysiologic mechanisms if we do not also act aggressively to reduce the higher prevalence of hypertension among certain subgroups of blacks in the U.S. population.

NOTES

This chapter was made possible by a Research Initiation Grant from The Pennsylvania State University, University Park, PA.

1. National Center For Health Statistics. *Health in The United States: 1984, Vital and Health Statistics* (U.S. Department of Health and Human Services), DHHS publication no.1 (PHS) 85-1232.

2. W.D. Hall, E. Saunders, and N.B. Shulman, *Hypertension in Blacks: Epidemiology Pathophysiology, and Treatment* (Chicago: Year Book Medical Publishers, 1985).

3. M. Marmot and W. Winkelstein, "Epidemiologic Observations on Intervention Trials for Prevention of Coronary Heart Disease," *American Journal of Epidemiology,* Vol. 101 (1975), pp. 177- 181.

4. S.A. James, S.A. Hartnett, and W.D. Kalsbeek, "John Henryism and Blood Pressure Differences Among Black Men," *Journal of Behavioral Medicine,* Vol. 6 (1983), pp. 259-278.

5. C.D. Jenkins, S.J. Zyzanski, and R.H. Rosenman, *Jenkins Activity Survey* (New York: Psychological Corporation, 1979).

6. W.C. Matney and D.L. Johnson, *America's Black Population: 1970-1982. A Statistical View,* special Publication by the Bureau of the census, (U.S. Government Printing Office), Publication no. P10/POP-83-1.

7. F.J. deCastro, R. Biesbroeck, C. Erickson, P. Farrell, W. Leong, D. Murphy, and R. Green, "Hypertension in Adolescents: A Significantly High Prevalence Among Students Attending an Inner City School," *Clinical Pediatrics,* Vol. 15 (1976), pp. 24-26.

8. D. Goldring, S. Londe, M. Sivakoff, A. Hernandez, C. Britton, and S. Choi, "Blood Pressure and the Relation of Age, Sex, Weight, Height, and Race to Blood Pressure in Children 14 to 18 Years of Age," *Journal of Pediatrics,* Vol. 91 (1977), pp. 884-889.

9. W.R. Harlan, A.L. Hull, R.L. Schmouder, J.R. Landis, F.E. Thompson, and F.A. Larkin, "Blood Pressure and Nutrition in Adults: The National Health and Nutrition Examination Survey," *American Journal of Epidemiology,* Vol. 120, no. 1 (1984), pp. 17-28.

10. National Center for Health Statistics, "Dietary Intake And Cardiovascular Risk Factors, Part I. Blood Pressure Correlates: United States 1971-1975," *Vital and Health Statistics,* series 11, no. 226, DHHS Publication no. (PHS)83-1676.

11. B.A. Blumenstein, M.B. Douglas, and W.D. Hall, "Blood Pressure Changes in Oral Contraceptive Use: A Study of 2676 Black Women in the Southeastern United States," *American Journal of Epidemiology,* Vol. 112, No 4 (1980), pp. 539-552. J.A. Pritchard and S.A. Pritchard, "Blood Pressure Response to Estrogen-Progestin Oral Contraceptives after Pregnancy-induced Hypertension," *American Journal of Obstetrics and Gynecology,* Vol. 129 (1977), pp. 733-739.

12. Blumenstein, Douglas, and Hall (1980), pp. 539-552.

13. J. Wilder, "The Law of Initial Values (LIV). Basimetric Approach (Law of Initial Values) to Biological Rhythms. Part III," *Annals of New York Academy of Science*, Vol. 98 (1962), pp. 1211-1220.

14. G.D. Friedman, "Oral Contraceptives and Hypertension," *Contrib Nephrol,* Vol. 8 (1977), pp. 213-220.

15. James, Hartnett, and Kalsbeck (1983), pp. 259-278. E. Harburg, E.H. Blakelock, Jr., and P.J. Roeper, "Resentful and Reflective Coping with Arbitrary Authority and Blood Pressure: Detroit," *Psychosomatic Medicine*, Vol. 41 (1971), pp. 89-202; S.L. Syme, T.W. Oakes, G.D. Friedman, R. Feldman, A.B. Sieglaub, and M. Collen, "Social Class and Racial Differences in Blood Pressure," *American Journal of Public Health,* Vol. 64 (1979), pp. 619-620; E. Harburg, J.C. Erfurt, L.S. Hauenstein, C. Chape, W.J. Schull, and M. A Schork, "Socioecological Stress, Suppressed Hostility, Skin Color, and Black-White Male Blood Pressure: Detroit," *Psychosomatic Medicine,* Vol. 35 (1973), pp. 276-296. A. M. Ostfeld and R.B. Shekelle, "Psychological Variables and Blood Pressure," in J. Stamler, R. Stamler, and T.N. Pullman, eds., *The Epidemiology of Hypertension* (New York: Grune and Stratton, 1967).

16. E. Harburg, J.C. Erfurt, L.S. Hauenstein, C. Chape, W.J. Schull, and M. A. Schork, "Socioecological Stressor Areas and Black-White Blood Pressure: Detroit," *Journal of Chronic Disease,* Vol. 26 (1973), pp. 596-611.

17. J.A. Morrison, P. Khoury, K. Kelly, M.J. Mellies, E. Parrish, G. Heiss, H. Tyroler, and C.J. Glueck, "Studies of Blood Pressure in School Children (Ages 6-19) and Their Parents in an integrated Suburban School District," *American Journal of Epidemiology,* Vol. 111 (1980), pp. 156-165; A.F. Brunswick and P. Collette, "Psychophysical Correlates of Elevated Blood Pressure: A Study of Urban Black Adolescents," *Journal of Human Stress,*Vol. 3 (1977), pp. 19-31; deCastro, et al., pp. 24-26. L.B. Reichman, B.M. Cooper, S. Blumenthal, G. Block, D. O'Hare, A.D. Chaves, M.H. Alerman, Q.B. Deming, S.J. Farber, and G.E. Thompson, "Hypertension Testing among High School Students. I. Surveillance Procedures and Results," *Journal of Chronic Disease,* Vol. 28 (1975), pp. 161-171; J.M. Kotchen, T.A. Kotchen, N.C. Schwertman, and L.H. Kuller, "Blood Pressure Distributions of Urban Adolescents," *American Journal of Epidemiology,* Vol. 99 (1974), pp. 315-324; M.M. Kilcoyne, R.W. Richter, and P.A. Alsup, "Adolescent Hypertension. I. Detection and Prevalence," *Circulation*, Vol. 50 (1974), pp. 758-764; M. Kilcoyne, "Hypertension and Heart Disease in the Urban Community," *Bulletin of New York Academy of Medicine,* Vol. 49 (1973), pp. 501-509.

18. Kotchen et al. (1974), pp. 315-324.

19. Ostfeld and Shekelle, (1967).

20. Harburg et al., (1973), pp. 596-611.

21. Harburg, Blakelock, and Cooper (1979), pp. 189–202.

22. Syme, et al. (1979) pp. 619-620.

23. James, Hartnett, and Kalsbeek, pp. 259-278.

24. I. Waldron, S.J. Zyzanski, R.B. Shekelle, and C.D. Jenkins, "Type A Behavior in Employed Men and Women," *Journal of Psychosomatic Research,* Vol. 22 (1978), pp. 79-87.

25. B.C. Myers, *Coronary Heart Disease Risk Factor Variables in Black and White Females Aged 18-24 Years,* dissertation (Eugene, OR: Microform Publications, 1986).

26. Matney and Johnson (1970-1982).

27. L.M. Verbrugge, "Marital Status and Health," *Journal of Marriage and the Family,* Vol. 41. (1979), pp. 267-284.

11

THE EMPLOYED BLACK: THE DYNAMICS OF WORK-FAMILY TENSION

Leanor Boulin Johnson

The interrelationship of job stressors, job strain, and marital strain among black police officers is examined using a "Work-Family Tension Model." Perceived job stressors, such as differential treatment based on racial status, tended to affect job strain. Furthermore, job stressors (direct/indirect) and job strain tended to influence the level of marital interaction and potential for separation and divorce. The implications these findings have for work organizations are discussed.

Twenty years of heated debate among scholars, policy makers, and social service workers has followed Moynihan's thesis on the etiological forces affecting the instability of black families.[1] While the debate took many directions, few scholars concurred with Moynihan that blacks lacked the discipline and necessary familial values to maintain the future existence of their communities. Instead, most argued that economic factors (e.g., black male unemployment and underemployment) prevented blacks from creating and maintaining a traditional family life.

Today, the crisis of black families has intensified. During the 1960-1980 period, black male separation and divorce rates rose from 8 percent to 13 percent; and intact marriages fell from 71 percent to 61 percent. Partly because of this marital instability trend, barely one-half of all black families with children include both parents. Concurrently, unemployment among black families continued to exceed that of white families.[2] Because divorce and singlehood rates tend to be associated with unemployment and lower income, employment/economic determinism continues to be the most commonly quoted explanation of the declining status of black families. Bureau of the Census data clearly show that among blacks ages 35-44, those without income (presumably unemployed) are less likely

217

than those with income to be married with spouse present (30 percent vs. 64 percent). Further, Glick and Staples report correlations between income and marital status. Glick found that for both black and nonblack men, the proportion with intact marriages tended to increase as income increased, particularly at the lower income levels. Staples notes that the marital rate of men earning $5,000 was 30 percent compared to 55 percent for those earning $15-20,000.[3]

Despite family researchers' focus on poverty and unemployment, there is impressive evidence that the level of family stability and satisfaction is also a function of the working conditions of the gainfully employed. Scholars have begun to document this work-family link among white families.

Piotrowski, for example, studied work-family psychological tensions. Her case studies of thirty members of thirteen working and lower-middle class families unveiled a detailed picture of the many ways work life spills over into family life. She concluded that working conditions affected the emotional life of the families she interviewed. Those workers who had gratifying jobs that affirmed their self-worth arrived home emotionally available to their family members. In contrast, those workers who had stressful and boring jobs arrived home with insufficient energy to deal positively with their wives and children. The emotionally depleted worker tended to isolate himself or vent his frustration and anger upon family members undeserving of such treatment.[4] Bray, Campbell, Grant, and Scanzoni studies are consistent with Piotrowski's. Bray et al. found that 19 percent of voluntary terminations from the American Telephone and Telegraph Company during the first eight years of their study were attributable to "home/personal" reasons. Presumably these workers quit in order to preserve the well-being of their families. Finally, Scanzoni found a positive relationship between the husband's success in the occupational system and marital satisfaction and stability.[5]

In contrast with those studies, Crosby and Crouter focused on spillover from family to work. Crosby found that positive home experiences were associated with positive work experiences. Crouter's interviews with thirty-eight men and seventeen women showed that they were able to give specific examples of how negative conditions at home (e.g., family member's illness or death) negatively affected their work life (e.g., tardiness, absenteeism, inattentiveness).[6]

In sum, these studies suggest a *Spillover/Generalization* model of work-family interaction. Experiences at work are carried over into home life or generalized (i.e., positive to positive/negative to negative) to nonwork domains. Similarly, nonwork experiences affect work life either positively or negatively. This model is commonly used to describe the effect of unemployment on black family life. However, not all family theorists agree that work stressors produce family strain. Two other models, discussed below, also receive support from family theorists: Compensatory-nonwork and Segmentation.

The *Compensatory-Nonwork* model assumes that individuals engage in nonwork (e.g., leisure and family life) activities to compensate for work deprivation experiences. Adherents of this model would argue that blacks look to the family to compensate for difficult work experiences. For instance, many black households depend on the income of multiple workers (e.g., husband, wife, and children) in order to economically survive. They also expect unfair treatment on the job. Knowing that the labor of each family member is important and that they must deal in a hostile society, great significance is placed on family members and interactions.[7] The family (extended and nuclear) serves as a balm, a safety valve for damaged souls and for workers whose labor has been undervalued. The resilience of black families through the ages speaks in support of this model. In fact, the contemporary indictment of unemployment and poverty for hindering marital formation and stability is not historically justified. Recent historical revisionists note that black families have survived periods of severe hardship. During the hardships of slavery, the adjustment to emancipation, and the geographical separations of families during the great migration North, the overwhelming majority of black families were headed by two parents.[8] Rather than being a home breaker, adversity tended to draw families closer together as they struggled to survive.[9] Family compensation is seen as the mechanism for black survival.

The *Segmentation* model assumes that the work and family domain are independent of each other. The segmentation argument derives strength from Parsonian theory. Parsons and his followers suggested that the family unit is isolated from work by virtue of its specialization, particularly family division of labor based on gender. The male struggles to capture a decent salary in a highly competitive job market, and finds rest in a home maintained by a nurturing woman.[10] But what happens when both work outside the home or when expected nurturance is not the model experience? The Parsonian orientation to this model assumes traditional gender roles and certainly does not hold for many families today—and

FIGURE 1
Work-Family Tension Model

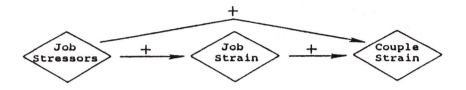

never really reflected the family functioning of most black couples. Moynihan's conclusion that the black family perpetuates its own pathology (i.e., independent of external forces) represents a segmented explanation of black family life.[11]

A CONCEPTUAL MODEL

Each of the three models discussed provides partial insight into the process by which some individuals may orchestrate work and family life. Given the abundance of assertions[12] emphasizing the link between labor force participation and marital stability among contemporary blacks, the Spillover/Generalization model is used here to explore work–family linkages. Figure 1 illustrates the hypothetical relationships derived from the "spillover" model and the major factors investigated.

This conceptual model suggests there is a positive (+) direct link from the work environment to individual and family strains. It is assumed, for example, that workers who experience adverse treatment on the job will experience job and couple (i.e., marital) strain. Increases in job stressors are assumed to directly and indirectly (e.g., as mediated by job strain) create greater couple tension. Furthermore, job strain has a direct impact upon couple strain—high job strain results in high couple strain.

OBJECTIVES

If white families experience work-family spillover, what about the black employed? They not only experience the work conditions of workers of all colors, but they must deal with the hidden bruises of race. Through social osmosis they may unknowingly internalize the bruises to their self-esteem. As Peters and Messey note, blacks are subjected to constant threats or periodic occurrences of discrimination, intimidation, or denial because of their race. Subtly or overtly they experience pervasive "Mundane Extreme Environmental Stress" (The Mees Effect).[13] Lazarus, a psychologist, believes that it is this type of stress—the everyday annoyances, daily little hassles and series of small tragedies—that contributes more to illness, depression, and burnout than major life changes.[14] Research has not adequately addressed the relationship between The Mees Effect within the job environment and the strain of black workers. To what extent does the perception of adverse treatment on the job impact upon an individual's job strain? Are the families of black workers receptacles for negative work experiences? More specifically, does the working environment have any direct or indirect affect on couple interaction or on their divorce and separation potential? From the perspective of the "work-family tension model," this study explores the effect which adverse treatment on the job has on job strain and marital quality.

WORK-FAMILY ISSUES: THE POLICE OCCUPATION

The above work-family linkage will be explored through examining the lives of black police officers. Why study police officers? Surely they do not represent the black workers in America. First, there is no such entity as *the* black family or *the* black worker. Black families and workers cut across all economic, social, religious, occupational, linguistic backgrounds. The various backgrounds are woven together by a common black experience. Rather than being solid black, these families represent shades of black. The police officer represents one shade. Our focus is on the thread that binds them to all ethnic minorities (i.e., the sociohistorical experiences shared by all peoples of color—racism, discrimination, and disenfranchisement).

Secondly, the police occupation was selected because it provides an ideal setting for studying work-family issues. Police officers are part of a highly organized and traditional structure which makes heavy demands on its members. Inherent in the police job are potential sources of work-family tensions—heavy demands on time (e.g., shift rotations), commitment, and emotional and physical energies. For instance, officers' emotional and psychological energies are drained not only from dealing with irate citizens, human tragedies, and threat to their own health and life, but also from shift rotations that disrupt their body rhythm and create a general level of fatigue. Concurrently, the family also requires its share of energy and attention. Compliance with work expectations may make it difficult or impossible to comply with family demands or even to dispassionately consider such demands.

In addition to these stressors, black officers' emotions may be further depleted because of their newcomer and minority status within the department. Being relatively recent (i.e., in the early 1970s they began entering an occupation which was established during colonial times) and often unwanted newcomers to police departments, black officers may experience more job stressors than the average white officer. While the majority of officers (black and white) expressed concern over the limited opportunities for job advancement, recent litigation by black police officers across the United States testifies to their perception of differential access to hiring and the mistreatment within the workplace. Both in and outside the department, blacks may find a cool reception when invoking their authority as law enforcers. They may exhibit ego-defensive behavior which may manifest itself in a variety of ways (e.g., acting tougher than they feel); or they may experience resentment, prejudice, and discrimination from the higher status group. Fear of harmful consequences to oneself may inhibit direct reactions to perceived mistreatment—creating a sense of powerlessness within the workplace. More insidious than overt discrimination are the nonhostile withdrawals or "psychological distancing" between those black and white officers who have not previously experienced interracial contact. This distancing may be expressed through telling ethnic jokes or confining interracial interactions to only job-related tasks. A corresponding tendency may be a defensive withdrawal on the part of blacks.[15] The dynamics of such interactions provide ample reasons for black officers to feel that they are unwelcome.

The results from the present survey of police officers suggest the extent to which they experienced adverse treatment on the job. Black officers, on the average, were significantly more likely to perceive annoying or unfair treatment. Their perception is reflected in their responses to several survey questions. Specifically, blacks more than their white colleauges felt that: (a) they were informally barred from certain assignments because of their race; (b) other officers tried to intimidate them; (c) unwanted racial jokes were made in their presence; (d) compared to others they were more apt to be penalized for their mistakes; (e) the actions of other officers of their race affected how they themselves were judged; and (f) they were more closely watched by their department. No doubt these perceptions tend to increase individual stress and decrease feelings of acceptance—making black officers' work lives relatively more difficult.[16]

Thus, emotional or psychological coping resources are heavily taxed among black police officers.[17] They must deal not only with the work-family conflict inherent in the job, but also with the added burden of being viewed as outsiders within a relatively closed and sometimes hostile occupational environment. It is this added stressor, this sense of being an outsider, that for many black workers may be a factor shaping the interpersonal dynamics between black couples. In sum, the police occupation provides the necessary elements for studying work-family linkages.

While examining the influence of job stress on black police, this study will test the general empirical model of positive linkages between workplace stress and perceived marital quality. If this general model can be supported with this special group, then it should be useful in extending our understanding of work–family tension among other stressful occupations.

STUDY VARIABLES

The three concepts—job stressors, job strain and couple strain—were measured by a number of items and scales. The indicators for job stressors were three items that reflected the degree to which the officers felt they were: (a) more penalized than other officers for their mistakes; (b) judged by the actions of other officers of their race; and (c) barred from certain assignments because of their race.

Job strain was measured by four scales: (a) internal burnout (e.g., feelings of fatigue and emotional depletion); (b) projected (external) burnout (e.g., treating civilians impersonally or becoming callous towards people; (c) transfer withdrawal (e.g., desires to quit the department or retire early). Transfer withdrawal consisted of two items and the remaining scales consisted of four to seven items.

Two scales, couple interaction and separation/divorce potential, measured couple strain. The six items composing couple interaction dealt with the officers' report of the degree to which they successfully communicated with their spouse, got what they wanted out of the relationship, received from or gave to their spouse emotional support, had an enjoyable sex life, and engaged in affectionate behavior. Separation/divorce potential was also composed of six items that tested the degree to which they considered divorce.[18] These items ranged from suggesting divorce to their spouse or a friend, to consulting an attorney, to actual separation.

Using Cronbach's alpha, each of the six scales had a reliability exceeding .70. The zero-order correlations among these variables are presented in Table 1.

SUBJECTS, SAMPLING AND PROCEDURE

The present sample consists of 92 (57 males and 42 females) black police officers of which 61 percent were married (includes those living together and separated). This sample was selected from a larger cross-sectional sample of over 700 black and white police officers from two police departments. In 1983 the officers voluntarily responded to a mailed survey. The survey instrument contained 333 items. These items were developed from information gathered from police-ride-alongs, over 65 in-depth interviews with officers and their spouses, an advisory panel of police officers/administrators and academicians, police stress workshops, and pretesting in three sites. The instrument was randomly administered to a large urban department as well as nonrandomly given to members of a black police organization and a second department.

The black officers had joined two large U.S. East coast police forces after 1969. Slightly more than half of the sample was under age 30, and 72 percent had joined the department prior to age 26. Only a third earned over $25,000 which reflected their tenure (three quarters were on the force less than 6 years). A fifth were married less than 3 years, 37 percent, 3 to 5 years, a fifth, 6 to 8 years, and 24 percent, 9 or more years. The majority of the officers (58 percent) had been married once and 11 percent more than once. Of those who had multiple marriages or who were currently separated or divorced (the latter not included in this study), a third felt that police work affected their decisions to separate or divorce. Among the 95 percent of spouses gainfully employed, 6 percent were also police officers, and an additional third were in jobs with rotating or non-day work schedules.[19]

Work-Family Tension: A Path Model

Path analysis. The interrelations among the three concepts (job stress, job strain, couple strain) were explored, using basic path analytic techniques. The path diagram in Figure 2 represents a series of multiple regression statistical analyses. Each of the job strain variables were re-

TABLE 1
Correlates, Means and Standard Deviations of the Study Variables

JOB STRAIN	JOB STRAIN — Internal Burnout	Projected Burnout	Transfer	Quit	COUPLE RELATIONSHIP — Spouse Interaction	Divorce Potential	DIFFERENTIAL TREATMENT — More Penalized	Judged by race	Barred because of race	Mean	SD
Internal Burnout		.5964 (88) p= .000	-.3720 (85) p= .000	.4562 (84) p= .000	-.3274 (52) p= .018	.4523 (46) p= .002	.1666 (80) p= .140	.1080 (79) p= .343	.3284 (80) p= .003	3.9	1.34
Projected Burnout			-.2585 (86) p= .016	.2940 (84) p= .007	-.4721 (54) p= .000	.4460 (48) p= .001	.1528 (81) p= .173	.2665 (80) p= .017	.1824 (81) p= .103	3.1	1.39
Transfer				-.3147 (85) p= .003	.1881 (52) p= .182	-.2152 (47) p= .146	-.2413 (81) p= .030	-.2098 (80) p= .062	-.2286 (81) p= .040	4.7	1.70
Quit					-.4079 (51) p= .003	.3398 (45) p= .022	.3822 (79) p= .001	.0845 (78) p= .462	.2864 (79) p= .010	2.3	1.52
COUPLE RELATIONSHIP Spouse Interaction						-.5697 (46) p= .000	-.1459 (49) p= .317	-.1885 (49) p= .195	-.1951 (49) p= .179	5.8	1.50
Divorce Potential							.1882 (45) p= .216	.1857 (45) p= .222	.2239 (45) p= .139	2.2	1.65
DIFFERENTIAL TREATMENT More Penalized than Others								.1861 (82) p= .094	.3779 (83) p= .000	3.9	2.08
Judged by race									.3213 (82) p= .003	4.7	1.95
Barred because of race										4.4	2.10

TABLE 2
Interrelationship of Job Stressors, Job Strain, and Couple Strain: A Path Model

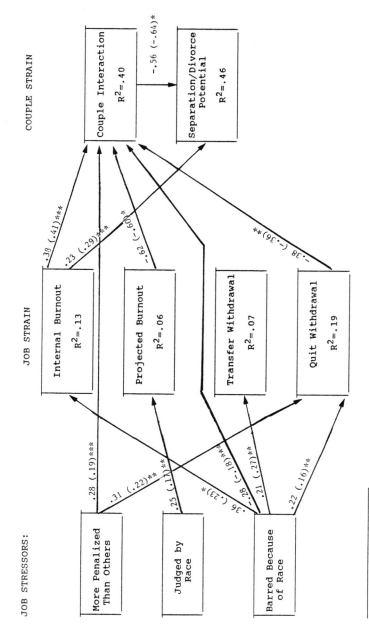

NOTE: The numbers within the parentheses are standardized coefficients.

* ≤ .01   ** ≤ .05   *** ≤ .10

gressed on all the job stress variables, couple interaction was regressed on all the antecedent variables, and separation/divorce potential was regressed on couple interaction and all possible antecedent variables.

The lines and arrowheads establish relations and directions of the influence; and the number associated with each arrow quantifies the strength of the relationship. Each of the boxes under job and couple strain contains an R^2 which represents the percentage of variance explained by the associated independent variable(s).

Findings. Figure 2 presents only the statistically significant relationships among the study variables. Overall, the findings support the spillover/generalization model. Job stressors have both direct and indirect influences on couple interaction. Couple strain is directly increased for officers who perceive that they are being penalized more than their coworkers or are being barred from certain assignments for racial reasons. Although being judged by the actions of other black officers does not directly affect couple strain, its effect is mediated by projected burnout. It appears that dual projections are operating. Officers stating that other officers are projecting the behavior of other black officers onto them, appear in turn to project their own inner feelings of frustration/burnout against others (e.g., citizens). This dual projection has a moderate indirect negative impact on couple interaction $(-.16)$.[20]

Of the three job stressors, being barred from job assignments for racial reasons had the most pervasive impact on individual job and couple strain. Apart from its direct effect (cited above) as well as its direct impact on desire to transfer to another assignment, it indirectly influences both couple interaction (mediated by internal burnout) and the potential for separation and divorce (mediated by desire to quit the department).

Three of the four job strain factors had direct effects on couple strain. Projected burnout had a powerful impact on couple interaction $(-.60)$ and a strong indirect impact on the potential for separation and divorce $(-.38)$. The other two factors, internal burnout and quit withdrawal (i.e., the desire to quit or retire early), were similar in the strength of their impact on couple interaction, but only one was in the expected direction. First, as expected, the higher the desire to quit, the lower the couple interaction. In an earlier analysis it was found that the quit withdrawal factor has a more profound effect on the marriages of black officers than on their white counterparts. This reflects, perhaps, the reality of the job market—there are less job opportunities for blacks than whites. Thus, conversations concerning quitting a steady job when so many blacks are without jobs can present serious interaction problems for black couples.

Second, our conceptual model postulated not only a link between job and family tension, but a positive flow between these two domains. The path diagram shows, however, that in one case, internal burnout, job strain markedly increased couple interaction rather than lowering it (apparent support for the compensatory model). This is particularly perplexing given that the potential for separation and divorce increased as internal burnout increased.[21] Also, separation/divorce potential was inversely related to couple interaction. Perhaps the opposite effects can be explained by the duration of the burnout. For example, burnout expressed over a short term may elicit a spouse's sympathy and emotional support; whereas long term internal burnout may deplete the emotional energies of the couple. After a period of time, a once sympathetic spouse may demand that his/her partner snap out of the depression and do something to eliminate the stressors. This withdrawal of support may come at a time when internal burnout is most intense. Thus, the partner experiencing job strain may feel betrayed and resentful—concluding that the stressors are beyond control; and if his/her partner cannot provide support what is the point of maintaining the relationship? The reaction to loss of support is probably intensified among blacks who have high and perhaps unrealistic expectations of the families' ability or willingness to absorb painful experiences. The critical point and specific conditions under which internal burnout may work against a marriage is in need of further study. Such studies should use longitudinal data in order to most effectively assess the effect of lengthy burnout.

Finally, each of the job strain factors is affected by at least one of the job stressors and in the expected direction (i.e., increased job stress is associated with increased job strain). However, with the exception of desires to quit the department ($R^2 = .19$), a negligible amount of the job strain variance is explained (R^2 range: .07 to .13). While this model captures only a small portion of the influences impacting upon job strain, it accounts for nearly one-half and 40 percent of the variance in separation and divorce potential and couple interaction, respectively. This is particularly impressive given that the model does not account for the many personal attributes (e.g., communication style, personality and physical attractiveness), which contribute to the success of a marriage. The link between job stress and family tensions is clearly supported.

POLICY IMPLICATIONS

The results indicate that job stressors in the form of differential treatment affect job strain. Thus, institutions should accept responsibility for the consequences of such treatment within the workplace by providing systematic programs aimed at confronting individual prejudices and improving the work environment. Consciousness-raising education that exposes specific barriers to effective communication between minority and majority groups could facilitate black officers' integration into the department. Such education should sensitize the majority and minority group to what each considers to be offensive language, attitudes and practices.

When developing human relations workshops the particular work setting should be taken into consideration. Racial prejudice and discrimination may be found anywhere, but programs must be preceded by feasibility assessments which consider the unique context and structural situation in which they occur. Careful consideration should be given to the content of packaged seminars/programs. Packaged programs should be modified to conform to accepted organizational principles (improving performance evaluation and leadership, strengthening group cohesion). Nieva and Gutek note that when programs conform to principles of a particular workplace they are more likely to be perceived as legitimate, possible, and acceptable.[22]

Generally, short-term workshops aimed at individuals or small groups are easy to implement, relatively inexpensive and present little or no threat to organizational management. Thus, it is not surprising that the overwhelming majority of remedy programs treat the effect of stress on the individual police officers. Organizational reform takes a back seat to other alternatives—despite the fact that studies show that if the organizational structure remains unchanged the gains from individual training sessions tend to be limited.[23] In order to counteract the tendency for nonorganizational reform, participants in these workshops should include employees who occupy influential positions and who have authority over the mechanisms for implementing institutional changes. Otherwise, change if it occurs at all, will be a slow process.[24]

Given that the findings also showed job stressors contributing to family strain, work organizations should also offer family services. However, while human relations workshops are not new to work settings, seminars that do not specifically address labor-management interactions or job performance may meet with resistance. Most work institutions are not willing to invest money and time in projects (e.g., marriage counseling and marriage enrichment seminars) that do not directly relate to profit, productivity, or serving their client. The "organizational man" philosophy and the belief that work and family life are segregated still guide the action of many managers. Hence, an employee who allows home problems to affect work productivity, is perceived as imbalanced, out of control, and in need of being replaced. Only recently have work organizations begun to both acknowledge the reality of the linkage between work and family and to admit that this link occurs among many workers.[25] The evidence in this chapter can provide a rationale for establishing family seminars within the workplace.

Since the work-family issue is relatively new, only a few work organizations have initiated concrete programs/services.[26] Several police departments have, for example, been vanguards in providing psychological services not only to individual officers but to their spouses as well. However, few have employed professionals who are skilled in relating to the specific problems many blacks encounter. Smith notes that the average counselor follows a set of conventional principles that do not take into account the impact of race. Conventional counseling focuses on intrapsychical problems, internal resolutions, and talk; instead, counselors need to emphasize the conditions to which minorities must adjust, external resolutions, the desirability of action. Counselors must also be sensitive to the client's degree of acculturation into the white majority cultural system and the client's belief about the culturally sanctioned ways of coping with problems and marshaling support.[27] For example, in an earlier report on black and white police officers, the present author found racial differences in sources of support.[28] Black officers relied much more on their informal networks, whereas white officers tended to rely more on their supervisor and squad. Further, friend support affected the couple relationship of blacks, but not whites.

If departments want to be responsive to the needs of all officers, they must include minorities on those committees responsible for hiring counselors. Only then will they be able to optimize the chances of hiring counselors trained in addressing not only intrapsychic factors, but the sociocultural context that often precipitates the onset of intrapsychic strain.

NOTES

This article was made possible by financial support from the Ford Foundation Postdoctoral Fellowship for Minorities, and computer support from The Catholic University of America. Initial data gathering was made possible by a National Institute of Mental Health Grant. Additional assistance was received from Dr. Veronica Nieva and typists Sonja Ouellette of Westat, Inc., and Mary Redondo and Jean Welch of Arizona State University. For special assistance on earlier drafts, the author wishes to thank Dr. Willie Melton of Michigan Technological University, Dr. Michael Wilson of Westat, Inc., Dr. Paul Glick of Arizona State University, and Dr. Robert Staples of the University of

California at San Francisco

The author takes full responsibility for the final content of this manuscript.

1. D. Moynihan, *The Negro Family: The Case For National Action* (U.S. Department of Labor, Office of Policy Planning, 1966).

2. Adjusting for inflation, there has not been an absolute increase in income for blacks nor whites. However, whites have had a relative economic gain over blacks. Black-white median income ratio dropped from 61 percent in 1969 to 57 percent in 1985. See P. Glick, "A Demographic Picture of Black Families" in *Black Families* (2nd ed.), H. McAdoo, editor, (Newbury Park, Calif: Sage, 1988), pp. 111-132; R. Staples, "Changes in Black Family Structure: The Conflict Between Family Ideology And Structural Conditions." Paper presented at the Marie Ferguson Peters Lecture (Conn: University of Connecticut); U.S. Census Bureau, *America's Black Population, 1970 to 1982: A Statistical View,* (Washington, D.C.: Government Printing Office, 1983), Series P10/83; Bureau of Labor Statistics, *Marital And Family Patterns Of Workers: An Update*, (Washington, D.C.: Department of Labor, May 1983).

3. P. Glick, "A Demographic Picture": R. Staples, "Changes in Black Families," Bureau of the Census, *Marital Characteristics: 1980 Census Population,* (Washington D.C.: U.S. Department of Commerce, March 1985), Report RCBO-2-4c.

4. C.S. Piotrowski, *Work And The Family* (New York: Free Press, 1979).

5. D.W. Bray, R.J. Campbell, and D.L. Grant, *Formative Years in Business; A Long Term AT&T Study Of Managerial Lives* (New York: Wiley, 1974), U.R. Burk and P. Bradshaw, "Occupational and Life Satisfaction And The Family," *Small Group Behavior* 12 (August 1981): 329-375; J. Scanzoni. *Sex Roles, Women's Work, And Marital Conflict* (Lexington, Mass: Lexington Books, 1978).

6. F. Crosby, "Job Satisfaction And Domestic Life," in *Management Of Work And Personal Life,* M.D. Lee and R.N. Kanungo, editors. (New York: Praeger, 1984); A. Crouter, "Spillover From Family to Work: The Neglected Side Of The Work-Family Interface," *Human Relations,* 37 (June, 1984): 425-442.

7. Studies consistently show that blacks as compared to whites have more significant others and stronger kinship support systems. See S.L. Hofferth, "Kin Networks, Race, and Family Structure," *Journal of Marriage and the Family* 46 (November, 1984): 791-806; H.P. McAdoo, editor, *Black Families* (Newbury Park, Calif: Sage, 1981); R. Hill, *Strengths of Black Families* (New York: Emerson Hall, 1971).

8. See H. Gutman, "The Gutman Report," in *The New York Review of Books* (September 30, 1976): 18-22, 27; P. Lammermeier, "The Urban Black Family Of The Nineteenth Century: A Study Of Black Family Structure In The Ohio Valley, 1850-1880," *Journal of Marriage and the Family* 35 (August, 1973): 446-447.

9. Some scholars have attempted to answer the query as to why it is that poverty and unemployment create family disorganization in contemporary society but built family strength in an earlier era. Some argue that under slavery blacks were exploited but fully employed. Because they were valued as property, the white masters assured them the minimum subsistence of meals, lodging and clothing. For the sake of worker morale, families were generally preserved, see G.M. Frederickson, "The Gutman Report," in *The New York Review of Books* (September 30, 1976). Fogel and Engerman extend the nonexploitation argument by claiming that slaves were willing collaborators in a capitalist enterprise. They worked for real incentives, which included upward mobility within the slave system and protection of their families, see R.S. Fogel and S. Engerman, *Time On The Cross: The Economics Of American Negro Slavery* (Boston: Little Brown). Yet, it is generally agreed that emancipation brought massive unemployment and meager wages— and the family still survived. In response to this fact it is argued that post-slavery families were often able to make ends meet by combined efforts of family members working at

3

multiple jobs. These scholars conclude that today, competition for the most menial jobs is keen. And now it is almost impossible to overcome poverty and unemployment, see *Ebony*, Special Issue, "The Crisis Of The Black Family," XLI (October, 1986); J.H. Franklin, "A Historical Note on Black Families," in *Black Families*, (2nd Edition, H.P. McAdoo, editor, (Newbury Park, Calif: Sage, 1988).

10. T. Parsons, *The Social Structure* (New York: Harper and Row, 1959).

11. R. Moynihan, *The Negro Family*

12. P. Glick, "A Demographic"; D. Moynihan, *The Negro Family;* R. Staples, "Changes in Black Family."

13. M. Peters and G. Massey, "Mundane Extreme Environmental Stress," in *Social Stress And The Family: Advances and Developments in Family Stress Theory And Research*, H. McCubbin, M. Sussman, and J. Patterson, editors (New York: Haworth, 1983).

14. R. Lazarus, *Psychological Stress And The Coping Process* (New York: McGraw Hill, 1966).

15. I. Katz, J. Goldston, and L. Benjamin, "Behavior and Productivity in Bi-Racial Work Groups," in *Minority-Group Relations*, D.L. Ford, Jr., editor (Calif: University Associates, 1976), pp. 49-72.

16. Kanter and others note that blacks in predominately white work settings have high visibility and suffer from "overobservation." The responses to the pressure brought on by overobservation include overachievement or low self-disclosure. Overachievement increases visibility which results in more pressure and even perhaps, resentment from the dominant group. The overachiever may respond by minimizing achievement. Second, blacks may feel that they cannot reveal their true selves. Recounting weaknesses in informal work groups can backfire (i.e., instead of receiving support, mistakes may be used against them). Smith notes that an individual who suppresses his or her true capabilities becomes estranged from himself or herself. Self-estrangement can precipitate the onset of emotional disorders and psychopathology. See E.M. Smith, "Ethnic Minorities: Life Stress, Social Support, and Mental Health Issues," *The Counseling Psychologist* 13 (October, 1985): 537-579.

17. For further discussion of the effect racism has on black coping and mental health, see Peters and Massey, "Mundane Extreme"; Smith, "Ethnic Minorities."

18. The separation/divorce scale is a modification of a scale presented in A. Booth, D. Johnson, and J.N. Edwards, "Measuring Marital Instability," *Journal of Marriage and the Family* 45 (May, 1983): 387-403.

19. Although spouse data are not included in the present analyses, the reader may find knowledge of the spouses' work profile useful in data interpretation.

20. The indirect coefficient is derived from multiplying the coefficients associated with the two different paths connecting the exogenous variable (e.g., judged by race) to the final dependent variable (e.g., couple interaction). Alternatively, the total effect minus the direct effect will produce the same results.

21. Multicollinearity was suspected since the correlation between projected burnout and internal burnout was .596; and these two variables had opposite sign effects on couple interaction. Thus, the data were submitted to an SAS diagnostic which (unlike the correlation matrix) was able to identify any collinearity with three or more variables and within the intercept (the most common cause of collinearity) (Belseoy, 1980). The results showed no problem with multicollinearity in the model.

22. V.F. Nieva and B.A. Gutek, *Women And Work: Psychological Perspective* (New York: Praeger, 1981).

23. W.C. Terry, "Police Stress," in *Thinking About Police Contemporary Issues*, C.B. Klockars, editor (New York: McGraw-Hill, 1983).

24. J. Ford, Jr., *Minority-Group Relations* (Calif: University Associates, 1976; V.F. Nieva and B.A. Gutek, *Women and Work*.

25. An earlier report showed not only work affecting family relations, but family contributing to work strain. See L.B. Johnson, V.F. Nieva, M.J. Wilson, *Police Work-Home Stress Study* (Rockville, MD: Westat, Inc, 1985).

26. L.B. Johnson, *Corporations and Families: Changing Family* (Washington, D.C.: Youth Policy Institute, The Catholic University of America, 1986).

27. E.M. Smith, "Ethnic Minorities."

28. Johnson, Nieva, and Wilson, *Police Work-Home Stress*.

12

VALUES, BELIEFS, AND WELFARE RECIPIENCY: IS THERE A CONNECTION?

Lois Benjamin and James B. Stewart

Relationships between values/beliefs and welfare recipiency and work attachment are examined using a sample of black and white women. The concept of self-efficacy, i.e. perceived ability to produce and regulate events is used to model paths of influence between values/ beliefs and observable behaviors. No racial differences are found in the determinants of current labor force status and previous work history. Race is also found to have no significant impact on the probability of receiving public assistance. The explanatory power of measures of self-efficacy is found to be minimal with respect to receipt of public assistance or the duration of receipt of assistance.

This study examines relationships between the values and beliefs of individuals and welfare recipiency and work attachment in a sample of black and white women. Special attention is focused on determining whether differences exist between black and white women in the values-behavior linkages. The relative power of "individual" and "structural" explanations of welfare dependency is also explored.

The present analysis differs from most economic studies by its relaxation of the traditional economics assumption that tastes and preferences are given. This assumption potentially leads to overconcentration on the effect of pecuniary and nonpecuniary incentives on behavior. This focus can be seen in economic analyses of welfare which typically explore the degree to which public assistance benefits constitute incentives for out-of-wedlock births, weaken labor market attachment, and reinforce the "cycle" of poverty.[1]

In this investigation, insights from psychology and sociology are used to develop metrics that proxy values and beliefs. These metrics are included as explanatory variables in models examining factors affecting (a) probability of receiving public assistance benefits and (b) duration of receipt of assistance. Traditional measures of the opportunity costs of alternative decisions are also included in the models. A secondary thrust of the present investigation is to determine if illness exacerbates welfare dependency.

The availability of measures of values and beliefs for black and white women allows us to test the Moynihan hypothesis advanced in 1965 that characterized the population of low income black families as "a tangle of pathology".[2] Moynihan saw the matriarchal structure of black families as the center of this "tangle of pathology."

The Moynihan perspective has been resurrected in recent years and, as a consequence, the focus of the present investigation is timely. We find no significant differences in determinants of current labor force status and previous work history between the black and white women in the sample. The metrics proxying values and belief were found, in general, to have little explanatory power in predicting either the probability of receipt of public assistance or the duration of receipt of assistance. Moreover, no differences were found between black and white women in the effect of values and beliefs on public assistance receipt. These findings suggest that "structural" explanations of welfare "dependency" may be a more useful guide for policy development than approaches emphasizing changing recipients' values.

In the second section, literature from relevant sociological and psychological literature is reviewed. The review is used to motivate a conceptual model that identifies specific paths of possible influence of values and beliefs on economic behavior. The data base and the operationalization of the variables in the conceptual model are presented in the third section along with the descriptive statistics. The results are presented in the fourth section and the implications of the study are presented in the conclusion.

VALUES, BELIEFS, AND ECONOMIC BEHAVIOR: AN OVERVIEW

The conception of self-efficacy, developed by Bandura, provides a connection to the economic focus on behavior in most studies of welfare and recipiency.[3] Bandura suggests that minority status creates a limited sense of "personal efficacy to produce and to regulate events in their lives"[4] The implication, according to Bandura, is that "[p]eople avoid activities that they believe exceed their coping abilities, but they undertake and perform assuredly those that they judge themselves capable of managing."[5] In many respects, the notion of self-efficacy clarifies the metaphorical "culture of poverty" by specifying the linkage between an individual's world view and/or sense of mastery over the environment and observable behavior.

The conception of "personal efficacy" thus provides a vehicle for operationalizing the linkage between values, beliefs, and observable behavior of interest to economists. Gurin, Gurin and Morrison's distinction between "personal control" and "ideology" aids in the application of Bandura's formulation.[6] Personal control refers to individuals' beliefs about capacities to exercise control over their own lives, while ideology connotes beliefs about the role of internal and external forces in the distribution of rewards in society.

This distinction is relevant for the examination of alternative approaches to explaining welfare dependency. "Structural" explanations de-emphasize the sense of self-efficacy as the critical important link in a causal explanatory chain of welfare dependence. Rather, structural constraints limiting the opportunities available to recipients are seen as the principle source of an individual's inability to escape poverty. These structural constraints can take a variety of forms, from systemic patterns of institutional discrimination to specific circumstances facing an individual household.

Although the two explanations need not be wholly competitive, they generate different interpretations of a variety of phenomena including the relationship between household composition and welfare dependency. The culture of poverty perspective would suggest that the greater prevalence of the extended family and associated patterns among blacks reinforce detachment from external social support structures. In contrast, the structural constraints model focuses on the functional aspects of extended households and resource sharing among blacks and other identifiable culture groups in militating against oppressive structures. A large body of literature documents the overall importance of the extended family among blacks.[7] Extensive patterns of resource-sharing among blacks have also been documented.[8] Hayes and Mindel reported, for example, that black families received more help from relatives than white families.[9]

Comparisons of factors affecting patterns of welfare dependence and work attachment by race must be sensitive to the extent to which intragroup differences in personal characteristics and household composition generate intragroup variation in observable behavior. To illustrate, Stewart found:[10]

a) The impact of child-bearing on the work effort of young never-married black females varies across household types and age grouping;

b) Mothers who live in extended households work more than mothers who live in nonextended households;

c) Older mothers work more than younger mothers;

d) Young women with no children work less than older women with no children.

Economists generally ignore the possible linkage between welfare recipiency, health status, and work attachment. Prince found that welfare recipients are likely to perceive their health as poor or fair more often than those persons not on welfare.[11] This finding raises the question of whether some recipients might adopt a "sick role" to make dependency legitimate. Cole and Lejeune found that welfare mothers were more likely to adopt the sick role than working class black women, particularly if they lacked hope of getting off welfare. They concluded that the sick role may offer an alternative status for individuals who lack other socially approved statuses.[12]

In contrast, the structural model of welfare dependence would suggest that differential illness reporting by welfare recipients is either a result of the stress caused by confronting the structural barriers or a precondition (constraint) that exacerbates limitations on opportunities rather than a condition consciously or unconsciously associated with efforts to legitimize detachment from the world of work.

It is well-known that an individual's familial or extrafamilial social support systems are intervening variables in moderating the effects of stressful life events on physical or emotional well being.[13] Some evidence suggests that the cultural repertoire of different groups varies in capacity to militate against particular stressful events and health problems. Mirowsky and Ross found that Mexicans had lower psychological distress than blacks or whites, which they attributed to Mexicans' stronger extended kinship network.[14] Wolinsky implied that different cultural traditions accounted for findings that whites make more use of preventive maintenance in dental care than blacks, even when class differences are accounted for.[15]

The preceding discussion has identified several mechanisms through which racial-cultural differences potentially contribute to variations in the linkages among an individual's world view, health status, work attachment, and welfare dependency. These various paths of influence are depicted in Figure 1.

FIGURE 1

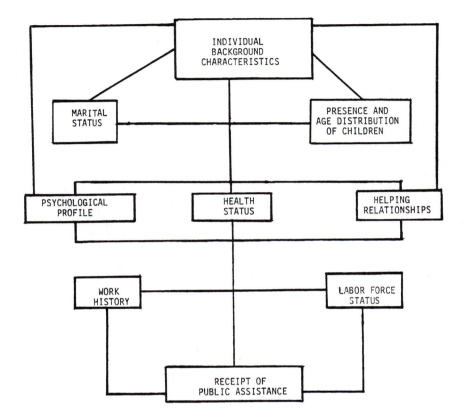

The paths of influence of particular interest in Figure 1 are (a) the factors affecting sense of self-efficacy, (b) the effects of self-efficacy and health status on current force status and previous work history, (c) the effects of self-efficacy, health status, labor status, and work history on the probability of receiving public assistance and the duration of receipt, and (d) the connections among self-efficacy, labor force status, work history, and receipt of public assistance and reported health status.

The data base used to construct the variables designed to capture the influences of the factors identified in Figure 1 is described in the next section. The empirical models used to test the strengths of various effects on each of the paths are also specified.

DATA BASE, MODEL SPECIFICATION/VARIABLE CONSTRUCTION, AND DESCRIPTIVE STATISTICS

A. Data Base

The data used in this investigation were collected through a structured interview designed to elucidate the circumstances of welfare recipients. The survey was administered over a four month period in 1982 to a sample of "low income" residents of public housing complexes in the Dayton-Springfield, Ohio SMSA. The choice of residents of public housing complexes provided general comparability in the environmental circumstances facing respondents. Efforts were made to interview all residents of eight complexes on lists provided by the Dayton Housing Authority. Interviews were conducted on a one-to-one basis by a team of eight undergraduate students trained in survey techniques. The questionnaire required an average of two and a half hours to administer. This process yielded 290 female respondents; 79.0 percent (229) black, 21.0 percent (61) white.

All of the variables used in the investigation were taken directly from responses to survey items. As indicated previously, the parameters of special concern are (a) welfare recipiency, (b) labor force status, (c) sense of self-efficacy, and (d) health status. The construction of the dependent variables used as proxies for each of these parameters is described first. The independent variables in the empirical models used to analyze paths of influence are then specified.

B. Model Specification/Variable Construction

1. Dependent Variables
   (a) Welfare Dependency/Welfare Recipiency
Two measures of linkage to the welfare system are used. The first measure, ONWEL, is a dichotomous indicator of whether an individual was receiving public assistance at the time of the survey (1 = Yes, 0 = No). The second measure, TMEWEL, is a coded indicator of the number of months a respondent had been receiving assistance at the same time of the survey. TMEWEL ranges from 1 (less than six months) to 6 (4-5 years).
   (b) Labor Force Status
Two dichotomous measures of labor force activity are used, current labor force participation status, WKSTAT, (1 = In Labor Force, 0 = No) and FULTJB which is assigned the value 1 if a respondent reported ever having a full time job and 0 otherwise.

(c) Sense of Self-Efficacy

Two separate sets of metrics were developed to measure the sense of self-efficacy depicted in Figure 1. This was accomplished by using principal components analysis to generate composite measures from raw data. The questions used to develop the metrics are shown in Tables 1 and 2, as well as the coefficients obtained from the analysis. The first group of indicators, BELIEF1, BELIEF2, and BELIEF3, emphasizes basic values and perceptions of self-worth. The second group of measures, WKORIENT1, WKORIENT2, WKORIENT3, WKORIENT4, and WKORIENT5, focuses more specifically on values related to work effort, expected patterns of upward mobility, the commitment to planning as a way of attaining goals, and perceptions of mastery over the environment. The question "In getting ahead, would you say that hard work is important to most people?" is common to both sets of metrics.

(d) Health Status

Although we are principally concerned with the impact of health status on economic behavior, factors affecting reported health status are also explored. This approach provides a means for interpreting the direction of causation. Two separate dichotomous measures of health were developed from the responses to questions about diagnosed cases of the following health problems: (a) arthritis or rheumatism, (b) ulcers, (c) cancer, (d) high blood pressure, (e) liver ailments, (f) kidney ailments, (g) stroke, (h) nervous condition, (i) diabetes, and/or (j) hardening of the arteries. The first health measure, HLTH1, was assigned the value 1 if a respondent indicated that at least one of the health problems restricted activities a great deal, and 0 otherwise. The second measure, HLTH2, was assigned the value 1 if a respondent indicated that at least one of the health problems listed above restricted activities moderately, but not a great deal, and 0 otherwise.

2. Model Specification and Independent Variables

(a) Model Specification

The structure of the empirical models of the factors affecting each of the dependent variables is presented schematically in Figure 2. Depending on the structure of the dependent variable, either standard multiple regression or logistical multiple regression techniques were used to estimate the models. Prior to the description of independent variables, it is useful to note special features of the estimation process. The models presented in columns (1) and (2) were estimated for each of the constructed measures of self-efficacy—three general belief indicators and five work orientation indicators. The model specification allows interaction between general beliefs and work orientation.

TABLE 1
Principal Component Eigenvectors
General Beliefs

Content	BELIEF1	BELIEF2	BELIEF3
1. In Getting Ahead Would You Say That Hard Work Is Important To Most People (1 = Yes; 0 = No)	-.50	-.46	.61
2. If You Were Guaranteed An Adequate Income Would You Work, Not Work, Not Sure If You Would Work (1 = Work; 2 = Not Sure, 3 = Not Work)	.51	.32	.78
3. I Am A Useful Person (1 = Almost Always True; 2 = Often True; 3 = Not Often True; 4 = Never True)	.59	-.15	-.15
4. I Feel That My Life Is Not Very Useful (1 = Almost Always True; 2 = Often True; 3 = Not Often True; 4 = Never True)	-.37	.82	.01
Proportion of Variation Explained	.36	.24	.21

The possibility that health status influences either or both types of beliefs is accounted for. The formulation assumes that values are shaped primarily by structural conditions rather than by behavioral responses to those conditions and that no differences across race exist in factors affecting self-efficacy.

The model specification for the analysis of present and historical labor force attachment is identical and allows for possible differences between blacks and whites. Discrimination is one factor that could generate such differences.

To account for simultaneity among labor force participation, welfare

TABLE 2
Principal Component Eigenvectors
Work Orientation

Content	WKORIENT1	WKORIENT2	WKORIENT3	WKORIENT4	WKORIENT5
1. Is Hard Work Important To You (1 = Yes; 2 = Not Sure; 3 = No)	-.16	-.01	-.53	.66	.08
2. In Getting Ahead Would You Say That Hard Work Is Important To Most People (1 = Yes; 0 = No)	.32	.35	-.12	-.46	.005
3. Which Statement Comes Closer To The Way You Really Feel (1 = The Rich Get Richer and The Poor Get Poorer; 2 = Everyone Has The Same Opportunities If He/She Has The Ability And Desire to Make It)	-.25	-.19	-.15	-.29	.89
4. Most People Make It In Our Society Through Working Hard (1 = Yes; 0 = No)	.63	-.23	-.30	.02	.08
5. Most People Make It In Our Society By Beating the System ((1 = Yes; 0 = No)	-.19	-.53	.52	.11	-.04

recipiency/dependency, and health status, the predicted value of WK-STAT (WKSTAT*) rather than the actual value is used in the examination of the factors affecting welfare recipiency and health status.

The examination of the factors affecting probability of receiving assistance and duration of recipiency differ only in inclusion of an additional variable to test for differences by race in the latter analysis.

The model examining factors affecting the probability of illness reporting (Column 7) were estimated separately for HLTH1 and HLTH2. Actual rather than predicted values of the health status indicators are used as arguments in the other models.

TABLE 2 *(Continued)*

6. Most People Make It In Our Society Both By Working Hard And Beating The System (1 = Yes; 0 = No)	-.44	.61	.05	.02	.01
7. Do You Think It's Better To (1 = Plan Your Life A Good Ways Ahead Or 2 = Would You Say Life Is Too Much A Matter Of Luck To Plan Ahead)	.31	.28	.24	.48	.33
8. When I Think Of Life Nowadays (1 = I Can Make Things Happen; 0 = I Can't Control Things Or Life Depends On Luck)	.29	.24	.51	.17	.27
Proportion of Variation Explained	.22	.19	.14	.13	.11

(b) Independent Variables

To facilitate presentation, the description of independent variables is organized to correspond to the variable categories in Figure 1. Descriptions of self-efficacy and health status indicators are not repeated.

(1) Individual Background Characteristics

The two background characteristics used are the respondent's age and educational level, measured by two coded variables, AGE, and EDU-LEV, respectively.

(2) Marital Status

To examine marital status effects, separate dichotomous indicators were constructed indicating if a respondent was married with spouse present (MAR), separated (SEP), or divorced (DIV). This alogrithm treats never married women as the reference group.

(3) Presence and Age Distribution of Children

Four dummy variables are used to capture the effects of differences in children's age distribution on welfare dependency and health status. CHUN-SIX indicates the presence of children under six, CH6-12 is assigned the

FIGURE 2
Structure of Empirical Models

Independent Variables In Models	Dependent Variable in Model			
	(1) Self Worth (BELIEF1-3)	(2) Work Orientation (WKORIENT1-5)	(3) Current Labor Force Status (WKSTAT)	(4) Previous Employment Experience (FULTJB)
AGE	X	X	X	X
EDULEV	X	X	X	X
CHUNSIX	X	X	X	X
CH6-12	X	X	X	X
CH12-18	X	X	X	X
CHUN6-18	X	X	X	X
MAR	X	X	X	X
DIV	X	X	X	X
SEP	X	X	X	X
EXT	X	X	X	X
EXTHLP			X	X
FAMHLP			X	X
BELIEF1-3		X		
WKORIENT1-5	X			
FULTJB			X	
WKSTAT*				X
ONWEL				
TMEWEL				
HLTH1	X	X	X	X
HLTH2	X	X	X	X
RACE			X	X
RACE*ONWEL				
RACE*HLTH			X	X

FIGURE 2 (*Continued*)

	Dependent Variable in Model		
	(5)	(6)	(7)
Independent Variables In Models	Current Receipt of Public Assistance (ONWEL)	Duration of Receipt of Assistance (TMEWEL)	Reporting of Health Problems (HLTH1,2)
AGE	X	X	X
EDULEV	X	X	X
CHUNSIX	X	X	X
CH6-12	X	X	X
CH12-18	X	X	X
CHUN6-18	X	X	X
MAR	X	X	X
DIV	X	X	X
SEP	X	X	X
EXT	X	X	X
EXTHLP	X	X	X
FAMHLP	X	X	X
BELIEF1-3	X	X	X
WKORIENT1-5	X	X	X
FULTJB	X	X	X
WKSTAT*	X	X	X
ONWEL			X
TMEWEL			
HLTH1	X	X	
HLTH2	X	X	
RACE	X	X	
RACE*ONWEL		X	X
RACE*HLTH		X	X

value 1 for cases where children are between 6 and 12 years old, and the presence of children between 12 and 18 years old is indicated by CH12-18. The fourth dummy variable CHUN6-18, indicates the presence of children that span the entire age range. This algorithm treats women without children as the reference group. The disaggregation to segment age range effects introduces some potential multicollinearity problems, especially between the variables CHUNSIX and CHUN6-18. Given that these variables function essentially as control variables in the investigation, special efforts to correct the multicollinearity are not undertaken.

(4) Helping Relationships

The variables focusing on helping relationships focus on extended family structure and resource sharing. The variable EXT is assigned the value 1 if the respondent indicated that relatives other than members of the immediate family live in the residence, and 0 otherwise. The variable EXTWCH is assigned the value 1 if relatives other than members of the immediate family live in the household and these relatives have children living with them. As would be expected, these variables are highly colinear. Efforts to correct this problem were not pursued since they serve essentially as control variables.

Two indicators of familial support patterns are included, EXTHLP and FAMHLP. The former measures the magnitude of help and is assigned the value 1 if a respondent indicated that the family was a "great help" or a "lot of help" to the respondent and 0 if it was indicated that family was "only a little help" to the respondent. FAMHLP measures frequency of the provision of help and was developed from responses to the question was "How often do people in your family help you out?" Responses were coded from 0, indicating never, to 4, indicating a high frequency of help provision.

(5) Racial Differences

We test for racial differences by including the variable RACE, a dummy variable assigned the value 1 if the respondent is black and 0 if white. A variable is also included to allow for the possibility that blacks reporting health problems display distinct patterns. This variable RACE*HLTH is defined as 1 if a respondent is black and reports experiencing an illness that either moderately or severely restricts activity.

Descriptive Statistics

The variable means and standard deviations for the subsample of all black and white respondents are shown in columns (1)—(4) of table 3.

TABLE 3
Means and Standard Deviation

| | Complete Sample | | | | Welfare Recipients | | | |
| | BLACK | | WHITE | | BLACK | | WHITE | |
Variable	(1) Mean	(2) Std. Dev.	(3) Mean	(4) Std. Dev.	(5) Mean	(6) Std. Dev.	(7) Mean	(8) Std. Dev.
ONWEL	.61	.49	.74	.44	-	-	-	-
TMEWEL	2.92	2.63	1.95	1.79	3.29	1.52	2.44	1.31
HLTH1	.21	.41	.31	.47	.15	.36	.33	.48
HLTH2	.15	.36	.21	.41	.16	.37	.20	.40
AGE	5.40	2.08	5.52	1.82	4.94	1.88	5.36	1.64
EDULEV	7.04	1.52	6.61	1.60	7.14	1.33	6.31	1.64
MAR	.09	.28	.33	.47	.06	.24	.29	.46
DIV	.24	.43	.38	.49	.24	.43	.38	.49
SEP	.12	.33	.08	.28	.11	.31	.11	.32
CHUNSIX	.35	.48	.36	.48	.48	.50	.38	.49
CH6-12	.13	.33	.15	.36	.17	.38	.18	.39
CH12-18	.15	.36	.11	.32	.09	.29	.13	.34
CHUN6-18	.18	.39	.28	.45	.18	.38	.27	.45
EXT	.09	.29	.08	.28	.12	.33	.04	.21
EXTWCH	.05	.22	.03	.18	.08	.28	.02	.15
EXTHLP	1.34	1.07	1.05	1.19	1.42	1.07	1.11	1.25
FAMHLP	3.16	1.04	3.21	1.08	3.20	.92	3.20	1.12

TABLE 3 *(Continued)*

| | Complete Sample | | | | Welfare Recipients | | | |
| | BLACK | | WHITE | | BLACK | | WHITE | |
Variable	(1) Mean	(2) Std. Dev.	(3) Mean	(4) Std. Dev.	(5) Mean	(6) Std. Dev.	(7) Mean	(8) Std. Dev.
BELIEF1	-.12	.72	-.21	.64	-.13	.69	-.15	.65
BELIEF2	2.42	.74	2.32	.72	2.39	.72	2.27	.71
BELIEF3	1.25	.45	1.25	.33	1.25	.43	1.20	.28
WKORIENT1	1.19	.66	1.11	.61	1.20	.66	1.07	.61
WKORIENT2	.64	.52	.62	.58	.66	.54	.55	.60
WKORIENT3	-.54	.57	-.39	.43	-.53	.57	-.43	.43
WKORIENT4	.76	.57	.57	.45	.79	.58	.53	.46
WKORIENT5	1.12	.46	1.10	.40	1.11	.46	1.06	.40
FULTJB	.84	.37	.92	.28	.81	.39	.89	.32
WKSTAT	.13	.16	.11	.17	.10	.13	.09	.14
WKSTAT*	.13	.16	.11	.17	.10	.13	.09	.14
N	229		61		142		45	

*Measures explicitly computed to produce linear variation by RACE

Several interesting patterns can be observed. A significant majority of the sample were on welfare at the time of the survey. White respondents had a higher probability of receiving public assistance currently, but black respondents were longer-term welfare recipients. Black respondents were slightly younger and had completed more years of formal education than white respondents. A significantly higher proportion of black respondents had never married, while a larger proportion of white respondents reported that they were married. Little difference in patterns of extendedness exist for the entire sample. While white respondents had a higher probability of having held a full time job at some time, black respondents tended to display a slightly higher labor force participation rate. Finally, white respondents were significantly more likely than black respondents to report health problems either significantly or moderately restricting activity.

The variable means and standard deviations for the subset of black and white welfare recipients are presented in columns (5)—(8) of Table 3. In comparison to the entire sample, the group of welfare recipients was slightly younger for both blacks and whites, with a larger difference for blacks. For blacks, welfare recipients were slightly more educated than nonrecipients, while the reverse was true among whites. Marital status does not vary markedly between welfare recipients and nonrecipients for either blacks or whites. The subset of black welfare recipients has a significantly higher proportion of preschool age children than that of nonrecipients, in contrast to the subsample of whites. Black welfare recipients were more likely to live in an extended familial configuration than any other subgroup, but patterns of support provided by relatives do not vary significantly across the subpopulations.

Differences in work experience and current labor force status are not dramatic between recipients and nonrecipients for either blacks or whites. Blacks were less likely than whites to report that illnesses moderately or severely restricts activity. Little variation exists among the subpopulations relative to the various psychological metrics that were constructed.

These basic patterns are useful for interpreting the results of the selected phases of the empirical analysis presented below.

RESULTS

Detailed results are presented only for the analyses of (a) factors affecting work history and labor market status, (b) factors affecting receipt of public assistance, and (c) factors affecting duration of receipt of public assistance.[16] In general, the results suggest that there is a linkage between self-efficacy and illness reporting, but it was not possible to identify particular self-efficacy profiles associated with adoption of the sick role.

The results also indicate that neither welfare recipiency per se nor length of time of receipt of assistance is associated with increased illness-reporting probability. Work history also has no indicated impact on the probability of reporting illnesses while, as would be expected, individuals with a higher predicted probability of being in the labor force have a lower probability of reporting illnesses. The results provide no support for the hypothesis that differences between blacks and whites exist for the probability of reporting illnesses. This finding is at variance with those of previous studies.

Although the results of the analysis of factors affecting sense of self-efficacy are not presented in detail, they are of interest because they provide evidence on the direction of causation between self-efficacy and "successful" economic functioning. In general, other than the companion subset of self-efficacy indicators, none of the variables is a consistent predictor of differences in either sense of mastery or work orientation. AGE is the most reliable background indicator, but its coefficient is significant in only a minority of cases. Reporting severe health-related activity restrictions appears to affect general beliefs but not work orientation. Although economic parameters and personal characteristisc have little indicated impact on self-efficacy metrics, the reverse direction of causation may occur. This possibility is examined below in the discussion of the principal results.

A. Determinants of Work History and Labor Force Status

The results obtained from analyzing factors affecting work history and current labor force status are presented in Table 4. Educational level is the only consistent predictor of the probability of a respondent both having held a full-time job and being currently employed. Married women are more likely to be currently employed than other women, but are no more likely to have had a work history that includes full time employment. Neither the presence nor the age distribution of children influences work history and only the presence of children under six significantly reduces current labor force participation.

Interestingly, there is only one statistically significant coefficient for the indicators of general world view and none for those measures associated with work orientation. This suggests the absence of a measurable influence of values and beliefs on labor market bahavior for this sample.

TABLE 4
Analysis of Factors Affecting Previous Work History
and Current Labor Force Status

Variable	FULTJB		WKSTAT	
	Coeff.	Std. E.	Coeff.	Std. E.
AGE	.164	.151	.115	.165
EDULEV	.401*	.139	.499*	.240
MAR	8.395	20.725	1.610*	.692
DIV	.491	.600	1.028	.669
SEP	-.027	.705	.091	.861
HLTH1	.744	.633	-.123	1.752
HLTH2	-.279	.534	.207	1.327
CHUNSIX	-.204	.610	-1.260*	.616
CH6-12	-.051	.767	-.968	.843
CH12-18	.573	.918	.143	.765
CHUN6-18	-.514	.696	-.442	.678
EXT	1.038	1.092	.708	.961
EXTWCH	.580	1.554	**	**
EXTHLP	-.062	.191	-.148	.233
FAMHLP	-.383	.261	.294	.238
RACE	-.141	.588	.663	.658
RACE*HLTH	**	**	-1.872	1.625
BELIEF1	-.160	.451	-1.758	1.137
BELIEF2	-.132	.360	.330	.689
BELIEF3	1.590*	.763	-3.066	2.561
WKORIENT1	-.619	.492	.522	.661
WKORIENT2	-.449	.481	.440	.630
WKORIENT3	.336	.490	-.331	.563
WKORIENT4	.840	.762	-1.589	1.180
WKORIENT5	.849	.426	.162	.516
INTERCEPT	-1.988	2.210	-4.316	4.177
N =	290		290	
-2 LOG L -	191.43		156.75	

*Significant at the 90% Level of Confidence or Better
**Limited Dispersion Precluded Computation of Standard Error

No statistically significant differences between women reporting health problems and those not reporting such problems are present for either work history or current labor market status.

Neither living in an extended family setting nor patterns of family support, have statistically significant impacts on either the probability of having held a full-time job or current employment. Finally, there are no significant differences for RACE per se. In addition, there is no evidence that black women reporting health problems have either different work histories or lower current labor force participation than any other subset in the sample.

B. Determinants of Welfare Recipiency

The results obtained from analyzing patterns of welfare recipiency are shown in Table 5. Younger women have a higher probability of receiving assistance. At the same time, being divorced or separated is also associated with increased probability of receiving welfare. Respondents living in an extended arrangement that includes relatives' children have an indicated higher probability of receiving assistance. This probability reflects the particularly vulnerable economic position of women in such settings. It should also be noted that neither the presence of nor the degree of support provided through helping networks has a significant effect on the probability of receiving assistance. This suggests that support from family and friends is not a substitute for government aid. Level of education has no indicated effect on the probability of receiving assistance. This result is to be expected since the socioeconomic class of women in the sample is fairly homogeneous.

One particularly interesting result is that neither work history nor predicted labor force status have statistically significant coefficients. These findings do not result from multicollinearity problems. The correlation coefficient between WKSTAT* and FULTJB is only .08. This low correlation reflects in part the low correlation between actual labor force status (WKSTAT) and FULTJB (.15).

The indicators of self-efficacy exhibit extremely weak explanatory power. None of the coefficients of the self-efficacy metrics have statistically significant coefficients. This suggests that observed behavior leading to and/or associated with receipt of public assistance may not be significantly related to the values and sense of self-efficacy of recipients in this sample.

The absence of a direct linkage between welfare recipiency and reporting of illness, is reaffirmed. Neither the coefficient of HLTH1, nor that of HLTH2 is significant. Moreover, the insignificant coefficient obtained for RACE*HLTH indicates no differences in the probability of reporting illnesses for black women reporting health problems. The coefficient of RACE is also statistically insignificant. Thus, when appropriate controls are introduced, there is no difference between blacks and

TABLE 5
Analysis of Factors Affecting the Probability of Welfare Recipient Status

Variable	Coefficient	Std. Error
AGE	-.309*	.110
EDULEV	-.072	.116
RACE	-.518	.459
RACE*HLTH	.463	1.015
HLTH1	-.297	1.087
HLTH2	-.272	.881
CHUNSIX	2.225*	.515
CH6-12	2.623*	.618
CH12-18	.767	.532
CHUN6-18	1.609*	.491
MAR	-.149	.626
DIV	.977*	.477
SEP	.905*	.546
EXT	-.441	.650
EXTWCH	2.824*	1.253
EXTHLP	-.036	.138
FAMHLP	-.055	.149
BELIEF1	-.229	.370
BELIEF2	-.281	.287
BELIEF3	.254	.481
WKORIENT1	.340	.389
WKORIENT2	-.200	.350
WKORIENT3	.452	.379
WKORIENT4	-.392	.608
WKORIENT5	-.022	.342
FULTJB	-.598	.462
WKSTAT*	-.471	1.654
INTERCEPT	2.353	1.567

N =   290
-2 Log L -   299.91

*Significant at the 90% Level of Confidence or Better

whites in the probability of receiving public assistance. Consequently, the pattern of a greater proportion of white respondents receiving public assistance, reflected in the variable means in Table 3, is eliminated when relevant factors are controlled.

C. Duration of Welfare Recipiency

Table 6 contains the results of the analysis of factors affecting the length of time individuals have been receiving public assistance. Neither marital status nor patterns of extendedness nor patterns of family support display significant explanatory power in contrast to the results reported in Table 5. The latter two results suggest that the capacity of social networks to provide support is limited and erodes over time. As was the case in the analysis of current recipiency status, current labor force participation and work history have no statistically significant effects.

In comparison to the results in Table 5, the measures of self-efficacy display slightly more explanatory power; however, only two of the work orientation metrics have significant coefficients. The coefficient of RACE is positive and statistically significant. This finding is consistent with basic patterns reflected by the means presented in Table 3 indicating that blacks tend to have been longer-term recipients of public assistance than whites. It contrasts, however, with the conclusion that blacks are no more likely to be current recipients of public assistance than whites.

As can be seen from the insignificance of the coefficient of RACE*HLTH, there is no support for the hypothesis that black women reporting health problems are likely to be longer-term recipients of public assistance than other women. This finding parallels that obtained in the anlaysis of factors affecting the likelihood of receiving public assistance. As is the case in Table 5, neither the coefficient of HLTH1, nor that of HLTH2, is statistically significant. Thus, in general, there is no indication that a linkage exists between the likelihood of reporting illnesses and long-term receipt of public assistance.

CONCLUSIONS

This analysis has examined the extent to which systematic differences exist between blacks and whites in the relationship among values/beliefs work attachment, and welfare dependency. Specific paths by which various outcomes are generated were hypothesized and modeled. The paths of influence of particular concern are (a) the determinants of a sense of

TABLE 6
Analysis of Factors Affecting Period of Welfare Recipiency

Variable	Coefficient	Std. Error
AGE	.207*	.088
EDULEV	-.013	.094
RACE	.931*	.301
RACE*HLTH	-.176	.705
HLTH1	.473	.764
HLTH2	.212	.583
CHUNSIX	.897	.540
CH6-12	1.767*	.540
CH12-18	.810	.531
CHUN6-18	1.199*	.502
MAR	-.449	.472
DIV	-.154	.346
SEP	-.132	.404
EXT	-.405	.496
EXTWCH	.354	.588
EXTHLP	-.020	.102
FAMHLP	-.149	.118
BELIEF1	-.125	.278
BELIEF2	-.349	.222
BELIEF3	.384	.373
WKORIENT1	-.481*	.294
WKORIENT2	.044	.247
WKORIENT3	-.350	.282
WKORIENT4	.761*	.435
WKORIENT5	-.321	.254
FULTJB	-.455	.295
WKSTAT*	-.412	1.440
INTERCEPT	2.272*	1.238

N =   184
F =   2.49

R^2 =   .30

*Significant at the 90% Level of Confidence or Better

self-efficacy, (b) the extent to which self-efficacy and health status affect current labor force status and previous work history, and (c) the extent to which self-efficacy, health status, expected labor status and work history affect the probability of receiving public assistance and the duration of receipt. In considering each path of influence, the extent to which racial differences exist was a major thrust of the inquiry.

No racial differences were found vis a vis the determinants of current labor force status and previous work history. Race was also found to have no significant impact on the probability of receiving public assistance. Weak evidence was found to suggest that blacks tend to be longer-term welfare recipients than whites.

Measures of self-efficacy were found to have virtually no explanatory power vis a vis the probability of receipt and the duration of assistance. No evidence was indicated to suggest that previous full-time employment militates against long-term receipt of public assistance and no support was found for the hypothesis that a higher probability of labor force participation reduces welfare dependency nor for the hypothesis that previous full-time employment reduces probability of receiving public assistance. Age and presence of young children were the most consistent predictors of welfare recipiency status and length of receipt of aid. Programs that require welfare recipients to work in order to receive benefits clearly have the potential to alter some of the patterns observed in this investigation. It will be recalled from Table 3 that only about 10 percent of the recipients were currently working. Linking benefits to work effort will put additional pressure on social support networks that provide child care. Efforts of women to attend school will also be affected.

We find no support for the hypothesis that a linkage exists between welfare recipiency and the reporting of illnesses. We do find support for the hypothesis that health status affects sense of self-efficacy and that self-efficacy affects the reporting of illnesses. The presence of health problems was found to have no significant impact on either the probability of receiving assistance or on the duration of receipt of assistance. Blacks reporting health problems were found to be no more likely to receive assistance or to receive such assistance for a longer period than other women.

Several of these findings are at variance with those reported by other analysts. This may result, in part, from special characteristics of the sample used in the investigation.

At the minimum, however, this analysis suggests the need for additional research refining the approach used in the present investigation. Improvement of the various metrics, and in particular, the psychological/value indicators would improve the capability of identifying and interpreting effects of the linkages explored in this investigation. Ideally, subsequent research should be conducted with a longitudinal data base that would allow changes in welfare recipiency status, in household composition, in health status, and in values/psychological orientation to be tracked. Such a research design would be of tremendous benefit in generating a consensus as to the magnitude and extent of race-associated differences in illness reporting and welfare dependency.

Irrespective of these caveats, this investigation suggests that the principal direction of research and intervention models should focus on identifying structural barriers to escaping dependency and designing coordinated labor market, housing, educational, and child care policies. While efforts to enhance the sense of self-efficacy can potentially complement efforts to de-activate structural barriers, the findings of this study suggest that self-efficacy enhancement alone will be insufficient to address the magnitude of the problems faced by low-income families. Developing an effective intervention strategy along the lines suggested is likely to be increasingly difficult, however, given the current political climate and patterns of structural discrimination. Recognition of the primacy of structural constraints can hopefully, however, provide additional momentum for continuing efforts to improve the quality of life for black families.

NOTES

1. See for example Marjorie Honig, "AFDC Income, Recipient Rates and Family Dissolution," *Journal of Human Resources*, Volume 9 (1974), pp. 303-322; and Lawrence Southwick, "The Effect of Welfare Programs on Family Stability," *Review of Social Economy*, Volume 36 (1978), pp. 19-39.

2. Daniel Moynihan, "The Negro Family: The Case for National Action," in Lee Rainwater and William Yancy, eds., *The Moynihan Report and the Politics of Controversy*, (Cambridge, MA: Harvard University Press, 1967).

3. Albert Bandura, "Self-Efficacy Mechanism in Human Agency," *American Psychologist*, Volume 37 (1982), pp. 122-147; Albert Bandura, "Self-Efficacy: Toward a Unifying Theory of Behavioral Change," *Psychological Review*, Volume 84 (1977), pp. 191-215; and Albert Bandura, "Fearful Expectations and Avoidant Actions as Coeffects of Perceived Self-Inefficacy," *American Psychologist*, Volume 41 (1986), pp. 1389-1391.

4. Bandura (1982), p. 122.

5. Bandura (1982), p. 123

6. Patricia Gurin, Gerald Gurin, and Betty M. Morrison, "Personal and Ideological Aspects of Internal and External Control, *Social Psycology*, Volume 41 (1978), pp. 275-296.

7. See for example Joyce Aschenbrenner, "Extended Families Among Black Americans," *Comparative Family Studies* (1973), pp. 257-268; Andrew Billingsley, *Black Families in White America*, (Englewood Cliffs, N.J.: Prentice-Hall, 1968); and Carol Stack, *All Our Kin*, (New York: Harper and Row, 1974).

8. See for example D. Brewington and J. Comerford, *A Look at the Kin Family Network of Black and White Families*, (master's research paper, Howard University of Social Work, 1974); and Robert Hill and Lawrence B. Shackelford, "The Black Extended Family Revisited," *Urban League Review* (1975), p. 1.

9. William Hays and Charles Mindel, "Extended Kinship Relations in Black and White Families," *Journal of Marriage and the Family*, Volume 35 (1973).

10. James B. Stewart, "Some Factors Determining the Work Effort of Single Black Women," *Review of Social Economy*, Volume 40 (1981), pp. 30-44.

11. Edgar O. Prince, "Welfare Status, Illness and Subjective Health Definition," *American Journal of Public Health*, Volume 68 (1978), pp. 865-870.

12. Stephen Cole and Robert Lejeune, "Illness and Legitimation of Failure," *American Sociological Review*, Volume 37 (1972), pp. 347-356.

13. See for example Sidney Cobb, "Social Support as a Moderator of Life Stress," *Psychosomatic Medicine*, Volume 38 (1976), pp. 300-314; Susan Gore, "The Effects of Social Support in Moderating the Health Consequences of Unemployment," *Journal of Health and Social Behavior*, Volume 19 (1978), pp. 157–165; and Scott Henderson, "The Social Network, Support and Neurosis: The Function of Attachment in Adult Life," *British Journal of Psychiatry*, Volume 131 (1977), pp. 185-191.

14. John Mirowsky III and Catherine E. Ross, "Minority Status, Ethnic Culture, and Distress: A Comparison of Blacks, Whites, Mexicans and Mexican Americans," *American Journal of Sociology*, Volume 86 (1980), pp. 479-495.

15. Frederic D. Wolinsky, "Racial Differences in Illness Behavior," *Journal of Community Health*, Volume 8 (1982), pp. 87-101.

16. Complete results of the analysis of factors affecting reporting of illnesses can be obtained from the author upon request.

Part V

Intracultural Perspectives

INTRODUCTION

Earlier the point was made that as work on this volume progressed it became apparent that it is necessary to write about *black families* lest the implication reside that there exists an authentic, monolithic black family. A major purpose of this book is to demonstrate that individual family units have responded differently to their sociohistorical experiences. The variations that distinguish black families in the United States likewise attend other families of African origin. The chapters in this section provide a basis for comparisons of the form and functioning of black families in the United States, the Caribbean, and Nigeria, as these families have responded to distinct societal conventions.

Austin, in the first chapter, for example, demonstrates that father-absence, which occurs with unusual frequency among African-descended people in the Caribbean, is not attended by the apparent stigma and negative social and economic consequences that black-American families suffer. He looks systematically at several arguments that have been advanced in support of the contention that father-absence is harmful to their offspring, and particularly so to the male offspring. Austin's data allow the conclusion that the proposed harmful effects are not invariant among families in St. Vincent. Rather, he reports that in some instances father-absent youth have higher aspirations and performances. Austin suggests that this effect may be owed to low stigmatization of father-absence in St. Vincent.

Okpala's chapter then addresses the relationship between child care and female employment in urban Nigeria. He focuses specifically on the "noneconomic" theory of households that proposes that powerful local norms of female seclusion severely restrict women from engaging in economic activity outside the family and on the issue of the choices women face in Third World nations. Of all factors implicated, Okpala notes that family composition, that is, presence of young children, a paid baby-sitter, or relative in the household, is a critical factor influencing mothers employment rate. He concludes that mothers with paid babysitters, as contrasted with other sources of child care, spend a greater part of their married life and of their available daily hours in outside employment. As help from relatives does not significantly affect rate of employment, Okpala concludes that the influence is likely due rather to the nature of such help.

Continuing the themes of Austin's and Okpala's chapters, Millette, in the last chapter in this section, notes that the purposes of marriage in the Caribbean differ from the purposes for which Americans marry. In the Caribbean, reproduction remains as the main function and marriage constitutes an alliance between two families or bodies of kin. Americans, Millette suggests, marry to fulfill new functions of friendship and emotional support needs that have been occasioned by the high mobility of U.S. society. These distinctions provide a base for conflict between Old and New World behaviors.

Millette divides West Indian families in the United States into three groups: "Maintainers," "Social Isolates," and "Social Strivers," and examines how these families are coping with migration, technology, discrimination, prejudice, and the loss of social status and personhood. He concludes that West Indian migration to the United States has resulted in normlessness and redefinition of the marital contract and, further, that the family structure of the "Social Isolates" is least affected, while the "Striver" families are experiencing the most conflict.

Together, the chapters in this section provide important complementary portraits of the differing social realities of black families who have a common African heritage.

13

FAMILY ENVIRONMENT, EDUCATIONAL ASPIRATION, AND PERFORMANCE IN ST. VINCENT

Roy L. Austin

Father-absence occurs with unusual frequency among people of African descent in the Caribbean. Yet concern over possibly harmful effects of this condition to children and society which is most obvious in the United States is not informed by scientific findings from this region. The present study yielded no evidence that father-absence retards the aspiration or performance of secondary school students in St. Vincent, West Indies, although twelve different groupings of the available cases were analyzed. Findings from this and some American studies suggest that father-absence is not harmful if it is not strongly condemned by the culture with which youths identify.

A high rate of father-absence resulting from illegitimacy and serial mating in many Caribbean territories encouraged an early interest among researchers in the consequences of father-absence in these territories.[1] But there are no recent systematic studies of this subject in this region, and the few older studies yielded conflicting answers on the likely adverse effects of father-absence and/or illegitimacy. Thus, two studies suggest that the lower status ascribed to a man's "outside" relative to his legitimate children[2] seems to have eventuated in a lower likelihood of delaying gratification[3] and of performing well in school[4] for father- absent than father-present children. But Simey[5] had earlier stated that illegitimate children suffer no harmful consequences from this status.

Even in the colonial period when European-derived norms were more dominant, it was observed that "the actual amount of stigma suffered by the average illegitimate child cannot be great, relative to legitimate children in his same stratum and neighborhood."[6] In recent years, not only has there been a deliberate effort to develop norms more suited to local circumstances, but there is some evidence that the rates of illegitimacy and, presumably, father-absence have increased. For example, in St. Lucia,[7] the island closest geographically to the one studied, illegitimacy rates between 1955 and 1961 ranged form 60.7 percent to 72.8 percent. But in 1979 and 1980, St. Lucia's rates are 82.6 percent and 87 percent respectively.[8] And it is reasonable to expect that the stigma attached to illegitimacy and father-absence should decrease as these conditions become less deviant statistically (that is, more common). Therefore, the present study tries to determine whether father-absence is related to educational aspiration and performance for any socioeconomic/gender group of secondary school students in 1982 in St. Vincent.

The results of the proposed study may have implications beyond the Caribbean. Presently, there is great concern in the United States over the high rates of father-absence in the black family. Juvenile delinquency, poor school performance, perpetuation of the cycle of poverty, and mental illness are but a few of the social problems claimed to result from father absence.[9] And syndicated newspaper columnists,[10] television journalists[11] and academics[12] have lamented the ready denunciations of the Moynihan[13] report which with a different reception might have slowed the "deterioration" of the black family. But it may be more productive to note that few analyses of the "crises" in the black family in America are informed by research findings on black families in other countries despite recognition that female-headed families are also unusually frequent in the Caribbean, Brazil, and on the Caribbean coast of Central America.[14] For instance, the controversial argument that welfare benefits induce black women to choose female-headed families[15] is less convincing when the high frequency of female-headship in the Caribbean is considered. Welfare payments similar to AFDC do not occur in the Caribbean. Caribbean findings on the effects of father-absence may likewise aid understanding of American results and/or make them more compelling.

THEORETICAL CONSIDERATIONS

Several arguments have been been advanced to support the claim that father-absence is harmful to children.[16] One account holds that the absence of the father creates economic hardship for the family.[17] In order to meet financial needs, the mother may join the labor force and leave the children unsuitably supervised, a state believed to produce behavioral problems. Or, children may enter the labor force at an early age and show a corresponding decline in educational aspiration and achievement. This argument accepts that father-absence causes undesirable attitudes in or actions by children.

However, a second socioeconomic argument regards any findings of a relationship between father-absence and undesirable characteristics as spurious. The position in this instance is that background variables such as income and education are related to both father-absence and the undesirable characteristics and are said to account for the relationship between these latter variables.

A third argument, derived from socializaion theory, emphasizes the importance of a male role model for the proper psychological development of the child. Males are expected to be harmed more than females because the male role model is more critical to the psychosexual development of males. A review of the literature by Hetherington et al.[18] revealed some empirical support for this expectation.

A fourth perspective regards the stigma of illegitimacy, divorce and abandonment by a parent as the crucial adverse factor. A variant of this view is that the trauma of divorce or abandonment has a damaging psychological impact due to extreme anger or feelings of loss. The stigma variant of this fourth perspective was the major impetus for the present study. It was reasoned that father-absence is unlikely to have negative effects in groups for whom it is not statistically deviant. At the least, the effect should be weaker for such groups than for others. And the high rate of illegitimacy and father-absence in lower class families in the Caribbean suggested that negative effects should be nonexistent in this group.

Each explanation of the expected relationship between father-absence and a harmful consequence implies a finding that depends on a group's socio-economic status. If the stigma explanation is valid, higher SES groups should show more harm in those situations where father-absence is more deviant at this level, as it usually is. If the economic hardship explanation is valid, youths from poorer families should be more likely than more advantaged youths to be harmed. And if it is socialization in the absence of a male role model that is the major difficulty, harm should be similar across SES groups, as McLanahan[19] states.

PREVIOUS RELEVANT STUDIES

The results of several American studies suggest that father-absence may have no harmful effects on lower class black youths. Some of these studies are summarized by Herzog and Sudia.[20] Included in their summary are studies of delinquency by Eisner,[21] Burgess and Price[22] and Willie.[23] In predominantly white areas of San Francisco, Eisner reported greater delinquency among father-absent youths except at the lowest income level, in 1960 data. In predominantly black areas, father-absence was associated with greater delinquency only in the upper-middle income group. The relationship was reversed at the lower-middle income level and tended toward reversal at the lowest and highest income levels.

Eisner's results are somewhat similar to Austin's[24] from 1964 Western Contra Costa County, California data. Austin found that father-absent white girls with higher occupation fathers but not those with lower occupation fathers were more likely to be delinquent than father-present white girls. There was no relationship between father-absence and delinquency for black girls regardless of their fathers' occupational level. Austin also found a reversal, the father-absent being less likely to be delinquent among black girls whose fathers fell in the longest of three unemployment categories.

Studies of school achievement and related variables summarized by Herzog and Sudia[25] also suggest that father-absence may have no harmful effects on lower-class black youths. For instance, Hess et al.[26] found no relationship between father-absence and scores on the Stanford-Binet I.Q. test for preschool low-income black children. The national study by Coleman[27] reported no effect of father-absence on school performance except among Chinese, Mexicans and Puerto Ricans. Wasserman[28] found no relationship between father-absence and school achievement or school attitude for black boys in a low-income housing project. And Mackler's[29] results with school achievement for a "typical" Harlem school were similar.

A review of the literature by Hetherington et al.[30] also suggests that the achievement of black children will not suffer because of father-absence. According to these researchers "most studies of black children reveal small and nonsignificant effects of one-parent rearing on achievement tests" (p. 261). In addition, they provide possible reasons for these findings, including smaller variability in test scores, the prevalence of father-absence, and the presence of kin or others who serve as a parent surrogate. For white youths too, father-absence has sometimes been found to affect an educational variable only among those most likely to feel stigmatized, the higher social classes. Thus, Turner[31] reported a relationship between family completeness and ambition only in upper-class neighborhoods. He concluded that the incomplete family inhibits ambition only in areas where middle-class values are most fully entrenched.

Of course there are American studies that have found harmful effects for father-absence among blacks and nonblacks.[32] But only the findings of McLanahan,[33] a recent study with particular relevance for the Caribbean, will be summarized. McLanahan found that the likelihood that black youths would be in school was less for those living with widowed, divorced and separated mothers than for those in two-parent households. This negative effect of single parenthood did not, however, hold for black youths living with never-married mothers. McLanahan viewed this finding and the decrease in the effect of the father's absence over time for the other types of father-absence as contrary to the absence of a male role model hypothesis. In addition, the absence of a negative effect for youths with never-married mothers suggests that Caribbean data might yield a finding of no effect because of the high frequency with which father-absence results from illegitimacy.

Another important result in McLanahan's study is that, among black youths, graduation from high school seemed to be negatively affected by a parent's absence only among children whose families received no public support. There is a fairly widespread belief in America that welfare does more harm than good for families. This belief is questioned by McLanahan's findings.

As previously indicated, Caribbean studies are sometimes consistent with American findings of no harmful effect of father-absence on lower class black children. But there are few quantitative examinations of this question using Caribbean data. One study of particular interest is Herzog's,[34] which was conducted in Barbados. This researcher found a tendency for father-absent boys to perform better than father-present on external tests (Chicago I.Q., Gates reading and Gates arithmetic) but differences were not statistically significant. Of three local tests (comprehension, composition and arithmetic), father-present boys performed significantly better on the arithemtic test. These results and teachers' ratings of attitude toward schoolwork and behavior in school led Herzog to conclude that the father-present boys are more cooperative and perform better on routine tasks. But the father-absent boys are mischievous and perform better on novel tasks.

A study of more marginal relevance that utilized Trinidadian data is reported by Dyer.[35] This researcher distinguished what the parent does (educational environment) from what the parent has (social background). The Index of Educational Environment yielded zero order correlation coefficients of .67 and .78 with achievement in each of two schools. Much weaker coefficients of $-.07$ and .01 were obtained for the relationship between the Index of Social Background and Achievement. A regresson analysis also showed the contribution of social background to the prediction of achievement to be much smaller than the contribution of educational environment, and statistically insignificant. Assuming that father-absence is a social background variable, one would expect it to contribute little or nothing to the explanation of achievement in these Trinidad schools.

However, there is some indirect evidence in two Caribbean studies by Mischel[36] that father-absence might be related to aspiration and need-achievement in younger children (ages 8 and 9) although not in older children (ages 11-14). In one of these studies, younger father-absent children in Grenada and Trinidad, but not older ones, were less likely to delay reinforcement than father-present children. In the other study which included only the older children in Trinidad, delayed reinforcement was associated with higher need-achievement which was significantly related to aspiration. There is a suggested relationship between father-absence and need-achievement/aspiration if it is assumed that younger children would have shown the same results as older children if they had been used in the second study.

The relatively detailed summary of the Caribbean studies should indicate some obvious shortcomings which necessitate more studies in this geographical/cultural region. First, Mischel and Dyer provide only indirect evidence on the relatinship of father-absence to variables of interest.[37] Further, father-absence was not included in Dyer's study and its duration was unknown in Mischel's studies. The single quantitative study with direct evidence on the question of interest is based on data collected in 1963.[38] That study possesses recognized strengths, such as fine gradations in duration of father-absence and a measure of socioeconomic status based on physical characteristics of the home. This measure of socioeconomic status avoids the problems of studies using indicators such as family status before the father's absence occurred or the mother's occupation.[39] In addition to using an indicator of economic status suited to father-absent households as Herzog does, the data that will be analyzed in the present study are much more recent, 1982.

DATA AND METHOD

Setting and Respondents' Characteristics

In June, 1982, questionnaires were administered in classrooms to students of the eight secondary schools in Kingstown, the capital of St. Vincent. Four hundred and eighty-six usuable questionnaires were returned by students whose ages ranged from 13 through 20 with a median age of 15.7. Eighty-four percent of the students were in form[40] 4 or 5 (usually indicating four or five years of secondary school), the remainder being in form 6 (9.5 percent) or 3 (1.2 percent) or having failed to indicate their form.

Seventy-two percent of the students classified themselves as black, 4.3 percent as mixtures of black and white, 3.7 percent as Indian and 1.9 percent each as Carib (a descendant of the island's earliest inhabitants) and white. Nine percent who designated themselves as mixed did not indicate the racial/ethnic groups involved. Groups constituting less than 1.9 percent of the population were black/Indian, Indian/white and Chinese. In addition, 5.1 percent gave no racial ethnic derivation. While the undesignated mixed group and the unknown are omitted, 90. 41 percent of the students are black or a mixture of black and another racial/ethnic group.

Variables, Measurement and Validity

The independent variables used in the analysis are sex, economic status and father-absence. There were two indicators of both status and father-absence but one indicator will in each case be used only to examine the validity of the other. Sex was measured by asking respondents to indicate whether they are male or female. The other independent variables were measured as follows:

Family's Economic Situation (FES). Is the wealth of your home such that it is easy for you to obtain clothing, books, toys, sports equipment and other things youths like to have? 1. Always, 2. Usually, 3. Sometimes, 4. Hardly ever, 5. Never

Parents' Economic Status (PES). Compared with the parents of most students in this island's secondary schools, how do your parents stand financially? 1. Very high, 2. Above average, 3. Average, 4. Below average, 5. Poor.

Extended Father-Absence (EFA). With whom have you lived for most of your life? 1. Mother and father, 2. Mother and stepfather, 3. Father and stepmother, 4. Mother, 5. Foster parent(s), 6. Other (write in).

Current Father-Absence (CFA). With whom do you live now? Categories are the same as for Extended Father-Absence.

The dependent variables are aspiration and performance but expectation was used to examine the validity of the aspiration indicator. Likewise aspiration and performance were used to examine the validity of each other. These variables were measured as follows:

Aspiration (ASP). If it were completely up to you what educational level would you like to attain? 1. Ordinary level G.C.E.[2], 2. Advanced level G.C. E., 3. B.A. or B.S., 4. M.A. or M.S. 5. Ph.D. or M.D., 6. Other (write in).

Expectation (EXP). What educational level do you expect to attain? Categories are the same as for Aspiration.

Performance (PERF). Compared with other students with whom you took exams in the last two years, how would rate your performance? 1. Excellent (top 20%), 2. Above average, 3. Average, 4. Below average, 5. Poor (bottom 20%).

Questions have been raised about what constitutes a suitable indicator of a family's economic condition where some families have only one parent. I regard the family's economic situation as more appropriate than the usual indicator of father's and or mother's income because the contribution of an absent parent to the home will not be known. It is also unlikely that youths would know their parents' income, especially in Third World countries where income may accrue from sources such as overseas remittance from relatives and the occasional sale of home-made products or home-grown produce. Still, it might be expected that an estimate of parents' economic status (Categories 1 & 2 and 4 & 5 were collapsed to provide 3 categories in all) would correlate strongly and positively with family's economic situation (Categories 4 and 5 were collapsed); and this occurs for the St. Vincent data, the zero order correlation coefficient between these indicators being .40 and significant at the 0.00 level.

Of the two indicators of father-absence, that distinguishing extended absence from other situations is felt to be better for the purpose at hand. The main reason for this choice is that illegitimacy, which is common in St. Vincent, is likely to be reflected in lengthy father-absence. Also, the role model hypothesis is more likely to hold in this situation than a stress hypothesis; and the role model hypothesis assumes lengthy father-absence. However, one would expect a strong positive association between extended father-absence and current father-absence. Using only the mother and father versus mother-only categories, the zero order correlation coefficient was .82 and the significance level was 0.00.

The associations among the indicators of the dependent variables also suggest that they are valid. Aspiration and expectation were reduced to three categories by collapsing categories 3, 4 and 5 which had relatively few cases. The zero order correlation coefficient between these variables was .57 and it was significant at the 0.00 level. The relationship between performance and aspiration also showed better performers to have higher aspirations, the zero order correlation coefficient being .16 and significant at the 0.00 level.

Statistical Procedure

The procedure used is analysis of variance with extended father-absence as the independent variable of primary interest while sex of respondent and family's economic situation are controlled. The inclusion of sex of respondent will provide an idea of the tenability of the role model hypothesis. Significant interaction in which boys with absent fathers have lower aspirations and/or poorer performance support this hypothesis. A finding of no significant interaction or interaction in which girls with absent fathers suffer greater harm will reject the hypothesis. Of course, father-absence may not be related to the education variables under any of the conditions examined.

Analyses will be conducted on all available cases and within sex groups. Similar analyses involving only two economic status groups at a time will attempt to uncover any concealed relationships worthy of attention. In each instance, one of the economic status groups will be that with the most favorable aspiration and performance. F-ratios with a probability level of .05 or lower will be regarded as statistically significant. But given the large reduction in cases for most analyses, the lowest beta to attain sigificance with all cases will be considered as substantial for other analyses.

RESULTS

Table 1 shows that extended father-absence is not significantly related to aspiration.[41] Also, the aspiration of the one-parent students is slightly higher than that of two-parent students.

However, sex is significantly related to aspiration, boys having higher aspiration than girls. Further, this relationship is not affected by family economic situation or extended father-absence because the eta and beta are the same, .12. Family economic situation is also significantly related

TABLE 1
Analysis of Variance and Multiple Classification Analysis
for All Cases with Aspiration as the Dependent Variable

Grand Mean = 2.23		Unadjusted		Adjusted for Independents		
Variables	N	Mean	Eta	Mean	Beta	Sig.F
Sex						
Male	172	2.31		2.32		
Female	192	2.15		2.15		
			.12		.12	.02
FES						
1. High	33	2.19		2.19		
2.	95	2.45		2.45		
3.	209	2.16		2.16		
4. Low	27	2.08		2.08		
			.18		.18	.01
EFA						
Ma & Pa	257	2.22		2.22		
Ma	107	2.25		2.25		
			.02		.02	.74

Interactions: Sex by Wealth with a significance level of .148 comes closest to being significant.

to aspiration, that relationship being stronger (eta and beta are each .18) than the relationship between sex and aspiration. The highest aspiration is found among the group of students that is second highest in economic well-being. The most economically advantaged group is closer in aspiration to the two lowest groups than to this second highest group.

Table 2 shows that none of the three independent variables used in Table 1 is significantly related to performance. However, as occurred for aspiration, what miniscule relationship exists between extended father-absence and performance favors one-parent students. That is, no evidence exists to suggest harm to the father-absent on the variables of aspiration and performance.

TABLE 2
Analysis of Variance and Multiple Classification Analysis for All Cases
with Performance as the Dependent Variable.

Grand Mean = 1.65		Unadjusted		Adjusted for Independents		
Variables	N	Mean	Eta	Mean	Beta	Sig.F
Sex						
Male	179	1.63		1.63		
Female	193	1.67		1.67		
			.04		.04	.48
FES						
1. High	35	1.60		1.60		
2.	94	1.60		1.60		
3.	214	1.67		1.67		
4. Low	29	1.72		1.72		
			.06		.06	.69
EFA						
Ma & Pa	258	1.66		1.66		
Ma	114	1.63		1.63		
			.02		.02	.74

Interactions: Wealth by EFA with a significance level of .250 comes closest to being significant.

While interactions did not prove to be significant, the significant relationships yielded with sex and family economic situation suggest that further exploration might produce patterns worthy of attention. Besides, because of the relatively small number of cases (364 for the aspiration analysis) and the use of almost all potential respondents from selected educational levels, the statistical significance of interactions should be given less weight in determining the importance of differential group patterns. Therefore, analyses were conducted within sexual groups as well as by comparing the economic group with the highest aspiration with each of the others separately.

In Table 3, neither family economic situation nor extended father-absence is significantly related to aspiration among boys. But the eta and

TABLE 3
Analysis of Variance and Multiple Classification Analysis for Boys and Girls Separately for the Four Economic Groups.

| | | BOYS | | | | | | GIRLS | | | | |
| | | Unadjusted | | Adjusted for Independent | | | | Unadjusted | | Adjusted for Independent | | |
Variables	N	Mean	Eta	Mean	Beta	Sig.F	N	Mean	Eta	Mean	Beta	Sig.F
FES												
1. High	15	2.53		2.53			18	1.89		1.89		
2.	44	2.43		2.43			51	2.46		2.46		
3.	101	2.24		2.24			108	2.07		2.07		
4. Low	12	2.16		2.16			15	2.00		2.00		
			.15		.15	.26			.26		.26	.00
EFA												
Ma & Pa	121	2.29		2.29			136	2.15		2.15		
Ma	51	2.35		2.35			56	2.15		2.15		
			.04		.04	.61			0.0		0.0	.97

Grand Mean = 2.31

Grand Mean = 2.15

beta of .15 for family economic situation suggests the effect of the reduction in cases by examining only one sex. In Table 1, an eta of .12 for sex was statistically significant at the .02 level while an eta of .18 for family economic situation was significant at the .01 level. Therefore, there seems to be an important difference in the aspiration level of boys from different economic backgrounds. Boys from the highest economic group have the highest aspiration; and the aspiration level declines as family economic situation worsens. However, any attempt to use a sample size argument to support the importance of extended father-absence will fail because the eta and beta are each .04. Besides, once again, it is the father-present students who have the lower aspiration level.

For girls, the relationship between family economic situation and aspiration is statistically significant and stronger than the same relationship for boys (Table 3). The relationship for girls also differs from that for boys in that the economically most advantaged girls hold the lowest aspiration. For the other economic groups, the level of aspiration declines as the economic situation worsens. The sizeable difference in the strength of the relationship for boys and girls and the unexpected pattern of the relationship for girls support the decisions to proceed with further analysis. However, the relationship between extended father-absence and aspiration for girls is the same as for both sexes together, insignificant in every sense.

When performance is the dependent variable (no table shown), the results for boys are similar to those with aspiration as the dependent variable. Neither family economic situation nor extended father-absence is significantly related to performance. Now, however, the relationship with family economic situation is also substantively insignificant, being given by an eta and a beta of .07. The lowest economic group claims a slightly better performance than the others. The relationship for extended father-absence is given by an eta and a beta of .06, the father-absent claiming the better performance.

For girls, when performance is the dependent variable (no table shown), there is also no statistically significant relationship with either family economic situation or extended father-absence. The eta and beta of .15 each with family economic situation, however, suggest substantive significance. The best performance is shown by the second highest economic group (mean = 1.52) while the highest economic group shows the next best performance (mean = 1.61). The next to lowest and lowest economic groups had means of 1.74 and 1.73, respectively. The eta and beta for extended father-absence are .02 and .03, respectively, father-present girls showing slightly better performance (means = 1.66 and 1.69).

Results so far show that family economic situation tends to be positively related to aspiration and performance, but among girls the economically most advantaged group is not the one with the most favorable standing on these variables. Instead, it is the second wealthiest group of girls that shows the highest aspiration and the best performance. Therefore, analyses allowing a comparison of only these two groups of girls were conducted with boys and girls together and then separately. With the two sexes together (no table shown), sex and extended father-absence showed no significant relationship to aspiration. But boys showed a higher level of aspiration than girls and the father-absent a higher level than the father-present (betas of .11 and .08, respectively). The higher economic group had a significantly lower level of aspiration than the lower economic group (eta and beta each = .17). Furthermore, the first instance of a significant interaction occurred, that being between sex and family economic situation.

The analysis restricted to the two highest economic groups also shows the strongest association for extended father-absence so far, this occurring with performance (no table shown). Although the relationship was not statistically significant, the eta and beta are each .15. However, contrary to the expectation of harm for the father-absent, this group shows the better performance (means = 1.46 and 1.67). Neither sex nor family economic situation was significantly related to performance, statistically or substantively.

The nature of the significant sex by family economic situation interaction for the two highest economic groups is revealed in Table 4. The relationship between family economic situation and aspiration for girls (eta and beta = .36) is much stronger than that for boys (eta and beta each = .07). And it is the wealthier girls who show the lower aspiration. Wealthier boys show higher aspiration. The other relationships shown in this table add no important information.

With the two highest economic groups and boys and girls separated, there is one observation of importance about performance (no table shown). The sizeable relationship between extended father-absence and performance holds especially for boys. While this relationship is not statistically significant, the eta and beta are each .19. For girls, the eta and beta are each .12. In both cases, the father-absent students claim better performance than the father-present.

The second set of analyses (no table shown) involving only two eco-

TABLE 4

Analysis of Variance and Multiple Classification Analysis for Boys and Girls Separately for the Two Highest Economic Groups. Aspiration is the Dependent Variable.

| Variables | BOYS | | | | | | GIRLS | | | | | |
| | N | Unadjusted | | Adjusted for Independent | | | N | Unadjusted | | Adjusted for Independent | | |
		Mean	Eta	Mean	Beta	Sig.F		Mean	Eta	Mean	Beta	Sig.F
FES												
1. High	15	2.54		2.54			18	1.88		1.89		
2.	44	2.43		2.43			51	2.45		2.45		
			.07		.07	.60			.36		.36	.00
EFA												
Ma & Pa	42	2.43		2.43			49	2.26		2.26		
Ma	17	2.53		2.53			20	2.40		2.39		
			.07		.07	.58			.09		.08	.47

Grand Mean = 2.46   Grand Mean = 2.30

nomic groups covers the second highest economic group and the lowest (2 and 4 in Table 1). When all the cases are included, the higher economic group shows significantly higher aspiration (beta .27) and substantially better performance (beta .13). The beta for extended father-absence and performance reaches .10, father-absent students reporting better performance. But with aspiration, this relationship is given by a beta of only .01.

For boys in economic groups 2 and 4, the father-absent have higher aspiration (beta = .10) and better performance (beta = .12), but family economic situation is substantially related only to aspiration (beta = .16). For girls, family economic situation is substantially related to aspiration (beta = .27) and performance (beta = .13), weathier girls showing higher aspiration and better performance. And extended father-absence shows a note-worthy relationship only to performance (beta = .11), the father-absent, as before, reporting the better performance.

The final set of analyses (no tables shown) involving two economic groups covers the two middle groups (2 and 3 in Table1). The findings of note include a significant interaction between sex and family economic situation with performance. Only for girls is there a significant relationship between family economic situation and performance (beta = .16). For boys, this relationship reaches a beta of only .06. Also, although there was not significant sex and family economic situation interaction with aspiration, the difference in aspiration between wealthier and less wealthy girls (beta = .25) was substantially greater than between these two groups of boys (beta = .12). The wealthier in both cases had the higher aspiration.

Finally, aspiration and performance were slightly more favorable for father-absent than father-present boys (beta = .08 and .06, respectively). The reverse held for girls (betas = .03 and .07, respectively).

Since the emphasis herein is on the effect of father absence, the findings for this variable are summarized in Table 5. The table shows that of the 24 relationships examined, 18 favor the father-absent, four favor the father-present and two favor neither. That is, more than four times as many results show higher aspiration or better performance for the father-absent than the father-present. Also, it is only among girls that the father-present are favored. In addition, Table 5 shows four substantial (beta = .12 or greater) and two notable (beta = .10 or .11) relationships, all favoring the father-absent and occurring for performance. Of the four relationships favoring the father-present, the strongest reaches a beta of only .07 while the remainder are less than .04. Therefore, any evidence of a relationship

TABLE 5
Summary of Betas and F-ratio Probability Levels for the Relationships of Extended Father-absence to Aspiration and Performance

		ASPIRATION			PERFORMANCE	
ALL CASES	All Cases	Boys	Girls	All Cases	Boys	Girls
Prob	.75	.61	.97	.74	.43	.72
Beta	.02 FA	.04 FA	.00	.02 FA	.06 FA	.03 FP
FES 1 & 2						
Prob	.37	.58	.46	.09	.15	.35
Beta	.08 FA	.07 FA	.08 FA	.15 FA	.19 FA	.12 FA
FES 2 & 3						
Prob	.68	.31	.67	.96	.46	.39
Beta	.02 FA	.08 FA	.03 FP	.00	.06 FA	.07 FP
FES 2 & 4						
Prob	.60	.48	.92	.25	.39	.45
Beta	.05 FA	.09 FA	.01 FP	.11 FA	.12 FA	.10 FA

FA = Father-absent youths claim higher Aspiration or better Performance
FP = Father-present youths claim higher Aspiration or better Peformance
Substantial Beta = .12 or stronger.
Notable Beta = .10 or .11.

between father-absence and the educational variables suggests that father-absence helps rather than hurts, especially boys and with performance.

SUMMARY AND CONCLUSIONS

At least three explanations have been proposed for an expected harmful effect of father-absence on children. One of these, the stigma explanation, is supported by many studies showing that lower-class black American children suffer no harm from father-absence while more advantaged blacks and whites are harmed. These results may be accounted for by the relatively low stigma where the condition usually stigmatized is relatively common in a group or community. This situation of likely low stigmatization of father-absence holds in St. Vincent because of a high incidence of this phenomenon due to a high rate of illegitimacy. Therefore, any harmful consequences of father-absence for the youths of this Caribbean island are more likely to result from economic hardship or absence of a male role model, the other two explanations.

The present study conducted 24 separate analyses seeking evidence that father-absence might be related to educational aspiration and/or performance. Analyses included those of the entire group of secondary school respondents and boys and girls separately. Also, there were three subdivisions of the respondents, each having two different economic groups, and for each subdivision, all of the cases as well as boys and girls separately were examined. There are only six instances in which relationships were considered notable or substantial and all showed higher aspiration or better performance for the father-absent. However, no relationship between father-absence and aspiration or performance was statistically significant.

None of the three explanations of harmful consequences of father-absence is supported by the St. Vincent data. Apparently, father-absence has no harmful consequences on aspiration or performance on this island. But it may be objected that these results occur because of the low stigma. However, this objection must assume that such stigma as might exist in St. Vincent is similar across economic groups.

Sex and family economic status were both significantly related to aspiration in the entire group of respondents, but not to performance. Boys have higher aspirations than girls, and wealthier students have higher aspirations than economically disadvantaged students. However, the highest aspiration is found among the second wealthiest, the aspiration of the wealthiest being slightly higher than but closer to the two economically more disadvantaged groups.

The higher aspiration of boys is not surprising, given the relative recency of the elimination of legal discrimination against women in running for political office, voting and wages.[42] Also, the patriarchal European family early became the norm in the Caribbean and as recently as 1975 male dominance was noted in the Eastern Caribbean.[43] In addition, the data used in the present study show fathers to be 2.6 times as likely as mothers to hold a college degree. Moreover, certain beliefs and expectations hinder the encouragement of high educational aspirations among girls. For instance, money spent on the education of girls is sometimes considered a bad investment because they will cease working early to raise families. Also, sons are expected to support parents who are without other means of support. But girls often perform this function although they are expected to be less likely to do so.[44] It is, of course, noteworthy that girls did not claim poorer performance than boys. Therefore, the sexual difference in aspiration should not be attributed to differing educational potential.

The positive relationship between family economic situation and aspiration is also not surprising. There have been sufficient previous studies showing this pattern.[45] But the relatively low aspiration for the wealthiest is unusual. While there was originally no significant interaction involving sex or family economic situation, further exploration of the data produced some significant interactions that made this unusual finding more understandable.

It is only among girls that the second wealthiest group shows the highest aspiration. Indeed, the wealthiest group of girls has the lowest level of aspiration among girls as well as boys. And when the two wealthiest groups alone are examined there is significant interaction between sex and family economic situation on aspiration. The relationship between family economic situation and aspiration was much stronger and significant only for girls. Wealthier girls showed lower aspiration. Among these two economic groups too, the second wealthiest group of girls performed substantially better than the wealthiest. There was no relationship for boys.

Analyses of the two other economic combinations (2 and 4; 2 and 3) also show stronger relationships between family economic situation and aspiration or performance for girls than for boys. For groups 2 and 4 combined, the sex by family economic situation with performance interaction is significant. But the relationships are all positive as expected.

The low aspiration of the wealthiest girls in the secondary school population in St. Vincent restricts the talent available for development in the very group most likely to be able to afford higher education. Casual observation suggests that these girls may expect no especially desirable outcomes from becoming exceptionally well educated. Their economic standing in the society already accords them high status and, perhaps, makes them highly attractive potential spouses. They may expect to inherit financial security or to marry into this position. Wealthy men in St. Vincent seem to place little emphasis on the eductional attainment of wives. Indeed, men in St. Vincent may generally be less concerned about the education of potential spouses than are men in developed countries.

However, in the Vincentian setting, father-absence, contrary to what might be expected from the flood of recent pronouncements on this conditon in the United States, does not limit the aspiration or performance of students. Father-absence may even enhance the achievement of some Vincentians. And an effort to determine how this occurs would be a worthy project. Meanwhile, the absence of a harmful effect for this disliked condition is more convincing because of the many subdivisions of the data in which it occurred. Additionally, relationships with other independent variables agree with the findings of other studies or are explainable.

Taken together, the empirical evidence from St. Vincent and some from America discussed earlier suggest that father-absence need not be educationally harmful to children. Perhaps, it is the relatively low stigma attached to this condition in St. Vincent that makes it harmless. Likewise, opposed findings in America may result from differences between communities in the extent to which they consider father-absence disgraceful. The American communities in which children experience little or no harm may be isolated from and/or little attached to the dominant culture. Therefore, the loud, clear and frequent condemnation of father-absence in America may have an effect which is the opposite of that intended by creating an atmosphere that adversely affects some father-absent children.

NOTES

This article is a revised version of a paper presented at the Caribbean Studies Association meeting in Venezuela, May 1986. I appreciate the cooperation of the principals and students of the secondary schools in Kingstown, St. Vincent and the assistance of Bentley Brown.

1. T.S. Simey, *Welfare and Planning in the West Indies* (Oxford: Clarendon Press, 1956); Edith Clarke, *My Mother who Fathered Me* (London: George Allen and Unwin Ltd., 1957); Walter Mischel "Father-Absence and Delay of Gratification: Cross-Cultural Comparisons," *Journal of Abnormal and Social Psychology* 63, 1 (1961), pp. 116-124.

2. William J. Goode, "Illegitimacy in the Caribbean Social Structure," *American Sociological Review* 25, 1 (1960), pp. 21-30.

3. Walter Mischel, op. cit.

4. John D. Herzog, "Father-Absence and Boys' School Performance in Barbados," *Human Organization* 33 (Spring 1974), pp. 71-83. Based on 1963 data.

5. T.S. Simey, op. cit.

6. William J. Goode, op. cit.

7. No recent figures on illegitimacy were available for St. Vincent, the island studied. But earlier figures show a higher rate for this island than for St. Lucia. During the 1955-64 decade, St. Vincent had illegitimacy rates ranging from 73 percent (1960) to 79.2 percent (1959), with eight of the ten years exceeding 75 percent. *U.N. Demographic Yearbook*, 1965.

8. *U.N. Demographic Yearbook*, 1981.

9. T.P. Monahan, "Family Status and the Delinquent Child: A Reappraisal and Some New Findings," *Social Forces* 35 (March 1957), pp. 250-258; F. Riessman, *The Culturally Deprived Child* (New York: Harper, 1962); Daniel P. Moynihan, *The Negro Family: The Case for National Action* (Washington, D.C.: U.S. Department of Labor, Government Printing Office, 1965); Oscar Lewis, "Culture of Poverty,"*Scientific American* 215 (1966), pp. 19-25; C.E. Vincent, "Mental Health and the Family," *Journal of Marriage*

and the Family 29 (1967): pp. 18-39; David Rosenthal and James Hansen, "Comparison of Adolescents' Perceptions and Behaviors in Single- and Two-Parent Families," *Journal of Youth and Adolescence* 9, 5 (1980), pp. 407-417.

10. David Broder, "It's Time to Take a Serious Look at the Family Unit," *Centre Daily Times* (January 27, 1986); Ellen Goodman, "Black Family Headed for Destruction," *Centre Daily Times* (January 28, 1986).

11. William D. Moyers, "The Vanishing Family: Crisis in Black America," *Columbia Broadcasting Service* (January 25, 1986).

12. William J. Wilson, "The Black Underclass," *The Wilson Quarterly* (Spring, 1984), pp. 88-99).

13. Daniel P. Moynihan, op. cit.

14. Nancie L. Solein, "Household and Family in the Caribbean: Some Definitions and Concepts," *Social and Economic Studies* 9, 1 (1960), pp. 101-106.

15. William A. Darity, Jr. and Samuel L. Myers, Jr., "Does Welfare Dependency Cause Female Headship? The Case of the Black Family," *Journal of Marriage and the Family* 46 4 (1984), pp. 765-779.

16. Elizabeth Herzog and Cecilia E. Sudia, "Children in Fatherless Families," in *Child Development Research*, Vol. 3, Bettye M. Caldwell and Henry N. Riccinti, editors. (Chicago: University of Chicago Press, 1973). Sara McLanahan, "Family Structure and the Reproduction of Poverty," *American Journal of Sociology* 90, 4 (1985), pp. 873-901.

17. L. Rainwater and W.L. Yancey, *The Moynihan Report and the Politics of Controversy* (Cambridge, MA: MIT Press, 1967).

18. E. Mavis Hetherington, Kathleen Camera and David Featherman, "Achievement and Intellectual Functioning of Children in One-Parent Households," in *Achievement and Achievement Motives*, Janet T. Spence, editor. (San Francisco: Freeman and Company, 1983).

19. Sara McLanahan, op. cit.

20. Elizabeth Herzog and Cecilia E. Sudia, op. cit.

21. V. Eisner, "Effects of Parents in the Home on Delinquency," *Public Health Reports* 81 (1966), pp. 905-910.

22. M.E. Burgess and D.O. Price, *An American Dependency Challenge* (Chicago: American Public Welfare Association, 1963).

23. Charles Willie, "The Relative Contribution of Family Status and Economic Status to Juvenile Delinquency," *Social Problems* 14 (1967), pp. 326-335.

24. Roy L. Austin, "Race, Father-Absence and Female Delinquency," *Criminology* 15 (February, 1978), pp. 487-504.

25. Elizabeth Herzog and Cecilia E. Sudia, op. cit.

26. R.D. Hess, V.C. Shipman, J.E. Brophy and R.M. Bear, *The Cognitive Environments of Urban Preschool Children* (Chicago: Graduate School of Education, University of Chicago, 1968).

27. John S. Coleman, *Equality of Educational Opportunity* (Washington, D.C.: U.S. Department of Health Education and Welfare; Office of Education, OE-38001, National Center for Educational Statistics).

28. H.L. Wasserman, *Father-Absent and Father-Present Lower Class Negro Families:A Comparative Study of Family Functioning* (Ph.D. Dissertation, Florence Heller Graduate School for Advanced Studies in Social Welfare, Brandeis University, 1968).

29. B. Mackler, *The Little Black School House: Success and Failure in a Ghetto School* (Final Report. Department of Urban Affairs, Hunter College of the City University of New York).

30. Hetherington, et. al., op. cit.

31. Ralph H. Turner, "Some Family Determinants of Ambition," *Sociology and Social Research* 46 (July 1962), pp. 397-411.

32. Wesley W. Jenkins, "An Experimental Study of the Relationship of Legitimate Status to School and Personal and Social Adjustment of Negro Children," *American Journal of Sociology* 64 (September 1958), pp. 169-173; J.W. Santrack, "Relation of Type and Onset of Father-Absence to Cognitive Development," *Child Development* 43 (1972), pp. 455-469; H.L. Wasserman, "A Comparative Study of School Performance Among Boys from Broken and Intact Black Families," *Journal of Negro Education* 41 (1972), pp. 137-141; M. Chapman, "Father-Absence, Stepfathers, and the Cognitive Performance of College Students," *Child Development* 48 (1977), pp. 1155-1158.

33. McLanahan, op. cit.

34. Herzog, op. cit.

35. P.B. Dyer, "The Effect of the Home on the School in Trinidad," *Social and Economic Studies* 17 (December), pp. 435-441.

36. Walter Mischel, "Father-Absence and Delay of Gratification: Cross-Cultural Comparisons," *Journal of Abnormal and Social Psychology* 63, 1 (1961), pp. 116-124; Walter Mischel, "Delay of Gratification, Need for Achievement, and Acquiescence in Another Culture," *Journal of Abnormal and Social Psychology* 62, 3 (1961), pp. 543-552.

37. Dyer, op. cit. Mischel, op. cit.

38. John D. Herzog, op. cit.

39. Hetherington, et. al., op. cit.

40. A "form" is similar to a grade in the United States but the term is used only for secondary school grade levels. Students making normal progress require one year to complete a form.

41. Current father-absence was also not significantly related to either aspiration or performance. Betas were .01 and .07 with aspiration and performance, respectively. Data collected by the present author in 1975 in three Caribbean islands including St. Vincent also show no significant relationship between extended father-absence and aspiration or performance.

42. Roy L. Austin, "Understanding Calypso Content: A Critique and an Alternative Explanation," *Caribbean Quarterly* 22 (June-September 1976), pp. 74-83.

43. Roy L. Austin and Elaine Porter, "Adolescent Perception of Parental Power in Three Caribbean Islands," *Social and Economic Studies* 29 (June'September 1980), pp. 247-263.

44. Yehudi A. Cohen, "Four Categories of Interpersonal Relationships in the Family and Community in a Jamaican Village," *Anthropological Quarterly* 3, 4 (1955), pp. 121-147.

45. William H. Sewell, Archibald O. Haller and Murray Strauss, "Social Status and Educational and Occupational Aspiration," *American Sociological Review* 22 (February 1957), pp. 67-73; William Sewell and Vimal P. Shah, "Social Class, Parental Encouragement and Educational Aspirations," *American Journal of Sociology* 73 (1968), pp. 559-572; David Shapiro and Joan E. Crowley, "Aspirations and Expectations of Youth in the United States. Part 2. Employment Activity," *Youth and Society* 14 (September 1982), pp. 33-58; Richard G. Lomax and Paula S. Gammil, "Sex Differences and Perceived Parental Influence on Student Occupational and Educational Aspirations," *Sociological Perspectives* 27 (October 1984), pp. 465-472.

14

CHILD CARE AND FEMALE EMPLOYMENT IN URBAN NIGERIA

Amon O. Okpala

Several factors influence female employment in most societies. They include family economic pressures, employability, earning potential, labor market environment and family composition. Several studies have been done on the influence of all factors but the last, family composition, that is, whether the mother has a baby-sitter. If the answer is a "yes," then the probability that she will engage in an economic activity increases.

This article addresses the question of the role of the child-care on female employment. The results show that the influence of child-care on female employment in Lagos depends on the nature of such help.

Attempts continue to be made to adapt the economic theory of the household in examining time-allocation behavior of households of Third World Nations.[1] Since the pioneer work by Gary S. Becker and Reuben Gronau, time allocation patterns of women from less-developed nations have received special attention.[2] This increased attention raises two serious issues: the first relates to what motivates or governs their time allocation decisions, that is, whether their decisions are governed by economic constraints or exclusively by noneconomic constraints such as religious practices and customs. The noneconomic theory, as opposed to the economic theory of the household emphasizes that powerful local norms of female seclusion restrict women severely from engaging in any form of economic activity outside the family.[3] The second issue relates to the choice that women face in the Third World nations.[4]

There is a need to identify appropriately the choice structure that women face in any given society, but that by itself is quite incomplete in explaining time-allocation behavior of Nigerian urban women. To fully understand the reasons behind the time-allocation behavior of Nigerian urban women requires more precise measurements of the economic and noneconomic variables; especially the role of parental surrogates[5] need to be carefully examined. This study examines exclusively the role of parental surrogates (sometimes referred to as family compositon) in explaining the time-allocation behavior of Nigerian urban women.

Several factors influence female labor force participation (FLFP).* They include family economic pressures, employability and earning potential of the family, market environment and family composition. A family's economic pressure is often measured by the husband's income. The probability that a woman would want to work in Nigerian society decreases if the husband's income is high, implying that the higher the income of the husband, the lower the probability that the wife will engage in formal work. Employability refers to a woman's ability to perform certain tasks for which there is a demand. A woman with some occupational skills is more likely to be employed. Earning potential is somewhat related to employability. If a woman can earn a high income, she is more likely to work. In this study, wife's potential income (WPI) and the number of years of schooling are used as proxies for earning potential and employability respectively.

Another factor mentioned above that may influence FLFP is the labor market environment. If the job market is such that it is not difficult to find a job, more women may choose to work and if the job market is bad, married women usually fall out of the labor force in Nigerian society. The last factor, family composition, is quite important in influencing mothers' employment rate. Family composition refers to whether the woman concerned has young children or not, whether she has a paid baby-sitter or a

EXHIBIT 1
DEFINITIONS

BSH—babysitting help from a relative
EW—wife's educational level measured in years of preschooling
FLFP—female labor force participation rate
MCA—multiple classification analysis
OLS—ordinary least squares
PBS—paid babysitter
PHDW—percentage of hours of daily work
PWYW—percentage of years worked since marriage
WPI—wife's potential income
YW—wife's income
HDW—hours of daily work

---

*See Exhibit 1 for list of abbreviations.

relative helping her in baby-sitting and household activities. If the answers to the last two conditions are "YES," then the probability that she will engage in an economic activity increases. So far, few empirical studies (especially in Third World nations) have tried to examine the influence of family composition on the employment of mothers. This study will address the family composition issue.

The remainder of the article is organized as follows. Section II outlines the economic framework of households. This framework is used in deriving the economic model of this study. Section III presents the survey data used in the article. Section IV explains the results of the multiple classification analysis (MCA) and the empirical estimates of the model. The final section summarizes the results.

II. HOUSEHOLD ECONOMIC MODEL.

According to the modern economic theory of the family, the household unit is viewed as making collective decisions that determine the behavior of each member. Assume that a household consists of only the husband (h), wife (w) and children. Given this, the household's aim is assumed to be that of maximization of utility from child services (C), other goods and services (G) and leisure (L_i, where $i = h,w$) of the husband and wife. As much, a household attempts to maximize utility subject to the constraints it faces—child services competing with other goods, plus the leisure time of wife and husband. Formally, the household utility function can be expressed as:

$$U = U(C, G, L_h, L_w) \quad \dots\dots\dots\dots\dots\dots\dots\dots\dots\dots\dots\dots (1)$$

Assume that (C) which refers to child services are home-produced and (G) which represents other goods are market-produced goods. Also, assume that home-produced goods are produced by utilizing some inputs (X); which are purchased at the market by utilizing wife's time only (T_{wc}). Child services can be expressed as:

$$C = C(X, T_{wc}) \quad \dots\dots\dots\dots\dots\dots\dots\dots\dots\dots\dots\dots\dots (2)$$

If the total time constraints are Y_i (where $i = h,w$); Y_h and Y_w represent the total time available to the husband and wife respectively: then the amount of time spent by each member for market work (M), home production of child services (C), and leisure (L) cannot exceed their respective total time available. These can be expressed as:

$$Y_h = T_{hm} + L_h \dots\dots\dots\dots\dots\dots\dots\dots\dots\dots\dots\dots (3)$$

$$Y_w = T_{wm} + T_{wc} + L_w \dots\dots\dots\dots\dots\dots\dots\dots\dots\dots (4)$$

Where T_{hm} and T_{wm} are time allocations for market work for husband and wife respectively. T_{wc}, T_{wm} and L_w depends on the availability of parental surrogates (P_s).[6] For a woman not employed, her time allocation should be distributed between leisure and home nonmarket production because $T_{wm} = 0$. Assume that wage rate for the husband and wife are Y_h and Y_w respectively, then their incomes are $Y_h T_{hm}$ and $Y_w T_{wm}$ respectively. Total family income (I) can be expressed as:

$$I = Y_h T_{hm} + Y_w T_{wm} + V \dots\dots\dots\dots\dots\dots\dots\dots\dots\dots (5)$$

where V is household's nonlabor income. This represents the income constraint of a household.

The economic model then assumes that the objective of each household is to maximize utility, subject to the income constraints of the household and the prices of the inputs purchased. This model yields a system of reduced-form equations for endogenous variables as functions of individual, household, market, and community constraints that set prices for goods and services that households produce and consume.[7] Of interest here is the reduced form of equation for a woman's time allocation in market production. The reduced equation could be expressed as:

$$T_{wm} = T_{wm}(Y_h, Y_w, V, P_x, P_g, Y_h, Y_w, P_s) \dots\dots\dots\dots\dots (6)$$

where P_x, P_g, represent prices of inputs purchased by households in nonmarket production and expenditure on market goods respectively. Due to lack of adequate data, the empirical model used in this study can be expressed as:

$$FLFP = \alpha_0 + \alpha_1 PBS + \alpha_2 BSH + \sum_{i=1}^{m} \beta_i X_i + \epsilon. \dots\dots\dots\dots\dots (7)$$

where FLFP (female labor force participation rate) represents either PWY[8] (the percentage of years worked since marriage) or PHDW (percentage of hours of daily work); X_i are the control variables (which include wife's education, wife's potential income,[9] wife's age, and the log of husband's income). PBS represents paid babysitter and BSH represents baby-sitting help from a relative. BSH and PBS are dummy variables in which values of "0" were assigned if respondents do not have baby-sitting help from either a relative of a paid baby-sitter, and the value of "1" is assigned otherwise respectively. These two variables are of major importance in determining the level of conflict between child-rearing and market employment. This is because most Nigerian women (like most Third World women) often have female relatives or paid maids living with them or close by, helping them in household and baby-sitting duties. The argument is that the compatibility of child-care and market work will considerably depend on whether relatives or older siblings are available to care for preschool children and whether the household can afford paid house maids.[10]

III. DATA AND THEIR CHARACTERISTICS

The data for this study are drawn from a sample of 568 households surveyed during the summer of 1983 in Lagos, Nigeria. According to the United Nations 1975 estimates, Lagos's territory was estimated to be inhabited by about 1.5 million people by 1985: the U. S. Bureau of Census estimated Lagos's population at about six million people. As a commercial center, Lagos draws immigrants from other parts of Nigeria and West African nations. As such, Lagos is made up of people of diverse ethnic origin who migrated mainly for economic reasons. By 1983, there were many postprimary educational institutions in Lagos, including some colleges of arts and science and a federal university. There are numerous manufacturing and construction industries, banking facilities, state offices, federal government offices and many foreign embassies. The indigenous people of Lagos are the Yorubas.

The women surveyed were within the age group of 15–49. The women cover all economic and sociological backgrounds prevalent in Lagos. They include the highly educated professionals, those who completed or attended high schools and those who completed or atttended elementary schools. The survey lacks information from those with no formal education. Probably, Lagos population lacks a good representation of that group. Surprisingly, all my respondents indicated that they have some years of formal education. The sample was stratified by measures of household monthly income and physical areas. Blocks were selected randomly within an area and clusters of dwellings were chosen from each block. As such, this sample is a fairly accurate representation of the population of households in Lagos.

The survey reveals that the fertility of Lagos women is quite high, which is quite consistent with other household surveys of different regions of Nigeria.[11] When the respondents are divided into two subgroups, the employed (this includes the civil servants and the self-employed) and the unemployed, a different pattern exists. For the employed women, the mean number of children born is 4.1 while for the unemployed women (or housewives) the mean is 5.0. The survey also reveals that 60 percent of all respondents have a relative who is helping in child care and housework activities. Also, 24 percent of all respondents indicate that they have a paid babysitter. When the respondents were grouped according to the types of economic activities they perform, an interesting pattern is observed.[12] More than 70 percent of the respondents who are employed in the civil service sector of the economy indicate that they have either a relative helping in child care/household activities or a paid babysitter. In contrast, about 50 percent of the rest of the respondents (i.e., the self-employed and the unemployed women) agree to the same question.

IV. EMPIRICAL RESULTS

Two methods are employed in analyzing the influence of child care availability on the employment of urban Nigerian women: the Multiple Classification Analysis (MCA) and Ordinary Least Square Regression (OLS). Tables I and II show various results of the MCA. Two dependent variables were employed—PWYW and HDW—the hours spent daily in any income earning activity that occurs outside the home. Four explanatory variables were utilized: baby-sitting help from a relative (BSH), paid baby-sitter (PBS), wife's educational level measured in years of schooling (EW), and wife's income (YW).

The results of the analysis shown in Tables I and II, reveal that the impact of the independent variables on PWYW and HDW is consistently positive both for the adjusted and unadjusted means. From Table I, about 136 respondents with a paid babysitter have spent more than half of their married life in income earning activities, while those without a paid babysitter have spent less than half of their married life in income earning

TABLE I
Multiple Classification Analysis of Effects of Four Independent Variables on PWYW.
(For All Respondents)

Variables + Categories	N	Mean	Adjusted Mean
PBS			
No	422	0.48	0.51
Yes	136	0.61	0.52
BSH			
No	194	0.53	0.53
Yes	364	0.51	0.51
EW			
< 9	166	0.28	0.42
9-14	263	0.55	0.53
15+	129	0.72	0.58
YW			
< 125	158	0.14	0.20
125-240	144	0.60	0.59
241-360	118	0.66	0.63
360+	138	0.71	0.68

Grand Mean: 0.51

R^2 :   0.386

NOTE: EW was subdivided according to respondent's educational achievements. EW <9 relates to respondents with some/completed primary school; EW (9-14) relates to those who attended or completed secondary school; and EW (15+) is for respondents that attended or completed university education.

YW represents different income levels, measured in naira (which is Nigerian currency). Categories were chosen mainly to maximize the differences among categories with respect to the dependent variables and also maintain fairly similar numbers of respondents in each category.

activities. Table II also reveals that respondents with a paid babysitter, on the average day worked longer hours than those without a paid babysitter. For the BSH, there seems to be lack of a substantial impact in all the cases as illustrated on Tables I and II, coupled with a lack of consistency. In most of the results, respondents with some babysitting help from a relative worked fewer hours daily or worked a lesser percentage of their married life than respondents with no such help from a relative. This is surprising, because one would expect that mothers who enjoy the privilege of having a relative helping them in babysitting activities would be more able to participate in income-earning activities outside the home. This may be due to the nature of babysitting help from relatives; they are in most situations very unreliable. There is no guarantee that a relative helping in babysitting activities will be faithful in her duties for the

TABLE II
Multiple Classification Analysis of Effects of Four Independent Variables on HDW
(For All Respondents)

Variables + Categories	N	Mean	Adjusted Mean
PBS			
No	422	5.45	5.69
Yes	136	7.16	6.43
BSH			
No	194	5.97	5.86
Yes	364	5.82	5.87
EW			
< 9	166	3.97	5.63
9–14	263	6.47	6.20
15+	129	7.09	5.51
YW			
< 125	158	1.85	1.98
125–240	144	7.05	6.93
241–360	118	7.24	7.22
360+	138	8.08	8.07

Grand Mean: 5.87

R^2 :   0.512

required period of time. For EW and YW, their individual impacts on the employment rate of mothers is as expected. For the two measures of FLFP rate employed, as illustrated in Tables I and II, positive effects are observed.

These tables of MCA results (i.e., I and II) give useful information about FLFP differences among categories of the explanatory variables, but the technique does not provide one with the summary measure for the net effects of an explanatory variable. Thus, OLS regression was utilized also. The model utilized is illustrated in equation 7 in section II above. Tables III to V show the regression results for the impact of PBS and BSH on PWYW and PHDW.

The regression results in Table III indicate that PBS has a positive, significant effect on PWYW and PHDW when all respondents were regressed together. When the respondents were grouped according to their age groups, a slightly different result occurs.[13] For the respondents

TABLE III
OLS Regresssion Coefficient of Two Explanatory Variables for Two FLFP Measures
(For All Respondents)

Explanatory Variables	Dependent Variables			
	PWYW		PHDW	
For All Respondents				
1) PBS	0.090	(2.44)	0.058	(3.90)
BSH	0.002	(0.07)	0.008	(0.57)
R^2	0.2613		0.1687	
All Respondents Aged 35 or Less. N = 374.				
2) PBS	0.078	(1.67)	0.066	(3.65)
BSH	-0.001	(-0.02)	0.001	(0.07)
R^2	0.2417		0.1752	
All Respondents Aged 36 or Above. N = 184.				
3) PBS	0.111	(1.87)	0.052	(2.00)
BSH	-0.005	(-0.09)	0.017	(0.72)
R^2	0.3135		0.2199	

Note: Ratios of regression coefficients to standard errors in parentheses.

Note: Ratios of regression coefficients to standard errors in parentheses.

aged 35 or less, PBS showed a positive impact on both PWYW and PHDW; but the significance level is higher in the latter case. A different picture is observed with the results of the regression analysis of the impact of BSH on both PWYW as shown in Table III. Mixed results were observed; a positive effect occurred in most cases. Only in two situations did BSH have a negative influence on FLFP. In any case, all the influences were highly insignificant.

These results are quite consistent with the MCA results shown earlier in Tables I and II. PBS showed a strong positive influence on both PWYW and PHDW while inconsistent and insignificant results were observed with the case of BSH's influence on PWYW and PHDW. These findings further help in showing that mothers with paid babysitters are usually more able to engage in some form of income earning activities.

Table IV shows the regression results for civil servants. The same model employed in the previous analysis was utilized here. For all the subgroups, PBS showed a consistent positive influence on both PWYW and PHDW. PBS showed a significant positive influence on PHDW when all the respondents that are civil servants were analyzed together. But when the civil servants were grouped according to their age groups, PBS was insignificantly related to PWYW and highly significantly related to

TABLE IV
OLS Regression Coefficient of Two Explanatory Variables for Two FLFP Measures
(For Civil Servants Only)

Explanatory Variables	Dependent Variables			
	PWYW		PHDW	
For All Civil Servants.				
1) PBS	0.061	(1.56)	0.021	(2.89)
BSH	-0.029	(-0.81)	-0.004	(-0.57)
R^2	0.2058		0.1320	
Civil Servants Aged 35 or Less. N = 207.				
2) PBS	0.013	(0.27)	0.020	(2.27)
BSH	-0.039	(-0.90)	-0.013	(-1.55)
R^2	0.1981		0.1519	
Civil Servants Aged 36 or Above. N = 78.				
3) PBS	0.172	(2.49)	0.026	(1.99)
BSH	-0.011	(-0.17)	0.018	(1.36)
R^2	0.2925		0.1978	

Note: Ratios of regression coefficients to standard errors in parentheses.

PHDW for civil servants aged 35 or less. For much older civil servants (36 years old or more) PBS was positively related to PWYW at a 99 percent significance level; also PBS's impact on PHDW was positively significant at a 95 percent level. The regression results indicate that among the older women who are employed in the civil service sector, PBS do have a greater impact on PWYW than on PHDW. And finally, the results show that BSH lacks a clear-cut consistent influence on either PWYW or PHDW for all respondents that are civil servants. Table V shows the regression results of respondents who are businesswomen. The model employed in the analysis shown in Table V is similar to the one utilized in two previous cases. The regression results give no clearly defined pattern that can help in explaining the influence of either PBS or BSH on the two FLFP measures employed. The lack of a consistent pattern can be explained by the nature of the economic activities performed by this group of respondents. They are all self-employed in their individual economic activities; as such, they are not under any person's code of conduct, and can very well have a flexible work time. Also, their respective economic activities can be quite compatible with child-rearing responsibilities. In some instances, as one drives through Lagos streets,

TABLE V
OLS Regression Coefficient of Two Explanatory Variables for Two FLFP Measures
(For Businesswomen Only)

Explanatory Variables	Dependent Variables			
	PWYW		PHDW	
For All Businesswomen.				
1) PBS	−0.029	(−0.45)	0.027	(1.47)
BSH	−0.006	(−0.09)	−0.042	(−2.27)
R^2	0.0522		0.0923	
Businesswomen Aged 35 or Less. N = 83.				
2) PBS	0.061	(0.65)	0.040	(1.47)
BSH	0.111	(1.10)	−0.021	(−0.71)
R^2	0.0786		0.0985	
Businesswomen Aged 36 or Above. N = 56.				
3) PBS	−0.058	(−0.59)	0.040	(1.65)
BSH	−0.054	(−0.54)	−0.53	(−2.20)
R^2	0.1280		0.1619	

Note: Ratios of regression coefficients to standard errors in parentheses.

one can often observe some of these petty-traders, or the hair dressers attending customers in their shops with their infants nearby. In such situations, any form of baby-sitting help may not have a very significant impact on a mother's working rate.

CONCLUSION

The question addressed in this article is: What influence, if any, does child care have on female employment? It is generally believed that the compatibility of child care and mother's market work will greatly depend on the availability of child care help in the household. Consequently, mothers with child care help will be more willing to engage in market work outside the home.

The results of this study do indicate that mothers with paid babysitters spend a greater part of their married life in income-generating activities; they also spend on the average more hours daily in income-generating activities that are performed outside the home. This result is quite pronounced for the civil servants, mainly because of the nature of civil service jobs, which are highly incompatible with child-rearing activities. As a result, baby-sitting help will have a significant impact on the time spent on market work for this category of respondents. The results indicate that PBS has a significant and positive influence on both PWYW and PHDW when the civil servants data was analyzed. The results from the analysis of businesswomen do not show any clearly defined pattern.

It was also observed that BSH does not have a significant impact on the work participation rate of mothers in the labor force. This rather surprising finding may be due to the nature of such babysitting help from relatives. First, there is always the possibility that a relative helping in babysitting care can easily terminate such activity without the necessary quit notices that are required if the babysitter is paid. Second, in most cases nowadays, when a relative is helping in babysitting duties it is usually agreed upon (especially if the babysitter is a teenager) that he/she be put through high school education. This cuts down on the number of hours he/she spends on actual babysitting duties.

In view of these findings, the influence of child care on female employment (and consequently on fertility) in Lagos will greatly depend on the nature of such help.

NOTES

Helpful comments were received on early drafts from Professor Herman E. Daly of Louisiana State University, Dr. Pozyhil O. James of Fayetteville State University, and the anonymous RBPE referee. The author is responsible for the final content.

1. Shahidur R. Khandker, "Determinants of Women's Time Allocation in Rural Bangladesh," *Economic Development and Cultural Change*, 37 (October 1988): 111-126.

2. Gary S. Becker, "A Theory of the Allocation of Time," *Economic Journal*, 75 (September, 1965): 493-517; and Reuben Gronau, "The Intrafamily Allocation of Time: The Value of the Housewives' Time," *AER* 68 (September 1973): 634-651.

3. See Mead Cain, S. Khanam and Shamsun Nahar, "Class Patriarchy and Women's Work in Bangladesh," *Population and Development Review*, 5 (September 1979): 405-38.

4. In his study of Bangladesh women, Shahidur R. Khandker found out that a two-way choice structure is more appropriate for describing women's work patterns. S. R. Khandker, "Determinants of Women's Time Allocation in Rural Bangladesh," *Economic Development & Cultural Change*, 37 (October 1988): 111-126. The two-way choice structure is whether "to work" in the labor force as a self-employed person in family enterprise and paid employment in nonfamilial market production, both producing cash income, or "to work" exclusively for home production.

5. Parental surrogates refer to the availability of different forms of child care help inside or outside the household.

6. This paper assumes that the two child-care variables employed in this analysis are explanatory variables. One can argue otherwise. My objective here is not to determine the direction of causation; although important, I leave that to others to explore.

7. Shahidur R. Khandker, "Determinants of Women's Time Allocation in Rural Bangladesh," *Economic Development and Cultural Change*, 37 (October 1988): 115.

8. This variable measures the amount of women's time as a percentage of married life for any type of work.

9. To estimate wife's potential wage, I used the wages and background characteristics of working women—this gave me a subsample of 285 women. The dependent variable used in this regression is the natural logarithm of income. The natural logarithm of income is chosen because the distribution of wages tends to approach a log-normal density function in most societies. The independnet variables used are wife's education (EW), wife's education squared (EWSQ), age at marriage (WAM), age (AGE), age squared (AGESQ), and husband's educatinnal attainment (EH), which was employed as an index of husband's occupational status/earning potential.

10. Karen O. Mason and V. T. Palan, "Female Employment and Fertility in Peninsular Malaysia: The Maternal Role Incompatibility Hypothesis Reconsidered," *Demography*, 18 (November, 1981): 551.

11. See Changing African Family Project (CAFN)—Nigerian segment, J. C. Caldwell, "The Study of Fertility Change in Tropical Africa," Occasional Papers, 7 (1974), World Fertility Survey; Nigerian Family Study, John C. Caldwell and Pat Caldwell, "The Role of Marital Sexual Abstinence in Determining Fertility: A Study of the Yoruba in Nigeria," *Population Studies*, 31 (July 1977).

12. The questionnaire utilized here addresses itself to three types of economic activities. The three main groups are: females employed in the civil service sector, the self-employed women and the unemployed housewives. The civil service category includes women working in government ministries, and private corporations: it embraces all types of activities from clerical and teaching jobs to women in top managerial positions. These types of jobs are grouped together because they have similar service conditions, code of conduct and similar work organization. The self-employed category includes different varieties of economic activities performed by women. They own their businesses and their activities may be either petty-trading, hair dressing, or sewing. The third category includes women who are unemployed and in most cases do not engage in any economic activity outside the home.

13. See A. Adewuyi, "Child Care and Female Employment in a Nigerian Metropolis: The Role of the Under-Six's," *Nigerian Journal of Economic and Social Studies*, 22 (July 1980). This study examined the influence of child care on female employment rates of mothers by age of the youngest child. In this article, the focus is on the age distribution among women surveyed and the role played by child care in employment. This will help show if difference in employment rate exist between younger and other mothers. It is quite reasonable to say that younger mothers are the ones most likely to have younger children, and as such, babysitting help may influence their participation rates.

15

WEST INDIAN FAMILIES IN THE UNITED STATES

Robert E. Millette

Immigrants to the United States face a variety of challenges. Those immigrants distinguished by their African descent face an additional challenge that inheres in the racial stratification of this society. Such is the case for West Indian immigrants to the United States. The subject of this chapter is the effects on West Indian families' form and functioning that result from efforts to become acculturated. These families are termed: "Maintainers," "Social Isolates," and "Social Strivers," consistent with their predominant modes of adaptation to the African-American and white co-culturals of the United States. It is concluded that Social Isolates experience less family conflict since they are willing to relinquish traditional role behaviors and adopt many of the norms and values of the host society.

INTRODUCTION

In the West Indies the main function of the family is reproduction. As in Africa, marriage in the Caribbean is an alliance between two families or bodies of kin.[1] In America, on the other hand, "modern marriage is called upon to fulfill new functions of friendship and emotional support, partly as a result of mobility and isolation of the couple and partly in response to new cultural expectations stimulated by the changing status of women and other trends."[2] With the emphasis on happiness and self-actualization, American couples seek mates who will be good companions and for whom they feel affection.

The purpose of this chapter is to examine how West Indian families are coping with the culture conflict of the Old and the New World ways of behavior. More specifically, we will examine how the Maintainers, the Social Isolates, and the Social Strivers[3] are "managing" the companionship type of family with its emphasis on affection and consensus.[4]

DATA COLLECTED

The bulk of the data for this article was collected during the summer of 1986. A questionnaire consisting of open and closed-ended questions was mailed to five hundred West Indians in the New York, New Jersey, Pennsylvania, Washington, D.C., and Delaware areas. The sample was randomly selected from a mailing list of thirteen thousand West Indians. Additionally, library data was gathered from the Research Institute for the Study of Man (New York), Brooklyn Public Library, Lincoln University Library (Special Collections), and Florida International University and from structured and unstructured interviews with 25 divorced West Indian families.

WEST INDIAN MIGRATION

West Indian immigration to the United States dates back to the mid-nineteenth century. Between 1820 and 1970, Charles reports that about 1 million (roughly 2 percent) of the legal immigrants to the United States came from the English-speaking Caribbean.[5] By 1974, some 16 percent of the 394,861 immigrants in the United States were West Indians. The U.S. Immigration reports (1959–1973) show that in this immigrant group women outnumber men and that the group is composed largely of professional, clerical, managerial, sales, craftsmen, operatives, and laborers. The percentage of professionals has decreased since 1967. The 1965 U.S. Immigration and Nationality Act has been responsible for a large influx of household workers. Thousands of West Indians have used domestic work as a means of getting permanent residence (a green card). Therefore, West Indian women from the lower and middle and as well as from upper strata of their societies are found working as domestic servants in metropolitan New York and New Jersey.

Data from the Immigration and Naturalization Service indicate that migrants from the English-speaking Caribbean tend to migrate in family groups less frequently than do most other migrants. Dominguez reports: "Of a total of 384,685 immigrants admitted to the United States between 1967 and 1973, there were 277,444 (59.1 percent) who were classified as housewives, children or other individuals with no reported occupation."[6] An examination of the 1970 census data shows that Caribbean families have been able to improve their economic position in the United States. The median income for these families (excluding Cubans and Puerto

Ricans) was $8,296. Palmer notes that although this median income was substantially greater than that of black American families, it was below the $9,327 for all American families.[7]

This apparent economic success has not resulted in social and political acceptance by the larger society. Most West Indians, regardless of economical, educational, or political achievements, are viewed by both black and white Americans as something of an oddity. In order to deal with the inequalities that confront them and to forge a new way of life, the majority of West Indians reject the American stratification system. These individuals have been labeled *Maintainers*[8] and comprise the first group examined in this chapter.

A second group, the *Social Isolates,* feel that their countrymen refuse to acknowledge their success because of their countrymen's knowledge of their past. More specifically, the Social Isolates' claim for social recognition among their community is rejected. Therefore, they seek out American friends, especially those who share similar culture, experiences, and rejection.

The *Social Strivers,* a third group, accept the American stratification system. However, unlike the Maintainers and the Social Isolates, they engage in both American and West Indian activities.

Within the context of these constructs, the impact of migration, social change, and technology on West Indian families in the United States is examined. To facilitate understanding of the foregoing, a brief review of the literature and examination of the conditions and structure of West Indian families before they migrated to the United States is offered.

HOUSEHOLD AND FAMILY

The research literature on the West Indian family structure is, at best, sketchy. The first comprehensive study was conducted by Herskovits, and the main focus of his work was to examine the persistence of Africanism in the New World. "They were not studies of Caribbean family structure, but of family forms among the descendants of Africans, and the relation of those forms to the general structural features of African societies."[9] Herskovits and Du Bois looked to Africa and the Institution of slavery for explanations of an Afro-American social organization.[10]

Frazier, on the other hand, did not view American blacks as displaced Africans. Instead, he regarded them as Americans trying to forge a new way of life in a society that is hostile, discriminatory, and oppressive. He said that deviations from normal American patterns of behavior were due to the hostile climate that blacks are confronted with in the South."[11] Myrdal puts it more strongly when he said that "in practically all its divergencies, American Negro culture is not something independent of general American culture. It is a distorted development, or a pathological condition, of the general American culture."[12] Frazier also documents the fact that American blacks had rebuilt a stable family structure along the lines of paternalism.[13]

A close examination of the Caribbean family structure uncovers the existence of paternalism as well as certain aspects of African residues. Therefore, these two approaches became attractive to both American and Caribbean social scientists. Most of these earlier researchers aligned with either Frazier's of Herskovits's approach. Henriques accepts Frazier's thesis that the economic and social conditions of slavery precluded development of stable nuclear families. He said that the high incidence of conjugal turnover, illegitimacy, and maternal households was due primarily to the economically and socially depressed condition of the West Indian family.[14] In the 1950s, social scientists concentrated their research on explaining the high illegitimacy rates, extraresidential mating, matrifocal arrangements, and casual mating.[15]

The earlier approaches were limited in scope because they failed to explore the relationships between consensual and legal cohabitation. Matthews (1953) said that the nonlegal union came about as a result of slavery and the plantation system. Such relationships, which might appear to be disorganized, are the free choices of the people. The decisions of most West Indian men and women to enter into nonlegal relationships must be examined within the social context in which they are made. Marriage is connected with the attainment of a certain socioeconomic standing, a demonstration of ambition and social adulthood. It is also considered by the majority of West Indians as the ideal.

This chapter is not intended to continue the Frazier and Herskovits debate, since such an approach would obscure examination of the elements and relations that give West Indian families their particular qualities and form.[16] Rather, the intent is to capture the world that West Indians have constructed to cope with slavery, the plantation system, and the social and domestic forms of socialization that existed in the Caribbean. A companion task is examination and analysis of how West Indian families in North America are coping with migration, technology, discrimination, prejudice, and the loss of social status and personhood in the United States.

SOCIAL ARRANGEMENTS

In the Caribbean, the man is the major wage earner and the final authority in all major decisions. As the breadwinner and authority figure, he is expected to provide adequately for his family's physical, social, economical, and psychological needs. Smith concludes that "a man with any pride cannot see his wife and children inadequately housed or fed, nor can he allow others to take advantage of them without taking the offender to court."[17] For a man to feel that he is unable to support his family is intolerable, since familial support is the basis for the respect and authority that is afforded him. Smith was partly correct when he said:

> In the lowest status group the only basis for male authority in the household unit is the husband/father's contribution to the economic foundation of the group, and further that where there is both insecurity in jobs where males are concerned and opportunities for women to engage in money-making activities, including farming, there is likely to develop a situation where men's roles are structurally marginal in the complex of domestic relations.[18]

These economic considerations, while very important, are not the only determinants of male authority. The Caribbean social structure says that the man must be the authority figure in his household and in society. The larger society frowns on women who are assertive. West Indian men, therefore, do everything in their power to maintain their manhood. Because of the social stigma attached to a man being a "mama's boy," women date and marry men who are strong, dependable, and willing to take on the responsibilities of being the head of the household.[19]

In the Caribbean, headship corresponds with the ownership of the house. The household head is the person the community as well as the household members regard as head of the domestic unit. It sometimes happens that the woman who is the dominant member of a household is not formally recognized as the head. "Headship is formal leadership and entails formal responsibility. . . ."[20] The head of the household among West Indian folk: (a) owns the house and land; (b) decides who may visit or stay in the household; and (c) has the prominent role of the household group. In a study of Grenville, a small town on the eastern coast of Grenada, Smith found that "few married males are not heads of their own homes . . . and that women with absent spouses tend to assert headhip of their own homes."[21]

Moses supports the claim by Smith and others that "economic contributions from women need not result in higher status, especially if existing cultural traditions define their activities as less prestigious than those of men."[22] For most elite, middle class, lower class, and elite working class families, the husband is considered the head of the household and the ultimate authority figure. The man continues to be the head of the household even though he is away from the island for several years.

SEXUAL EXCLUSIVITY

Caribbean men who control their wives' and mistresses' sexual activities are accorded higher status by the society. Men who are unable to have their women to themselves are viewed as weak and are therefore ranked lower. It is socially acceptable however, for men to have legal wives and several mistresses. Smith reports there is also a well-marked pattern of extramarital mating on the part of high status males. Along with the middle class emphasis upon respectable patterns of behavior that differentiate them from the lower classes, there is an old and pervasive pattern of sexual license for men. . . . The Europeans set the pattern of mating outside marriage by their willingness to take black or colored mistresses. . . .[23]

Girls and women, on the other hand, are expected to be "pure" while boys and men "sow their wild oats."[24] Open instances of infidelity among Caribbean women are quite low. A woman who is unfaithful to her husband or common law husband runs the risk of losing his support and of breaking up her relations with her children.[25]

The society laughs at men who are upwardly mobile and are unable to hold onto their women. Men whose wives or mistresses have extramarital affairs are labelled "soffee." A soffee is a man who is unable to satisfy his woman sexually. And to be labeled sexually weak could mean a loss of social, political, and economical status. Therefore, the insistence of West Indian men on sexual exclusivity of the woman has much more to do with the maintenance of status than with morality.

West Indian men use violence, or the threat of violence, to prevent their wives, keepers, or mistresses from extramarital sexual affairs. They also withhold economic support, use blackmail (the loss of jobs, the loss of upper class contacts, the loss of promotion), and the threat of removing the children's names from their wills to prevent their wives or keepers from engaging in extramarital affairs.

The social status that is attached to marriage keeps West Indian women in their place. Married women tolerate the double standards so that they can be seen in the eyes of the larger society as "good women." Good women are those who accept the authority of their husbands (legal or extra-legal) are responsible parents, take care of their family's domestic needs (cook, clean, sew, wash, iron), and do not "run around with every Tom, Dick, and Harry." The "good woman" label also applies to extralegal relationships. For example, women who are "faithful concubines," "keepers,"[26] "Christian families," or "companionate unions"[27] are also expected to obey their husbands and to take care of the domestic needs of their husbands and children. Women in nonlegal relationships want to be labeled good women, since "good women" are the ones whom most men will eventually marry. Marriage "is indeed valued as the appropriate status for mature and independent couples of middle or senior years. . . ." Thus, in the West Indian communities marriage has dual meanings, as a condition of personal status and as the most esteemed form of mating.[28] Furthermore, marriage grants full adult status to the individuals who are marrying, as well as complete emancipation from parental control.[29]

In America the man is no longer the major wage earner. The societal and religious restrictions that maintain leadership, authority, sexual exclusivity, and obedience have been redefined in America. This redefinition of the situation means that West Indian families have to adjust to the changes that are occurring in the larger society. The rest of this chapter will discuss the changes that have occurred.

Our research indicates that the West Indian families are experiencing severe marital and interpersonal problems in the following areas:

(a) The double standards as they relate to extramarital affairs, domestic arrangements, financial responsibility, sex, and in-law meddling. However, most family problems are kept secret.

(b) Infidelity heads the list of complaints among Caribbean women. Seventy-five percent of the respondents (N = 55) told us that their husband's relationship with his mistress has become public knowledge.

(c) Several male respondents complained about their wives or women questioning their manhood. "We have always had a wife and a mistress on the side," one told us, and "For my wife to now insist that I cannot have an outside woman is a direct attack on my manhood. I am the man and therefore should be free to do as I please."[30]

(d) The women who complained the most were better educated, upwardly mobile urban dwellers. Women who attended church regularly told us that they are constantly praying for their husbands who are living in sin. This rationalization of wanting to help their husbands has helped to maintain marital stability and the continuance of the double standard.

THE IMPACT OF MIGRATION

Sociologists such as Burgess and Locke,[31] Edwards,[32] Frazier,[33] and Ogburn and Nimkof[34] have agreed that industrialization destroys traditional family structure. The city affords comparative freedom from the religious restraints imposed by the churches, freedom from neighborhood organizations, freedom from gossip, and freedom from the mores and folkways of the Caribbean. However, this new freedom creates a sense of normlessness. And since tradition and sentiment no longer furnish the guide for living, they were forced to make their own variations of conduct and thereby develop rational attitudes toward their new environment. More specifically, Burgess and Locke[35] and Merton[36] suggest that a group will form new norms in a normless situation and that these new norms will be formulated around predominant values. Since the predominant value in America is equality between men and women,[37] we can expect that equality would become an important factor for Caribbean-American families. Women are now openly seeking equality in sexual freedom, decision making, ownership of property, and the running of the household. Furthermore, they are demanding that their husbands assist with cooking, cleaning, caring for children, and other household chores.

The effect of migration has had tremendous effects, as can be seen in the distinct socialization patterns of West Indian families. These patterns have been conceptualized as those of Maintainers, Social Isolates, and Social Strivers. The rest of this chapter will explore how these groups are coping or failing to cope with the changes that are occurring.

THE MAINTAINERS

The Maintainers are West Indians who reject the West Indian stratification system, values, norms, and beliefs:

There is a strict hierarchical structure among members of this group. Membership is based not on personal achievement in America but on a careful evaluation of one's past, old friendship ties, family name, skin color, and social class. . . . The ex-businessman, ex-schoolmaster, ex-minister of government, the ex-lawyer or the ex-chief of police usually provide the leadership for this clique. The ideologies that hold the Maintainers together are reverence for the past, a total rejection of the American stratification system, and the quest to maintain the old society in the new world. . . .[38]

The Maintainers also feel that "a man must hold on to his West Indian values. A respondent told us that 'in this country, the man has to be tough. We cannot let those damn women dominate us. You give them an inch and they want a mile. What would my friends in Grenada say if they hear that my wife is dominating me? I will not allow any woman to tell me how to run my house."[39] This strict reverence for the past is causing serious marital problems.

Change in this group, for both men and women, is very slow. Because of the clique system that has emerged, the Maintainers are able to retain the majority of their culture. Unlike Shibutani and Kwan[40] and Park,[41] we did not find that industrial cities are the "graveyards to traditions." However, there is some loosening of social, religious, cultural, and communal values. As a result of the reduced influence of the community, the anonymity that the larger society provides, and the quest for equality, both men and women are experimenting with marital structures and forms that were immoral, degrading, and downright ridiculous in the West Indies. For example, extramarital sex and extramarital dating have increased among this group. The fear of punishment or social and communal threats as an instrument of controlling extramarital sex no longer works. The majority of the women interviewed told us that wife beating would not be tolerated in the United States. Mrs. W.S. said that she is not afraid of her husband. "He tried to beat me once. I immediately got on the telephone and called the cops. Since this incident, he realized that I was not joking. Few women will tolerate wife beatings. New York, thank God, has taught us."

The definition of what constitutes a "good husband" has also changed. The respondents told us that they want their husbands to possess the following qualities:

(a) ability to take care of their family.
(b) ability to be affectionate.
(c) ability to head a family that provides companionship, happiness, freedom and self actualization.

Kamarovsky observes that "modern marriage is called upon to fulfill new functions of friendship and emotional support, partly as a result of mobility and isolation of the couple and partly in response to new cultural expectations stimulated by the changing status of women and other trends."[42]

Sex and sexual activities are seldom discussed by the Maintainers. For example, 68 percent of the women told us that their husbands reprimanded them when they tried to discuss sex. Any attempts on the part of these women to enjoy the sexual act were forbidden. The church in medieval England, as well as in the Caribbean, taught that sexual desires were evil and that passionate love was to be condemned. "Even between husband and wife such impulses were regarded as sinful . . . hence the use of contraceptives was obviously evil, because they could have no other purpose than to facilitate the enjoyment of sex without helping to perpetuate the species. . . ."[43]

With the emphasis on equality, self-actualization, and freedom, the majority of these women told us that they no longer view sex as only a reproductive act. Such concepts as "satisfaction," "fun," "enjoyment," "pleasure," and "sensation" were used by these women to describe what they expect to get from the sexual act. "This expectation put a new binder on husbands and created new complexities when the woman did not find the satisfaction to which she now felt entitled in the bonds of a proper monogamous marriage."[44] About 25 percent of women in Maintainer families have engaged or are engaging in extramarital relationships. These relationships have not, in many instances, led to a large rate of divorce or separation, since most of the husbands are unaware of their wives' outside activities. However, in instances where the outside relationships became known to husbands, they separated from or divorced their wives.

The double standard concerning sexual exclusivity continues among the Maintainers. The men are determined to maintain the same levels of authority and control that they had in the Caribbean. They told us that they will not "give up their manhood." Many claim that they would divorce their spouse rather than be humiliated by her. Men continue to demand that their wives be "loyal, obedient, and accept their responsibilities as housewives, mothers, entertainers, and nurses.'' More specifically, they expect their wives to see them as the boss—the sole authority figure. Ninety-five percent of the men that we interviewed said that they were engaged in at least 1 outside sexual relationship. Ten percent were involved in as many as 10 to 15. Blackwell's observation that urbanization permitted experimentation with social relationships between the sexes is salient here.[45] In spite of their extramarital relationships, the women interviewed continue to see themselves as ''good women.'' Their husbands, on the other hand, are refusing, in the face of changing values, norms, and roles, to change or alter their definition of the situation. When asked to rate their relationship, 35 percent of the women and 30 percent of the men said that they were very satisfied; 45 percent of the women and 37 percent of the men said they were satisfied. The women who said that they were dissatisfied told us that they are ''giving their husband time to change . . . time to realize that he cannot run the family as he did in the Caribbean.'' Only 5 percent of the men that we interviewed (the Maintainers) said that they have considered divorcing their wives. Divorce and to a lesser extent separation are partly controlled by the West Indian community. Family considerations in America, as well as in the Caribbean, the fear of family rejection, and the influence of earlier religious, cultural, and social socialization are responsible for the low divorce rate among West Indian families, especially among the Maintainers. For example, the techniques for socialization of boys in the Maintainer family continue to saddle many of them with irrational and damaging anxieties about their ability to implement the male role. These boys are finding out that many of the things that they observe and learn from their fathers are not acceptable in the larger American society.

THE SOCIAL ISOLATES

The Social Isolates are successful educationally and professionally. However, their successes are not always recognized and regarded by other West Indians. This lack of recognition causes them to withdraw mentally and sometimes physically from the West Indian community. The Social Isolates socialize with individuals who see them as successful individuals and who are not overly interested in their past. Their new friends are usually black Americans from the Deep South—Alabama, Mississippi, North and South Carolina, Virginia, and Louisiana.[46]

Social isolation is used by the Social Isolates to cover up for their inability to compete with the Strivers, who are recognized by the majority of their countrymen as West Indian leaders. The refusal of the West Indian community to accept and recognize the Social Isolates for their achievements in America is due to the rigid stratification system that exists in the Caribbean. Family name, geographical location, skin color, and kinship ties continue to be important indicators for assigning social status.[47] The Social Isolates are constantly reminded of their past lower class status through jokes, direct confrontation, and others' refusal to accept them as equals. Unlike the Maintainers, the Social Isolates try to forget their past. As a result, they are better socially adjusted to deal with the problems of the larger society.

Of the three family types, the Social Isolates are best able to deal with the marital changes with which they have been confronted. Unlike the Maintainers, the men are more involved in the day-to-day running of the family and in the division of labor.

The Social Isolates are experiencing fewer marital conflicts in the areas of sexual exclusivity, authority, and child rearing. In great contrast with the Maintainers, only 5 percent of the Social Isolate families were very dissatisfied with their relationships. Both men and women in this family type said that their lives were centered around having a good family. An interviewee told us, "My countrymen have refused to accept me, America has discriminated against me, my family envies my profession and economic successes . . . my wife, however, respects and admires me and my children give me all the encouragement and support that I need to succeed as a contractor . . . it's only fair that I return the support and love that I receive from them."[48] Such sentiment is widespread among the Social Isolates. Their families become the one thing that gives them, both men and women, a sense of self-worth. Family relationships, therefore, are guarded carefully and cherished.

This group registered the lowest percentage of extramarital sex. Respect, admiration, fear of jeopardizing the relationship, and concern for what the community would say were given as reasons why these individuals do not engage in outside relationships. Headship and authority were areas where the Social Isolates experienced less conflict than the Maintainers and Strivers. In this family, the man is considered the head of the household. However, we found that decision making is a shared process. This supports the findings by McAdoo that black American fathers are moving toward an egalitarian relationship in the decision making and power relationship in the home.[49]

THE STRIVERS

The Strivers accept the American stratification system. Unlike the Maintainers, they engage in both American and West Indian activities.[50] And like the Social Isolates, they were members of the Caribbean middle, lower, and upper classes. In America, they are the college-educated, the laborers, the plumbers, the professionals, and the community leaders. The distinguishing characteristic of the Strivers is their quest for success and leadership.

In the Caribbean, the Strivers were usually teachers, bankers, civil servants, policemen, politicians, small farmers, and small businessmen. Even though they were successful in their respective countries, they were generally locked into dead end positions. The Strivers' dreams of attending college or university, getting a management position, or becoming an investor are realized in America. The Strivers view America as their opportunity for achieving higher status and social honor. Needless to say, they fully accept the American dream and certain aspects of the American culture.

The Strivers are progressive and liberal in areas such as education, politics, employment, and economics, but quite conservative in their views of the family and child rearing. This refusal to change and to accept the new definitions of the situation, as they relate to Caribbean families, are causing severe marital strains for both husbands and wives. Most male Strivers insist on maintaining the old West Indian family structure in the new society. They, like the Maintainers, are determined that their wives remain submissive, loyal, obedient, and dependent. The Strivers continued to see themselves as the sole wage earners and the authority figures. Any departure from "the traditional marital contract" is viewed as a direct attack on their manhood.

The women in this group are upwardly mobile and are quick to point out that "the old West Indian way of life has no place in America." They insist that the American family structure, which stresses equality for everyone, is superior to the authoritarian structures that were commonplace in the Caribbean. After approximately one year in the United States, they seek equality in the following areas: (a) decision making (b) household chores (e.g., housecleaning, cooking, and taking care of the children) (c) freedom to do what they please, and (d) exclusive sex rights over their men.

This indicates that the new societal and marital scripts have changed.

Women are now demanding equality, freedom, self-actualization, self-respect, and the ability to do as they please socially, economically and sexually. They are no longer prepared to accept the familial system that they were accustomed to in the Caribbean. Additionally, these women are looking for relationships that are exciting, fulfilling, and romantic.

Both West Indian men and women have described their American counterparts as sexually excitable, aggressive, loving, romantic, and caring. Both groups told us that they will "venture out" if their spouses are unable to satisfy their sexual desires. The maintenance of the Striver family is no longer governed by the regularity of the man's employment. Several of the women believe that they would be better off by themselves. Whether this belief is true or imagined, these women felt that they are capable of attracting mates that are more compatible and upwardly mobile. Male Strivers have similar feelings and expectations.[51] Scott seems to have captured this well when she said that "as work, and husbands, moved out of the home, women were destined to become discontented and eventually to work out a new pattern of usefulness for themselves."

For the Strivers, economic and political successes resulted in serious familial problems. Like the Sicilians in Gabaccia's study referred to in the following quote, the Strivers claimed that New York destroyed the family. "Mobility influenced the ways in which immigrants pursued their social ideals, freed in so many other ways from the restraints imposed by Sicilian agrotowns. Anxieties about privacy and the compensatory myth of male dominance gradually disappeared as immigrants built new social networks in New York."[52]

CONCLUSION

The three family structures discussed in this chapter are all influenced by the norms and values of the American society. The family structure of the Social Isolate is the one least influenced by migration. Both men and women in this group are committed to developing relationships that are beneficial to the entire family. The willingness of Striver women to accept their husbands as the heads of the households and the willingness of the men to treat their wives as equal partners are mainly responsible for the marital stability of this family structure. The refusal of the Maintainers to accept the new definition of the situation is causing severe marital strains. Even though changes are slow in the Maintainer family, women are, nevertheless, questioning the authority of their husbands, insisting that they do not engage in extramarital affairs, and demanding a say in the running of the family.

The Striver family is experiencing the most conflict. Both husbands and wives place great emphasis on self-actualization, success, happiness, and freedom. The traditional marital contract that maintained marital stability in the Caribbean is not applicable in America. Like the Maintainers, the Strivers continue to experiment with extramarital sex. However, the men, in both groups, see their wives' infidelity as a direct attack on their manhood.

West Indian migration to America has resulted in normlessness and a redefinition of the traditional marital contract, at least as it was defined and practiced in the Caribbean. The Strivers, Maintainers, and Social Isolates are presently developing new norms to cope with the changes that they are experiencing. The data presented throughout this paper indicate that West Indian men are more reluctant than West Indian women to accept the new definition of the situation. Their refusal to assimilate and internalize the American value system of equality, freedom, and justice for all is causing and will continue to cause marital problems for the Strivers, Maintainers, and Social Isolates.

The Social Isolates have accepted assimilation and have internalized many of the norms and values of the larger society. They have, like the Cubans, "adjusted well to the United States as a host country—according to indices of social organization family stability, upward mobility, dependency. . . ."[53] We should point out that our conclusions are based on a pilot study. We will study this family type further to see if they "repress or displace hostile feelings"[54] in order to present a sense of marital stability. We agree with Simmel, as quoted by Coser, that

> . . . it is necessary for one to probe beneath behavioral manifestations in order to disclose the full extent of social reality . . . the lack of conflict in a relationship cannot be taken to indicate that the relationship is stable and secure or that it is free from potential disruptive strains. We must concern ourselves with latent as well as manifest elements within a relationship if its full meaning is to be disclosed analytically.[55]

NOTES

1. A.R. Radcliffe-Brown, "African Kinship," in A.R. Radcliffe-Brown and D. Forde, eds., *African Systems of Kinship and Marriage* (London: Oxford U. Press, 1950).

2. M. Kamarovsky, *Blue Collar Marriage* (New York: Random House, 1967).

3. R.E. Millette, *New Grenada in Brooklyn, Social Stratification and Adaptation Among First Generation Immigrants* (New York: Associated Faculty Press, 1987/in press).

4. E.W. Burgess and H.J. Locke, *The Family: From Institution to Companionship* (New York: American Books, 1953).

5. H.J. Charles, "Patterns of West Indian Emigration, 1880-1970," mimeographed paper presented at the Atlantic History and Culture Seminar, Johns Hopkins University.

6. V.R. Dominiquez, *From Neighbor to Stranger: The Dilemma of Caribbean People in the United States,* Antilles Research Program, Yale University, 1975, p. 14.

7. R. Palmer, "Migration from the Caribbean to the States: The Economic Status of the Immigrants," in R.S. Bryce-Laporte and D.M. Mortimer, eds., *Caribbean Immigration to the United States* (Washington, DC: Research Institute on Immigration, Smithsonian Institute, 1976).

8. Millette (1987/in press).

9. R.T. Smith, "Culture and Social Structure in the Caribbean: Some Recent Work on Family and Kinship Studies," In M.M. Horowitz, ed., *Peoples and Cultures of the Caribbean* (New York: Natural History Press, 1971).

10. M.J. Herskovits, *The Myth of the Negro Past* (Boston: Beacon, 1958); W.E.B. Du Bois, *The Negro American Family* (New York: New American Library, 1969).

11. E.F. Frazier, *The Negro Family in the United States* (Chicago: Univerisity of Chicago Press, 1966).

12. Gunnar Myrdal, *An American Dilemma: The Negro Problem in Modern Democracy* (New York: Harper and Row, 1944), p. 28.

13. Frazier, (1966).

14. F. Henriques, "West Indian Family Organization," in L. Comitas & D. Lowenthal, eds., *Work and Family Life: West Indian Perspective* (New York: Anchor, 1973).

15. R.T. Smith, "The Family in the Caribbean," in V. Rubin, ed., *Caribbean Studies: A Symposium.* Jamica Institute of Social and Economic Research, University of the West Indies, 1957.

16. Comitas and Lowenthal, (1973).

17. R.T. Smith, *The Negro Family in British Guiana: Family Structure and Social Status in the Villages* (New York: Humanities Press, 1965).

18. Ibid.

19. Millette, (1987 in press).

20. M.G. Smith, *West Indian Family Structure* (Seattle: University of Washington Press, 1962), p. 16.

21. Ibid.

22. Y.T. Moses, "Female Status and Male Dominance in the West Indian Community," in C. Steady, ed., *The Black Woman Cross Culturally* (Cambridge, MA: Schenkman Publishing Company, 1981).

23. Smith (1971).

24. S.A. Queen and J.B. Adams, *The Family in Various Cultures* (New York: J.B. Lippincott Company, 1952).

25. Smith, (1965).

26. Henriques (1973).

27. T.S. Simey, *Welfare and Planning in the West Indies* (London: Oxford University Press, 1946).

28. E. Clarke, "Variations in Jamaican Domestic Patterns," in Comitas and Lowenthal (1973).

29. Cohen, Y.A.

30. Interview with Mr. H.S. July 1986.

31. Burgess and Locke (1953).

32. J.H. Edwards, ed., *The Family and Change* (New York: Alfred A. Knopf, 1960).

33. Frazier (Chicago, 1966).

34. W.F. Ogburn and M.F. Nimkoff, *Technology and the Changing Family* (Boston: Houghton Mifflin, 1955).

35. Burgess and Locke (1953).

36. R. Merton, *Social Theory and Social Structure* (Glencoe: Illinois: Free Press, 1957).

37. See Robin M. Williams, *American Society, A Social Interpretation*, 2nd Edition (New York: Alfred A. Knopf, 1960) pp. 409-417.

38. Millette (1987/in press).

39. Ibid.

40. T. Shibutani and K.M. Kwan, *Ethnic Stratification: A Comparative Approach* (London: MacMillan, 1965).

41. R.E. Park, *"Racial Assimilation in Secondary Groups,"* in *Race and Culture: Essays in the Sociology of Contemporary Man* (London: Free Press, 1950).

42. Kamarovsky (1967).

43. Queen and Adams (1952).

44. A.F. Scott, *The Southern Lady: From Pedestal to Politics 1830-1930* (Chicago: University of Chicago Press, 1970).

45. J.E. Blakwell, *The Black Community: Diversity and Unity* (New York: Dodd, Mead and Company, 1975).

46. Millette (1987/in press).

47. Ibid.

48. Ibid.

49. J.L. McAdoo, "Involvement of Fathers in the Socialization of Black Children," in H.P. McAdoo, ed., *Black Families* (Beverly Hills: Sage 1981).

50. Millette (1987/in press).

51. Scott (1970).

52. D.R. Gabaccia, *From Sicily to Elizabeth Street: Housing and Social Change Among Italian Immigrants, 1880-1930*. (New York: State University of New York Press, 1984).

53. Dominiquez (1975).

54. L. Coser, *The Functions of Social Conflict* (New York: Free Press, 1956).

55. Ibid.

Part VI

Policy and Social Service Delivery Systems

INTRODUCTION

The intransigence of an inadequate and unresponsive social service delivery system poses a continuing impediment in black families' quest for equity and survival. Sociopsychological investigations and literature prior to the late 1960s commonly stereotyped, trivialized, and ultimately pathologized black family units as complex deviations from a unilaterally ordained norm. Rarely did researchers and writers examine and appreciate the specificity of black families. Rarely were the form and function of these units viewed as normative responses to an oppressive social and economic system. How black families differed or deviated from white families—the deviant hypothesis—has shaped both scholarly inquiry and the consequent development and implementation of public policy recommendations. Compare, for example, the recommendation of Moynihan to the national administration that it pursue a policy toward African-Americans of benign neglect.

Much of the recent scholarship portrays black families as they are, a contrast to earlier foci on what these families' are not. Those recent works challenge the ideological perspective that holds black families as deviant. Further, they offer alternative theories and perspectives for studying these families. The newer theoretical perspectives and conceptualizations have been derived from documentations of black families form and function, and although they are variously termed, they essentially focus on the actual strengths and dynamics of black families. The emergent perspective, termed *cultural variation,* carries the assertion that these differential family structures are legitimate *and* are required in a pluralistic society in order to meet fully the needs of family members as well as those of the social system. Ironically, some of the forms: "female-headed households," "latchkey children," and "unwed single parents," currently enjoy legitimacy as they have been adapted by non-black American "families."

Recent scholarship on black families has produced a portrait of families that, although historically obliged to enter by the narrow door, have distinct values, philosophies, strengths, aspirations, and consonant behaviors. Despite ample and consistent demonstrations of the distinct ethos of black Americans and black families, social service delivery systems have not been revised or adapted to offer adequate, sensitive interventions that address blacks' specificity.

Continuing the thesis of the other chapters in this volume, the authors in this section focus on the characteristics of black families as related to these families' sociocultural history and traditions. The writers propose models of social service intervention that respect and incorporate this history and tradition. Gibbs's chapter "Developing Intervention Models for Black Families: Linking Theory and Research," presents the broader conceptualization of interventions—one that accommodates advocacy and education roles that enable black families and their members to deal effectively at successive societal levels: macro—encompassing the economic and political systems in which all of the other levels are embedded; mezzo—the level of local government and societal institutions and employers with whom black families have direct contract; micro—encompassing kinship and social networks with whom the family functions daily; and finally, the individual level, where individual motivation, knowledge, and behavior are concomitants of one's responsibility for change.

Gibbs's thesis is that problems faced by black families are best understood as the interaction between historical patterns of adaptation, current social policies, environmental stress, and the families' coping strategies. As she sets forth the relationship between theoretical perspectives and empirical research in developing appropriate and potentially effective intervention models, Gibbs argues that the chronicity and pervasiveness of inequities require multiple levels of intervention.

Gibbs's notions have concordance with those of Solomon. In "Counseling Black Families at Inner-City Church Sites," Solomon reports experiences from an intervention model and argues persuasively that the appropriate intervention model is one that empowers black families to solve their own problems rather than simplistically providing service to problem families. Solomon also notes the failure of existing service delivery systems both in terms of physical versus "psychological" access and appropriate interventions. The primary purpose of the intervention model that she devised was to stimulate referral of unserved and underserved persons who utilize informal and often nonprofessional community resources. The focus of the counseling provided at the church sites was teaching or empowering clients to take control over aspects of their lives.

The example of interventions and the results reported by Solomon suggest again that the success of a counseling intervention is dependent upon the appropriateness of the intervention.

In the final chapter, "Empowering Black Families," Cheatham focuses on the documented evidence of black families' characteristics and experiences and argues that Africentrism, as a heuristic device, has greater legitimacy than the currently imposed normative, Eurocentric model of service intervention. He suggests that practitioners need not necessarily abandon existing models of intervention but that we must, at least, extend and refine these models to serve the needs of black—and, in fact, all nontraditional—clients. Although it has explicit utility beyond the mental-health helping professions, the proposed model intentionally is focused rather narrowly on counseling and psychotherapeutic interventions intended to empower black families.

These chapters collectively argue the utility of the cultural variation perspective in theoretical and practical models for service delivery to black families.

16

DEVELOPING INTERVENTION MODELS FOR BLACK FAMILIES: LINKING THEORY AND RESEARCH

Jewelle Taylor Gibbs

Revived interest in the status of black families presages a movement beyond the inuring "tangle of pathology" thesis, dominant in public policy decisions during the past two decades. Demographic profiles of these families confirm chronic and pervasive problems of poverty, inadequate housing, welfare dependency, and similar poverty-related social problems. This profile however, does not provide an adequate understanding of the economic context that gives life and longevity to these problems. In this chapter, explication is provided of the relationship between theoretical perspectives and empirical research on black families. This understanding must inform the development of intervention models. Advanced, among several propositions concerning appropriate intervention strategies, is the proposition that problems currently experienced by black families have multiple causation, are embedded in a complex sociopolitical-economic context, and must be approached through several levels of intervention.

INTRODUCTION

Since the Reagan administration assumed the reins of government in 1980, attitudes toward the poor and minorities in this country have been reflected in social policies that are regressive and punitive, resulting in reduced benefits, weakened civil rights, and increased barriers to equal opportunity in American society. Concomitant with these policies there have been a revival of interest in the status and problems of the black family, which has experienced a form of "benign neglect" ever since the end of the Johnson administration and the War on Poverty. This renewed interest in the problems of the black family, as documented in numerous television shows, magazine and newspaper articles, and scholarly symposia, recalls echoes of the earlier debate on the black family that was sparked by Moynihan's controversial essay on the subject two decades earlier.[1]

The predominant theme of these discussions about the black family has been the alleged deteriorating condition of this segment of the population, buttressed by an array of statistics on negative social indicators in the areas of education, employment, crime and delinquency, teenage pregnancy, substance abuse, and inner-city violence. Unfortunately, these statistics are rarely presented in the context of the historical antecedents, the current sociopolitical environment, and the changing economic structure, which have contributed so significantly and so adversely to the so-called "breakdown of the black family."

As Benjamin and Stewart point out in their chapter in this volume, the demographic profile of American blacks certainly confirms the fact that many families live in poverty, are plagued by unemployment, are headed by single women, are welfare-dependent, and experience more chronic illnesses, inadequate housing problems, and other poverty-related social problems. What these statistics fail to show, however, is the noxious impact on the black family of over 350 years of slavery and discrimination, prejudice and exclusion, economic exploitation and unemployment, poverty and deprivation, and unequal access to the material, social, cultural, and political benefits of American society.

The chronicity and pervasiveness of these inequities experienced by the black family for so many generations have created the need for multiple levels of intervention so that these families will be able to function effectively in this society. The goal of this chapter is to explicate the relationship between theoretical perspectives and empirical research on the black family in developing models of intervention that are appropriate and potentially effective in addressing the problems of black families in contemporary America.

The author will set forth the following propositions concerning intervention strategies with black families:

(a) that the current problems experienced by black families, as outlined above and elsewhere in this volume, are multiply determined, embedded in a very complex sociopolitical-economic context and must be approached at several levels of intervention;

(b) that current policies and programs are inadequate, inappropriate, and inefficient to address the multiple social and economic problems of black families;

(c) that there are barriers to the use of traditional social and mental health services that have further reduced their effectiveness and have frequently resulted in an exacerbation of existing problems;

(d) that there is an urgent need for innovative models of service delivery for troubled black families in order to prevent further widespread deterioration and dysfunction; and

(e) that policymakers and helping professionals need to understand the cultural, social-structural, and environmental forces impinging on black families in order to design policies and intervention strategies that will achieve maximum results with minimum resistance.

This discussion will focus primarily on the problems experienced by low income and working class black families, who constitute the majority of black families, but it is important to note that there is no single stereotypical "black family," but rather a great diversity of families with different cultural backgrounds, socioeconomic levels, regional loyalties, political and religious affiliations, and levels of acculturation and assimilation into the dominant majority culture. However, low income black families are the ones most likely to need or to utilize publicly funded social and mental-health services and also the ones most likely to suffer when these services are unavailable, underfunded, or unresponsive.

THEORETICAL CONCEPTIONS OF THE BLACK FAMILY

Several scholars have proposed classificatory schemes for the analysis of the black family; these schemes are very similar and generally have overlapping categories.[2] Allen makes the important distinction between conceptual approaches and ideological perspectives in the study of black families, noting that there are three major ideological perspectives: the cultural deviant, the cultural equivalent, and the cultural variant.[3] Briefly, the cultural deviant perspective views black families as deviating from the normative patterns and values of white middle class families; thus they are labeled as pathological and dysfunctional as compared to an "ideal norm." This perspective has its historical roots in the work of E. Franklin Frazier, a black sociologist who asserted that the integrity of the black family was damaged severely by the impact of slavery and discrimination.[4] Later advocates of this viewpoint were Moynihan, Rainwater, and Schulz.[5]

The cultural equivalent perspective emphasizes similarities in "universal patterns" and values between black and white families, attributing any observed differences to social class influences. While this view deemphasizes racial differences, it also fails to recognize legitimate cultural differences between racial groups with unique historical and social experiences. Proponents of this view are Jesse Bernard, who refers to "culturally white Black families," and Scanzoni, who argues that SES accounts for most of the differences between black and white families.[6]

Finally, the cultural variant perspective views the black family as a distinctive cultural form that has evolved in America from a fusion of elements from African culture and adaptations to slavery, segregation, rural southern culture, and urban northern ghetto life. Advocates of this viewpoint include Billingsley, who describes the black community as an "ethnic subsociety," Stack, who documents the function of extended kinship networks, and Nobles, whose theory of "Africanity" proposes that African customs and values have been incorporated into black family structure and functioning.[7]

These ideological perspectives have shaped the scholarly inquiry of generations of social scientists, historians, and public policy specialists conducting research on the black family. In more recent years, the cultural variant perspective has gained more prominence and more intellectual respectability as black social scientists have developed their own conceptual paradigms and have challenged the underlying negative or paternalistic assumptions of the other two perspectives. However, this perspective alone does not sufficiently explain the current social problems besetting the black family. Young black males in the 15–25 age range are particularly vulnerable to significant social problems, which frequently result in their inability to participate in the labor market, their involvement in an underworld of crime and drugs, and their failure to assume paternal responsibility for the children they have fathered.[8] These problems, as well as the high rates of school dropouts, unemployment, and teenage pregnancy, can be better understood if they are conceptualized as an interaction between historical patterns of adaptation, current social policies, environmental stress, and coping strategies utilized by black family members.[9]

One of the major problems with all of the ideological perspectives on the black family is that they have not been subjected to rigorous empirical tests to determine their validity. This lack of empirical validation may be attributed to at least four factors that make it difficult to test the concepts. First, the perspectives are themselves very broad, complex, and derived from a combination of sociological, psychological, and anthropological concepts. Second, the concepts, such as "pathological norms," "dysfunctional behaviors," "deviant lifestyles," "culturally white," "Africanity," and "ethnic subsociety," are often difficult, if not impossible, to operationalize and to measure objectively. Third, it is difficult to study families in their natural environments to assess their roles, functions, values, and interpersonal relationships, yet observation of families in controlled laboratory settings does not yield the type of qualitative data needed for an in-depth assessment of family functioning. Fourth, a family is a heterogeneous collection of individuals and even most of the systems theorists will admit that these individuals have personalities, values, behaviors, and goals that are unique and make it very difficult to identify and evaluate shared common properties of the black family *as a system* for intervention.

Notwithstanding these difficulties inherent in testing theoretical concepts about the black family, there are three types of research that have enlarged our understanding of black family social structure, functions, and dynamics, i.e., ethnographic studies, social-psychological studies, and clinical studies. These studies, as recently reviewed by Allen, Johnson, Mathis, and Staples and Mirande, have investigated a number of topics, ranging from marital satisfaction and child-rearing patterns to intergenerational mobility and social support networks.[10] For the purpose of this chapter, four issues have been selected for discussion in order to illustrate their relationship to theoretical concepts, on the one hand, and their implications for intervention, on the other hand. These issues are: (a) marital satisfaction and stability, (b) child-rearing and socialization patterns, (c) teenage pregnancy and parenting, and (d) family conflict and help-seeking patterns.

REVIEW OF FOUR AREAS OF RESEARCH ON THE BLACK FAMILY

This section will review research in four selected areas of black family functioning, selected in terms of their relevance to current social problems and their clear implications for social policy and/or social service delivery systems. Social service programs in this context will include federal, state, and local social welfare programs and services, programs sponsored by private industry, nonprofit agencies, voluntary organizations, and churches, and public and privately funded health and mental health services.

Marital Satisfaction and Stability

This is a crucial aspect of family functioning, since the family's health and well-being are determined to a large extent by the quality of the marital relationship.

In their study of marital status and life satisfaction in a large probability sample of black women and their mates, Ball and Robbins found that married women were not significantly more satisfied with their lives than widowed, divorced, or single women, once they controlled for age, education, income, health, and social participation.[11] However, married men had the lowest mean satisfaction score of all marital statuses, significantly lower than the satisfaction level of nonmarried men. Other studies of marital status and life satisfaction among blacks have not found significant differences between currently married and not married black men and women.[12]

The implication from these studies is that marriage among blacks is not related to higher levels of life satisfaction or happiness as it has been consistently found among whites.[13] This may reflect several factors, such as the greater difficulties black males have in fulfilling their economic obligations to their families, the more frequent tendency of black women to marry men who have less education and lower occupational status, and the persistent and pervasive racism that particularly undermines the competence and confidence of black males in this society.[14]

The idea that the satisfaction of the black male in the marital dyad may be strongly influenced by his power in the relationship is supported by the results of a study of black married couples by Gray-Little, who found that husband-dominant couples most frequently reported the highest level of marital quality, as measured by marital satisfaction, positive regard for the spouse, and reciprocity.[15] While several scholars have described black couples as more egalitarian than white couples, others have found that blacks and whites of the same socioeconomic level display similar variations in marital power.[16] However, two factors that have been consistently associated with lower marital satisfaction have been membership in a minority group and low socioeconomic status, both of which impact on black couples.[17]

Studies of black marital dyads indicate that marital satisfaction is inversely related to economic stresses.[18] Dissatisfaction with marriage among black couples increases as income and education decrease, but very poor black women rated their marital relationship very low as a source of satisfaction.[19] Black wives in ''blue collar'' marriages were less satisfied than their white counterparts with their relationships.[20] Black women also had greater marital instability than whites in a study of welfare recipients.

The relationship between economic status and marital satisfaction is also amply documented by studies of Liebow and Belle.[21] Since marital satisfaction apparently decreases as income and education decrease and family size increases, the clear implication is that a high proportion of black marriages are significantly stressed due to poverty, unemployment, and lack of opportunity for mobility. This would account for both the high rate of marital dissolution and the high rate of mothers who remain single by choice.[22]

As Wilson and Neckerman point out, the ratio of marriageable males to eligible black females is very low in the age groups where family formation is most likely to occur, i.e., 18–24 and 25–39. A marriageable male is defined by these authors as one who is gainfully employed and able to support a wife and family. They attribute the low ratio of eligible black males in the marriage pool to the attrition of black males through violent and accidental deaths, substance abuse addiction, unemployment, incarceration, and other social factors that make them ineligible for marriage. Thus, for the past forty years (since the end of World War II), black women have had a diminishing pool of eligible black men to marry. In addition, black widows and divorcées are less likely to remarry than white women of comparable status, so that the total number of black female head of households is increased by these two demographic trends.[23]

Even when black women do marry, they are frequently in the position of having more education, a higher-status occupation, and a more stable source of income than their mates. This disparity may contribute to marital dissatisfaction and ultimately result in marital dissolution. This same phenomonoen may underlie the statistics on the dissolution of low income and working class black families, who are more vulnerable to economic stresses.

Contrary to conceptions of the black family as a matriarchy or as a preferred matrifocal arrangement, historians have documented the preference for a two-parent family before and since the days of slavery.[24] Thus, there seems ample evidence from both historical and sociological research that black families have traditionally been headed by two parents, except in periods when marriage was not legally permitted for blacks (during slavery) or when there has been severe economic instability in the country and/or high rates of unemployment among adult black males.

This evidence leads to the rejection of the cultural deviant theory of black family structure and support for the cultural variant prospective, which assumes that the emergence of the single-parent family and the female-headed household is an adaptation to economic forces, discrimination in employment, and punitive social welfare eligibility criteria rather than an active rejection of the norms of the dominant society.

One of the factors that has allowed the female-headed household to survive in the black community has been the cultural tradition of extended kinship relationships and strong social support networks.[25] These networks have functioned rather successfully to provide emotional support, child care, economic resources, and social relationships for black families of all social classes; they have been particularly crucial to the maintenance of functioning for the low income black family. These networks may reflect the influence of African tribal customs, as some scholars have suggested, or they may simply reflect a creative and resilient response to conditions of black community life both in the rural South and the urban North.[26]

On the other hand, there is also some evidence to support the "cultural equivalent" theory in the studies that indicate that black and white couples of the same socioeconomic level have similar patterns of power and similar levels of marital satisfaction. Moreover, the traditional pattern of husband-dominant marital dyads appears to be related to greater satisfaction among black and white couples. There is clearly a need for further research that will disentangle the effects of race, socioeconomic status, and level of acculturation or assimilation on marital roles, marital satisfaction, and marital stability.

The implications for intervention of this interaction effect of race and socioeconomic status on the marital satisfaction and stability of black couples will be discussed later.

Teenage Pregnancy and Parenting

The problem of "children having children" among unwed black teenage girls has been the focus of intense attention and debate in the past decade. As statistics have shown that over 80 percent of the babies born to black teen mothers are born out-of-wedlock, health professionals, policymakers, and civil rights leaders have expressed concern over the impact of this phenomenon on black youth and the implications for the black family.[27] Even though the actual rate of childbearing in this group declined during the 1970s and early 1980s, the adolescent age cohort had increased in size by 20 percent due to the coming of age of the "baby boomers," so that there were simply more girls having babies. In 1980, nearly 1 of 10 black adolescent females had a baby and 27 percent of this group were giving birth to a second or higher-order child.[28]

Childbearing among teenagers has many negative consequences.[29] First, there are negative consequences for the teen mothers themselves, physically, psychologically, and economically. Pregnancy interferes with the normal adolescent developmental-maturational process, so these girls are at greater risk than older first-time mothers for prenatal, perinatal, and postnatal health problems.[30] Psychologically, they are still in the process of forming a psychosocial identity, yet motherhood imposes on them a premature adult role, resulting in a foreclosure of identity development for many who become invested in the motherhood role and fail to explore other options. Economically, they will experience less mobility and less economic stability over their adult lives, primarily because they are more likely to drop out of school after they become pregnant.[31] In fact, these teen mothers are more likely to have more children out-of-wedlock and larger families and to spend part of their adult lives on welfare than those young women who delay pregnancy.[32]

Second, there are negative consequences for the children born to teen mothers. Infant mortality rates are higher for this age group, and if the infant survives, he is more likely to be born with low birthweight, medical problems, and developmental disabilities.[33] These children are also at greater risk for child abuse from immature parents and, as they enter preschool and elementary school, may have lower IQ scores and more deviant behavior than children born to older mothers. However, educational and occupational outcomes of these mothers are improved for girls who live with their parents for at least five years after the birth of a child.[34]

Third, there may be negative consequencs for the whole family and for the father of the child, particularly if he is also an adolescent. A new baby in the family may initially be a novelty and create a bond between the teenager and her mother, but studies have also found that the addition of another member to an often overcrowded and overburdened family unit will result in greater household conflict and tension, intensify sibling rivalry, and strain economic resources in the family.[35] Young men who become fathers in their teens are more likely to drop out of school, to have less occupational mobility, to marry at an earlier age, and to have larger families eventually.[36] Among those young couples who do marry, they are more likely to have marital difficulties than their later-married peers, and the chances that they will separate within five years are very high.[37]

While some authors have suggested that high fertility rates among black women, including unwed teenagers, can be justified in terms of a strategy for cultural survival, the overriding issues for these adolescent mothers is that they do not have the physical or mental maturity nor the economic resources to bear and raise a child successfully. Moreover, in a highly industrialized and competitive society, adolescent childbearing places both females and males at a distinct disadvantage in terms of educational and occupational mobility and relegates many of them to a permanent position at the bottom of the social pyramid, where they will spend a great part of their young adult lives either unemployed, on welfare, or at marginal subsistence levels.

Teenage pregnancy has been correlated to many factors, including earlier onset of sexual activity, low school achievement, low educational aspirations, race, poverty, and lack of knowledge about sex education or ineffective contraception.[38] Many of these factors are amenable to intervention, but they are also related to a host of other variables that are often ignored in planning intervention programs. For black teenagers, in particular, culturally reinforced attitudes and values toward sexual activity and fertility must be taken into account if intervention strategies are to be effective.[39] For example, ethnographic studies suggest that for many black teenagers, childbearing represents a path to adulthood and a socially legitimized role in the community, where other options may not be perceived as possible or probable.

Finally, continued high rates of out-of-wedlock teenage pregnancy create a vicious cycle of welfare dependency, family instability, and community disorganization in the black community. The fact that the pregnancy rate for white adolescent females is increasing and contributing to the highest teenage pregnancy rate of all industrialized nations does not vitiate the point about negative outcomes for black teenage mothers.[40] However, the increasing pregnancy rate among white teenagers certainly suggests that there are no significant differences in sexual activity between black and white adolescents, but more likely differences in cultural attitudes toward birth control and pregnancy.

Thus, the high rate of pregnancy among black adolescent females can be viewed as support for the theory of cultural variance, reflecting more liberal attitudes than whites about sexual activity at an earlier age, more negative attitudes toward contraception and abortion, and more tolerant attitudes toward having babies out-of-wedlock. As pointed out earlier, it is important to recognize the relationship of out-of-wedlock pregnancy to black male unemployment, since many young black women may feel they are making a rational choice not to marry a young man who cannot support a family.

Further, as the sexual attitudes and behaviors of white adolescent females change in the direction of earlier sexual activity, fewer abortions, and more frequent decisions to keep their babies, black and white patterns in this area may begin to converge and cultural differences will be minimized.

Implications of these factors in planning intervention and prevention programs aimed at reducing the rate of first-time pregnancies in black female adolescents, as well as the rate of higher-order pregnancies among unwed teen mothers, will be discussed in the next section.

Child-rearing and Socialization Patterns

The issue of child-rearing patterns and the socialization of black children is especially relevant to the future stability and well-being of the black family. Two issues that reflect family values and attitudes are of growing concern to the black community, i.e., educational achievement and aspirations of children in the public schools and antisocial behaviors of youth in the community. While it is difficult to make direct linkages between socialization patterns, values, and behaviors, it is important to use research findings as a basis for interpreting observed behaviors. It is equally important to analyze the contribution of environmental factors, social expectations, and opportunity structures on the achievement, aspirations, and social behaviors of black children and youth. Since the majority of black children will spend part of their youth in a single-parent family, it is also essential to provide these parents with helpful information and constructive techniques to assist them in socializing their children.[41]

Studies of child-rearing techniques among black parents indicate that there are strong similarities to white parents of the same socioeconomic level, but there are also significant differences that reflect different cultural values and attitudes on major dimensions of behavior.[42] While earlier studies suggested, for example, that black parents were less supportive and less controlling than white middle class parents, more recent studies, controlling for class, found that black working class parents were both highly supportive and highly controlling of their children compared to white and Chicano parents.[43]

Contrary to the stereotype of permissive child rearing, black parents of all social classes tend to be more authoritarian than white parents in their disciplinary techniques, including the use of physical punishment.[44] There is a consensus among these researchers that black parents use strict, rather harsh techniques in order to socialize obedience to authority in their children so that they will develop coping strategies to deal with the dominant white society. Unfortunately, this emphasis on conformity and obedience to authority may be counterproductive for students in competitive classrooms, where dialogue with teachers and individual competition with one's classmates is rewarded. Thus, many black parents may unwittingly reinforce behaviors at home that are not functional in the classroom and result in placing their children at a competitive disadvantage from their initial entry into elementary school.

Since many black families have two working parents or are headed by a single parent, children are socialized to be autonomous and independent earlier than in comparable white families.[45] This emphasis on early independence begins with early toilet training and extends to early assumption of household chores, including child care of younger siblings. Although this encourages autonomy in some children, especially firstborn females, who often serve as mother substitutes for their younger siblings, it also may have negative consequences for the development of age-appropriate interests and experiences, as well as causing the "parentified child" syndrome, which may result in identity foreclosure for many young girls. (An interesting research question to investigate is the relationship, if any, between birth order, early child-care responsibilities, and subsequent teenage pregnancy in black adolescent females.) However, contrary to stereotypes in the mass media about the neglectful black parents, a recent survey indicates that black parents at all income levels are less likely than white parents to leave their children at home without supervision while they are working. This may reflect the greater tendency of blacks to live with or near extended family members who can offer child-care services.[46] Nevertheless, too many black low income children are without adult supervision for most of the work week and these "latchkey" children are particularly vulnerable to truancy, school failure, sexual exploitation, and delinquency.[47]

Flexibility in sex roles and sharing in decision making are also encouraged by black parents as their children grow into adolescents, especially in working class and middle class families.[48] These socialization practices result in less gender-specific behaviors as children are expected to perform household chores according to their age and competence rather than their sex. Although there is no conscious intention to promote androgynous children, personality studies have found that black adolescents show both "masculine" and "feminine" traits such as flexibility, independence, and emotional expressiveness.[49]

Finally, black parents devote a great deal of energy, directly and indirectly, in communicating a sense of racial identity to their children, but this process is a two-edged sword. On the one hand, black parents must inculcate into their children a sense of positive self-esteem, self-worth, and pride in their ethnicity, while at the same time they must prepare them to understand and cope with the social devaluation of their race (and often their social class and lifestyle also) and the prejudice and discrimination that they will inevitably experience in their multiple encounters with the dominant society.[50] Several authors have pointed out that many parents are successful at transmitting this complex process, as can be inferred from the recent studies showing that black youngsters rate their self-esteem as high or higher than that of comparable whites.[51]

In spite of empirical findings that many black children do report high levels of self-esteem on standardized scales, several leading mental-health researchers have proposed a connection between the suppressed anger and hostility of many blacks, who have experienced persistent discrimination or humiliation from whites, and the eruption of aggressive, antisocial behaviors.[52]Spurlock notes that many black children display aggressive behavior as a way of coping with the intolerable conflicts engendered by racial discrimination.[53] She further states that this aggressive behavior can evolve into antisocial behavior, which is supported by the increasing rate of juvenile delinquency and youth violence in black inner-city communities.[54] On the other hand, Spurlock suggests that another common response to discrimination is constricted behavior and depression among black children, which is often the underlying cause of poor school performance, underachievement, classroom disruption, or just simply "giving up" to passivity and alienation.[55]

In summary, child-rearing patterns and socialization techniques of black parents may vary along social class lines, but there are some common elements that reflect historical factors and current social realities. By focusing on the development of conformity and obedience to authority, many black parents fail to promote the qualities of assertiveness, inquisitiveness, creativity, and intellectual curiosity, which are necessary to compete effectively in middle class oriented classrooms. By expecting older children to assume adult household responsibilities and child care prematurely, black parents promote independence and pseudo-maturity at the expense of educational achievement and age-appropriate developmental behaviors. It is reasonable to assume that some of the problems black children experience in schools are the result of burdensome responsibilities at home and/or lack of parental supervision, resulting in poor performance, suspension or expulsion, and ultimate withdrawal from school.

These patterns of child-rearing and socialization techniques developed in response to slavery, discrimination, and poverty in this society. While they may have been adaptive for blacks in segregated or in adverse economic situations, they may have also reinforced some behaviors that are maladaptive and dysfunctional in integrated and more advantageous economic environments. Thus, while these patterns may reflect a culturally variant adaptation to social and economic factors, they may be viewed as maladaptive in a broader social context where blacks are evaluated by the same criteria as whites, particularly in educational and employment settings.

The implications of these child-rearing patterns and socialization techniques in terms of intervention programs to improve educational outcomes and to reduce antisocial behaviors in the classroom and in the community will be discussed in the next section.

Family Conflict

Studies of family dynamics and interpersonal relationships in black families have yielded conflicting results, with some studies portraying black families as chaotic, disorganized, and full of conflict,[56] while other studies have found them to be flexible, competent, and cooperative.[57] Obviously these studies began with different theoretical assumptions, used different methodological approaches, sampled different populations, and interpreted their data along different dimensions with unique sets of relevant variables. Nonetheless, according to researchers in the field, family conflict occurs in all types of families and family violence cuts across all races and socioeconomic groups. However, reported rates of family violence are higher among minorities and poor families because they are more vulnerable to detection and arrest by the police and referral to public agencies for some form of intervention.

There is a perception, fostered by the sensationalism of the mass media, that family violence has been increasing in the black community, but it is difficult to obtain hard data to support this perception. The perception may be partially due to a number of related factors, i.e., victimization rates in the inner cities are higher than in the suburbs, homicide is the leading cause of death among black youth in the 15–24 age group, and black teenagers account for a disproportionate share of the violent crime committed in this country.[58] However, these problems may be more appropriately viewed as community problems rather than problems of the black family, although they certainly impact negatively on the functioning of black families who live in many urban areas.

Ethnographic and clinical studies of low income black families indicate that family conflicts are sometimes settled by physical violence, but this pattern of dealing with conflict may be more related to social class attitudes rather than to race.[59] As economic problems and unemployment increase, levels of family violence (spouse abuse, child abuse, elder abuse) tend to rise in the general society, so it is predictable that family violence would increase among black families, who are the most vulnerable to economic dislocation and unemployment. For example, in a recent survey of children's agencies in San Francisco, it was noted that there has been a dramatic increase recently in the number of black children who have been removed from their homes due to parental neglect or abuse.[60]

While family conflict and violence is not unique to black families, their strategies for coping with it may be rooted in particular cultural beliefs and attitudes. As many authors have noted, blacks have developed a set of beliefs and attitudes about handling their psychological problems and dysfunctional behaviors that reflect a tradition of stoicism, endurance, and religious faith.[61] Surveys of help-seeking behaviors among blacks indicate that they would generally confide in a minister, relative, or friend or some other sources of informal help before they would seek professional help for a range of problems.[62]

As earlier noted, one of the major sources of help for the troubled black family is their extended kinship network. These networks offer emotional support and function as therapeutic communities in times of psychological distress.[63] Networks composed of friends and neighbors complement the kinship networks and are especially important for female-headed households with meager resources.[64] While these networks have both negative as well as positive effects on their members, they are an integral and important element in maintaining the economic stability, social cohesiveness, and positive mental health of these families.

Fraternal organizations and social clubs are also an important source of support and self-esteem for working and middle class blacks, who often derive a sense of social status and community recognition from membership in these groups.[65] These groups also function as vehicles for advocacy and social change, serving as legitimate outlets for the aspirations and goals of upwardly mobile black families.

Finally, the black church is an important source of help for black families, who often view their minister as a counselor, community leader, and advocate.[66] The minister and the black church are very valuable resources to black families, although the church has become less central in the black community as its role in urban inner-city communities has been replaced by government programs and other voluntary organizations that provide social services once exclusively provided by the church. Moreover, few black ministers have had training in pastoral counseling, and they are unlikely to have the knowledge and skills to deal with the complex issues and problems experienced by many low income black families. Despite the lack of training, black ministers are frequently sought out for their advice by troubled families. As Barbarin points out: "Personal religiosity and involvement in organized religion may enhance coping by providing a basis for optimism.. . ."[67]

In summary, contemporary black families are particularly vulnerable to stress and conflict due to high rates of unemployment, social discrimination, and punitive social welfare policies. These stresses may be channeled into spouse abuse, child abuse, substance abuse, delinquency and criminal behavior, homicide, or suicide. Some of these acts occur within the family context, while others take place in the outside community. Yet, whether they are internally or externally directed acts of violence, they take an extremely high toll on the black community and create the perception that inner cities are unsafe and unpredictable places to be.

The high rate of interpersonal violence that occurs in the most disadvantaged sectors of the black community is not unique to low income ethnic communities in this country, as similar patterns can be found among Mexican-Americans, Puerto Ricans, and American Indians. However, it is also true that low income blacks are more likely than whites to be arrested and convicted for crimes of violence, primarily because they are more vulnerable to the vagaries of the criminal justice system. Thus, behavior that may appear deviant from the normative behavior of middle class Americans must be evaluated in the context of an inner-city environment that breeds frustration and hostility without a process for grievances to be addressed through legitimate channels. While it may be stretching a point to label this behavior as a variant form of cultural adaptation, it is important to view the functional significance of family violence as a channel for blacks to displace the anger and rage they experience toward the wider society upon their own family members and peers, resulting in the deflection of this hostility from the white community.[68]

Due to a set of historical and social circumstances, black families have developed ways of coping with their problems through alternative social institutions such as the church, kinship networks, and social support networks and fraternal organizations. Blacks do not tend to seek help from traditional mental-health agencies or sources until other avenues of help have been exhausted. This pattern may prove in the future to be quite functional in view of the steady erosion of publicly funded services, the general conservative trend in the country, and the elimination of many of the programs initiated during the Johnson administration.

The implications of these help-seeking attitudes and patterns for developing intervention programs to address the issue of family conflict and violence will be discussed in the next section.

DEVELOPING MODELS OF INTERVENTION

The four problem issues reviewed in the previous sections share several underlying elements. First, they are all correlated to economic stability, generally increasing in severity as economic stability decreases. Second, they are variant forms of problems affecting all American families, but their particular expression reflects an adaptation to social discrimination and cultural isolation from the dominant white society in some way. Third, they have been exacerbated by recent trends in politics, cutbacks in social welfare programs, and structural changes in the economy that have fostered the growth of an unschooled and unskilled underclass.

In developing intervention models to address these problems, four levels of intervention must be considered: (a) macro-level policies, (b) mezzo-level programs and services, (c) micro-level support systems, and (d) individual level change. All of these levels are interdependent, as Bronfrenbrenner notes, so that change in one level will impact on all the other levels.[69]

Macro-Level Intervention

This level is significant because it encompasses the economic and political systems in which all the other levels are embedded. It is the level of *primary prevention* in terms of promoting family stability. In order to effect major changes in the structure and functioning of the black family, it is imperative to institute a comprehensive family policy that will replace the current antiquated welfare system with a guaranteed minimum income for all families, adequate housing, comprehensive health services, and opportunities for productive employment for all citizens.[70] Such a comprehensive program would eliminate humiliating eligibility criteria, restore the self-esteem of many black parents, and improve the overall quality of life for all black families. Presumably, if such a comprehensive program were actually put in place, the improved economic stability and healthier social environment would result in more stable families, lower rates of divorce, lower rates of crime and delinquency, lower rates of teenage pregnancy, and an overall reduction in social pathology. Since the research indicates that marital satisfaction and marital stability are related to economic self-sufficiency and security, a full employment policy with adequate safeguards for affirmative action and occupational mobility would contribute more to the stability of black marriages than any other macro-level policy. However, changes in the macro structure are not sufficient by themselves to ensure such gains in the status of the black family. They must be complemented by changes at the other three levels of intervention.

Mezzo-Level Intervention

This level is the intermediate level of social institutions such as local government agencies, schools, businesses, health agencies, and churches. It includes primary prevention and early intervention approaches to family stability. These institutions provide jobs, education, services, and religious affiliation to black families, yet they are very often insensitive to the needs and problems of these families. In order to respond more effectively to these needs, these institutions must form alliances with community organizations to develop innovative solutions to the problems of youth education, employment, housing, and delivery of social and health services. This would involve sincere efforts to understand cultural differences in behaviors, attitudes, and values, to communicate expectations that problems can be solved and that people can take control of their own communities, and to share their expertise to help solve chronic community problems that will eventually undermine the broader society.

Black churches are in the forefront of some of the most innovative programs, including using their facilities to house a comprehensive range of social services for all age groups, including child care, senior citizens' programs, after-school cultural and recreational programs, and voter education programs.[71] The Carnegie Corporation recently awarded grants to help train black clergymen to be more effective in serving inner-city parishes.[72]

Businesses in many urban areas have developed partnership programs with local schools to provide supplies, tutors, and financial assistance for enriched programs in a model of "adopt-a-school" programs as established in cities like Chicago and Washington, D.C. Through the Private

Industry Council, many businesses now offer part-time and summer jobs to minority youth, enabling them to stay in school and to develop skills that will lead to entry-level jobs upon their graduation from high school.[73]

To address the problem of teenage pregnancy, some communities have set up school-based clinics in the junior and senior high schools to provide contraceptive advice, family planning information, and general counseling.[74] In a recent study conducted in Baltimore by researchers at Johns Hopkins University, teenage girls who had received sex education and contraceptives in a school-based clinic were found to have increased their use of effective contraception over a 28-month period and to have decreased their rate of pregnancy by 30 percent, as compared with a control group of girls who did not receive the contraceptives or participate in the program.[75] There was also a mean delay in the onset of sexual activity in the participants of seven months during this period. Follow-up studies of the effects of these school-based family-planning clinics have generally found them to be one of the most effective methods of reducing the rates of first-time pregnancies among low income black adolescent females, suggesting that access to services and availability of contraceptives in a nonthreatening environment is one of the best strategies of intervention for this problem.

Further, many organizations have recognized the need to address the issue of black male sexual attitudes and behaviors in order to promote greater sexual responsibility. Programs such as the National Urban League's Adolescent Male Responsibility Project promote information about contraception to delay the first pregnancy and provide values about responsible sexuality and parenting for those teenagers who do bear children.

These programs of prevention and early intervention to address teenage sexuality and pregnancy have recognized the relationship between effective contraception to delay pregnancy and perceptions of opportunity for productive adult roles. Thus, the links between educational achievement, employment opportunities, and responsible sexual behavior need to be developed and supported in a variety of organizational programs.

Micro-Level Intervention

This is the level of the family and those social relationships that impinge directly on the individual's behavior and daily functioning, thus it would include kinship and social support networks that are characterized by propinquity, frequency, and intensity. Providing adequate economic resources and increasing access to social institutions will not guarantee that black families will function effectively. This third source of intervention is the provision of direct social and mental-health services that are culturally sensitive, easily accessible, and affordable. This is the level of treatment for families which are dysfunctional in some way.

For several decades, traditional social and mental health services have been frequently criticized for their lack of flexibility in service delivery and for their costs. Even with the advent of the community mental-health centers with their emphasis on innovative and affordable services, blacks have still received poorer service by less-well-trained professionals for briefer periods of time.[76]

In recent years, a number of innovative programs have been instituted to provide more appropriate and effective services for black families. For example, services have been offered in storefront clinics and community centers in black neighborhoods; paraprofessionals have been used both for peer counseling and for community outreach programs; advocacy and self-help groups have been developed to address chronic community issues and problems.

In the field of family therapy, new techniques have been developed by black clinicians to respond to the communication patterns, attitudes, and values of black families.[77] Knowledge of the dynamics in interpersonal relationships between black clients and authority figures has contributed to modified conceptual models of treatment in both individual and family therapy.[78] Conversely, black families have demonstrated that they can benefit from insight-oriented techniques as well as a systems approach if therapists are warm, empathic, and sensitive to cultural nuances in treatment.

At this level of intervention, the dysfunctional patterns in vulnerable black families can be addressed through the provision of appropriate social and mental-health services. Intervention might be directed to child-rearing techniques that place too much emphasis on harsh discipline or premature autonomy, which may cause problems for black children in the school setting. Alternately, intervention might be directed to the resolution of family conflict through community-based mediation techniques rather than traditional family-therapy techniques. The choice of intervention or treatment strategies for behavioral or psychological conflicts in the black family should take into account the preference of many blacks for informal or nontraditional sources of help, such as the minister and the family doctor. Mental-health and social welfare professionals would increase their effectiveness if they routinely consulted with these community professionals in planning the delivery of services to black families.

Individual Level of Intervention

This is the level of individual responsibility for change. Unless the individual has the motivation for change, the knowledge of how to use the resources, and the social environment that reinforces his change efforts, none of the other modifications will work. This is the most difficult level for social policymakers, helping professionals, and educators to evaluate and to monitor, yet it is at this level that change must occur to ensure that change will be transmitted to the next generation of black families.

For example, a concerted effort must be made by parents, educators, and religious institutions to reinforce the values of black youth in a number of areas, e.g., the importance of education, the importance of personal effort, the importance of delaying sexual activity, the importance of avoiding drugs, and the importance of resisting involvement in delinquency. However, these values cannot be reinforced in a vacuum, i.e., they must be linked to major changes in the educational system that would offer black youth real options for learning in supportive environments; they must be linked to increased perceptions of opportunity for meaningful adult roles through encouraging hard work and the delay of sexual gratification for future rewards; they must be linked to the development of youth employment opportunities to provide legitimate earnings and self-respect rather than income from the underworld of drugs and delinquency.

Finally, successful black adults in well-functioning families must be willing to share their values and their resources and to serve as mentors and role models for black youth in vulnerable high-risk families. Since many successful black families have moved out of the inner cities and loosened their ties with black social and civic organizations in these communities, the least advantaged families do not have regular contact with the most advantaged families, so they cannot benefit from the values, aspirations, and experiences of those who have struggled to achieve some measure of success in the dominant society. Successful blacks can participate in strengthening inner-city families through very specific activities such as offering part-time jobs to black youth, serving as tutors and classroom teaching aides, organizing cultural programs and field trips, sponsoring athletic teams and extracurricular activities, serving as Big Brothers and Big Sisters, and teaching parent-education classes. Perhaps through these joint ventures, those blacks who have learned effective survival strategies will be able to transmit the skills as well as the underlying values to those blacks who have been isolated from the mainstream of American life.

SUMMARY AND CONCLUSION

This chapter has focused on the linkages between theories and empirical research on the black family and the implications of these linkages for developing models of intervention. First, three major ideological perspectives on the black family were briefly summarized, i.e., the cultural deviant, the cultural equivalent, and the cultural variant. Second, the research on four problem issues was briefly reviewed in terms of these theoretical concepts. Third, four levels of intervention, i.e., macro, mezzo, micro, and individual, were described in terms of addressing the four types of problems discussed.

The problems currently facing black families are gradually spreading to all American families who are economically disadvantaged.[79] However, black families are especially vulnerable because of the dual handicap of race and poverty. Since demographic trends indicate that black youth will constitute a larger proportion of all youth in the twenty-first century, it is important for social policy planners, educators, and mental-health professionals to develop policies and programs that focus on prevention and early intervention strategies to reduce social and economic risks for black families.

In order to develop a comprehensive, multitiered intervention approach, it is necessary to go beyond a clinical model that focuses on pathology and treatment. First, the levels of prevention and intervention must be addressed through government-sponsored social welfare policies and programs, creative initiatives of the business sector, cooperative ventures of voluntary organizations and churches, and innovative programs of social welfare, mental-health, and educational agencies.

Second, the training of service providers at all levels (e.g., educators, health and mental-health professionals, social service providers, police and probation officers) needs to be seriously modified to include substantial information about the history and culture of blacks, the structure and functioning of the black family, black communication and expressive styles, and the adaptive behaviors of blacks to American society.[80]

Third, black families must become more aggressive advocates for change through the political process. Black leaders need to find more effective ways of increasing black participation in the political system at all levels so that legislators will be more responsive to the needs of the black community in education, employment, housing, health, and other areas.

Fourth, blacks must learn to work harmoniously with Third World groups to maximize their political power in order to gain social and economic equality of opportunity. Without such coalitions, progress will be slow and ethnic groups will compete for smaller shares of the nation's wealth.

Fifth, the black community must assume ultimate responsibility for the many dysfunctional behaviors that currently paralyze it, e.g., high school dropout rates, teenage pregnancy, substance abuse, delinquency, and violent crime. The "black community" is composed of many black families, who can organize crime watches in their neighborhoods, discourage drug dealers by turning them in to the police, educate young people about sexual responsibility and family planning, and bring political pressure for improved police protection and safer neighborhoods. Macro-level policy changes and mezzo-level program initiatives will prove to be effective only if they are supplemented and reinforced by micro-level modifications in family and individual attitudes, values, and behaviors within the black community.

In conclusion, while the debate over the most appropriate theoretical approach to the black family continues to escalate, the problems of the black family continue to proliferate. It is this author's hope that black scholars will become more active participants in the public policy debate and in proposing solutions for the problems of the black family in an increasingly complex society, moving toward the twenty-first century of high technology, international interdependence, and space travel, where survival will depend on multiple skills, economic self-sufficiency, and integration into the mainstream society.

NOTES

1. D.P. Moynihan, *The Negro Family: The Case for National Action* (Washington, DC: U.S. Department of Labor, 1965).

2. W.R. Allen, "The Search for Applicable Theories of Black Family Life," *Journal of Marriage and the Family*, Vol. 40 (1978), pp. 117–129; A. Billingsley, *Black Families in White America* (Englewood Cliffs, NJ: Prentice Hall, 1968); R. Staples, "Towards a Sociology of the Black Family: A Theoretical and Methodological Assessment," *Journal of Marriage and the Family,* Vol. 33 (1971), pp. 119–138.

3. Allen (1978).

4. E.F. Frazier, *The Negro Family in the United States* (Chicago: University of Chicago Press, 1966).

5. Moynihan (1965); L. Rainwater, "Crucible of Identity: The Lower-Class Negro Family," *Daedalus,* Vol. 95 (1966), pp. 172–216; D. Schulz, *Coming Up Black: Patterns of Ghetto Socialization* (Englewood Cliffs, NJ: Prentice-Hall, 1969).

6. J. Bernard, *Marriage and Family Among Negroes* (Englewood Cliffs, NJ: Prentice-Hall, 1966); J. Scanzoni, *The Black Family in Modern Society* (Boston: Allyn and Bacon, 1971).

7. Billingsley (1962); C. Stack, *All Our Kin: Strategies for Survival in a Black Community* (New York: Harper and Row, 1974); W. Nobles, "African Root and American Fruit: The Black Family," *Journal of Social and Behavioral Sciences,* Vol. 20 (1974), pp. 52–64.

8. N.A. Casenave, "Black Men in America: The Quest for Manhood," in H.P. McAdoo, ed., *Black Families* (Beverly Hills: Sage, 1981; L.E. Gary, "Utilization of Network Systems in the Black Community," in A.E. Johnson, ed., *The Black Experience: Considerations for Health and Human Services* (Davis, CA: International Dialogue Press, 1983); D. Glasgow, *The Black Underclass* (New York: Vintage Books, 1981); E. Liebow, *Tally's Corner: A Study of Negro Street Corner Men* (Boston, MA: Little Brown, 1967).

9. J.T. Gibbs, *Young, Black and Male in America: An Endangered Species* (Dover, MA: Auburn House, 1988).

10. Allen (1978); A. Mathis, "Contrasting Approaches to the Study of Black Families," *Journal of Marriage and the Family,* Vol. 40 (1978), pp. 667–676; R. Staples and A. Mirande, "Racial and Cultural Variations Among American Families: A Decennial Review of the Literature on Minority Families," *Journal of Marriage and the Family,* Vol. 42 (1980), pp. 887–903.

11. R.E. Ball and L. Robbins, "Marital Status and Life Satisfaction Among Black Americans," *Journal of Marriage and the Family,* Vol. 48 (1986), pp. 389–394.

12. A. Campbell, P. Converse, and W. Rodgers, *The Quality of American Life* (New York: Russell Sage, 1986); N. Glenn, "The Well–Being of Persons Remarried After Divorce," *Journal of Family Issues,* Vol. 2 (1981), pp. 61–75.

13. Campbell, Converse, and Rodgers (1986); J. Veroff, G. Douvan, and R. Kulka, *The Inner American: A Self-Portrait from 1957-1976* (New York: Basic Books, 1981).

14. Cazenave (1981); Staples (1971); D.Y. Wilkinson and R.L. Taylor, eds., *The Black Male in America* (Chicago: Nelson Hall, 1977).

15. B. Gray-Little, "Marital Quality and Power Processes Among Black Couples," *Journal of Marriage and the Family,* Vol. 44 (1982), pp. 633–646.

16. J. Heiss, *The Case of the Black Family: A Sociological Inquiry* (New York: Columbia University Press, 1975); R. Hill, *The Strengths of Black Families* (New York: Emerson Hall, 1971); K.T. Dietrich, "A Re-Examination of the Myth of the Black Matriarchy," *Journal of Marriage and the Family,* Vol. 37 (1975): 367–374; D. Mack, "The Power Relationship in Black Families and White Families," in R. Staples, ed., *The Black Family: Essays and Studies* (Belmont, CA: Wadsworth, 1978); C.F. Willie and S.L. Greenblatt, "Four 'Classic' Studies of Power Relationships in Black Families: A Review and Look to the Future," *Journal of Marriage and the Family,* Vol. 40 (1978), pp. 691–694.

17. M.W. Hicks and M. Platt, "Marital Happiness and Stability: A Review of Research in the Sixties," *Journal of Marriage and the Family,* Vol. 32 (1970), pp. 553–574; R.A. Lewis and G.B. Spanier, "Theorizing About the Quality and Stability of Marriage," in W. Burr et al., eds., *Contemporary Theories About the Family* Vol 1: *Research-Based Theories* (New York: Free Press, 1979).

18. Renne, K.S. "Correlates of Dissatisfaction in Marriage," *Journal of Marriage and the Family,* Vol. 32 (1970), pp. 54–67; J. Scanzoni, (1971).

19. D. Belle, ed., *Lives in Stress: Women and Depression* (Beverly Hills: Sage Pub., 1982); Renne (1970).

20. R.O. Blood and D.M. Wolfe, *Husbands and Wives* (Glencoe, IL: Free Press, 1960).

21. Belle (1982); Liebow (1967); Scanzoni (1971).

22. J. Wilson and K. Neckerman, "Poverty and Family Structure: The Widening Gap Between Evidence and Public Policy Issues," Paper presented at conference on Poverty and Family Policy: Retrospect and Prospects, Williamsburg, VA, December 1984.

23. Ibid.

24. H. Gutman, *The Black Family in Slavery and Freedom, 1750-1925* (New York: Pantheon, 1976); P.J. Lammermeier, "The Urban Black Family in the 19th Century: A Study of Black Family Structure in the Ohio Valley, 1850-1880," *Journal of Marriage and the Family,* Vol. 35 (1972) pp. 440–456; E. Pleck, "The Two-Parent Household: Black Family Structure in Late 19th Century Boston," in M. Gordon, ed., *The American Family in Socio-Historical Perspective* (New York: St. Martin's Press, 1972).

25. J. Aschenbrenner, *Lifelines: Black Families in Chicago* (New York: Holt, Rinehart and Winston, 1975); Billingsley (1968); J.M. Lewis and J. G. Looney, *The Long Struggle: Well-Functioning Working Class Black Families* (New York: Brunner/Mazel, 1983); McAdoo, (1981).

26. Allen (1978); Nobles (1974).

27. Children's Defense Fund, *Welfare and Teen Pregnancy: What Do We Know?* (Washington, DC: CDF, 1986).

28. Ibid.

29. C. Chilman, *Adolescent Sexuality in a Changing American Society* (New York: John Wiley and Sons, 1983); F. Furstenberg, *Unplanned Parenthood: The Social Consequences of Teenage Childbearing* (New York: Free Press, 1976).

30. Chilman (1983).

31. J. Card and L. Wise, "Teenage Mothers and Teenage Fathers: The Impact of Early Child-Bearing on the Parents' Personal and Professional Lives," *Family Planning Perspectives,* Vol. 10 (1978), pp. 199–205.

32. Children's Defense Fund (1986).

33. Ibid.

34. F. Furstenberg, R. Loncoln, and J. Menken, *Teenage Sexuality, Pregnancy and Childrearing* (Philadelphia: University of Pennsylvania Press, 1981).

35. Chilman (1983), J. Ladner, *Tomorrow's Tomorrow: The Black Woman* (New York: Doubleday, 1971).

36. Card and Wise (1978); Furstenberg (1976).

37. Furstenberg (1976).

38. Chilman (1983); Furstenberg (1976).

39. S. Clark, L. Zabin, and J. Hardy, "Sex, Contraception, and Parenthood: Experiences and Attitudes Among Urban Black Young Men," *Family Planning Perspectives*

Vol. 16 (1984), pp. 77–82; J.T. Gibbs, "Psychosocial Correlates of Sexual Attitudes and Behaviors in Urban Early Adolescent Females: Implications for Intervention," *Journal of Social Work and Human Sexuality*, Vol. 5 (1986), pp. 81–97; Ladner (1971).

40. Children's Defense Fund, *A Children's Defense Budget* (Washington, DC: CDF, 1988).

41. Ibid.

42. Allen (1978); Staples and Mirande (1980); K.W. Bartz and E.S. Levine, "Childrearing by Black Parents: A Description and Comparison to Anglo and Chicano Parents," *Journal of Marriage and the Family*, Vol. 40 (1978), pp. 709–719; M.F. Peters, "Parenting in Black Families With Young Children: A Historical Perspective," in McAdoo (1981).

43. Bernard (1966).

44. Bartz and Levine (1978); I.D. Cahill, "Child-Rearing Practices in Lower Socio-Economic Ethnic Groups," *Dissertation Abstracts*, Vol. 27 (1966), p. 3139; M.D. Durrett, S.O'Bryant, and J.W. Pennebaker, "Child-Rearing Reports of White, Black and Mexican-American Families," *Developmental Psychology*, Vol. 11 (1975), pp. 871–878; Peters (1981).

45. Bartz and Levine (1978); D. Lewis, "The Black Family: Socialization and Sex Roles," *Phylon* Vol. 36 (1975), pp. 221–237; Peters (1981); Staples and Mirande (1980).

46. Ladner (1971); E. Martin and J. Martin, *The Black Extended Family* (Chicago: University of Chicago Press, 1978); Stack (1974).

47. Children's Defense Fund (1988).

48. Bartz and Levine (1978); Lewis (1975); Peters (1981); Staples and Mirande (1980).

49. Allen (1978).

50. L. Chestang, "Racial and Personal Identity in the Black Experience," in B. White, ed., *Color in a White Society* (Silver Spring, MD: NASW Publications, 1984); A. Jenkins, *The Psychology of the Afro-American* (New York: Pergamon Press, 1982); J. Spurlock, "Black Child Development and Socialization," in Johnson (1983).

51. Gibbs (1986); G.J. Powell, "Self-Concept in White and Black Children," in C.V. Willie, B.M. Kramer, and B.S. Brown, eds., *Racism and Mental Health* (Pittsburgh: University of Pittsburgh Press, 1973); M. Rosenberg and R. Simmons, *Black and White Self-Esteem: The Urban School Child* (Washington, DC: American Sociological Association, 1971); R. L. Taylor, "Psychosocial Development Among Black Children and Youth: A Reexamination," *American Journal of Orthopsychiatry* 46 (1976): 4–19.

52. W.H. Grier and P.M. Cobbs, *Black Rage* (New York: Basic Books, 1968); Jenkins (1982).

53. Spurlock (1983).

54. J.T. Gibbs, "Black Adolescents and Youth: An Endangered Species," *American Journal of Orthopsychiatry*, Vol. 54 (1984), pp. 6–21.

55. Spurlock (1983).

56. S. Minuchin, *Families of the Slums* (New York: Basic Books, 1967); Rainwater (1966); Schulz (1969).

57. Aschenbrenner (1979); Lewis (1975); Lewis and Looney (1983); Stack (1974).

58. Gibbs (1988); U.S. Department of Health and Human Services. Report of the Secretary's Task Force on Black and Minority Health, Washington, D.C., 1986.

59. Cazenave (1981); Minuchin (1967); Rainwater (1966); C. Sager, T. Brayboy, and B. Waxenberg, *Black Ghetto Family in Therapy* (New York: Grove Press, 1970); Schulz (1969).

60. Coleman Children and Youth Services, *Window on the Future: Executive Summary* (San Francisco, CA: Coleman Children and Youth Services, 1983).

61. Billingsley (1968); Hill (1971); McAdoo (1981).

62. Gary (1983); H.W. Neighbors and J.S. Jackson, "The Use of Informal and Formal Help: Four Patterns of Illness Behavior in the Black Community," *American Journal of Community Psychology,* Vol. 12 (1984), pp. 629–644.

63. Aschenbrenner (1975); McAdoo (1981); Martin and Martin (1978); Stack (1974).

64. Belle (1982); Lewis and Looney (1983); Gary (1983); Ladner (1971).

65. C.V. Willie, *A New Look at Black Families* (Bayside, NY: General Hall, 1976); Billingsley (1968).

66. Billingsley, (1968); Frazier (1966); Hill, (1971); Lewis (1975); Willie (1968).

67. O.A. Barbarin, "Coping With Ecological Transitions by Black Families: A Psychosocial Model," *Journal of Community Psychology,* Vol. 11 (1983); p. 319.

68. Grier and Cobbs (1968).

69. U. Bronfenbrenner, *The Ecology of Human Development: Experiments by Nature and Design* (Cambridge, MA: Harvard University Press, 1979).

70. Children's Defense Fund (1988); M.W. Edelman, *Families in Peril: An Agenda for Social Change* (Cambridge, MA: Harvard University Press, 1987); D.P. Moynihan, *Family and Nation* (New York: Harcourt Brace and Jovanovich, 1986).

71. B.B. Solomon, "Innovations in Service Delivery to Black Clients," in Johnson (1983).

72. Carnegie Corporation of New York, *Annual Report 1986* (New York: Carnegie Corporation, 1986).

73. Committee for Economic Development, *Children in Need. Investment Strategies for the Educationally Disadvantaged* (New York: Committee for Economic Development, 1987).

74. F. Furstenberg (1976); Chilman (1983); Children's Defense Fund (1988).

75. L. Zabin, M. Hersch, E. Smith, and J. Hardy, "Adolescent Sexual Attitudes and Behaviors: Are They Consistent?," *Family Planning Perspectives,* Vol. 12 (1984), pp. 230–237.

76. E.E. Jones and S.J. Korchin, eds., *Minority Mental Health* (New York: Praeger, 1982); L. Snowden, ed., *Reaching the Underserved: Mental Health Needs of Neglected Populations* (Beverly Hills CA: Sage, 1982).

77. N. Boyd, "Family Therapy with Black Families," in Jones and Korchin (1982); E. Pinderhughes, "Afro-American Families and the Victim System," in M. McGoldrick, J.K. Pearce, and J. Giordano, eds., *Ethnicity and Family Therapy* (New York: Guilford Press, 1982).

78. J.T. Gibbs, "City Girls: Psychosocial Adjustment of Urban Black Adolescent Females," *SAGE: A Scholarly Journal on Black Women,* Vol. 2 (1985a), pp. 28–36; Jenkins (1982); Pinderhughes (1982).

79. Edelman (1987); Moynihan (1986).

80. J.T. Gibbs, "Treatment Relationships With Black Clients: Interpersonal vs. Instrumental Strategies," in C. Germain, ed., *Advances in Clinical Social Work Practice* (Silver Spring, MD: NASW, 1985b).

17

COUNSELING BLACK FAMILIES AT INNER-CITY CHURCH SITES

Barbara Bryant Solomon

The author presents a community-based professional intervention model devised to assist ethnic minority (primarily black) families' and their members' effective dealing with various societal institutions and agencies. Development of the model is based primarily on the pervasive perception that services for these families need to be more culturally syntonic. Recognizing the central role of the church and emerging theoretical perspectives on interrelationships of individuals, their support systems, and the larger society, as well, a church site was selected for the demonstration project. It is concluded, from this study of strategies that these families use and that were focused and enhanced in the counseling process, that it is in black families' best interest to effect balance between help-providing interventions and interventions that empower these families to solve their problems.

From January 1981 to June 1983, a research and demonstration project was conducted in the south central areas of Los Angeles, California, to assist individuals and families referred to a counseling program at church sites for help with problems in social and emotional functioning.[1] Problem solving with these clients involved a model of professional helping that focused on strategies aimed at helping individuals and families deal more effectively with such institutions as schools, police, welfare departments, health agencies, the courts, and other community agencies. Although this chapter is most concerned with the program as an example of the application of contemporary theoretical perspectives on services to black families, the services were available to anyone—single or in a family—who was referred for social or psychological counseling. More important, however, since blacks constituted the predominant racial/

ethnic group to be served, counseling was focused primarily on transactions with external, often oppressive social systems rather than on intrapsychic processes, family relationships, or the relationship with the counselor.

The black community in Los Angeles is both similar to and different from most other black communities in large urban areas in the United States. The percentage of blacks in the total population of the city of Los Angeles is smaller—only approximately 17 percent. On the other hand, despite two decades of fair housing legislation and the dispersal of at least some predominantly middle and upper middle class blacks throughout all areas of the city, the large majority of the black population is still located in low income neighborhoods in the south central area. These neighborhoods, unlike black inner cities in the north and east, are, for the most part, low-density single-family and small apartment buildings rather than high-rise, high-density multifamily complexes. There is a large and growing Hispanic population in this still predominantly black area of the city with which public and private services must be shared. The one social institution that remains intransigently monoracial is the Protestant church.

THE NATURE OF SERVICE DELIVERY TO BLACK FAMILIES

A phenomenon shared with every other urban black community is the strong perception that services to black individuals and families provided in traditional social service and mental-health agencies are ineffective, inadequate, and insensitive to the realities of lives of black families. Reasons proposed for the substandard delivery of services have been varied, but a persistent theme is that middle class white values, norms, and role expectations are imposed in the manner in which professional services are structured; therefore, more culturally syntonic service delivery systems are needed.

Lenrow reports a comparative analysis of natural helping and professional helping. Natural helping is that which is provided in informal support systems by relatives, neighbors, friends, church organizations, and so on. Lenrow concludes that there is nothing inherent in professional helping that is incompatible with helping that is experienced by oppressed minority persons in their informal social networks.[2] There is a core set of professional values, such as impartiality, rationality, empirical knowledge, and ethics, committed to the dignity of the individual and to public welfare. However, there are institutionalized practices that are destructive of the professional values described above. Such practices include bureaucratic organization, economic self-interest, narrow preoccupation with techniques, and defensive self-aggrandizement, which ignore potential sources of help outside the profession. Therefore, it is important to reduce the extent to which clinical social work services reflect these institutionalized practices.

There is evidence that clergy along with physicians are consulted more frequently than other professionals for help with personal problems. They are the "gatekeepers" in the mental health and social service systems. However, there is also evidence that they do not often refer persons who seek help from them to social or mental health agencies despite the fact that the presenting problems may require skills they do not possess. However, at least one study of the relationship between the clergyman's educational level and his referral behavior indicated that there was a significant relationship between educational level and referral behavior; i.e., the less educated ministers made fewer referrals.[3] This suggested that education and training could increase the number of referrals made by ministers to the social and mental-health agency systems.

Meshack describes the involvement of black Baptist churches in the decades of the War on Poverty and Great Society programs: "Some churches took the lead in sponsoring business enterprises, opening job placement centers and conducting day nurseries for inner-city children. To these ministers and many more, the Church had become a base of operations to improve man's life in this world."[4] This history supports the feasibility of locating agency services in the black church, utilizing the minister as linking agent, and developing a counseling model that takes into account the unique ecological pattern of environmental and interpersonal relationships in black communities.

There is a precedent to this nontraditional placement of agency services. Joseph discusses the trend toward placing service delivery systems not only in the neighborhood but in neighborhood social structures that are part of the natural life space of the person—places where people intersect in the normal course of their lives, such as schools, housing complexes, shopping centers, and churches.[5] The church is by its very nature an identified community structure, close to individual and family life-cycle events. Since it intersects many service institutions both within the community of churches to which it belongs and in the public sector, it can serve to facilitate, integrate, and optimize service delivery.

The use of the minister as linking agent and the church as a service site is also justifiable given some emerging theoretical perspectives on the interrelationship of individuals, mediating or support systems, and the larger society. Berger and Neuhaus demonstrate that public policy has functioned to increase the strength of large bureaucratic structures.[6] At the same time, small structures (e.g., neighborhoods, churches, and voluntary associations) serve to help people relate to larger collectivities such as the welfare departments, probation departments, or medical institutions. Many of the social and emotional problems experienced in black families have been generated by their dysfunctional relationships with these larger collectivities.

The counseling program described in this chapter was developed to utilize the strengths of the church as an indigenous social institution with a strong service orientation. Ministers in the community—regardless of denominational affiliation—were invited to attend mental health training workshops that aimed to assist them in understanding the consequences of stress on individuals and families, to recognize emotional and social distress, and to develop competence in connecting persons who come to them for help with psychosocial problems to professional helpers. Sixty-one Protestant ministers of predominantly black congregations in south central Los Angeles participated in this training component.

THE THEORETICAL FRAMEWORK

Over the past two decades, the social work literature has included attempts to infuse a black or minority perspective into existing programs serving black individuals and families. Much of this literature has attempted to expand the profession's theoretical frameworks so that they more accurately explain black behavior, especially as influenced by the larger social environment. For example, Chestang and also Norton emphasize the importance of the simultaneous influence on blacks of the immediate "nurturing" environment (comprising subsystems of family, neighborhood, peer group, etcetera) and the wider dominant or "sustaining" system, also with a wide range of subsystems (e.g., justice, school, or work organizations).[7] This is consistent with the conceptualization of American society as an ethnosystem, i.e., a collectivity of interdependent ethnic groups, each defined by unique historical and/or cultural ties, and bound together by a single political system.

The common theme that permeates these expanded frameworks is that of social systems. The Task Force on Afro-American Content in Social Work Education has observed: "It [social systems] is an approach that has perhaps the greatest potential for incorporating what is known about the dynamic interactions between Afro-Americans and their environment.

However, the systems approach does not constitute a cohesive theory with tightly connecting propositions and unambiguous concepts. . . . At least a systems perspective provides a framework from which the appropriate questions may be asked and studied. . . .''[8]

The systems approach has been more definitively conceptualized in the recent literature describing ecological systems and their significance in planning and implementing delivery of services. From this perspective, people's needs or problem situations are viewed as outcomes of dysfunctional person-environment relationships.[9] They are also viewed as consequences of characteristics of the person, significant others, and their transactions with representatives of larger social institutions. Therefore, the focus of help is on transactional phenomena such as stress, coping, and social support as expressions of the relationships that exist between people and their environments. The goals of professional intervention are competence, autonomy, self-esteem, and relatedness as these may be defined in a particular cultural context. In order to achieve these positive goals, it is necessary to take into account the dynamics of such negative transactional outcomes as oppression and other injustices derived from the misuse of power. The concept of empowerment is consistent with this ecological systems approach. Racial minorities have clearly been stigmatized in the American social system. *Empowerment* refers to the reduction of a particular type of powerlessness, namely, an overriding sense of one's powerlessness to direct one's own life in a course leading to a reasonable personal gratification. This type of powerlessness is an insidious consequence of membership in a stigmatized group, i.e., a group that experiences negative valuation and discrimination in its transactions with the society's major institutions. It is perhaps safe to assume that most black families that come to social agencies for assistance have not escaped the insidious effect of society's negative valuation of them as members of a stigmatized collective.

Empowerment is essentially a set of activities that are engaged in by helping professionals and aimed at dealing with the power blocks experienced by negatively valued individuals or families. A power block is any act, event, or condition that disrupts the process whereby individuals develop effective personal and social skills.[10] Persons who belong to stigmatized collectives experience both direct and indirect power blocks. Indirect power blocks are those that are incorporated into the developmental experiences of the individual as mediated by significant others. These indirect power blocks may operate at three levels. At the primary level, negative valuations may become incorporated into family processes and prevent optimum development of personal resources such as self-esteem and cognitive skills among individual family members. At the secondary level, power blocks occur when limited personal resources due to blocks at the primary level act to limit the development of family members' interpersonal and technical skills. At the tertiary level, power blocks occur when limited interpersonal and technical skills reduce family members' effectiveness in performing valued social roles such as those of parents or employees.

On the other hand, members of oppressed minority groups often experience direct power blocks. These have not been incorporated into the developmental experiences of the individual but are applied directly by some agent of major social institutions. Direct power blocks can also be experienced at three levels. For example, at the primary level, families may not be provided access to resources needed to develop some critical personal resource, e.g., lack of access to good health care so that as a consequence family members do not have good health, a valued personal resource. At the secondary level, a power block may be directly applied to prevent family members from developing technical and interpersonal skills such as limitations placed on educational or management training opportunities. Consequently, promotions or other forms of career advancement may not be forthcoming. At the tertiary level, the valued social role itself is denied, e.g., discriminatory employment practices may prevent a father from obtaining a job adequate to support the family.

An empowerment approach to helping enables the individual to perceive himself as capable of exercising competence.[11] Furthermore, the empowered individual recognizes the opportunities that are available to him to gain control over the forces that determine the quality of his life. The exercise of competence further increases feelings of worth and dignity, so that giving and receiving of service is perceived as part of the public good rather than as a privilege for the few. It means acknowledging and enhancing the strengths that have been the basis for survival of black families despite tremendous suffering and hardship. Empowerment also means that feelings of powerlessness that have been internalized because of negative valuation by the larger society must be changed. Thus, in order to reach black families and empower them to deal more effectively with both the direct and indirect power blocks that have contributed to their problems in social functioning, it is clear that both nontraditional settings and nontraditional intervention strategies are required.

DESCRIPTION OF THE PROGRAM

The overall objective of the research and demonstration program was to develop a model of collaboration between inner-city churches and a family counseling agency that would be characterized by the following:

(a) services located at church sites, i.e., in a setting that is significantly different from traditional social or mental-health agency settings;
(b) services delivered so that at each stage of the counseling process the client would be "in control";
(c) a target population of persons with mental-health problems who would not go to traditional agencies, who had been dissatisfied with services received from a traditional agency, or who had habitually used the church and the minister as primary help source;
(d) a problem-solving strategy based on intervention not only with individuals and families but with external systems that are perceived as contributing to the etiology of the problem or to its solution.

The Counseling Sites

Three church sites were selected, with consideration given to the desirability of diversity in denominational affiliation, socioeconomic level of members, type of neighborhood, and size. A Pentecostal church was selected that was located in a low income neighborhood on a major business artery, although its surrounding area is largely residential. Its membership is predominantly low income and relatively small (approximately 250). Also selected was a Baptist church in a similar neighborhood. However, it has a large membership exceeding two thousand with greater diversity in socioeconomic level of members although still predominantly low income. Many of its members do not live in the immediate area but in more middle class neighborhoods many miles away. The church building extends for an entire city block. Much of the space was planned to accommodate educational and social programs including day care, youth employment service, and alternative school programs. Finally, a United Methodist church was selected that was located in a predominantly black middle class neighborhood. Its membership is predominantly middle and upper middle class and its size is relatively small (approximately four hundred) considering its extensive facilities, including many classrooms and a gymnasium that are largely unused during the week. A full-time clinical social worker was assigned to each of these churches. In addition, in order to increase access of clients to the program, a satellite office was opened at another Baptist church several miles from any of the three main sites.

In the selection of all sites for the program, the availability of space for individual and group counseling as well as for files and a secure telephone was of primary importance. The counseling rooms at each site were identified by the agency's name on the door. This was necessary to ensure that the services were perceived as community agency-sponsored rather than church-sponsored and therefore available to any member of the community rather than only to members of the particular church. It was anticipated, however, that the location of the counseling program at a church site would suggest the endorsement of the church a perhaps less bureaucratic, less culturally alien program of services.

The furnishing of the offices at each site was a critical aspect of the nontraditional approach to be taken in the program. Although desks were available to staff as well as file cabinets for records, these were placed at the periphery of the rooms used for counseling while the central area was furnished with sofas, chairs, and low tables with magazines and flowers. Thus, no interviews would be held with the client facing the counselor separated by a desk, nor were the counselor's degrees or professional memberships prominently displayed. Kitchen facilities at each site also made it possible to serve coffee, tea, and other refreshments to clients individually or in groups.

Resources

Staff of the counseling program included a coordinator of clinical services, three full-time licensed clinical social workers who provided the counseling services, and an administrative secretary. Staff were employed specifically for this project by a United Way family counseling agency that had been contracted to provide counseling services in the project. All staff were involved in a staff development program over the three-month period prior to initiation of the counseling program that focused on the practice model and its theoretical framework. The coordinator, the administrative secretary, and a clinical social worker were located at the Baptist church site. One social worker was assigned to each of the other two sites. All sites were connected by a telephone system that made it possible for all incoming telephone calls to be received by the administrative secretary. In addition, a telephone answering device was utilized and a clinical social worker was "on call" whenever the offices were closed in order to ensure maximum accessibility for clients.

Since the staff had been hired by the community agency, staff also had access to many of the agency's resources, including psychiatric consultation and an extensive staff development program. In addition, each church site provided staff with access to the resources of the church. These resources ranged from capital, i.e. duplicating machines, to human resources, i.e., volunteers who could provide emergency transportation of clients to homes, hospitals, or other community programs. Another major resource of the project was the Advisory Committee made up of ministers, laymen, and representatives of key community agencies.

Individuals and Families Served

Intensively during the initial phases of the project and to some extent in subsequent months, the counselors engaged in activities aimed at orienting the community to the target group for their services, i.e., those individuals or families who had refused or resisted going to traditional agencies for assistance, who had dropped out of service, or who had indicated that they would feel more comfortable in seeking help in the environment of the church or neighborhood. These activities included presentations to a variety of church organizations such as usher boards, missionary societies, choirs, and other service groups as well as presentations to other community agencies dealing with specific problem areas, e.g., child abuse, teenage pregnancy, health care, etcetera. However, it was soon apparent that there were tremendous pressures being applied to staff to accept clients who did not necessarily fit into the target population.

The changing economic environment was a major source of the pressure indicated above. Many agencies in the community were reducing services whereas more and more families were experiencing overwhelming stress from such sources as unemployment of heads of households, an increasing flow of drugs into the community, and a serious decline in the availability of affordable housing. Given the increasing demand for services, many agencies restricted eligibility to the most seriously disturbed individuals or families or the chronically mentally ill. Thus, there were fewer services available to those persons who were experiencing acute emotional disorders or involved in stressful situations that had not yet resulted in emotional breakdown. Table 17.1 presents the source of all

TABLE 17.1
Referrals to Counseling Component: January 1981–June 1983

Total Number of Referrals	775
Referral Source	
Self (Including Family Member)	121
Minister	48
Church Organization	194
Community (Agency or Individual)	412
Service Requested	
Liaison*	77
Counseling	698
For Whom	
Individual Adult	226
Individual Minor	256
Family	293

*Assistance in connecting to services not provided by the project (e.g., legal aid, residential treatment, ecetera.).

referrals received during the thirty months' duration of the research and demonstration program.

The largest proportion of referrals during the total program period was for services to families (defined as two or more persons who are related or in an interdependent relationship). It should also be noted that the category *individual adult* referred to single males and females whereas the category *individual minor* more often referred to teenagers either living independently or in foster homes. The most frequent presenting problems of individual adults were depression, anxiety reactions precipitated by employment problems or health problems, and substance abuse. The most frequent presenting problems of individual minors were problems in establishing independence, conflicts with school, and conflicts with peers (e.g., pressure from gang members). The most frequent presenting problems of families were child-parent problems, child-school problems, marital conflict, substance abuse, and problems in caring for elderly relatives.

The Counseling Model

Empowerment of individuals and families to effect positive changes in their lives was a universal goal regardless of the specific presenting problem. For example, the goal of ''empowering'' people led to a more intermediate goal of providing clients with opportunities to ''control'' the counseling process, which had to be further reduced to specific behaviors expected on the part of the counselor. For example, counselors were expected to be flexible in determining where and when clients would be seen so that if it were more convenient for a mother to be seen in a neighborhood park so that her children could be watched at play, this would be arranged.[12] Counselors were also expected to return all telephone calls received from clients or applicants for service when they were not available, rather than having clients or applicants be instructed to call later when the counselor was expected to be available. Thus, the client's power and control over the counseling process is measured by the extent that the client's needs take precedence over the agency's convenience.

In addition to giving maximum control of the counseling process to clients, another critical aspect of the counseling model was the focus of the counselor's activity on teaching clients to deal more effectively with those social institutions that makes decisions that affect their lives. This is based on the assumption that the majority of social and mental health problems presented by black clients—particularly low income clients— either generate or are generated by negative encounters with such institutions as schools, police, welfare departments, probation departments, health agencies, or other community agencies. Thus, clients who learn more effective ways of coping with these institutions would be expected to enhance subjective feelings of self-esteem and competence and at the same time reduce objective stressors such as school failure, loss of eligibility of public assistance, difficulties in obtaining health care, etcetera. Thus, counseling was not focused solely on the one-to-one relationship between the individual or family and the counselor but rather on the social network or ecological system in which individuals and their families interact. Spiegel describes a similar approach to counseling families as particularly useful with ethnic families.[13]

The method utilized by counselors to help clients to become more effective in system transactions was to implement one or more of four possible educational strategies: (a) the demonstration of new behaviors by the counselor in the counseling session that are to be used by the individual or family in the target system, (b) the rehearsal of the new behaviors by the individual or family in the counseling session, (c) the demonstration of the new behaviors by the counselor for the individual or the family in the target system and the assessment of the outcome, (d) implementation of the new behavior in the target system by the individual or the family followed by an assessment of the outcome. All four strategies are not necessarily implemented with each individual or family or for each relevant system.

The new behaviors are almost always aimed at helping the individual or family deal more effectively with potentially or actually oppressive systems. The selection of a particular strategy is based on the assessment of the transacting systems of person, family, significant others, and larger social systems involved in the problem situation. Thus, the counselor's skills should include the ability to assess how these transactions are influencing the presenting problem and what new client behaviors would be most likely to change the nature of the transactions to enhance feelings of competence and/or relieve system produced stress. When the behavior is actually demonstrated for the individual or family by the counselor, it may be viewed as a supportive intervention, i.e., supporting the client's effort to learn how to behave similarly and independently. Seven such interventions were conceptualized and utilized by the clinical social work staff.

Priming is defined as preparing a system (school, welfare department, etcetera) to respond differently and more positively to the client than it might otherwise respond. This strategy assumes that many of the systems with which families have negative encounters can respond more positively, but only under conditions that would be perceived as a "cost" to the system, i.e., any suggestions that the system was not adhering to is own policies and procedures or that the system was "caving in" to some external pressure.

A family was experiencing a great deal of family conflict. The junior high school-age son had become angry and even assaultive with his siblings and parents when he was feeling particularly stressed. The counselor pointed out to the parents that although he had not exhibited the behavior at schools, he might do so at any time and the school would very likely suspend him. The parents were, therefore, encouraged to discuss their son's reaction to the stressful situation at home and the fact that the family was in counseling with the school counselor and homeroom teacher. It should also be indicated that in the case of any unacceptable behavior, one of the parents or the counselor could be called to school to handle it. The mother was able to have this discussion with the school personnel, who agreed to handle any acting-out behavior on the part of her son as she had requested. Thus, the counselor assisted the family in priming the system so that it would respond differently and more positively than it would have done otherwise. After the school has already made a decision to suspend a child, there is a vested interest in implementing the decision even if good reasons are given for changing it. The cost would be the appearance of caving in to pressure or not adhering to established school policy. Most school bureaucracies would consider this cost too high.

Enabling refers to actions on the part of the counselor to provide information or contacts that will make it possible for the family to utilize its own resources more effectively. This strategy assumes that a family may have considerable resources that are not always recognized as useful in obtaining from a system what the family needs. A family attempting to obtain special support services for a child who was failing in school was frustrated until the counselor helped the parents to become aware of legal remedies available to them in this situation. Given this additional knowledge, the parents were able to confront the school authorities and obtain the services. Similarly, a single parent who could read only at a fifth grade level often experienced crisis situations due to the difficulty she encountered in reading utility bills, rental agreements, etcetera. The parent was helped to make a decision to enroll in a literacy program but in the meantime to perceive her teenage daughter as a resource able to intercept important written materials until the time that she could master basic reading and writing skills herself. The teenager viewed this request for her assistance as an acknowledgment of her own growing maturity.

Catalyzing refers to those actions taken by the counselor to obtain resources that are prerequisite to the family fully utilizing their existing resources. This strategy assumes that families have resources, but additional resources may be needed before their own can be fully utilized. For example, if a parent has job skills, he or she will need to be able to get an actual job before those skills can be used. One family who came to the counseling program for assistance had a relative who lived in another city but was willing to move in with the family and provide child care that the family could not otherwise afford. However, the family's apartment was too small to accommodate another adult and they had been unsuccessful in finding appropriate yet affordable housing. By finding a room for the relative in the same neighborhood, the social worker was able to obtain a resource that made it possible for the family to use their own extended family more effectively to meet their needs.

Linking refers to actions taken by the social worker to connect families to other groups, families, or social networks. It assumes that families can augment their own strengths by linking with others who can provide new perceptions and/or opportunities. Families may link with others to provide a collective power that can be more successful in confronting a system than that available to any individual family. For example, several parents who were experiencing difficulties in relating to the elementary school that their children were attending formed a support group that provided opportunities for their collective action in regard to such issues as corporal punishment and availability of support services.

Translating refers to worker activities aimed at helping families and the systems with which they interact clarify the purpose and consequences of that transaction. For example, a mother and three children, ages 7 to 13, were counseled for problems including the disruptive behavior of the 13-year-old son at home and school and the mother's depression over the custody battle in which she was involved with the father of the two younger children. The mother had a very hostile relationship with teachers and counselors in the school because she thought their actions in regard to the 13- year-old son indicated that they were racially prejudiced. The counselor arranged a meeting with the mother, the son, and the school counselor at which several interactions were modeled for the mother aimed at translating for the school counselor the mother's efforts to communicate her concerns about: (a) how to determine whether the school's actions in regard to her son were consistent with school policy or merely arbitrary, (b) how to be supportive of her son without being hostile or argumentative with school staff, and (c) how to support the school's efforts with her son without appearing to abandon him. The counselor was also able to translate for the mother her concerns about (a) how to be sensitive to students' special needs without appearing to condone misbehavior and (b) how to develop a collaborative rather than adversarial relationship with parents of students presenting behavior problems.

Negotiation refers to worker activities that seek to obtain agreement between client and others in the system regarding mutually acceptable rules governing their relationship and transactions. A family sought help for problems exacerbated by the mother's depression and difficulties on her job because of excessive absenteeism. She indicated that she was sure that her boss was planning to fire her soon. The counselor and client composed a letter that was sent by the counselor requesting a delay in any punitive action planned against this employee until she had had an opportunity to work through her problems in a time-limit counseling program. The employer called to indicate that "progress would need to be shown by the end of another month." The worker was able to increase this grace period to three months. This plan was accepted by the client. Thus, the negotiations were considered successful.

Collaboration occurs when the counselor joins with significant others or agencies to achieve some positive outcome for the client through their joint efforts that could not be achieved by any single agent or agency acting alone. For example, a parent-child conflict problem seemed to be related to the child's acting out because of reading difficulties. The counselor attempted first to assist the parent in obtaining tutorial services from the school. This was unsuccessful because of the assessment made by the school psychologist that the child's problems were emotional rather than educational and therefore she would not be able to utilize the school's tutorial program effectively. The parent was referred to the mental-health clinic operated by the public school system, but she refused to go. The worker was able, however, to arrange a meeting with the school psychologist and a staff member of a community agency providing a limited educational counseling service. It was finally determined that our program would provide family counseling to deal with the emotional problem and the community agency would simultaneously provide tutorial services based on the child's needs as indicated from the school's records of educational and psychological testing, which would be made available with parental consent to the agency. After six months, the school psychologist would reevaluate the child to determine whether she would be considered improved to the extent that she could utilize the school's tutorial program. This collaboration made it possible to maximize the use of public school and community agency resources for the benefit of the child.

EVALUATION

The strategies selected for the evaluation of the counseling component were determined by its primary objective, which was to stimulate the referral of unserved and underserved persons with social and mental-health problems. Ideally, within the contract agency comparisons could be made of persons referred to the regular program of individual and family counseling. However, eligibility for services in the regular program was determined to a large extent by sources of funding (e.g., State Office of Criminal Justice for counseling services to youth who had been diverted from the system and their families). Thus, its client pool would not reflect a "free market" system for agency services. Clearly, a study design in which alternative programs were compared to determine relative attractiveness to inner-city persons with social and mental-health problems was not possible under these circumstances. Although an effort was made to determine whether the program reached a different population of individuals and families from those served by traditional agencies, a major concern was also to analyze the service delivery of services in the counseling program at church sites to determine whether at least an embryonic technology for dealing with social and mental health problems in predominantly black inner cities could be discerned. Five questions were used to guide the analysis.

To what extent do ministers (or church organizations) refer persons to the counseling program at church sites as compared with referrals to other mental-health programs?

All available statistics regarding referral sources to agencies providing family counseling in Los Angeles County indicate only a negligible percentage that can be attributed to ministers or church organizations.[14] This is based on inferences made from the category "Other" in category sets of referral sources, which is almost always less than 2 percent and which contains, in addition to ministers or church organizations, such other rare referral sources as private physicians and lawyers. As indicated in Table 1, the percentage of ministers who served as referral source was 6 percent of all clients referred to the program. However, another 25 percent were referred by church organizations, which do not appear at all in the statistics of other counseling agencies. Thus 31 percent or nearly one-third of the referrals were from church-related sources. This is still perhaps a conservative figure, since the "Self" referred category often included persons who had heard about the program at church and had sought counseling on their own without the intercession of minister of church organization.

To what extent are persons referred for counseling services at church sites considered to be unserved or underserved?

Forty-seven percent or nearly one-half of church-referred clients indicated that they had not sought counseling from any other agency. This was in contrast to 28 percent of all other referrals who had not sought counseling before. The difference is statistically significant (p.$\langle$.001). These findings suggest that not only were ministers more likely to refer persons for counseling to this counseling program at church sites than to other counseling programs, but the persons referred were more likely to be persons who had not sought help from other counseling agencies.

To what extent are presenting problems of clients receiving counseling at a church site similar to or different from the social and emotional problems brought to traditional mental-health agencies?

As indicated, traditional agencies in the target community had set priorities for service that essentially ensured that only the most serious problems would be accepted for treatment. Thus, it would be expected that milder problems would be brought to the church-based counseling program. This was confirmed to some extent, but not without some contradictions. The presenting problems were almost always some problem in living, e.g., marital problems, child-parent conflict, family violence, substance abuse, adjustment to the chronic or terminal illness of a family member, etcetera. However, the persons involved also presented a wide range of emotional dysfunction, such as depression, anxiety reactions, and borderline personality. Some individuals presented more serious problems, such as dissociative reaction and severe depression.

There was no effort made to assess level of family functioning beyond the descriptive measure of presenting problem.

To what extent do clients who have received counseling at the church site compare their experience favorably or unfavorably with counseling received in traditional agency settings?

A random sample of 50 clients who had completed counseling were selected for a follow-up survey. Of the sample selected, 38 could be located and agreed to be interviewed. Seventeen clients (45 percent) had sought counseling from another agency for the same or different problem. An attitude toward counseling index was included in the semistructured interview schedule, and questions included in the index were addressed to both past and church-based counseling experiences. For those clients who had both past and church-based counseling, the mean score on the index for church-based counseling was significantly higher than the mean for past counseling (p.⟨.001).

The mean score for the 21 respondents who had received only church-based counseling was significantly more positive about that counseling than respondents who had received other counseling (p.⟨01). It could be speculated that the respondents who had received church-based counseling should have felt less positive, since they did not have a negative experience with other counseling as a point of comparison. However, the failure to seek assistance from traditional agencies may have reflected such strong negative stereotypes about a counseling process and the pressure within it for self-disclosure that the more positive attitude of these respondents could reflect instead a halo-effect based on the dissimilarity between the stereotype and what was actually experienced.

To what extent do counselors implement specific interventions into macrosystems (e.g, schools, health agencies, or welfare departments) with which clients have had problematical transactions?

Counselors were asked to select purposively each month for six consecutive months those active cases that best illustrated use of supportive interventions into external systems implemented by the counselor on behalf of the client. As a result, 64 cases were identified. The seven supportive interventions for which examples were sought were: (a) priming, (b) enabling, (c) linking, (d) catalyzing, (e) translating, (f) collaborating, and (g) negotiating. Given the sampling design, it was not possible to determine the extent to which counselors implemented specific interventions into specific systems. However, in those cases considered to be most illustrative of the use of these interventions it was possible to determine which of the interventions were utilized most frequently and which interventions had the most positive outcomes.

The most frequent strategy encountered in cases identified as most illustrative was priming, which was identified in 30 (47 percent) of the representative cases.

TABLE 17.2
Outcome of Selected Supportive Interventions

Strategy	No. of Cases	No. Positive	%
1. Priming	30	24	80%
2. Enabling	22	14	64%
3. Linking	22	20	82%
4. Catalyzing	16	11	69%
5. Translating	16	15	94%
6. Collaborating	6	6	100%
7. Negotiating	6	3	50%

CONCLUSION

An empowerment approach to families who are encountering problems in living is based essentially on assumptions of family strengths. At the same time, the empowerment model does not equate a need for assistance with signs of weakness or dependency. Perhaps most important, the assistance provided is more often directed toward increasing families' capacities to use their own resources more effectively, particularly in encounters with external social institutions. The importance of this latter fact is due to the major role played by these institutions in the development of excessive stress on individuals and on the whole families, which may contribute to an array of family problems.

The next page to be written in the social history of black families in the United States will probably document the emphasis placed on responses to the forces that have threatened to destroy it in the decade of the eighties. The responses have been made by multiple action systems: federal, state and local governments, nonprofit community service agencies, indigenous groups in black communities, and so on. There is no apparent consensus in these systems as to the most effective approach for empowerment of black families. There is considerable promise, however, that these responses will ultimately bring about a transformation of a significant number of families from powerless, unstable collectivities to strong, well-functioning centers of identity for its members. If so, it will be because there has been a fine balance achieved between the responsibility accepted and effectively implemented by government and the responsibility taken by members of families for each other. In addition, those professionals sanctioned by society to provide assistance to families will have understood the difference between providing services to problem families and empowering families to solve their problems.

NOTES

1. *Mental Health Services at Inner-City Churches,* Final Report to National Institute of Mental Health, January 1984, Grant #T24-MH16129.

2. P. Lenrow, "Dilemmas of Professional Helping: Discontinuities with Folk Helping Roles," in Lauren Wise, ed., *Altruism, Sympathy and Helping* (New York: Academic Press, 1978).

3. W.K. Bentz, "The Relationship Between Educational Background and the Referral Role of Ministers," *Sociology and Social Research,* Vol. 51, no. 2 (January 1967), pp. 199–208.

4. B.A. Meshack, *Is the Baptist Church Relevant to the Black Community* (San Francisco, CA: R and E Research Associates, 1976), p. 60.

5. Sister Mary Vicentia Joseph, "The Parish as Social Service and Social Action Center: An Ecological Systems Approach," *Social Thought* (Fall 1975), pp. 43–60.

6. P.L. Berger and R.J. Neuhaus, *To Empower People: The Roles of Mediating Structures in Public Policy* (Washington, DC: American Enterprise Institute for Public Policy Research, 1977).

7. L. Chestang, *Character Development in a Hostile Society* (Chicago: School of Social Service Administration, Occasional Paper 3, 1972); "Competencies and Knowledge in Clinical Social Work: A Dual Perspective," in Patricia Ewalt, ed., *Toward a Definition of Clinical Social Work Practice* (New York: National Association of Social Workers, 1980), pp. 1–12 D.G. Norton, *The Dual Perspective: Inclusion of Ethnic Minority Content in the Social Work Curriculum* (New York: Council on Social Work Education, 1978).

8. J.A. Bush, D.C. Norton, C.L. Sanders, and B.B. Solomon, "An Integrative Approach for the Inclusion of Content on Blacks in Social Work Education," in Jay Chun et al., eds., in *Mental Health and People of Color* (Washington, DC: Howard University Press, 1983), pp. 97–125.

9. C. B. Germain, "Using Social and Physical Environments," in Aaron Rosenblatt and Diana Waldfogel, eds., *Handbook of Clinical Social Work,* pp. 110–133.

10. B. Solomon, *Black Empowerment: Social Work in Oppressed Communities* (New York: Columbia University Press, 1976).

11. E.B. Pinderhughes and A.B. Pittman, "A Socio-Cultural Treatment Model: Empowerment of Worker and Client," in Mary Ward Day, ed., *The Socio-Cultural Dimensions of Mental Health* (New York: Vintage Press, 1985), pp. 82–111.

12. P. Pedersen, "The Cultural Role of Conceptual and Contextual Support Systems in Counseling," *American Mental Health Counselor's Association Journal,* Vol. 8, no.1, pp. 35–42.

13. J. Spiegel, "An Ecological Model of Ethnic Families," in M. McGoldrick, J. K. Pearce, and J. Giordino, eds., *Ethnicity and Family Therapy* (New York: Guilford Press, 1982), pp. 31–51.

14. Los Angeles County Mental Health Department, 1982.

18

EMPOWERING BLACK FAMILIES

Harold E. Cheatham

The chapters in this volume address the specific characteristics and dynamics of black families in America. They provide a synthesis of theoretical and empirical evidence on the structure and functioning of black families both as a by-product of and in response to societal constraints. This chapter continues that orientation in a critical discussion of perspectives prerequisite to effecting a mental-health service delivery system appropriate to black Americans. It argues, thus, that while the effort to derive a syncretic model for serving all people of color is a defensible and important proposition, it is too soon to ignore the specificity of blacks' historic and cultural experiences by such incorporation. Mental-health professionals need to attend to the specifics of the black experience and to the related service needs that lead to client empowerment.

No other ethnic group's experiences precisely parallel those of black Americans and, indeed, to focus on color without reference to history and culture has been termed a "scientific error."[1] The American version of slavery bound it inextricably to race.[2] Knowledge of "similar" groups is not a sufficient predicate for a specific intervention. That knowledge must be enriched and operationalized through coupling to actual experience with the groups' members.

The observable decline in openly espoused, ideological racism in the postsegregation period has encouraged some mental health professionals to champion a therapy that is applicable to all ethnic minorities.[3] This renewed expression focusing on clients' universal characteristics mutes the long history of intellectualized racism in America. Racism may be defined loosely as synonymous with race prejudice or discrimination or in a more restricted way as "a rationalized pseudoscientific theory positing the innate and permanent inferiority of (people of color)."[4] It is in the latter sense that racism, as it has forestalled the development of a truly egalitarian multiracial American society is used in this chapter.

The effects of structural racism persist in all aspects of American life and institutions, including the mental-health service delivery system. Accepting the call for a universal conceptualization fitted to all people of color forces the notion that black Americans are just another ethnic minority group. To accept this construction is also to move, in a very brief time, beyond the chronicled and uncorrected inadequacies of the mental-health care system to the illusion of color blindness.[5] Such movement, perhaps, is an appropriate objective. The thorny question is one of timing.

The dismantling of legal forms of segregation was hailed as portending "the declining significance of race."[6] Such optimistic predictions of the changing of American institutions misgauge both the legions of blacks who remain virtually unaffected by federal legislation and the initiatives that provided for equal employment opportunities and affirmative action. Marable suggested that during the "second reconstruction, 1945–1982," the social and economic conditions of most blacks remained unchanged or actually worsened.[7] He noted, further, that the deteriorating social environment had deleterious effects on the black family as indexed in the increased out-of-wedlock births, increased birth rate among the poor and uneducated, and increased incidence of single-parent and female-headed households. The postsegregation era also ushered in increases in black suicides and homicide. Consider, for example, that the black homicide rate increased in the 1960s from 21.9 per 100,000 deaths (a decline from 22.3 in 1910) to 35.5 in the 1970s. The 1970s rate for whites was 4.4 percent. By the 1980s, fully 54 percent of all homicide victims were black. Add to those grim statistics the observation by Marable and others[8] that the cruel paradox of desegregation is that black cultural forms and institutions experience a decline in status, quality, and viability. Those observations serve the conclusion that a color-blind, nonspecific intervention model is not in the best interest of black Americans at this historical juncture.

AFRICAN-AMERICAN BEGINNINGS

The slave legacy of blacks' experience of being poor, oppressed, and marginalized has a sturdy base in American history. Attitudes and attending behaviors of cultural superiority also have a long history. The institution of slavery, a manifestation of man's pride and of his quest for superiority over others and the environment, was old when Babylonia, Phoenicia, and Assyria were young.[9] The seventeenth century version of slavery, however, unlike its antecedents, was a manifestation of man's irrational power.[10] It brought slave trading to its "direst height"; other nations trafficked in human flesh, but none equaled the "cynical, degrading, gruesome, cold-blooded enterprise" that English seapower achieved.[11] Giddings asserted that American slavery was enabled by the confluence of religion, the laws of capitalism, and the psychological needs of white males. She wrote: "It was a seventeenth-century mind that had been shaped by the Renaissance, with its cult of individualism and the moral right to exploit those weaker than oneself; by the Protestant Reformation's ethic and evangelical piety, which separated body from soul; by the Age of Discovery which found a continent of people different from the explorers; and by the Commercial Revolution with its vision of wealth on a global scale."[12]

The slave experience, however, did not produce a monolithic black American. Mathis and Nobles contend that blacks, in response to chronic and systematized injustice and enforced isolation, created systems to meet the needs of their community.[13] The system that was created had its genesis in African form and tradition. The irony is that as cruel as slavery was, its legacy ensured the survival and preservation of African culture, albeit in revised form. Contrary to the predominant intent to destroy the vestiges of community and values, the oppressive system inadvertently enabled social organization, as it existed in the psyche of this people, to be actualized in America.

Unlike the Western philosophic system, the African tradition has no heavy emphasis on the individual; the individual's being is authenticated only in terms of others'. Nobles writes that there is a sense of corporate responsibility and collective destiny as epitomized in the traditional African self-concept: "I am because we are; and because we are, therefore, I am."[14] Further he argues that the philosophical linkages were retained even with transplantation to America, that a region's particular physical features facilitated retention of African orientations, and that rigidly enforced isolation of blacks allowed (perhaps even obligated) retention of their orientation.

The meticulously documented accounts provide further discussion of the characteristics of the slave community and its legacy for black Americans.[15] These writers focus on the distorted view of the plantation, a view that denies that the slave had a meaningful and distinctive culture and that also obscures the slave's inner life, thought, action, and sense of self. They demonstrate, instead, that the slave had a rather diversified personality, not a unidimensional one.

The slave held fast to African culture, practicing and enhancing its meaning and melding into American culture those aspects that had shared similarity. Strains of African culture in the current American culture are testimony to the notion that the African did not simply succumb to the vagaries of slavery. Forms were synthesized rather than relinquished. Among the examples of retained African form are religion that embodied elements similar to those of Europeans, and particularly animism, which enabled retention of African elements regardless of what or whom was worshipped.[16] The roots of the art forms termed *blues* and *jazz* have been assigned primarily to black Americans and authoritatively linked to Africa.[17] Blassingame further noted that language was imposed upon slaves but that the African linguistic style and timbre were retained and that not the least item of the slaves' distinct cultural inventory was the folktale, which is regarded as one of the African forms most resistant to European culture.

SLAVE PERSONALITY

In the exchange and adaptation process, there is considerable evidence that the slave held fast to the African cultural determinants of his status rather than accept the slaveholder's view of his place in society. This pervasive sense of self-efficacy,[18] together with the resilience of African cultural forms that were merged with American forms, provided a different view of slaves' existence and of black Americans' heritage.

The evidence is that slaves had social organization incorporating the norms of role ascription, social conformance, ethical conduct, group solidarity and defense, cooperation, accommodation and conflict, and similar sociological constructs.[19] This social and cultural organization, while differing from that of free peoples, nonetheless provided for the traditional functions of group solidarity and family organization, including established child-rearing practices.

Although family life had no legal status, it was one of the most important aspects of slave life as it benefited both the slaveholder and the slave. Some slaveholders encouraged organic family life as insurance against rebellion and runaways. The slave was able to observe traditional family practices, children were taught obedience to parents and elders, women had prescribed roles, and parents lavished affection on children.

Blassingame noted that black slave children learned about slavery vicariously as they were taught obedience, religiosity, morality, and obedience — even to slaveholders. The lessons were complex and contradictory, obliging children to be respectful and compliant but not to the point of unconditional submission. They were taught to distinguish situations in which allegiance to family and tradition were preeminent. This distinction was learned through the parents' modeling of "a shallow level of convenience" where required[20] and modeling of strength in the sanctity of the family. This dual identity behavior that is practiced by black Americans has been termed *mild dissociation*.[21]

The summary point from these observations is that much of what has been canonized about black families is in error as it fails to present this life from the view of the slave. No single theoretical conceptualization can capture the complexity of a racial or ethnic group. And while there is no single authentic black experience in America, there is evidence to support the commonality of experience borne of pervasive racism and color consciousness.[22] The truncated view of the slave and, hence, of the legacy of black Americans obligates conclusions and justifies, for some practitioners, behaviors and clinical interventions that ignore the unique characteristics of the person being treated. The perspective offered here is that there is no single black American profile, that the experiences of blacks in slavery and it successor forms — "Jim Crow," "separate but equal," "affirmative discrimination" gave rise to variegated personalities that are unique in their own right rather than being vulgar, pathologized caricatures of "ideal" Americans. Inherent in this perspective is the argument that observing the resiliency of black Americans forces the conclusion that they indeed embody heroic characteristics. As one observer put it, properly regarded, Chicken George and Aunt Jemima *are* heroic figures.

The Afrocentric construct is presented here as a heuristic device, as a fuller and more contemporary view of the predilections, as opposed to the presumed or ascribed characteristics, of black Americans. It does not seem necessary for one to accept this construct as valid *or* to argue it is invalid. What is suggested is that in the place of the negative and unauthenticated ascriptions, one might utilize this thesis as a starting point toward understanding and dealing clinically with the reality and complexity of black Americans.

As a coda, I have intended to demonstrate that the "black personality" accrues from a variety of primary sources. First among these is the residue from the African roots; second is blacks' immersion into American and, particularly, southern culture. The third source is learning adduced from the obligated adaptation to and manipulations of the new system (cf. Pinderhughes, 1982).

BLACK FAMILY CHARACTERISTICS

The slavery experience was an interlude rather than the beginning of black family life in America. Slavery, in fact, was a crucible for effecting a blend of African and American ethos—and, indeed, in reciprocal fashion. Black family form must be understood as a viable continuation of the African heritage and, as such, ought not be subjected to qualitative comparisons with those family forms from which it differs. The African cosmological sense of the universe—a "we" not an "I" orientation—coupled with philosophical principles of unity, cooperative effort, and mutual responsibility still characterizes black families.[23]

Functioning as a family transcended the corporate, nuclear household, and within the household the leadership and gender roles were not immutably fixed. Hence, the ascription of positive and negative valence to "patriarchy" and "matriarchy" is foreign to the African notion of unity. "The unity within the family disallowed any element which endangered its capacity to survive. A system where the family totally disintegrates because one member is lost (i.e., father or mother dies or abandons the unit) would be antithetical to the traditional principles which defined the African family."[24] Other scholars of this issue also assert that slaves retained and subsequently transmitted, to contemporary life, the essential African philosophy, perception of reality, and tradition.[25] Most scholars agree, however, that the Afrocentric orientation is not a pure form, but an amalgam. As black American families respond to structural racism, we witness a twentieth-century version of their rejection of the Eurocentric template.

Much has been written about black self-hatred—mostly from speculation and conjecture—and made credible by repetition. Where research evidence was gathered it often was without sound empirical basis and failed to examine the black self-concept in context, i.e., as a rational response to circular and reinforcing oppression.[26] Kardiner and Ovesey's conclusion about black behavior was based on their observations of a small sample of black psychotherapy patients in a Harlem hospital. Ignoring blacks' context and reality, they concluded that blacks were without a base for healthy self-concept but were rich in the elements for self-hatred.[27] That conclusion is now widely recognized as racist, as defined earlier in this chapter.

Such errors in outsiders' understanding of cultures they attempt to study or errors of "transubstantiation" and "conceptual incarceration"[28] have been perpetuated[29] with little reverence for blacks' vitality and resilience. Cogent, measured critiques of the scientific credence of blacks' personal disorganization and "distorted family life" are presented together with alternative constructions by Billingsley and McCarthy and Yancey.[30] These constructions force the conclusion that rather than self-hatred, there exists a vital self-concept and love of self without which black Americans would have been "neutralized." Giddings's account also makes this point. She wrote of black women poisoning slave masters and engaging in acts of incendiarism and spontaneous aborting of fetuses as acts of self-preservation.[31] An understanding of these critiques would suggest that Rev. Dr. Ben Chavis, who as an adult achieved civil rights ("Wilmington Ten") notoriety, was "crazy" in his response to structural racism when at age 11 he refused to yield to a South Carolina librarian's insistence that he could not borrow books.[32] He was not pathological, however. Rather, he epitomized black consciousness.

Foster and Perry, charging that most research evidence of blacks' negative self-concept is conceptual rather than explanatory, collected subjective data from respondents in a large, economically depressed metropolitan city. Despite blacks' dissatisfaction with some social and economic conditions, they reported higher self-esteem than did the whites in the study. Foster and Perry conclude that many blacks have positive self-concepts regardless of demographics and oppressive social, economic, and environmental conditions. They call on helping professionals to dispel the myth of blacks' negative self-evaluation and to treat the strengths.[33]

The American experience doubtless effected a heterogeneity among and within black families. The summary notion for this section is that despite the more familiar caricature, African values emphasizing collectivity, affiliation, sharing, spiritualityy, and obedience have been preserved and transmitted to black families.[34] The strengths of black families have been identified as: (a) strong kinship bonds as manifested in the capacity to absorb other individuals into the family structure (and) in informal adaptation, (b) a strong work orientation, (c) flexibility of family (members') roles, (d) high achievement orientation, and (e) religious orientation.[35] Bartz and Levine, comparing black to Anglo and Chicano child-rearing practices, suggest that these five values remain intact. They report that in contrast to Anglo and Chicano mothers, black mothers, across all economic levels, were stronger advocates of accelerated development of child responsibility and autonomy and were less permissive. Further, they note that black parents were least tolerant of wasted time, while also exhibiting the most supportive behavior, and that black mothers were highest, among these cohorts, on egalitarianism. They conclude that, consistent with earlier findings, black families exhibited a combination of high support, high control, open communications, and demands for mature behavior.[36]

The American Psychological Association stated that it is unethical to undertake therapy with clients whose sociocultural experience is significantly different from the therapist's own.[37] Despite this pronouncement, therapists in training are taught interventions that ignore the client's culture.[38] These basic discrepancies remain to be resolved.

EMPOWERMENT THROUGH APPROPRIATE INTERVENTION

Cultural Awareness

The black American is at once an individual and a member of a unique racial and cultural group. This uniqueness has been the subject of speculation and notable insistence that blacks' mental-health needs could not be served by nonblacks. Curiously, nearly two decades of research have not borne out this assertion. Rather, what has been demonstrated is that faulty and single construct research paradigms have produced mixed and contradictory results and that therapist skills and orientations, rather than specific ethnicity, are implicated in the low incidence and quality of psychological service delivery to black Americans.

Billingsley observes that American social scientists are much more American than social and much more social than scientific.[39] The substance of that criticism is repeated in the frequent observation that dominant theories of counseling and psychotherapy are bounded by culture, class, and language (*n.b.*, the terms *counseling* and *psychotherapy* are acknowledged as qualitatively different but for simplicity are used interchangeably here). Most intervention approaches assume that clients have an individual (versus group/nationalistic) orientation and are verbally and emotionally expressive, open, spontaneous, and insightful. Further, clients are assumed to value punctuality and long-range goal setting, and to distinguish psychological from somatic complaints.[40]

Proceeding from such assumptions, the helping professional doubtless will violate the black client's sense of integrity or ''world view.''[41] World view is defined as one's perception of one's relationship to persons and events. World view is affected by sociocultural experience—one's inventory of enabling and disabling events. The therapist and client are more likely than not to come from differing sociocultural and sociohistorical backgrounds. The variance between the world view of the therapist and the therapized makes all counseling interventions to some extent cross-cultural. Pedersen notes that experiences of misunderstanding, rejection, distrust, and negative transference are more likely to occur in cross-cultural dyads.[42]

The challenge for the helping professional is to be aware of, and sensitive to, the black client's distinctiveness and to utilize that awareness to develop, *with* the client, understanding of the client's expectations and needs. Blacks' lower incidence of use of mental-health facilities, frequent misdiagnosis, service by least qualified and least experienced staff, higher incidence of outpatient and chemotherapy treatment, and higher rate of unilateral termination have been demonstrated.[43] These findings attest to the continuation, within the therapy context, of the disabling experiences blacks face in the societal context. The challenge for the therapist is to empower the client through a therapy experience that negates the client's disabling experiences.

Despite nearly four centuries of adversity, black families have thrived. This fact is due, in part, to an obligated orientation to self-conscious, self-preservation. The unfinished business of providing this clientele with principled, sensitive, and committed mental-health service remains unfinished and, moreover, is in danger of being extinguished by calls for a single theoretical model sensitive to all people of color.[44] Blacks are products of their distinct sociocultural and sociohistorical experience. Counseling and therapy are specific, contractual events and, thus, must proceed on the basis of understanding of the client's cultural context. Training programs have yet to adequately prepare counselors and therapists for this boundary crossing.

While comprehensive empirical bases for such interventions are lacking, the available literature provides adequate demonstrations of starting points. Li-Repac, for example, presents evidence that the counselor's rating did not have a significant negative effect on the client's self-rating in therapy. Her evidence that the client tended to maintain a rather robust self-concept even during the experience of inefficient counseling provides refutation for the simplistic notion about who cannot serve whom.[45] That there are no demonstrations of incontrovertible negative effects from cross-cultural interventions suggests that meliorating factors can be identified. This is not to argue the converse proposition that crossing boundaries in therapy is a universal counselor/therapist capability. Rather, it is to petition that instead of awaiting the millennium, practitioners ought to garner encouragement to undertake interventions that utilize their training *and* that are tempered by the available findings in the considerable cross-cultural counseling and therapy literature.

FRAMEWORK FOR PSYCHOLOGICAL INTERVENTIONS WITH BLACK FAMILIES' MEMBERS

The therapist needs to observe caution not to intervene on other than a base that has been negotiated with the client. The therapist will not necessarily understand the values, mores, norms, assumptions, or even linguistic nuances of the client. The requirement, however, is for the therapist to understand these elements of the therapist's own cultural context and to utilize that understanding to derive an understanding and appreciation of the client's cultural context. Respect for what is important and culturally relevant to the client is prerequisite to effecting a successful helping intervention. Although some proficiencies appear to need special emphases in the cross-cultural dyad, the relevant counselor proficiencies are the enduring ones taught in professional preparation programs: genuineness, accurate empathy, unconditional positive regard, respect for the client, self-knowledge, and, not least of all, patience and humility. With this basic armamentarium, the therapist can approach the goal of enabling the client's improved psychological functioning in terms of the client's cultural context.

Expansive efforts to explain blacks' underutilization of mental-health facilities have proceeded through the study of the constructs *preference* and *expectancy*. These constructs have not been conceptually distinguished in the literature, however. Some researchers conclude that preference and expectancy are distinct constructs and that failure to accommodate the client's preference may produce effects independent of whether or not the client experiences therapy as beneficial. Preference suggests that the client (and counselor) has some desire or preference for the complementary person to have and utilize some specific characteristics deemed important to the helping relationship. Race is one such characteristic, and numerous studies have focused inconclusively on race as the salient feature in the therapy dyad.[46] *Expectancy* refers to the client's (and counselor's) preexisting and emerging notions about the process, roles, and responsibilities in therapy. By implication, these concerns include the results or therapy outcomes.

Preference, further, denotes client and counselor assumption of shared values, experiences, and perceptions. The more complex issue of which characteristics matter—race, gender, sociocultural experience, or counselor skill, style, and behavior among numerous such variables—awaits further research. Harrison and Atkinson provide comprehensive reviews of the preference and ethnic similarity research.[47] Atkinson reports that the inconclusive findings were evenly divided between those finding and not finding effects for ethnic similarity. The unavoidable conclusion is that while preference is an important constant in the therapy relationship, its effects may be transient and apparently can be disposed of effectively in an appropriate intervention.

Appropriate counseling or therapeutic intervention, further, may be facilitated by the therapist's recognition and understanding of the client's level or extent of acculturation. The historical period of consciousness raising termed the *Black Power* movement had profound effects upon blacks' *expression* of self. Hraba and Grant and Ward and Braun demonstrate in a replication of the classic Clark and Clark doll study that black children post—"Black Power" showed a preference for dolls of their own ethnicity. Self-concept apparently is not fixed; rather, it is altered by one's experiences[48] and by one's perceptions and management of those experiences. This observation is widely supported in the psychological literature, color notwithstanding.

Cross terms the process of blacks' positive reconceptualization of their "self" *Nigrescence*.[49] Specifically, he proposes conversion to blackness through five psychological stages, each characterized by unique cognitive, and affective stages. In Preencounter one thinks and behaves consistent with the culturally dominant Eurocentric frame of reference; in this stage whiteness is idealized and blackness is devalued. The second stage is Encounter, where one's experiences of social and personal events collide with one's existing "world view," causing fissures and deterioration. In the third stage, Immersion-Emersion, one "tries on" or idealizes blackness, generally valuing and immersing self in black experiences and denigrating "whiteness." In Internalization, the fourth stage, one incorporates aspects of the Immersion-Emersion experience and achieves inner security with blackness. Diminution of antiwhite sentiment and accompanying ideological flexibility are characteristic in the fourth stage also. In the fifth stage, termed *Internalization-Commitment,* the conversion is completed by the incorporation of the new ideology into one's self system. The new ideology or "world view," in turn, is reinforced through commitment to promoting and actualizing of group objectives.[50]

To achieve an appropriate counseling intervention, attention needs to be given to Cross's notion that the conversion process is descriptive of blacks' self-actualization under conditions of oppression. Conversion is attended by a wide range of affective states (i.e., inferiority, shame, guilt, rage) paralleling the stage of development. Individual blacks' perceptions of societal oppression, it must be noted, will differ; hence, adaptive or coping strategies will differ or be imperceptible. Thus, this model is proposed as helpful to the therapist for deriving a tentative understanding of the client's "worldview" or "minority identity development."[51]

ROLE INDUCTION/PREPARATION

The literature is conclusive about the benefits to therapy to be derived from preparing the client for the therapeutic intervention.[52] Specifically demonstrated is that when clients received an orientation to the therapeutic process and context, they have more positive attitudes toward therapy and also self-disclose more readily. Most clients have at least secondary knowledge of the format of psychological interventions. Accordingly, the therapist can proceed to collaboratively negotiate the terms for serving the client. For black families or their members there are two probabilities to be explored. The first is that as a direct experience, interacting with a mental-health helping professional is new. The second is that there is an expectation of a negative experience.[53] If either of these propositions is established, the therapist needs to provide time for clarification of the process, roles, rights, and responsibilities of both the client and therapist.

In this regard, Pedersen suggests that overemphasizing the importance of a person's behavior, oversimplifying social system variables, and approaching counseling primarily as a formal process are errors in cross-cultural counseling. He encourages the counselor "to differentiate formal and informal counseling approaches in terms of method and context."[54] The useful, possible variations for working with persons from cultures unfamiliar to the counselor include formal context and method, formal context and informal method, and so on, exhausting nine combinations. Essentially, the "interculturally skilled counselor" is called upon to provide for objectivity by appreciating and complementing the client's cultural context in the intervention paradigm. Pedersen concludes: "The culturally accurate interpretation of behaviors from the perspective of expectations and values will help the counselor manage both the complexity and dynamism of a client's personal cultural orientation." This sentiment echoes Stewart's idea that for a coherent image to the client to be established, the cross-culture counseling intervention should be extended horizontally to accommodate the clients' histories and futures and vertically to incorporate the cultural meaning.[55]

THEORETICAL ORIENTATION

The theoretical orientation of the therapist is of consequence in the therapeutic intervention. The specific nature of the intervention with black families suggests that the therapist's theoretical orientation is a critical ingredient. The emphasis in Western culture and, specifically, in the training of American psychological helpers focuses heavily on individual responsibility. These models of clinical intervention intrude on the therapist's development of coherent understanding of the client. For the black client, whose sociocultural experience is infused with themes of powerlessness and stress borne of being marginalized, a therapy focused on client responsibility is ill-suited. An example of such a therapy is Rational Emotive Therapy. This system's emphasis on the client's role in establishing and, hence, *dis*establishing the client's own psychological problems makes its utility questionable. When the goal of therapy is the development of behaviors that enhance the client's psychological functioning, ''self talk'' and similar elements of RET likely prolong accomplishing of the therapeutic goal.[56]

The psycholoanalytic-oriented therapies with emphasis on the client's inner feelings, likewise, would seem to have limited utility with black clients and particularly if the therapist adheres to the systems' traditional elements. Ridley addresses the paradox in treatment of black clients when self-disclosure is a treatment goal. Since self-disclosure heightens vulnerability, a black client is likely to engage in nondisclosure. In the paradigm that Ridley proposed, he noted that most blacks are located in the ''functional paranoia'' quadrant, suggesting that cautious, untrusting behavior has an appropriate and identifiable base. Hence, he concluded that while nondisclosure is a paradox, it is resolvable if the therapist is culturally skilled and professionally competent.[57]

Traditional psychoanalytic and behaviorally based conceptualizations of therapy do not recognize and incorporate the rich sociocultural experiences of black families and their members. Among those therapies with the most promise for serving blacks are those that set aside abstract theoretical notions of how therapy is done and, instead, adopt active, intervention-oriented strategies. Smith reports that, among practitioners, currently the most popular are those therapies that, as opposed to arid theoretical approaches, integrate affective, cognitive, and behavioral elements and that stress intervention strategies.[58] Such systems include the behavioral therapies that emphasize social functioning over inner feelings. The relatively realistic, objective, and extraspective orientation of the behavior therapist in contrast to the idealistic, subjective, and introspective orientation of the dynamic therapist seems better suited to the client who has been described in this chapter.[59] The psychological modeling (i.e., social learning theory) work of Rosenthal and Bandura and self-efficacy postulation of Bandura further support this notion. They conclude, without specific reference to client ethnicity, that performance-based treatment is superior to other interventions.[60]

For over two decades Albee has been an incisive critic of the status quo in mental-health service delivery. Championing a community mental-health model, he argues persuasively that reduction of unnecessary stress and the enhancement of self-esteem and support networks would reduce the incidence of psychological dysfunctioning. Further, he argues that the recognition that these disturbances are more social than biological in origin dictates reorganization of psychological services and adoption of a primary prevention model. In rhetorical style, which supports the observations presented in this chapter, Albee notes the parallel between the incidence of familial disruption and each American ethnic group's progression up the rungs of the socioeconomic ladder. Psychological dysfunction declines as economic status increases.[61] Part of the answer to this dilemma lies in the adoption of a humanistic perspective, that is, the more liberal view that human improvement is possible and that our vital role as mental-health providers empowers our clients. Jenkins also calls for reconceptualization of the psychological functioning of black Americans in terms of the humanistic perspective. He stresses the position of humanistic psychology that one cannot understand behavior without understanding the intent of that behavior.[62] This perspective does not require abandoning Western psychology's rich heritage. Rather, it calls for suffusing current conceptualizations with explicit humanistic constructs. These calls are particularly poignant when one considers the demonstrated deficiencies of the mental-health service accorded to the least powerful ethnic and racial groups.

THE INTERVENTION

As suggested earlier, the enduring tools of the counselor are those that are taught in professional preparation programs. Appropriate extensions and modifications are prerequisite to successful intervention with the black client and with black families. The following brief focus on five elements of the intervention is provided as an example.

Discussion of Role and Expectancy

With the black client who may or may not be familiar with the format and context of therapy, a discussion ought to be undertaken of the roles and responsibilities of both participants. What the client expects to happen in, and as a result of, therapy needs to be clarified and negotiated. The therapist needs to understand the use of self-disclosure and to be conversant with the suggestions of how the black client may respond to calls for self-disclosure.[63] The existence of power in this counseling dyad also must be understood and utilized.[64] Contrary to some conceptualizations, power in the counseling dyad is not neutral; nor is it mutual nor reciprocal until it has been recognized and negotiated. This negotiation may be facilitated through the therapist's willingness to note and modify the therapy setting to accommodate the client's comfort. Relinquishing elements of formality will also modify the power quotient.

Identification and Interpretation of the Situation

As in other interventions, the therapist moves next to establish with the client the situation and the meaning and dynamics that the client attaches to the situation that brought the client to therapy. A safe and indispensable assumption is that the client is aware of the client's own norms. The sensitive therapist enables an exploration of these norms and in that course does not violate the client's cultural anchor. This task is accomplished partly through tolerant, forebearing exploration with the client of the client's present and through equally tolerant projection of his or her future, that is, determining what is going on and what the client wants to do about it.

Deciding a Course of Resolution

Having established the situation and a tentative course of action, the next step is an inventory of the client's resources for effecting resolution. The extension of the counseling setting in the first stage will serve to facilitate the therapists' identifying with the client of those persons and networks to be included in the inventory of resources.

Trying Out for Legibility

The next stage in the process is to move from facsimile to repetitious practice of the new behaviors until they become client skills. Incorporation of the behaviors into the client's repertory is achieved through "guided practice and corrective feedback to assure skill transfer and confirmation of positive self expectations."[65] The therapist must be skilled or conscientious in efforts to provide the client with culture-relevant and culture-specific reinforcers. The therapist, again, might rely on learning derived from the earlier horizontal and vertical extension of the intervention to assist the therapist's identification of culture-specific reinforcers.[66]

Evaluation

The final stage is evaluation, with the client, of the fit of the new behaviors. As necessary, the process returns to identification and interpretation of the situation and then proceeds sensitively through subsequent stages.

SUMMARY AND CONCLUSIONS

I have argued that traditional concepts of psychological intervention ignore the cultural and contextual specificity of black families and their members and, thus, are inadequate to serve these clients. Further, reflecting the considerable literature on who can counsel whom and under what circumstances, I have contended that ethical, committed service delivery is predicated on the therapist's supplanting of the traditional therapeutic armamentaria with reflected understanding and appreciation of the client's cultural context. The goal of all counseling and therapy is to achieve long-term constructive outcomes. For the black client, with the modal experience of being disenfranchised and marginalized in American society, these outcomes are instated through empowerment. Empowering the client through therapeutic intervention means transcending subtle and unintended adjustment to the disabling, dysfunctional conventions of the "dominant culture." It means assisting the client to validate his or her sense of self-efficacy and ability to productively confront and dismantle disabling events.

The therapy intervention that empowers the client is one in which the caregiver is prepared to go beyond the traditional intervention to blend normative approaches with acceptable techniques.[67] Several models exist for transcending firm boundaries to make the connections that are prerequisite to assisting the client. Devore advocates a model that specifically acknowledges and utilizes the black client's support networks, the meaning of family and friends, and the role and meaning of the church. That family is important to nurturance of the individual sense of self and continuity is documented in a substantial literature. Not to establish the meaning of family to the client is to make a serious error. Draguns's notions focus on identifying and using culture-specific reinforcers without preoccupation with the traditional ethos of the profession. And Feuerstein in similar abandonment of constricting theoretical "oughts" provides impressive demonstration of Israeli children's improved psychological functioning when the intervention model was focused on making the environment legible to the client.[68]

In sum, to serve black families and their members, the therapist operates beyond encapsulation and demonstrates cultural awareness that takes into account thte sociocultural history of the black American. This history is rich in enduring ethnic characteristics and strengths that are vital sources for promoting blacks' psychological functioning and personal empowerment.

Principally, I have argued that empowerment of the black family can occur through empowering of its members. This argument sidesteps that which discounts the prospect of nonblacks doing counseling and therapy with blacks. It proposes that the ethical, committed helping professional potentially can provide functions traditionally reserved to the black family. Understanding the legacy of blacks' experience in America is a prerequisite to providing a beneficial intervention. While a traditional model may be an appropriate focus for black family members whose orientation is essentially Eurocentric, a model that incorporates understanding of black families' specific characteristics and dynamics is required for empowering the black family.

The revised model advocated here doesn't presume a "fourth force." It does move dramatically beyond the rhetoric and stereotyped attack on counselors' and therapists' inadequacy to suggest the development of a paradigm that is respectful of the client and replaces the pedestrian, detached, and intimidated treatment typically offered to black families' members.

NOTES

1. A. Hillard, "A Framework for Focused Counseling of the Afro-American Man," *Journal of Non-White Concerns*, Vol. 13 (1985), pp. 72–78.

2. See P. Giddings, *When and Where I Enter: The Impact of Black Women on Race and Sex in America*, (New York: Bantam Books, 1985).

3. D. Lum, *Social Work Practice and People of Color*, (Monterey, CA: Brooks-Cole Publishing Company, 1986).

4. G.M. Frederickson, *The Black Image in the White Mind: The Debate of Afro-American Character and Destiny, 1817-1914*, (New York: Harper and Row, 1971).

5. See for example F.X. Acosta, "Self-Described Reasons for Premature Termination of Psychotherapy by Mexican American, Black-American and Anglo-American Patients, *Journal of Psychology*, Vol. 103 (1980), pp. 129–134; V. Adebimpe, "Overview: White Norms in Psychiatric Diagnosis of Black Patients," *American Journal of Psychiatry*, Vol. 138 (1981), pp. 279–285; G.W. Albee, "Preventing Psychopathology and Promoting Human Potential," *American Psychologist*, Vol. 37 (1982), pp. 1043–1050; C.B. Block, "Diagnostic and Treatment Issues for Black Patients," *Clinical Psychologist*, Vol. 37 (1984), pp. 54–59; N. Boyd-Franklin, *Black Families in Therapy: A Multisystem Approach* (New York: Guilford Press, 1989); M.C. Maultsby, "A Historical View of Blacks' Distrust of Psychiatry," in S.M. Turner and R.T. Jones, eds., *Behavior Modification in Black Populations* (New York: Plenum Press, 1982), pp. 39–44; J.A. Mayo, "The Significance of Sociocultural Variables in the Psychiatric Treatment of Black Outpatients," *Comparative Psychiatry*, Vol. 15 (1974), pp. 471–482; A. Mitchell-Jackson, "Psychosocial Aspects of the Psychotherapeutic Process," in S.M. Turner and R.T. Jones, eds., *Behavior Modification in Black Populations* (New York: Plenum Press, 1982) pp. 39–55; A. Thomas, "Pseudo-Transference Reactions Due to Cultural Stereotyping," *American Journal of Orthopsychiatry*, Vol. 32 (1962), pp. 894–900; and A. Thomas and S. Sillen, *Racism in Psychiatry* (New York: Brunner Mazel, 1972).

6. W.J. Wilson, *The Declining Significance of Race* (Chicago: University of Chicago Press, 1978).

7. M. Marable, *Race, Reform, and Rebellion: The Second Reconstruction in Black America, 1945-1982* (Jackson: University Press of Mississippi, 1984).

8. See for example: H.H. Doddy, "The Status of Negro Public College," *Journal of Negro Education*, Vol. 31 (1962), pp. 370–385; V. Harding, "Toward the Black University," *Ebony*, (August 1970), pp. 156–159; A.C. Hill, "Black Education in the Seventies: A Lesson from the Past," in F.B. Barbour ed., *The Black Seventies* (Boston: Porter Sargent Publisher, 1970), pp. 51–67; and M. Jones, "The Responsibility of the Black College to the Black Community: Then and Now," *Daedalus*, Vol. 100 (1971), pp. 732–744.

9. S. Redding, *They Came in Chains: Americans from Africa*, Rev. ed. (Philadelphia: J.B. Lippincott, 1973).

10. E. Fromm, *The Sane Society* (New York: Holt, Rinehart and Winston, 1976).

11. See, for example: Doddy (1962); Harding (1976); Hill (1970); and Jones (1971).

12. See Giddings (1985).

13. A. Mathis, "Contrasting Approaches to the Study of Black Families," *Journal of Marriage and the Family*, Vol. 40 (1976), pp. 667–676. W.W. Nobles, "African Philosophy: Foundation for Black Psychology," in R. Jones, ed., *Black Psychology* (New York: Harper and Row, 1972), pp. 18–32.

14. Nobles (1972).

15. See Giddings (1985) and J. Blassingame, *The Slave Community: Plantation Life in the Antebellum South* (New York: Oxford University Press, 1979).

16. Nobles (1972).

17. N. Hentoff, *Jazz Is* (New York: Random House, 1976).

18. A. Bandura, "Self Efficacy Mechanism in Human Agency," *American Psychologist*, Vol. 11 (1982), pp. 122–147.

19. Mathis (1976); Nobles (1972); J. Blackwell, *The Black Community: Diversity and Unity* (New York: Harper and Row, 1975); W.W. Nobles, "African Root and American Fruit: The Black Family," *Journal of Social and Behavior Sciences*, Vol. 20 (1974), pp. 52–64.

20. See Blassingame (1979), p. 190.

21. C.A. Pinderhughes, "Racism in Psychotherapy," in C. Willie, B. Kramer, and B. Brown, eds., *Racism and Mental Health*, (Pittsburgh, PA: University of Pittsburgh Press, 1973); W. Devore, "Ethnic Reality: The Life Model and Work with Black Families" *Social Caseworker*, Vol. 64 (1983), pp. 525–531.

22. Blackwell (1975).

23. See Nobles (1974) pp. 54–55.

24. Ibid., p. 60.

25. See, for example: Blassingame (1979); E. Genovese, *Roll, Jordan, Roll: The World Slaves Made* (New York: Vintage Books, 1976); H.G. Gutman, *The Black Family in Slavery and Freedom, 1750-1925* (New York: Pantheon Books, 1976).

26. E.B. Pinderhughes, "Family Functioning of Afro Americans," *Social Work*, Vol. 27 (1982), pp. 91–96.

27. A. Kardiner and L. Ovesey, *Mark of Oppression: Exploration in the Personality of the Negro* (New York: Norton, 1951).

28. W.W. Nobles, "Toward an Empirical and Theoretical Framework for Defining Black Families," *Journal of Marriage and the Family*, Vol. 40 (1978), pp. 679–688.

29. See for example D.P. Moynihan, *The Negro Family: A Case for National Action* (Washington, DC: U.S. Department of Labor, 1965); A.A. Poussaint, "A Negro Psychiatrist Explains the Negro Psyche," *New York Times Magazine*, (August 1967); and A.A. Poussaint, "Why Blacks Kill Blacks," *Ebony*, Vol. 25 (1970), pp. 143–180.

30. See A. Billingsley, "Black Families and White Social Science," *Journal of Social Issues*, Vol. 26 (1970), pp. 127–142; J. McCarthy and W. Yancy, "Uncle Tom and Mr. Charlie: Metaphysical Pathos in the Study of Racism and Personal Discrimination," *American Journal of Sociology*, Vol. 76 (1971), pp. 648–672.

31. See Giddings (1985).

32. B. Chavis, Second Annual Dr. Martin Luther King, Jr. Lecture, Pennsylvania State University, April 2, 1986.

33. M. Foster and L.R. Perry, "Self Valuation Among Blacks," *Social Work*, Vol. 27 (1982), pp. 60–66.

34. Pinderhughes (1982).

35. Nobles (1972), p. 50.

36. K.W. Bartz and E.S. Levine, "Childrearing by Black Parents: A Description and Comparison to Anglo and Chicano Parents," *Journal of Marriage and the Family*, Vol. 40 (1978), p. 718.

37. F.E. Paradis, "Themes in Training Culturally Effective Psychotherapists," *Counselor Education and Supervision*, Vol. 21 (1983), pp. 136–151.

38. D.W. Sue, "Ethnic Minority Issues in Psychology: A Reexamination," *American Psychologist*, Vol. 38 (1983), pp. 583–592.

39. See Billingsley (1970); and McCarthy and Yancy (1971).

40. See for example, G. Seward, *Clinical Studies in Cultural Conflict* (New York: Ronald Press, 1970); L. Comas-Dias, J. D. Geller, B. Melgoze, and R. Baker, *Attitudes and Expectations About Mental Health Services Among Hispanics and Afro-Americans*, paper presented at ninetieth Annual Convention of the American Psychological Association. Washington, DC., August 1982, and D.W. Sue, "Counseling the Culturally Different: A Conceptual Analysis," *Personnel and Guidance Journal*, Vol. 55 (1977), pp. 422–425.

41. D.W. Sue, "World Views and Counseling," *Personnel and Guidance Journal*, Vol. 56 (1978), pp. 458–462.

42. P. Pedersen, "Four Dimensions of Cross-Cultural Skill in Counselor Training," *Personnel and Guidance Journal*, Vol. 56 (1978), pp. 480–484.

43. See Adebimpe (1981); Maultsby (1982); Mayo (1974); Thomas (1962); Thomas and Sillen (1972); and Comas-Dias et al., (1982). See also S. Sue, H. McKinney, D. Allen, and J. Hall, "Delivery of Mental Health Services to Black and White Clients." *Journal of Counsulting and Clinical Psychology*, Vol. 42 (1974), pp. 794–801; and J. Yamamoto, Q.C. James, and N. Palley, "Cultural Problems in Psychiatric Therapy," *Archives of General Psychiatry*, Vol. 19 (1968), pp. 45–59.

44. Lum (1986).

45. D. Li-Repac, "Cultural Influences on Clinical Perceptions," *Journal of Cross-Cultural Psychology*, Vol. II, pp. 327–342.

46. See P. Cimbolic, "Counselor Race and Experience Effects on Black Clients," *Journal of Consulting and Clinical Psychology*, Vol. 39 (1972), pp. 328–332; H.E. Cheatham and J. Patrick, "The Nature of Preference: Or Is It Choice?," *Journal of Counseling and Development*, Vol. 66 (1987), pp. 131–134; R. J. Grantham and M.E. Gordon, "The Nature of Preference," *Journal of Counseling and Development*, Vol. 64 (1986), pp. 396–400; J.B. Heitler, "Preparatory Techniques in Initiating Expressive Psychotherapy with Lower Class, Unsophisticated Clients," *Psychological Bulletin*, Vol. 83 (1976), pp. 339–352; E. Proctor and A. Rosen, "Expectations and Preferences for Counselor Race and Their Relation to Intermediate Treatment Outcomes." *Journal of Counseling Psychology*, Vol. 28 (1981), pp. 40–46; and F.X. Acosta, "Preference and Self-Disclosure in Relation to Psychotherapist Professional and Ethnic Identification," *Journal of Psychology*, Vol. 103 (1979), pp. 129–134. H.E. Cheatham, T.O. Shelton, and W. Ray, "Race, Gender, Causal Attribution and Help-Seeking Behavior," *Journal of College Student Personnel*, Vol. 28 (1987), pp. 559–568; G. Morten and D.R. Atkinson, "Minority Identity Development and Preference for Counselor Race," *Journal of Negro Education*, Vol. 52 (1983), pp. 156–161; Cimbolic (1972).

47. D.K. Harrison, "Race as a Counselor-Client Variable in Counseling and Psychotherapy: A Review of the Research," *Counseling Psychologist*, Vol. 5 (1975), pp. 124–133; D.R. Atkinson, G. Morten, and D. W. Sue, *Counseling American Minorities: A Cross Cultural Perspective* (Dubuque, LA: William C. Brown Publishers, 1979).

48. See J. Hraba and G. Grant, "Black Is Beautiful: A Reexamination of Racial Preference and Identification," *Journal of Personality and Social Psychology*, Vol. 16 (1970), pp. 378–402 and S.H. Ward and J. Braun, "Self-Esteem and Racial Preference in Black Children," *American Journal of Orthopsychiatry*, Vol. 42 (1972), pp. 644–647.

49. W.E. Cross, "The Negro-to-Black Conversion Experience: Toward a Psychology of Black Liberation," *Black World*, Vol. 20 (1971), pp. 13–27.

50. W.E. Cross, "The Thomas and Cross Models of Psychological Nigrescence: A Review," *Journal of Black Psychology*, Vol. 5 (1978), pp. 13–31.

51. G. Morten and D.R. Atkinson, "Minority Identity Development and Preference for Counselor Race," *Journal of Negro Education*, Vol. 52 (1983), pp. 156–161.

52. F.X. Acosta, J. Yamamoto, L.A. Evans, and W.M. Skilbeck, "Preparing Low-Income Hispanic, Black and White Patients for Psychotherapy: Evaluation of New Orientation Program," *Journal of Clinical Psychology*, Vol. 39 (1983), pp. 872–877; L.A. Evans, F.X. Acosta, J. Yamamoto, and J. Skilbeck, "Orienting Psychotherapists to Better Serve Low Income and Minority Patients," *Journal of Clinical Psychology*, Vol. 40 (1984), pp. 90–96; M. L. Friedlander and T.J. Kaul, "Preparing Clients for Counseling: Effects of Role Induction on Counseling Process and Outcome," *Journal of College Student Personnel*, Vol. 24 (1983), pp. 207–214.

53. See Maultsby (1982). See also J.G. Ponterotto, W.H. Anderson, and I.Z. Grieger, "Black Students' Attitudes Towards Counseling as a Function of Ethnic Identity," *Journal of Multi-Cultural Counseling,* Vol. 14 (1986), pp. 50–59, and F. Terrell and S. Terrell, "Race of Counselor, Client Sex, Cultural Mistrust Level, and Termination of Counseling Among Black Clients," *Journal of Counseling Psychology,* Vol. 31, pp. 371–375.

54. P. Pedersen, "The Cultural Role of Conceptual and Contextual Support Systems in Counseling" *American Mental Health Counselors Association,* Vol. 8 (1986), pp. 35–42.

55. E.C. Stewart, "Cultural Sensitivities in Counseling," in P.P. Pedersen, J. Draguns, W. Lonner, and S. Trimble, eds., *Counseling Across Cultures* (Honolulu: The East West Center, 1981), pp. 61–83.

56. A. Ellis, *Reason and Emotion in Psychotherapy* (Secaucus, NJ: Citadel Press, 1979).

57. C.R. Ridley, "Clinical Treatment of the Nondisclosing Black Client: A Therapeutic Paradox," *American Psychologist,* Vol. 39 (1984), pp. 1234–1244.

58. D. Smith, "Trends in Counseling and Psychotherapy," *American Psychologist,* Vol. 37 (1982), pp. 802–809.

59. See S.B. Messer and M. Winokur, "Some Limits to the Integration of Psychoanalytic and Behavior Therapy," *American Psychologist,* Vol. 35 (1980), pp. 818–827.

60. T. Rosenthal and A. Bandura, "Psychological Modeling: Theory and Practice," in A. Bergin and S. C. Garfield eds., *Handbook of Psychotherapy and Behavior Change* (New York: John Wiley and Sons, 1978); (1982).

61. Albee, G. "Preventing Psychopathology and Promoting Human Potential," *American Psychologist,* Vol. 37, pp. 1043–1050.

62. A.H. Jenkins, *The Psychology of the Afro-American: A Humanistic Approach* (New York: Pergamon Press, 1981).

63. Ridley (1984).

64. Pinerhughes (1973).

65. Jenkins (1981).

66. Stewart (1981).

67. Devore (1983); J. Draguns, "Counseling Across Cultures: Common Themes and Distinct Approaches," in R.B. Pederson, J.G. Draguns, J. Lorimer, and J.E. Trimble, eds., *Counseling Across Cultures* (Honolulu: University Press of Hawaii, 1981).

68. R. Feuerstein, *Instrumental Enrichment: An Introduction Program for Cognitive Modifiability* (Baltimore: University Park Press, 1979); J. Spiegel, "An Ecological Model of Ethnic Families," in M. McGoldrick, J.K. Pearce, and J. Giordano, eds., *Ethnicity and Family Therapy* (New York: Guilford Press, 1981), pp. 31–51.

RETROSPECTIVE AND EXEGESIS: BLACK FAMILIES RECONCEPTUALIZED

Harold E. Cheatham and James B. Stewart

Billingsley suggests that American social science is more American than social and more social than science.[1] That observation hearkens to the enduring notion that clear and substantial discrepancies exist in knowledge about black families. At issue is the fact that researchers have not viewed their studies of black families as cross-cultural and thus certainly have violated the cultural specificity of these families.

A preponderance of evidence argues that conceptual and contextual errors accompany the chronicles that describe nonwhite, non-Western phenomena. Definitional and terminological errors are inherent in theories of social science that are based on Western values. Dominant social science paradigms have been naturalistic and ahistoric, seeking conclusions that are absolute and universal. Sampson suggests that the dominance of Western thought and values has resulted in two paradigms. Paradigm I emerged from a male subculture and reflects such male values as individualism, achievement, mastery, and detachment. Paradigm II seeks conclusions that are historical, context-bound, concrete, and particularistic.[2]

A similar conceptualization of the deficiencies that inhere in Western-oriented theory and research has been advanced by Awa. He holds that there are three dominant theoretical approaches: (a) Index theory which results in measuring phenomena in strictly quantifiable terms and hence erring in presuming that the measurement yields a total assessment of the phenomena; (b) Differentiation theory, which errs in assuming a cultural universalism in that it describes phenomena as characterized by the emergence of role segmentation, institutional differentiation, and adoption of new values appropriate to each change, and (c) Diffusion theory which deals essentially with the process through which externally or exoge-neously induced change is incorporated into the belief and response patterns of those adopting the change.[3] In this regard, Warwick proposes that: ''Whatever its disciplinary origins and methodology, cross-cultural research is *always* [emphasis added] a form of social intervention.'' Warwick further defines social intervention as planned or unplanned acts that alter the characteristics or relationships of individuals or groups.[4] His notion, concurred with by Awa, is that the researchers' orientation affects the research problem chosen, how the problem is defined, and the operationalization of the variables. Enshrining observations and assumptions that negate ethnic pluralism and cultural diversity perpetuates ignorance of cultural diversity. Pedersen aptly summarizes the consequences, noting that: ignorance of cultural diversity leads to asking the wrong questions, lack of knowledge of the culture leads to wrong answers, and lack of culturally relevant skills for interventions leads to wrong actions.[5] Most existing models make no exceptions for nor accommodation to traditional values and how these values conflict with Western attitudes.

These observations together argue that black families are unlikely to be understood and appreciated as black families unless and until research paradigms account for blacks' cultural specificity. Rather, what exists in the literature regarding black families is stereotype and evolution of stereotype through successive theoretical formulations from *pathological* to *culturally deficient* to *culturally different*. And even in the latter case, the current formulation of cultural difference yet enjoys some status as a synonym of deficient. The consequent models have treated black families as discrepant variations from a Western template rather than as a legitimate family form.

Clearly it is no longer acceptable to presume that assumptions about culture and the human condition have universality. This volume was conceived and developed to provide a theoretical and methodological framework for understanding and serving black families. It was intended to address a void in conceptual knowledge and in methodological approaches—and as well, to serve to expedite the derivation of culture specific models for treatment interventions with black families. As such, this volume simultaneously provides a critique of existing knowledge and sets ground rules for a cohesive, unified approach to theorizing about and studying the black family.

These critiques of existing theoretical frameworks suggest the need for new approaches in theory testing and in the collection and analysis of quantitative and qualitative data on black families. As Frazier notes, data collection and analysis must be guided by a coherent theoretical framework.[6] In the emerging theoretical framework, a black family is a system interacting with other systems in social space. It is necessary, therefore, to examine both the relevant characteristics of the selected systems and the nature, extent, and configuration of these systems with the family. There, thus, is a need to integrate micro and macro perspectives in quantitative and qualitative research to recognize the symbiotic relationship between aggregate constraints on black family development and functioning of individual members within and outside the familial environs.

The work necessary to instate black families as the critically important developmental units that they are has only begun. The divergent schools of thought as represented in Du Bois's and Frazier's work as well as in the work of contemporary students of black families have been merged, even if tentatively, in this volume. The seminal works do not incorporate the diverse scholarship on black families. Those works, however, taken with the scholarship in this volume provide students and scholars of black families in the United States with fresh and potent frameworks.

A variety of quantitative and qualitative research is presented in this volume. Collectively it emanates from a wholistic systems framework consistent with that advocated above. The research is designed to facilitate proactive as contrasted with reactive intervention strategies. Moreover, the research is designed to lay a foundation from which interconnections can be examined systematically and from which various disciplinary components can be woven into a fresh perspective.

Finally, this volume has contributed to the task before us by bringing together established and emerging scholars. We might have provided chapters representing narrower perspectives, but we believe that a richer contribution emerges from the diverse scholarship represented here. Achieving a comprehensive critique of existing models is difficult, and achieving an exhaustive critique is even more difficult. Our concern has been to assist in generating models and theories that incorporate the nature of black families' self-definition as reflected in cultural form, values, and beliefs. These derivations, then, ought to obviate the notions and assumptions that interaction with the white West transformed black families — and particularly so in unilateral fashion, (i.e., with no reciprocal effects or modifications).

Ultimately, this volume's contributors argue for theory and models that restore the dignity and the vitality of black families. Further, they assert that diversity—even among black families—argues against treating them as if they constitute a single identity in a multiethnic society.

We do not contend that we have answered all of the questions, nor that we have eradicated destructive theoretical formulations concerning black families. We do hope that we provided some fresh foundation on which to raise the level of reflection, investigation, and, ultimately, knowledge about and treatment of black families.

NOTES

1. A. Billingsley, *Black Families in White America* (Englewood Cliffs, NJ: Prentice-Hall, 1968).
2. E.E. Sampson "Scientific Paradigms and Social Value: Wanted—A Scientific Revolution," *Journal of Personality and Social Psychology* 36 (1978), pp. 1332–1348.
3. N.E. Awa, "Ethnocentric Bias in Development Research," In M.K. Asante, E. Newmark, and C.A. Black, eds., *Handbook of Intercultural Communication* (Beverly Hills: Sage, 1979), pp. 263–281.
4. D.P. Warwick, "The Politics and Ethics of Cross-Cultural Research," in H.C. Triandis and W.W. Lambert, eds., *Handbook of Cross-Cultural Psychology: Perspectives,* Vol. 1 (Boston: Allyn-Bacon, 1980), pp. 319–371.
5. P.O. Pedersen, Interview, *Education Exchange,* (Syracuse, NY: Syracuse University Alumni News, Fall 1984).
6. E.F. Frazier, "Theoretical Structure of Sociology and Sociological Research," *British Journal of Sociology,* Vol. 4 (1953), pp. 292–311, reprinted in G.F. Edwards, ed., *E.F. Franklin Frazier on Race Relations* (Chicago: University of Chicago Press, 1968), pp. 3–29.

ABOUT THE EDITORS AND CONTRIBUTORS

THE EDITORS

HAROLD E. CHEATHAM is a member of the counselor education/counseling psychology faculty of the Pennsylvania State University, where he teaches cross-cultural counseling and directs the student personnel graduate program. Dr. Cheatham's research addresses mental-health service delivery to ethnic minorities and women and equity issues regarding these populations in U.S. higher education and the U.S. military. He has served on the editorial boards of a number of journals in his discipline. He is editor of a special issue of the *Journal of College Student Development* entitled *Blacks in U.S. Higher Education* and he is working on a book addressing collegiate programming for cultural pluralism.

JAMES B. STEWART is director of the black studies program at the Pennsylvania State University and a member of the faculty of labor studies and industrial relations. Dr. Stewart's research interests include economic development in minority communities and discrimination against racial and ethnic minorities. His work examining African-American families has appeared in numerous journals and he serves on the advisory panel of the "Changing Black Family" project of the Joint Center for Political Studies in Washington, D.C. He is editor of the *Review of Black Political Economy*.

THE CONTRIBUTORS

ROY L. AUSTIN is associate professor of sociology and administration of justice at the Pennsylvania State University. His publications are primarily in the area of crime and delinquency, including several with a concern with race. He has also published articles on various Caribbean subjects.

LOIS BENJAMIN is an associate professor of sociology at Central State University. Dr. Benjamin's research interests include the black family and racial stratification. Her forthcoming work, *The Color Line in the Twilight of the 20th Century* (to be published by Nelson-Hall) examines how racism is experienced by the black elite and their means of coping with it.

Noel A. Cazenave is an associate professor in the Department of Sociology of Temple University. Current research interests are the uses of social science expertise, social problems and social policy, poverty and inequality, political sociology, and community organization and protest. He is now planning a major research project that is tentatively titled, "Preparing for Battle: Social Science Experts and Their Conceptualization of Citizen Participation in the U.S. 'War on Poverty' and its Precursors; 1957–1968.''

Peggy Dilworth-Anderson is professor of child development and family relations at the University of North Carolina at Greensboro. Dr. Dilworth-Anderson's research has focused on intergenerational relations in the black family, with an emphasis on the elderly. She currently serves on the Board of Directors for the National Council on Family Relations and on the National Advisory Board of the Family Information Services. Among her publications is a special collection of articles with Harriet McAdoo on ethnic minority families published in *Family Relations*, July 1988.

Jewelle Taylor Gibbs is Associate Professor at the School of Social Welfare at the University of California at Berkeley. Dr. Gibbs is currently a member of the Advisory Board of the National Center for Children in Poverty. She served on the Task Panel on Special Populations of President Carter's Commission on Mental Health and on the Board of Directors of the American Orthopsychiatric Association. She was the recipient of the 1987 McCormick Award from the American Association of Suicidology for her scholarly contributions to minority suicide. She is the editor of *Young, Black and Male in America: An Endangered Species* (1988) and the co-author of *Children of Color: Psychological Interventions With Minority Youth* (1989).

Robert B. Hill is director of the Institute for Urban Research at Morgan State University. Dr. Hill is the author of *The Strengths of Black Families* (1971), *Black Families and the 1974–75 Depression* (1975), *Informal Adoption Among Black Families* (1977), and *The Illusion of Black Progress* (1978). He has served on several high-level panels, including the U.S. Bureau of the Census Advisory Committee on the Black Population in the 1980 Census; the 1981 White House Conference on Aging; the 1980 White House Conference on Families; and the National Academy of Sciences Committee on Child Development Research and Public Policy. Dr. Hill was formerly director of research of the National Urban League.

Leanor Boulin Johnson is an associate professor of Family Resources and

Human Development at Arizona State University. For the past four years she has been a principal investigator on a work-family linkage project funded by the National Institute of Mental Health. She has served as associate editor and reviewer for several journals, is a past director of the National Council on Family Relations and former chair of the Ethnic Minorities Section of this same organization. Dr. Boulin Johnson's research on black families, gender roles, sexuality, and work-family stress has appeared in numerous journals.

WILHELMINA A. LEIGH is a principal analyst at the Congressional Budget Office in Washington, D.C. An economist by training, Dr. Leigh wrote the monograph *Shelter Affordability for Blacks: Crisis or Clamor?* (1982) while a senior research associate with the research department of the National Urban League. She also has been a consultant to the Urban Institute and has taught at Harvard University, Howard University, and the University of Virginia. Her research has focused on many aspects of housing market problems and policies, in general, and of race and housing, in particular.

ROBERT E. MILLETTE is the chairperson of the Sociology/Human Services/ Criminal Justice Department at Lincoln University in Pennsylvania. Dr. Millette also chairs the Division of Social Sciences and Behavioral Studies. He is a member of the Editorial Advisory Board of Collegiate Press. His research interests include social stratification, the Caribbean and the family. Dr. Millette is the author of *The Grenada Revolution: Why It Failed?* (1985); *New Grenada in Brooklyn: Social Stratification and Adaption Among First Generation Immigrants* (in press); "The West Indian Family in Crisis"; and "Drug and Alcohol in Transit."

BARBEE C. MYERS is assistant professor in the Department of Health and Sport Science at Wake Forest University, where she teaches wellness and health promotions. Dr. Myers's research explores racial and sociocultural predictors of cardiovascular morbidity and mortality among adult women. She is active in the American College of Sports Medicine, the International Society on Hypertension in Blacks, and the Association of Black Cardiologists. Dr. Myers also serves on the editorial board of Urban Cardiology Journal.

AMON O. OKPALA is assistant professor of economics at Winston-Salem State University, Winston-Salem, North Carolina. He has published on Nigerian female labor force participation rate, economic and noneconomic determinants of fertility, and the economic implications of Nigerian population growth.

THOMAS G. POOLE is director of the Helen Eakin Eisenhower Chapel and affiliate assistant professor of religious studies at the Pennsylvania State University. Dr. Poole's teaching and research focus on African-American religion, theological ethics, and religion and social transformation. He is a member of the American Academy of Religion and the Society of Christian Ethics.

MITCHELL F. RICE is professor of public administration and political science at Louisiana State University, Baton Rouge. He holds the Ph.D. in government from Claremont Graduate School, Claremont, California. He has written extensively on black and minority health issues in *Social Science and Medicine, Health Policy, Journal of Health and Human Resources Administration, American Journal of Preventive Medicine, Urban League Review,* and other journals. He is co-editor of *Health Care Issues in Black America* (Greenwood Press, 1987) and *Contemporary Public Policy Perspectives and Black Americans* (Greenwood Press, 1984) and co-compiler of *Black American Health: An Annotated Bibliography* (Greenwood Press, 1987).

DIANA T. SLAUGHTER is associate professor of education and social policy and holds an appointment in the Department of African American Studies, Northwestern University. Dr. Slaughter's research interests include family influences on academic achievement, black education, and early intervention studies. She is co-editor (1987, with Edgar Epps) of a special issue of the *Journal of Negro Education* devoted to the black child's home environment and student achievement. She is co-editor (with Deborah Johnson) of the book, *Visible Now: Blacks in Private Schools* (1988), and editor of the book, *Black Children and Poverty: A Developmental Perspective* (1988).

RITA R. SMITH-WADE-EL is assistant chairperson and an associate professor in the Department of Psychology, Millersville University of Pennsylvania, where she teaches undergraduate courses in developmental, cognitive, and social psychology, racism, history and systems of psychology and graduate courses in statistics. Dr. Smith was a consulting psychologist at the Lancaster Career Development Center and consults in the areas of the black child/black families, child development, parenting, race relations, black culture, study skills, interpersonal relations, SAT preparation, and values clarification. Rita Smith-Wade El has published articles in the area of race and class differences in the predisposition to learned helplessness, race as a self scheme, blacks and mental health services, teenage pregnancy, and the ethnicity of the state-related social science curriculum, as well as co-authored an article on black male/female relationships.

BARBARA BRYANT SOLOMON is professor of social work and associate dean of the graduate school, University of Southern California. Dr. Solomon's primary research and teaching interests are social service delivery systems in health and mental health settings, particularly those serving minority and aged populations. She has received the Social Work Educator of the Year Award from the National Association of Social Workers.

MARGARET BEALE SPENCER is an associate professor in the Division of Educational Studies at Emory University and associate clinical professor of community medicine at Morehouse School of Medicine. Her minority-focused developmental research on identity and competence-formation processes for children and adolescents has been sponsored by NIMH and several private funding sources (e.g., Spencer Foundation, W.T. Grant Foundation, and the Carnegie Corporation of New York). Her publications include numerous articles and chapters, a co-edited volume (with G.K. Brookins and W.R. Allen), *Beginnings: Social and Affective Development of Black Children,* and a co-edited special issue of the journal *Child Development* (in press), on minority children and families. She is currently working on a volume on African-American children and families with Alex Pointsett. Professional activities include the National Academy of Sciences (panel membership), the Social Science Research Council, the W.T. Grant Foundation, and the National Black Child Development Institute (board member).

MICHAEL W. WILLIAMS is an assistant professor in the Department of Afro-American and African Studies at the University of North Carolina at Charlotte. His research interests include African-American families, race and ethnic relations, the sociology of knowledge, and Pan-Africanism. Dr. Williams's work has appeared in several journals. He is currently completing a study on the plight of African-American children raised in families with absent fathers.